West Virginia
and the
Captains of Industry

West Virginia
and the
Captains of Industry

by

John Alexander Williams

West Virginia University Press

Morgantown 2003

West Virginia University Press, Morgantown 26506

First edition published 1976, West Virginia University Library
First ed. rev. 2003
Printed in the United States of America

10 09 08 07 06 05 04 03   9 8 7 6 5 4 3 2 1

ISBN 0-937058-78-5 (alk. paper)

Library of Congress Cataloguing-in-Publication Data

West Virginia and the captains of industry / John Alexander Williams.
    p.   cm.
    1. United States History. South Atlantic States — West Virginia. 2.
Businessmen — West Virginia — History. 3. Industry — West Virginia —
History. 4. Camden, Johnson Newlon, 1828-1908. 5. Davis, Henry
Gassaway, 1823-1916. 5. Elkins, Stephen Benton, 1841-1911. 6. Scott,
Nathan Bay, 1841-1924. I. Title. II. Williams, John Alexander.
IN PROCESS

Library of Congress Control Number: 2003101826

Cover Design by Sara Pritchard
Cover photograph courtesy of West Virginia & Regional History
    Collection, West Virginia University Library.

Printed in USA by Bookmasters, Inc.

To my mother,
Mary Agnes Marsh Williams

Table of Contents

Acknowledgments

Anyone who peruses the footnotes of this volume will quickly discern that my greatest debt is to the archivists, past and present, who have assembled and organized the splendid collection of research materials housed in the West Virginia Collection of the West Virginia University Library. They include Charles Shetler, Jerry Ham, J. William Hess, and George Parkinson, the last two of whom have earned my gratitude also in the roles of counselors and friends. C. Vann Woodward guided this project in its embryonic dissertation stage at Yale University and made valuable suggestions for the improvement of a later version. Two eminent former colleagues, James W. Silver and John Wolf, also read parts of the manuscript, while Donald J. Mattheisen and William I. Davisson offered counsel in formulating the quantitative aspects of my research. At West Virginia University, Maurice Brooks and Paul Atkins contributed helpful criticism and suggestions to the final version of the book, and Donovan H. Bond and Robert Munn provided wise and patient guidance through the publishing process in 1976. Among the several typists who worked on one or more versions of this study at that time, I especially want to thank Carmela Rulli, Shirley Schneck, and Jane Yeager. Among friends whose contributions were more general than specific, I am particularly indebted to the late Ann and Dan Fisher.

It is again a pleasure to acknowledge the help of these kind people and to exonerate them from the defects in this study that persisted despite their care.

Appalachian State University
February 10, 2003

The New Dominion

In the last third of the nineteenth century the gods of war and commerce created a new American commonwealth in the heart of the Appalachian highlands. The state of West Virginia, created from fifty counties of Virginia during the Civil War, became the thirty-fifth daughter of the American Union on June 20, 1863. As the political institutions of the new state matured, it underwent another transition, an economic one. Beginning in late antebellum times, but at a much quickened pace after the Civil War, there emerged in the new state an industrial economy based on extracting the timber and fossil fuel resources of the Appalachian plateau. The conjunction of these trends was not a fortunate one. The creation of a new and unformed polity in a territory almost wholly subject to the social impact of extractive industry resulted in a phenomenon best described as a colonial political economy. By 1900, West Virginia business and politics were dominated by industrialists who marshalled both the political and economic resources of the state for use beyond its borders. The forging of this colonial political economy is the central concern of this book.

The beginning and the end of West Virginia's first century of statehood are well known, at least in outline, to scholars and other observers. The unique and dramatic circumstances surrounding the state's creation provides West Virginia's most distinctive mark on the nation's history and has absorbed by far the largest share of local historians' attention.[1] Modern "Appalachia," whose social and economic characteristics are more pervasive and concentrated in West Virginia than in any other state, has inspired even more abundant scrutiny. Beginning with the "discovery" of the region by scholars, journalists, and reformers around the time of the First World War, this scrutiny has continued with varying degrees of intensity through the present day.[2] The links between these two most common perceptions of West Virginia—between its fascinating but remote political beginnings and its troubled career in the twentieth century—remain dimly perceived, however. Consequently this study focuses upon the vital period of transition, beginning around 1880 when issues and leaders generated by decades of sectional conflict began yielding to new forces associated with emerging industrialism, and continuing to 1913, when West Virginia celebrated its semicentennial amid scenes of political and social turbulence in which may be clearly discerned the complex of social pathologies that would eventually be identified with "Appalachia." No adequate understanding of West Virginia history—or of Appalachia itself—can be formed without close examination of the changes of this period.

An important premise of the men who founded West Virginia was that political autonomy, coupled with the "boundless resources" locked in the West Virginia hills, would guarantee a future as rich as could be found in any other American commonwealth.[3] Fifty years later, articulate citizens, though shaken by a series of natural and social disasters, were less troubled by a clouded future than enthralled by the changes of the recent past. The state's more prosperous and patriotic citizens have continued throughout the twentieth century to launch embarrassed protests and demurrers against growing "outside" scrutiny of West Virginia's ills, but as human as well as natural resources began to take flight after World War II, it became increasingly hard to deny that the boundless future envisioned by the statemakers had failed to materialize. It is time then for historians as well as economists and sociologists to ask the question: What went wrong? What was done, or not done, to guarantee the failure of West Virginians' aspirations for their proportionate share of the national wealth?

The failure of West Virginia and its region to achieve a future as rich as Appalachia's natural resources once seemed certain to provide is partly explained by uncontrollable im-

2

pediments to a mature and balanced industrial economy. Considered within the context of a national economic system that directly or indirectly extends to most of the North American continent, Appalachia's reserves of energy are not matched by the array of complimentary assets that other American regions can provide. The mountain environment ①
has presented serious obstacles to economic growth at each stage of the region's development and probably will continue to do so unless the advocates of open-ended growth create a natural and aesthetic wasteland in order to accomplish their aims. Another factor to be considered is the general failure of ②
American capitalism's vision of economic progress to adapt to special circumstances such as those presented by this environment.[4] But West Virginia's fate was also the product of conscious and unconscious acts and decisions made by identi-③
fiable men, and the historian is obliged to include these as well as more impersonal forces in his assessment of the past.

This assessment of West Virginia history will focus upon four individuals in particular: Johnson N. Camden (1828-1908), a founder of West Virginia's oil industry, associ- *Camden*
ate of John D. Rockefeller and the Standard Oil Company, and a developer of railroad, coal, and timber enterprises in the northern and central parts of the state; Henry G. Davis *Davis*
(1823-1916) and his son-in-law, Stephen B. Elkins *Elkins*
(1841-1911), whose family coal and railroad empire developed originally in northeastern West Virginia and eventually extended through railroads, banks, and urban service enterprises to more than twenty localities; and Nathan B. Scott *Scott*
(1842-1924), a Wheeling glass manufacturer, banker, and mining magnate. These four were West Virginia's richest and most powerful men by 1900. They led both major political parties, Davis and Camden as Democrats, Elkins and Scott as Republicans. They represented the state in Congress and in other arenas of national politics. There were others like them in West Virginia—A. Brooks Fleming and Clarence W. Watson of the Fairmont (Consolidation) Coal Company, for example, or Davis Elkins, who worked successfully to extend his family's dual lease on power during the twentieth century. But

3

Camden, Davis, Scott, and particularly the elder Elkins were the originals. They perfected West Virginia's modern political system, subdued or co-opted local competitors for power, adapted the state's political representation along with its fuels and raw materials to the use of metropolitan industrialism, and trained their less powerful collaborators and successors to the work of a *comprador* middle class. As much as the men who brought the state to life in 1863, these four were the makers of West Virginia as it is today.

In many respects West Virginia's late nineteenth century development resembled that of other tributary regions of the American homeland, notably the mining states of the Rocky Mountain West. The facility with which Elkins transferred his base of political operations from New Mexico to West Virginia during the 1880s makes the comparison an obvious one. But there was one important difference. West Virginia at this time, unlike its western counterparts, was neither an empty or newly conquered territory. It had been occupied by Anglo-Americans for over a century. Thus these capitalists of the corporate and metropolitan economy encountered a provincial society whose leaders were variously willing and able to offer resistance to their search for political power. In one form or another, this resistance occasioned much of the political conflict in West Virginia between the time of Davis's and Camden's appearance in state politics after the Civil War and the industrialists' final accession to power at the end of the century.

This resistance was slow in getting under way, however, owing to the fact that Davis and Camden arrived on the West Virginia political scene at a moment of opportune disarray among their potential rivals. Both the Democratic and Republican parties were divided in 1866-1871: by local and national issues of Reconstruction; among former Whigs and former Democrats, former Unionists, Confederates, and Copperheads; between those who looked to the future and those who dwelt on the past. Camden's nominations for governor in 1868 and 1872 and Davis's election as the state's first

4

Democratic United States senator in 1871 occasioned cries of scorn and surprise among observers whose estimates of political worth was drawn in terms of the issues of the past decade. But these budding tycoons were superbly, if only temporarily, fitted to part the muddy waters of West Virginia politics. Having concentrated in recent years on the task of keeping their fledgling business enterprises out of the path of border warfare, they were able to engage the economic aspirations that united West Virginians while adopting ambiguous stands on the sectional and constitutional issues that divided them. No less important was the fact that they had cash to finance the Democracy's effort to shape its mixed bag of supporters into an effective majority at the polls. "I believe those who worked on during the dark days ought to be rewarded," Davis wrote following the Democratic victory of 1870.[5] And so they were.

There was much to support the frequent allusions to a Davis-Camden "ring" in West Virginia politics during and after Reconstruction. It is not clear how the two industrialists first encountered each other. Camden was chiefly concerned with oil producing and refining in the Parkersburg region during this period, while Davis, who apart from a brief residence at Piedmont, (West) Virginia, spent most of his time in his native Maryland, concentrated on the upper Potomac forests and coal measures lying on the opposite side of the state from Camden's domain.[6] Perhaps the two first met during the West Virginia Legislature's session at Wheeling in January 1866. Davis was a freshman member of the House of Delegates at this time, having sought the office for reasons involving his projected railroad. Camden also had business before the session. However they came together, the two were fast friends and political allies by 1868. Then and in later years they exchanged gifts, vacationed together at home and abroad, invested in one another's enterprises, and worked jointly as well as separately to strengthen the ties to national political leaders and to metropolitan suppliers of capital that underpinned their double careers in business and politics. Elkins fitted easily into the friendship after he married Hallie

5

Davis in 1875 and transferred his residence from New Mexico to Washington and New York.[7] Although Elkins would not interest himself in West Virginia politics until Davis gave the signal a decade later, he became a partner in the family's West Virginia and Maryland enterprises in 1877. Two years later he joined with Davis and Camden to purchase the "Caperton lands" in central West Virginia, a 90,000-acre tract acquired, appropriately enough, from the estate of a prominent antebellum land lawyer and Confederate politician. In making plans to develop this holding as a joint enterprise, and on hundreds of other occasions growing out of their private and public lives, the industrialists had ample opportunities to confer together. It is only because the far-flung character of their various activities led to frequent physical separations and hence to written exchanges among them that we know as much about their collaboration as we do.

The ascendancy of Davis and Camden was thus one of the features of West Virginia politics during and after Reconstruction, but it is important to understand that their ascendancy was rarely complete. A narrow Democratic victory in the state election of 1870 drove the Republican founders of West Virginia from power and left that party on the sidelines until Elkins took it in hand in 1888. Meanwhile the Democracy (as the party liked to call itself during these years) plunged into a bewildering variety of factional conflicts and shifting intraparty coalitions. Davis and Camden often won out in these combats, but just as often they lost. Frequently the result was to force one or both of the industrialists to make way for someone else at the top of the Democratic heap. Camden, for example, had little trouble getting the party's gubernatorial nomination in 1868, when it was worthless owing to the exclusion of former Confederates from the polls. But when he went after the nomination again on the eve of victory in 1870, he could not get it; when he got it in 1872, he was again defeated, this time by a fusion movement of Republicans and insurgent Democrats. He sought the junior senatorial seat in 1875 and was again defeated. Finally he won election to the Senate in 1881, only to be denied a second term after a bitter and protracted struggle in the legislature of 1887. Davis initially fared somewhat better. He managed to win his Senate seat with Camden's help in the fluid circumstances of 1871 and to hang on to it six years later, but only by virtue of his ability to marshal Republican support against a powerful Democratic rival. Thereafter Davis sought to cultivate the posture of a party statesman, above factionalism and so open to all as a compromise leader. Fearing defeat if he openly bid for reelection in 1883, he staged a painfully transparent "retirement" in hopes of luring enough factional candidates into the caucus to stalemate it and so permit his supporters to call for his return to Washington as a means of preserving unity. The strategy failed, however. All that was preserved was Davis's dignity. Deprived of a third term in the Senate, he was forced to watch from the sidelines as the tariff reform movement in Congress mounted an increasingly serious threat to the tariff on bituminous coal.

Three groups of West Virginia politicians contended with Davis and Camden for control of the Democracy during these years. One was comparable to those "Redeemers" who surfaced in other Southern and Border states at the end of Reconstruction. In West Virginia these men constituted a traditional type of leader, gifted in oratory and debate but unskilled in the sort of statewide organizational tactics in which the industrialists excelled. Most Redeemers were Confederate veterans or sympathizers. Most, too, were lawyers and specialists in the complex system of land registry that the state had inherited from Virginia. In the thirty years preceding the Civil War, such men and their predecessors had rewritten Virginia's land laws for their own benefit. Returning to power in 1870, they performed the same task for West Virginia at the constitutional convention of 1872. The resulting "Lawyer's Constitution" may not have been "gotten up to make litigation the principal business in West Virginia," as its Republican critics avowed. But the land title provisions of the new constitution entailed further confusion in land and tax policies and facilitated, under the supervision of "distinguished land attorneys," the eventual transfer of titles and mineral rights from small proprietors to mining and lumber corporations during the next three decades.[8]

Although Redeemer Democrats flourished on a local or regional basis, and were especially successful in judicial elections, few were as prominent as Davis or Camden in statewide politics. One exception was Charles James Faulkner, the principal architect of the 1872 constitution, who also helped to engineer Camden's gubernatorial defeat in the same year. Faulkner challenged Davis for the latter's senatorial seat in 1877 and divided the Democratic legislators, forcing Davis to turn to Republican support to carry him through. Another prominent Redeemer was Allen Caperton, an antebellum lawyer-legislator and member of the Confederate Senate. Although his speculative landholdings remained for Davis, Camden, and Elkins to develop after his death, Caperton nevertheless managed to claim the senatorial prize that Camden wanted in 1875.[9] The Redeemers indeed spoke for the southern and eastern West Virginia strongholds of Confederate sentiments and Virginia traditionalism and were usually conservative in their economic views; in fact, they yielded nothing to the industrialists in their anxiety to attract—and profit from—the investment capital needed to develop West Virginia's natural resources.

For their part, the industrialists preferred the sectional agitation on which the Redeemers thrived to the economic issues that surfaced during the 1870s in the platforms of the "Agrarian" wing of the Democracy. Camden, by virtue of his identification with Rockefeller and the Standard Oil Company, offered a particularly inviting target for anticorporation men, but most Agrarians lumped him and Davis together as representatives of "Monopoly and the cohesive power of public plunder."[10] Although they infrequently won office for themselves, Agrarian candidates often managed to stalemate a convention or caucus and force the selection of a compromise Democratic nominee, usually a Redeemer. As this suggests, there was a significant sectional component to the Agrarian appeal. Of the leading Agrarian spokesmen,

8

three (John J. Davis, Henry S. Walker, E. Willis Wilson) were former Copperheads and "Bitter Enders" who initially attacked Camden or Henry G. Davis for their moderation on the racial issues of Reconstruction. A fourth, Daniel B. Lucas, was instrumental in Camden's defeat for a second Senate term in 1887 and is remembered for his critiques of unregulated industrial capitalism during his brief tenure as a justice of the state supreme court. In all other respects, however, Lucas was the epitome of a Redeemer: distinguished Virginian ancestry and a graceful family home on the banks of the Shenandoah, a Charlottesville education, a heroic Confederate war record, some few volumes of poetry that mourned the Lost Cause and celebrated the glories of old Virginia (defined, in 1868, as extending from "Ohio to the Ocean's bounding main"). Notwithstanding the indisputably "Southern" character of Agrarian leaders, however, their greatest appeal was not to be found in the southern and eastern counties. A quantitative study of Democratic factional struggles over candidates or issues between 1872 and 1887 shows that Agrarians made inroads in Redeemer strongholds along the Virginia border but fared poorly in the backwoods districts of the interior. Their greatest proportionate strength came from economically advanced districts along the Ohio and Kanawha rivers and the Baltimore & Ohio Railroad, in other words, in the northern and western counties. In fact the Agrarians' greatest victory, the nomination of E. Willis Wilson for governor in 1884, was accomplished through an alliance with the Democrats of "ironhearted" city of Wheeling!

Finally, there was the first of several organizations known to West Virginia political lore as the Charleston Gang or Kanawha Ring. John E. Kenna, who outmaneuvered Davis to win election to the Senate in 1883, was a Confederate veteran, while many of his associates had Confederate records or connections. But in their capacities as members of the Charleston law firms of Chilton, MacCorkle & Chilton and Kenna & Watts, the Kanawha Ring proved adept at combining the traditional avocations of circuit-riding lawyers in the

9

southern interior with the practice of land and corporation law. Governor William A. MacCorkle explained why in his memoirs: "Almost every man needed advice about land titles, or some phase of his life in the fluxing condition of the country" after the southern interior was opened by the Chesapeake & Ohio Railroad in 1876. The railroad also needed legal advice, as did the eastern and British capitalists whose coal and lumber companies entered the region during the next decade. Much of the resulting litigation involved disputed land titles, and since it also involved nonresidents of the state, "It was almost a matter of course that cases could be removed from the state court to the Federal court," which sat in four northern West Virginia localities but only in Charleston in the south. The permanent fixture of the state capital in Charleston in 1885 brought state courts and departments of government there to enhance the Kanawha lawyers' opportunities. "I smiled, and the money came," wrote MacCorkle the millionaire in 1928.[11] Kenna died young in modest circumstances, but his associates prospered at the bar and as the owners of coalfield and Charleston real estate; they also managed to accumulate state and federal offices on a large scale after they won statewide prominence in the campaign of 1880. The combination of modern and traditional outlooks that the Kanawha Ring brought to West Virginia politics is conveyed by MacCorkle's analysis of his successful gubernatorial campaign in 1892. His pursuit of the nomination was a carefully prepared and disciplined assault on the "concatenation of organized power" wielded by Camden and Davis; the effort was financed by a friendly coal operator from Philadelphia. Then on the hustings "I appealed to the southern element largely, as I was southern born and my father had been in the southern army. . . . The southern people almost universally supported me."[12] Quantitative analysis of the Kanawha organization's performance in the state Democratic conventions of 1880 and 1884 and in third district congressional campaigns from 1878 to 1886 reinforces this impression of modern political methods wedded to traditional campaigning styles. The Kanawha Ring's

10

strength rested on its ability to mobilize support in the interior counties lying at a distance from the railroad and river transportation lines; they also formed temporary but useful alliances with Camden and the Redeemers. As early as 1880, however, they had lost effective control of their home base, yielding the wealthier agricultural and mining districts along the Kanawha River to Agrarian Democrats or Greenbackers, the city of Charleston to the Republicans.

There is no need here to trace the factional battles that broke out every time West Virginia Democrats met in convention to nominate a congressman or governor or in the legislature to elect a United States senator. What is important is what underlay these conflicts. Although sectional and economic issues were often at stake, there was also an underlying clash between different ways of conducting the business of politics.[13] Entrenched in the interior counties and in tradition-minded districts along the Virginia border was a pre-industrial political system, whose social basis was kinship, propinquity, and deference to neighborhood and district notables. It rested on face-to-face communications, with linkages provided by lawyers and other itinerants who followed the rough mountain trails through settlements whose residents were scattered along the watercourses, isolated even from nearby neighbors by the difficult character of the terrain. A Republican who sought to explain the failure of his party to win much support in central and southern West Virginia during the 1870s put his finger neatly on the cause: "It is exceedingly difficult to reach the voting masses of the state," he wrote:

> Thousands of the people live in remote and almost inaccessible mountain districts, where they have but few means of communicating with the outside world. Many of them are unable to read, and they are Democrats because they don't know any better. Of course among this class of people public speaking is the only kind of campaign work that accomplishes anything. . . .

And Republicans, he went on to say, were hampered by a lack of funds and of "home speakers."[14] George W. Atkinson, West Virginia's next (1897) Republican governor, spent

11

eight years of his youth in the Kanawha valley as the Charleston postmaster and editor of a Republican newspaper but failed to make headway in bids for elective office. Concluding that "this portion of West Virginia is bankrupt both financially and morally," Atkinson turned north in 1877 to Wheeling and Washington with the disgust of a frustrated missionary.[15] But for the young lawyers of the Kanawha Ring who, unlike Atkinson, were able to exploit the networks of backwoods connections and attitudes, the interior was not at all bankrupt.

Opposing the traditional political system, and gradually eroding its social base as railroads, lumber camps, and mines appeared in the interior plateau during the 1880s and '90s, was a modern system, one based on modern forms of communication and bureaucratic political linkages. Among its features were centralized and continuously functioning machinery for the recruitment of candidates and the conduct of election campaigns; regular propagandizing of followers and potential converts by means of newspapers and printed circulars; and mass meetings which often featured railroad excursions for voters who lived outside the larger cities and towns. The costs of these recurrent functions were met by the donated services of party workers, especially patronage appointees, and by contributions from wealthy followers and clients. The credit for inaugurating this system in West Virginia may actually belong to rival factions of eastern Virginia Democrats, who used both the federal patronage and newspaper propaganda in a frantic search for western allies on the eve of the Civil War. When the war swept away these beginnings, the Republican founders of West Virginia relaid the foundations of its modern politics. Following its reorganization under Elkins during the 1890s, the G.O.P. completed the shift from a pre-industrial system to a modern one. But it was the Democratic industrialists, Camden and Davis, who bore the brunt of the transition.

Against the pre-industrial networks of information and influence that survived in West Virginia, Camden and Davis manned the axes of modern communications. MacCorkle

12

considered it "an anomaly in politics" that neither could make a decent speech,[16] but investments in Democratic newspapers and gifts and loans to their editors added weight to their viewpoints and lent them the statesmanlike aura that they failed to project in person. They contributed financially to party campaign funds and to individual candidates, which added to the funds from national party agencies channeled through them, made them by far and away the largest source of "the sinews of war." As private employers, they could supply jobs, railroad passes, legal work, and other forms of private patronage. Camden also was able to control the flow of federal jobs after the election of Grover Cleveland made these available to Democrats in 1885. The industrialists enjoyed equivalent leverage in the party's organizational machinery. Despite the success of rival factions in the various contests for office, Camden, Davis, and their "Regular" followers maintained unbroken control of the committees that determined the sites and dates of nominating conventions, awarded credentials and wrote platforms, distributed campaign literature and funds—control that lasted from 1866 to 1892, when the Kanawha Ring wrested away the state party chairmanship for William E. Chilton. The industrialists themselves undertook to represent the state in national Democratic councils. Jointly or singly Davis and Camden led the delegations to every Democratic National Convention from 1868 to 1892, the single exception being 1872 when the convention met to endorse the Liberal Republican, Horace Greeley, an unpopular candidate in West Virginia. They also kept tabs on the key post of national committeeman and rotated it among themselves during the mid-eighties when no suitable lieutenant could be found.

Despite this formidable array of political resources, the industrialists still failed to tame their border Democracy. They were able to create a secure base in the towns along the railroads and rivers, especially in northern West Virginia, where the competition of a locally strong Republican party offered a further inducement to Democratic discipline. They headed the strongest and best organized of the party's factions, but this in itself was not enough. Davis and Camden commanded the lines of information and organization extending outward from Wheeling and other industrial centers. But beyond the reach of these media lay the pre-industrial and transitional communities whose networks of influence and information were commanded by Redeemer traditionalists. At the defiles between past and present stood the Agrarians and the Kanawha Ring, contending with each other and with the tycoons for mastery of West Virginia's future. Although each was weaker than the industrialists' "concatenation of organized power," one or more of the rival factions were usually able to disrupt the Regulars' calculations, forcing Camden or Davis to make way for someone else. Occasionally the Regulars met defeat at the hands of a rival leader, as in the cases of Senator Kenna or Governor Wilson. More commonly the result was stalemate, followed by compromise, with the office in question going to some Redeemer or Kanawha lawyer whose political style combined traditional Virginia practices with conservative economic views.

One such incident in 1882 produced the congressional career of William L. Wilson, who apart from Senators Davis and Elkins achieved a greater prominence in national politics than any West Virginia leader of his day. As fate would have it, it was Davis who groomed Wilson for his compromiser role for reasons connected with his own hopes of winning a third senatorial term. The strategy worked only too well from Davis's standpoint. Wilson's Confederate war record and polished oratorical style so entranced the rural voters who provided the Democratic majorities in his district that it became a difficult task to dislodge him after he developed views on the tariff issue that affronted Davis and other producers of West Virginia coal. Davis's attempt to discipline and then to defeat his most illustrious protege provides an ironic commentary on the vagaries of the changing political system with which the Democratic industrialists had to deal.

Time and progress in the form of advancing industrialism were on Davis and Camden's side during the 1880s. The

14

eastern valleys that produced many of their Redeemer and Agrarian rivals remained the richest agricultural lands in the state, but their share of West Virginia's population was declining and by 1890 they were losing their relative lead in agricultural wealth. West of the Allegheny Front, the advancing railroads were turning the interior bastions of backwoods politics into industrial communities of the sort where the tycoons' political resources were deployed to greatest effect. If Davis read these hopeful signs, however, he decided after 1887 to ignore them. Discouraged by two decades of factional struggle and confronted in the tariff reform movement by what he regarded as a drastic threat to his economic interests, he was no longer disposed to wait. When to his own political frustrations was added Camden's ousting from the Senate in 1887, he initiated a course of action that had far-reaching implications for the history of the Mountain State: It led to Elkins's entry into West Virginia politics, to his displacement of the statemakers and their heirs from the helm of the local Republican party, and thus to his and Scott's assumption of the places once held by Davis and Camden after the G.O.P. regained control of West Virginia in the election of 1894. These developments in turn led to the consolidation of the industrialists' power in both political parties by 1900, a state of affairs that was aptly described as a bipartisan "merger" operated by and for the leading business interests in the state.[17]

The task of tracing these developments in the following chapters will take us initially far from the borders of West Virginia, but that is only appropriate. The circuitous route by which Elkins traveled to power in his adopted home was a fitting comment on the colonial nature of the political economy that he and his colleagues helped to create there. Although the other captains of industry presented more plausible claims to actual residence in West Virginia than did Elkins, all four were "carpetbaggers" by traditional political standards. All were business and political associates or allies of integrated industrial concerns operated from Baltimore, Cleveland, Pittsburgh, or New York. As industrialists whose

15

personal business concerns extended from Alaska to Mexico, from California to New England, their real constituencies did not know the boundaries established by an eighteenth-century federalist constitution. Their primary concerns in politics were not local affairs; watchdogs of the type that the historian, Charles Henry Ambler, called "henchmen" were plentiful enough at Charleston and the courthouse towns, and as Ambler noted, the political "evils" of the day "were [more] pronounced among the lesser leaders" than among the industrialists themselves.[18] It was not their economic interest in local matters but the requirements for creating and maintaining a secure political base that led the industrialists to exert a transforming influence in West Virginia's political history. Their primary concern was the formation of national policy, especially that part that directly concerned their interstate business interests. This was why they concentrated on the Senate, since it offered the most enduring and influential basis for intervening in national policy formation in a day of nondescript presidents and closely contested electoral campaigns. Elkins and his colleagues thus placed West Virginia's Senate representation, like its coal, timber, oil, and natural gas, at the service of the metropolitan centers of industrial capitalism. Local political leaders, insofar as they collaborated in this development, settled for a colonial politics just as they settled for a colonial economy.

The formation of West Virginia's colonial political economy is the subject of the narrative that follows. The story begins with ex-Senator Davis at a moment when he is much preoccupied with the defense of the tariff on coal.

The Politics of Coal

Today the West Virginia coal industry is noted for the scars it leaves upon the hillsides, but its scar runs deep across the history books as well. Bituminous coal has been the leading industrial product of the state since the 1890s. Even before the industry assumed its present importance, the extent to which its anticipated growth fueled West Virginians' economic aspirations meant that few local politicians were in a position to overlook coal's interests. Thus during the 1880s, when the national leadership of the Democratic party debated and then embraced a reform program that seemed likely to lead to the removal of tariff protection for coal, West Virginia Democrats who were loyal to their party and loyal to their state found themselves in a dilemma. The social value of the tariff on coal to the state as well as to the nation could be called into question, but its economic value to individual producers of coal was undoubted. No one was less troubled on this point than Henry G. Davis. "Charity ought to begin and stay at home," was the view of this leading West Virginia Democrat and coal producer, stated with characteristic thrift of expression.[1] "It is my conviction," he stated, "that no party can succeed in this country for any length of time which places itself upon a free-trade platform, and I do not believe it ought to succeed."[2] When this warning went unheeded, he set out to prove his point.

What Davis eventually set out to do, in fact, was to sabotage his own political party in order to bring Elkins and the Republicans to power, where they might act in defense of the tariff on coal. The program is simply stated, but it was anything but simple in conception or execution, as this chapter will disclose. Davis approached this objective only after intricate maneuvers among fellow Democrats failed to contain the

17

tariff reform threat. Elkins in turn engaged in equally intricate maneuvers within his own party to place himself in a position to benefit from Davis's plan. These developments are worth a detailed exposition, however, despite their complexity. The tortuous path that Davis and Elkins followed to cement their power in West Virginia tells us much about the personalities and motives of the two men and also about the relationship between the political and business aspects of their careers. It is probably true also that this path took them to a point where they had greater influence on national politics and policies than any West Virginia leaders before or since.

The path begins where it will also end—with the tariff on coal.

As Davis saw it, the tariff question was not a "purely political" matter, even though he presented the issue to his fellow Democrats in a blunt political way. For him the tariff belonged to that "constructive" sphere of activities that he placed above partisan considerations.[3] It was a matter of principle, he insisted.[4] He declined to acknowledge the economic equation in his thinking, even though his self-interest in the tariff was patently visible to most observers and was directly thrown up to him on more than one occasion. Yet the economic equation was there, very much so, as his record as a U.S. senator reveals.

Davis first encountered the tariff issue as a freshman senator in 1872, when Congress attempted a modest revision of the Morrill Tariff of the Civil War. At that time his interest in the coal industry was limited to the shipments of his mercantile firm, H. G. Davis & Brother, (amounting to about 6,000 tons in 1875, the first year for which there are figures) and to his as-yet-undeveloped coal lands.[5] In the tariff debate of May 1872, he was either prudent or uninterested, even though the bituminous duty was pruned from $1.25 to $.75 per ton. He left the talking to his Republican colleague and to the Pennsylvania and Maryland senators and did not record a vote on the issue.[6] In 1875, when the Republicans carried an upward revision of the tariff on nearly everything

18

but coal, he voted with his party against them.[7] When tariff reform emerged as a more powerful movement during the 1880s, however, it found Davis's economic interests concentrated in coal and at a critical stage of development. Accordingly, his attitude stiffened. It is noteworthy that he assumed active leadership of the Democratic protectionists just at the moment when his secret campaign to win reelection was still pending, a time when a politician more prudent or less alarmed might have found it wise to keep silent.

While modern observers sometimes find the tariff uproar a sham battle, it was a deadly serious one as far as Davis was concerned, as it was for Elkins. Their reaction to the reform threat was conditioned by the nature of competition within the coal industry. The geographic juxtaposition of coalfields and waterways dictated the division of the United States into several fairly distinct regional markets. Although the West Virginia Central* always shipped a little coal to the Pittsburgh market, the western or "lake" trade, and the southern "river" or "Gulf" trades, its main outlet was the eastern or "seaboard" market, which served the railroads and industries of Maryland, Delaware, eastern Pennsylvania and New York, New Jersey, and New England. Prior to 1880 this market was practically the monopoly of producers in the Cumberland region of western Maryland and the Clearfield region of central Pennsylvania. But during the next six years, four major fields were opened to production. These included, besides Elk Garden (mined exclusively by the West Virginia Central), the Pocahontas field on the Norfolk & Western Railroad, Beech Creek on the New York Central east of Clearfield, and Reynoldsville on the Erie Railroad in northern Pennsylvania. In addition to these, some slightly older regions, like New River on the Chesapeake & Ohio in southern West Virginia, greatly expanded their production during these years. Con-

---

*"West Virginia Central" is used here to designate the Davis-Elkins coal and/or railroad operations as the context indicates, even though "Elk Garden" coal was marketed by family mining firms (notably Davis Coal & Coke Company) as well as by the railroad. All operating mining and railroad firms were consolidated under the West Virginia Central charter in 1899-1901.

sequently the tonnage arriving in the seaboard market rose sharply, from 5,600,000 tons in 1880 to an estimated 9,500,000 in 1885, to 10,500,000 in 1886.[8] Davis and Elkins's own production rose from 54,000 tons in 1880, representing the Maryland mines of H. G. Davis & Brother, to 456,000 in 1884, when the main line of their railroad was opened. The Elk Garden region's output was still dwarfed by the 2,500,000 tons of the parent Cumberland region, but the West Virginia Central was now the second largest producing firm in the Potomac valley, after the Consolidation Coal Company.[9]

In these circumstances prices fell as production mounted and were further depressed by the general business downturn that gathered speed after 1882. The f.o.b. price per ton at Baltimore, through which most Elk Garden coal was shipped until 1888, declined from $3.75 in 1881 to $2.90 in 1883, $2.25 in 1885, and $2.10 in 1886.[10] These were average market prices. Contract prices with large customers, often requiring producers to absorb part of the cost of delivery from tidewater to the point of destination, were even lower.[11] And the point of destination for Elk Garden coal was as often as not New England, precisely the market in which duty-free Canadian coal could be expected to have its greatest impact. Like all West Virginia seaboard producers, Davis and Elkins competed at a disadvantage with Pennsylvania mines in supplying coal to the Middle Atlantic states. They were farther from the markets and also farther from the sea, which meant that railroad freights constituted a larger component in their prices. However, lower southern wage rates, plus lower water freight differentials between Boston and the several tidewater railheads (chiefly New York harbor, Philadelphia, Baltimore, and Hampton Roads), smoothed the difference for southern coal in New England.[12] In 1885 Davis and Elkins sold 100,000 tons, nearly a quarter of their entire production, to the Boston & Maine Railroad. The same road took 50,000 tons the following year, the New Haven Railroad, 40,000, and the Housatonic Railroad in Connecticut, 30,000. Some other Elk Garden consumers were the

20

Maine Central, Kennebec, Naugatuck Valley, and New Haven & Northampton railroads.[13]

Although of a generally inferior quality to the best American grades, Cape Breton coal was sufficient for gas manufacturing and for many steam-raising purposes of these and other consumers. Under the Canadian reciprocity treaty that lapsed in 1866, Nova Scotia coal had commanded lower prices than domestic in the Boston market.[14] High wartime demand then protected American producers from adverse effects, but there was no likelihood of this happening now. Of the 1,300,000 tons received at Boston during 1887, only 14,000 came in from Canada, thanks to the tariff.[15] But with the tariff barrier down, Canadian coal might dominate the New England market. Which was, in fact, precisely what New England manufacturers who favored tariff reform hoped for.[16]

The bituminous producers sought to cope with their several problems collectively. Like their anthracite cousins, they established a pool, the Seaboard Steam Coal Association, that tried to stabilize prices by restraining production and dividing the market. Davis took a leading hand in the affairs of this organization, but it did not work very well. Especially during unprosperous periods, some member or other yielded to the temptation to increase volume at the expense of prices, whereupon the pool would collapse, only to revive again during times of prosperity.[17] On the political front, the organization created a lobbying wing as the tariff struggle approached a climax in 1893. This American Coal Trade Committee involved the seaboard industry generally, but Davis and Elkins quickly assumed the leadership of its Washington operations. Their political experience and bipartisan connections stood them well in this endeavor, but they encountered another set of difficulties. The anthracite industry, reflecting the compact arrangement of producing fields in northeastern Pennsylvania, was by that time highly concentrated, involving a handful of railroad-owned firms that neither needed nor sought tariff protection, anthracite coal being a virtual monopoly of the United States. Bituminous fields were

21

dispersed and firms small by comparison. Geographic dispersion encouraged a disparity of interests as well. Producers south of the Virginias did not compete in the seaboard market, nor did those of Ohio, Indiana, and Illinois. Western Pennsylvania mines, along with those of the Fairmont and Kanawha regions in West Virginia, competed mainly in the Pittsburgh, lake, and river trades. Moreover, western producers enjoyed the same prospective advantages in Ontario that Nova Scotia coal did in New England, which helps to explain why Representative William L. Scott of Pennsylvania, a bituminous magnate from Erie, was to be found among the congressional leaders of tariff reform. For these reasons, the seaboard bituminous producers lacked the advantage of wool growers, who had a dispersed and hence politically potent constituency united in a common interest. They also lacked the concentrated power that giant firms like Standard Oil or the American Sugar Refining Company could bring to bear on doubtful or pliant legislators.[18]

These circumstances, in the midst of a battle such as eventually took place in Congress in 1893-1894, could breed suspicion of even the best of friends. Senator Arthur Gorman, for example, Democratic boss of Maryland and majority leader in the Senate in 1894, was Davis's first cousin, a longtime friend and ally, and a stockholder in the Davis-Elkins firms, one of which his brother, Willie Gorman, managed. But Gorman was known in mysterious but generally acknowledged ways to be allied with the American Sugar Refining Company. Moreover, he was a professional politician who ranked party loyalty high among the political virtues. Camden, a senator again in 1894, also owned coal mines. But his first legislative loyalty was to Rockefeller; his mines were in the western-oriented Fairmont region; and he was suspected of speculating in sugar stocks during the tariff debate. Davis trusted but Elkins deeply distrusted each of these men during the crisis.[19] Both partners recognized an enemy in the Dominion Coal Company, a Boston-based firm organized shortly after Cleveland's second election to control over 90 percent of Nova Scotia bituminous production. Controlled by a

22

brother and business associates of William C. Whitney, Cleveland's secretary of the navy, the Dominion Company constituted a politically powerful rival nourished at the very breast of tariff reform.[20]

Viewed from Davis's position during the eighties, some of the disadvantages outlined above were prospective ones, but the fact that they later materialized helps to explain why he worked so tirelessly to head off a tariff confrontation and, just in case, to regain a voice in the Senate whose first allegiance was to his particular interests. And, as if the woes he and Elkins shared with other seaboard producers were not enough, they faced troubles that were peculiarly their own. Few businessmen were as dependent upon railroads as were the coal operators. Railroad rates were the biggest factor in determining coal prices—accounting for 45 percent of the market price at New York as Davis calculated it in 1881, with water freight between tidewater on Chesapeake Bay and New York harbor adding another 27 percent.[21] The carriers provided special cars, storage, and harbor facilities for coal shippers, and the way they allotted these facilities among competing firms could make or break a given producer. They were also consumers of coal. Because they dealt with larger railroads through the West Virginia Central, Davis and Elkins enjoyed the opportunity to make favorable interrailroad traffic arrangements such as the "mileage" arrangements with the B&O and later the Pennsylvania, by which the trunk lines' coal cars were used by the smaller road free of charge. They also negotiated rates with the trunk lines as connectors rather than as shippers. This meant that a favorable "pro-rating" arrangement by a trunk line with the West Virginia Central amounted to much the same thing as rebating. Any losses incurred by the Davis-Elkins railroad in setting these rates showed up as profits on the ledgers of the Davis-Elkins coal companies, which—unlike the railroad—were wholly owned by members of the family or close friends.[22]

As long as the B&O was led by Davis's old friend and former employer, John W. Garrett, the West Virginia Central enjoyed profitable relations with its principal outlet to market. But, as Elkins later noted, "Things change fast, & corporations fast friends today may be enemies tomorrow...."[23] Garrett died in September 1884 and after a Cromwellian interlude in which the presidency was held by his son, Robert, then by a professional manager, control of the trunk line passed in December 1888 to a syndicate representing Davis and Elkins's foremost competitor, the Consolidation Coal Company of Cumberland.[24] Their relations with the B&O had already begun to deteriorate during the presidency of Robert Garrett. In March 1886, Davis broke off a series of negotiations with Garrett over rebates, car interchange, and prorating, and announced his intention to build a new railroad from Piedmont to Cumberland to connect with the Pennsylvania system. The Piedmont & Cumberland Railroad was completed in the fall of 1887, after clearing legal and, in one instance, physical hurdles placed in its path by the B&O.[25] But the Cumberland-Philadelphia route was a mountainous, roundabout one, able to handle little more than one-third of the Davis-Elkins coal shipments to tidewater, even though their traffic agreement with the PRR called for one-half.[26] A reduced flow of traffic continued over the B&O under informal arrangements, with no special privileges, while the two sides transferred their battle to the courts in a series of suits and countersuits between Davis and Elkins and Alexander Shaw of Baltimore, Davis's original partner and the West Virginia Central's largest minority stockholder.[27] After Shaw was decisively beaten in 1893, he sold his holdings to Richard C. Kerens of Saint Louis, a Republican politician and associate of Elkins during the latter's business and political novitiate in the Southwest.[28]

It is also of interest that these changes in business relations affected Davis's relations with Camden. During the seventies, for reasons that will be explained at greater length in Chapter 5, Camden acted as a determined business enemy of B&O, working to tame it to the Standard Oil Company's ambition to control and limit West Virginia refinery and crude oil production and also to end the B&O's support of independent

24

refiners in Pennsylvania and Baltimore. The success of the strategy restricted Camden's managerial responsibilities in the oil industry and freed him to turn to other projects.[29] One was the Ohio River Railroad, paralleling the river from Wheeling to the mouth of the Kanawha and eventually to Huntington. Another was a narrow-gauge railroad (West Virginia & Pittsburgh) extending south from Clarksburg toward the interior lands acquired in his youth; a third involved the Monongah mine in the Fairmont region and collaboration with the Watson interests there; a fourth was the Caperton lands project, toward which the West Virginia & Pittsburgh made its way between 1879 and 1892.[30] All of these projects required the cooperation of the B&O for much the same reasons Davis had needed it during the developmental stages of his upper Potomac enterprises. This business realignment did not end the industrialists' sociable relationship. But the effect introduced a certain distance in place of the earlier comradeship. One result was a general "treaty" between the two "interests," signed at Baltimore in January 1890. By its terms Camden liquidated his holdings in the Davis-Elkins enterprises, as they did in his, and acquired full title to the Caperton lands. The agreement divided central and east-central West Virginia into spheres of interest, bounded by a line roughly parallel to but somewhat west of the Greenbrier valley, wherein the other would not tread.[31] Another result was Davis's less-than-ardent support of Camden in his contest with the Agrarians in the senatorial contest of 1887, a development that will be more fully discussed later.

Meanwhile, as the depression of the mid-eighties touched bottom, Davis and Elkins faced still other sources of distress, which Davis summed up in a letter of April 1886. "Owing to the severe Winter, and the consequent blocking of the harbor here [Baltimore] for a long time, the low prices obtaining for coal, . . . and the miners' strike now pending in our region," he wrote, "this company is having a hard time."[32] Business improved during 1887 but neither the price of coal nor Elk Garden production nor the value of West Virginia Central stocks and bonds had regained their earlier levels by the time

Grover Cleveland loosed his celebrated Tariff Message in December.[33] Davis was having a hard time in business and politics and was not about to acquiesce in tariff tampering simply out of loyalty to the Democratic party. Elkins was having Republican troubles of his own, for reasons that will forthwith be reviewed. At this point the political careers of the two men converged, as their business careers had earlier done, with important implications for West Virginia's future.

But for a handshake, so the story went, Stephen B. Elkins might have become the political boss of New Mexico instead of West Virginia. Elkins first went to that southwestern territory from Missouri as a young lawyer in 1864 and prospered there much in the same way that lawyers prospered in antebellum western Virginia—with an important difference. Thanks to the confusion in land titles arising from the transfer from Hispano-American to Anglo-American legal systems in 1848, New Mexican lawyers, like their Virginian counterparts, encountered abundant professional and speculative opportunities in land, especially those lawyers like Elkins who acquired a command of the Spanish language. Within a few years of his arrival in the West, he was an inside member of the "Santa Fe Ring" of attorneys who were eventually to engross some 80 percent of New Mexico's land-grant property.[34] The difference was that New Mexico was conquered territory and its native Indian and Spanish inhabitants subject peoples. Federal authorities filled the key territorial offices by appointment. Moreover, federal treaties and laws required confirmation by Congress to the territory's greatest temptation for land speculators: these were the 197 private grants that had been created (several of them suddenly and fraudulently on the eve of the Mexican cession) under earlier Hispanic regimes. Thus the shortest route to power in New Mexico lay through Washington.[35] Elkins learned the route well and employed it again when he turned to West Virginia in search of a new political home.

Apparently Elkins came to New Mexico as a Democrat. So his early correspondence would indicate, so also his middle name (Benton) and the fact that his father and older brothers served in the Confederate army. Elkins himself signed up in the Missouri (Union) Home Guards at Westport, his home near Kansas City. But like Camden and Davis he found the martial side of border warfare uninteresting and struck out on the Santa Fe Trail after a few months' service.[36] After the war, Thomas B. Catron, a boyhood friend and fellow lawyer, joined Elkins as his partner. Catron's conversion from border Democrat to territorial Republican is a matter of record, further suggesting that Elkins followed the same route. In any event, the two prospered in land, law, banking, and politics; Elkins advancing swiftly through a succession of territorial offices, Catron following at one or two paces behind.[37] In 1872, the "Ring" made Elkins its choice for territorial delegate to Congress. The following year he drew close to the font of power with two special purposes in mind. One was to secure congressional confirmation for 55 New Mexican land grants comprising 1,409,000 acres and to secure federal funds to survey others already confirmed. The second was to make New Mexico a state and so allow those who now held power in Santa Fe to consolidate their position without fear of further interference from the East.[38]

To this second purpose, and with the cooperation of his fellow delegate and land speculator, Jerome B. Chaffee of Colorado, Elkins submitted to the Forty-third Congress a New Mexico statehood bill, tied to the Colorado bill, which passed the House in May 1874. The Senate amended both bills, forcing a return to the House during the closing hours of the forty-third session. Colorado backers mustered the two-thirds vote required to bring their bill up out of order and the House concurred in the Senate amendments by a midnight vote on March 3-4, 1875; when the new state entered the Union in 1876, Chaffee returned to Washington as its first United States senator, an ambition that Elkins shared. New Mexico languished in territorial status for another thirty-six years, however.[39] The traditional explanation is that Elkins, wandering into the House a few days before the statehood vote at the conclusion of a particularly nasty

27

bloody-shirt speech, rushed up with his fellow Republicans to shake the speaker's hand, unwittingly alienating the Democratic votes needed to rescue the New Mexico bill.

That was the story. In fact this explanation rests on slender evidence and attributes to Elkins an impulsiveness he rarely betrayed in political affairs. New Mexican statehood may have failed for partisan reasons or because of racial prejudice against the territory's Spanish people and culture.[40] It may also have fallen victim to the maneuvers of the territory's land speculators. One of the Senate amendments required citizens of the territory to relinquish all claims to unappropriated public lands. This was a conventional provision, less objectionable in the case of Colorado. But, as Catron later noted, New Mexico's private land grants were far superior to the territory's vacant and arid public domain: They "were located by intelligent people according to their own selections and necessarily occupy the very best lands in the Territory—that is the bottom lands and land adjacent to water, which can be most easily and cheaply irrigated."[41] Since the process of congressional confirmation of the grants was incomplete in 1875, it is possible that Elkins and his clients feared the amendment as a possible future means of invalidating their claims. It is significant in this respect that Frank Hereford, a West Virginia Democratic congressman who at this point frequently acted with Elkins's prospective father-in-law, Senator Davis, voted against the New Mexico bill, and also that Speaker James G. Blaine, another Elkins ally, did not exert himself greatly in the bill's behalf.[42]

Whatever killed the New Mexico bill, its demise profoundly affected Elkins's future. After his second congressional term expired in 1877, he settled in Washington for three years as a professional lobbyist, earning upwards of $50,000 a year from clients like Collis P. Huntington, the Maxwell Land Grant & Railroad Company, and some of the mail contractors involved in the Star Route frauds—one of whom, Kerens, became a partner in his southwestern and West Virginia enterprises.[43] His marriage in 1875 and his entry into the Davis family firms in 1878 and 1880 gradually diverted

Elkins's acquisitive energies into more reputable channels as a railroad builder and coal producer.[44] But his early adventures left him with mud on his feet and habits that he could never quite shake off. A case in point involved the North American Commercial Company, a California firm whose major stockholders reportedly were Elkins and D. O. Mills of San Francisco. In 1889, exerting his and Davis's influence with members of the Harrison Cabinet, Elkins managed to secure for this firm a twenty-year lease on the federally owned Seal (Pribilot) Islands of Alaska. Adroitly he steered the company through the Bering Sea controversy with Great Britain and an attempt by the second Cleveland administration to take away some of its privileges.[45] The further details of this venture are of no special concern here but the fact of Elkins's interest in the fur seals should be borne in mind for its relevance to West Virginia matters at a later point.

Throughout this period Elkins enjoyed a growing reputation in national Republican politics, but his influence did not rest upon a local constituency. In 1880 he moved his family to New York and opened a business office hard by the national headquarters of Camden's friends in Standard Oil. Meanwhile his legal residence remained New Mexico and he represented that territory on the Republican National Committee as late as 1884.[46] His fame in metropolitan political circles derived not from geography but from a personal attachment to the most luminous star in Republican heavens, James Gillespie Blaine.

It was Elkins's intimate association with Blaine that most distinguished him from the other spoilsmen who crowded Washington during the era of the bonanzas. When the two men met, Blaine was Speaker of the House, Elkins a lowly territorial delegate, but the mutual attraction was immediate and lasting. Elkins himself possessed some of that "magnetism" by which Blaine's hold on people was commonly explained. He was a boon companion, a good talker, and—what is more—a good listener. More than once Blaine called him near to share his "hopes, fears perturbations confidences and distrusts."[47] In other ways Elkins appealed to the pride and weakness that warred within Blaine for mastery of his considerable abilities, especially to that tragic fascination with wealth, never strong enough to command him but always ready to divert him to tastes that taxed his income and get-rich-quick schemes that marred his reputation. Elkins provided some of the schemes, as well as solid opportunities for investment in West Virginia; he also made available the vicarious satisfaction that Blaine always enjoyed in associating with rich and successful men.[48] In return, Blaine was able to put Elkins and Davis in touch with some of his other businessmen friends, like A. J. Cassatt, Henry Villard, and Andrew Carnegie, whose acquaintance was useful in developing their West Virginia enterprises.[49] Elkins's association with Carnegie, Garret Hobart, W. W. Phelps, and B. F. Jones in Blaine's several campaigns for the presidential nomination helped to smooth his passage from the ranks of the territorial adventurers into the eastern business wing of the Republican party.

It was Elkins's talent as a political organizer that most attracted Blaine. "He seems to have an undoubted faith in management," observed James A. Garfield of the "Plumed Knight."[50] In the Republican national conventions of 1880 and 1884, Blaine's faith reposed chiefly in Elkins, who justified it by tireless efforts to realize his friend's presidential ambition. His most notable achievement was the vice-presidential deal with John A. Logan that gave Blaine the presidential nomination in 1884. This left Blaine breathless with gratitude and he promptly made Elkins the manager of his campaign for the presidency.[51] Elkins conducted a thoroughly professional canvass for votes and funds and was strong in opposition to Blaine's disastrous last-minute visit to New York.[52] The 1884 campaign left Elkins with a national reputation as a political strategist, an asset that played an important role in his translation from New Mexico and the lobby to West Virginia and the Senate in later years.

Throughout this period Elkins did not abandon the goal of a Senate seat and expected the toga as a reward for his services to Blaine. At first the two counted on passing a suitable New Mexico bill when Blaine could place behind it the full weight of the presidency. In an especially cryptic letter of 1879, full of references to "my 'pet lamb' " and its "good fleece of fine wool," he assured Elkins that "we will make you Senator from New Mexico in two years," adding, with typical indiscretion, "There's bribery for you on a huge scale!"[53] But as long as Blaine failed to gather his fleece, Elkins's career remained in suspense. Following Garfield's election in 1880, Blaine turned to the cabinet as a temporary outpost for his friend. Elkins was "a strong and valuable friend who may prove useful to you at odd times," he told Garfield in recommending Elkins for the secretaryship of the Interior. Numerous other friends of Elkins seconded the recommendation, but Garfield ignored it, perhaps because he recognized the more than casual interest of New Mexicans in the affairs of the department in question.[54] An unfriendly source, *The New York Sun,* suggested another reason for the President's decision: that Elkins, as "a banker in New Mexico, a railroad builder in West Virginia, a speculator in New York," could not be located on the political map.[55] There is evidence that this problem of geography had already begun to worry Blaine and Elkins in 1881. But in August of that year, with the wounded Garfield lying on his deathbed, Blaine warned that "Cabinet matters in the future are very uncertain and hence I do not wish you to take any decisive step touching your political *status* especially respecting domicile until matters are settled down. . . ." Apparently they had in mind a new cabinet possibility for Elkins, the postmaster-generalship, Star Route disclosures notwithstanding (or perhaps because of them).[56] In any event, Garfield's death left things in their "very unsettled condition," so far as Elkins's political prospects were concerned.

Despite the succession of hostile Republicans under Arthur and Blaine's defeat in 1884, there is no further indication that Elkins's thoughts were turning to West Virginia as a possible political home. For one thing, Davis was not yet ready to declare it open territory, as we shall see. Even if

Elkins was planning to relocate, he still had need of a powerful friend in Washington. The local Republican party was steadily healing its internal wounds and increasing its share of the vote in West Virginia during the eighties and Elkins would need to control the flow of federal patronage if he hoped to make a bloodless and rapid conquest. In this respect his hopes were still riding with Blaine early in 1887. But Blaine was behaving most uncharacteristically. "I have been giving no heed to political currents," he told Elkins in March, "think nothing of them, know nothing of them and am almost ready to say care nothing." In June the Plumed Knight sailed off for a year in Europe, telling Elkins that he had no stomach for another fight for the nomination.[57] Even if he had, the Republican chances of victory were not that great. The party was still divided along the bitter lines of 1884 and was without an issue against Cleveland.[58] It was also broke. Chairman B. F. Jones informed Elkins that national, state, and local committees were without funds and that "the American Iron & Steel Association is milked dry," along with other manufacturers.[59] It was in this context that Elkins joined Davis and another ex-senator, Benjamin Harrison of Indiana, in August 1887 at the family's summer retreat atop the Maryland Alleghenies for a conference that had momentous consequences for West Virginia and the nation.

The aura of power that clung to Davis and Elkins at this time derived in large part from the fame of their summer home, Deer Park, Maryland, as a political capital. With the cooperation of John W. Garrett of the B&O, Davis had made his mountaintop "farm" into a thriving summer resort, attracting mainly railroad executives and other Baltimore businessmen. The most prominent visitors, however, were the friends that he brought home from the Senate, among them Thurman, Sherman, and Pendleton of Ohio, McDonald and Harrison of Indiana, Windom of Minnesota, and Bayard of Delaware. Gorman and Camden were frequent visitors, while the other politicians, many of whom owned stock in the West Virginia Central, often dropped by on their way down to inspect their property. Elkins, himself quite a news maker at this time, had a "cottage" close to Davis's where he entertained Blaine, ex-President Grant, and lesser Republican dignitaries. Thus by 1884 the place was widely known as "A paradise of babies and lovers and politicians"—especially politicians. A series of tanbark paths connected the cottages with the little B&O station, allowing important visitors to slip through the woods unobserved by reporters who lined the veranda of the local hotel. This convenience was said to be of special value to Elkins when he was directing the Blaine campaign.[60]

The coming and going at Deer Park doubtless made for a good deal of innocent fun, not to mention good advertising for the property. The rich mixture of mountain air and political gossip was a big attraction, and the host was much impressed by his position amid all this bipartisan good fellowship. As Davis noted in his journal after the 1884 election, "Mr. Elkins (son-in-law) and Senator Gorman (cousin) were at the head of the [campaign] committees of Democrats and Republicans, so my relation to each is good and close."[61] It is clear that he expected to make use of his impressive national connections to restore his influence in West Virginia.

In one respect the Cleveland-Blaine campaign cost Davis a further setback in West Virginia. The Wheeling editor, Lewis Baker, irritated by a disagreement with Davis over Democratic strategy, became convinced that Davis was secretly working with Elkins and Blaine. When he received from Davis a $200 check and the message that "Elkins says you ought not to shout fraud at Blaine try and beat him but not abuse," Baker rushed into print and made his suspicion public. There followed an open break between the two men, and for Davis, the loss of a hitherto loyal and valuable ally.[62] Baker was not alone in his doubts about Davis's loyalty during the 1884 campaign.[63] Indeed, the latter's feelings were divided but the skeptics underestimated his ability to compartmentalize his interests into "personal" or "constructive" and "purely political" slots. As he expressed it, "my political feeling and acts were and are with Cleveland; my personal feeling with

33

Blaine."[64] Gorman advised him to remain in the background because of his "peculiar relations" with Elkins, but he contributed at least $2000 to the party war chest.[65] Visiting Albany at Cleveland's request on October 8, he was impressed by the candidate and redoubled his efforts to carry West Virginia.[66]

Following the Democratic victory, Davis moved to attach himself to the new administration. He trained his sights on a cabinet post, the postmaster generalship. In view of the well-known connection of that office with patronage it may be that Davis was impressed by now with the necessity of building up a stronger personal organization in West Virginia. Gorman conducted Davis's campaign, with support from Senators Bayard and Camden and the latter's brother-in-law, W. P. Thompson of Standard Oil, who took special pains to see that Davis's business relations with Elkins and Blaine were not "misunderstood" by Cleveland. They kept up the pressure throughout December and January; on February 6 Davis himself went to call on the president-elect. But in the end the appointment went to William F. Vilas of Wisconsin.[67] This was only the start of a bad year for Davis, for he did badly with patronage generally. His leading protege at home, C. Wood Dailey, lost out in the scramble for the top local jobs to John T. McGraw, a Camdenite, and C. C. Watts of the Kanawha Ring. "I see you and Kenna are doing well for [illegible] boys," he ruefully wrote Camden.[68] He tried counseling the administration at least to distribute the goods evenly among the West Virginia factions, but Cleveland continued to work through Camden and Kenna.[69] By September 1885 his own sights were lowered to "a suitable [diplomatic] mission. . . . I would not want to stay away long (say a year)," he told Secretary of State Bayard; "money not so much an object as honor."[70] Bayard had nothing to offer, however.

Ironically Davis's reputation for influence, if anything, prospered during this lean period and he was able to count the new president among the number of his powerful friends. Their personal relations endured a number of Washington dinners in wintertime and reached a high point in the summer of 1886 when Cleveland visited Deer Park. The occasion was a singular one, the first presidential honeymoon in American history. The bridegroom chose Deer Park for its convenience to Washington, a disastrous error as it turned out. Reporters swarmed over the place, filled the hotel, infested the shrubbery, and ruthlessly disregarded the presidential privacy. Under these trying circumstances, Davis did his best to make the visit a pleasant one. He dined his guests, took them on fishing trips and on carriage rides to view the magnificent scenery.[71] His hospitality was returned the following winter at Mrs. Cleveland's first state dinner, where he went in with Mrs. August Belmont.[72] But these social amenities produced no political results. A week after the dinner Davis called on Cleveland to try to interest him in his views on the tariff, but he was unsuccessful.[73] A few weeks later in March 1887 he called again at the White House in the interest of William Windom, whom he wanted named to the new Interstate Commerce Commission. This was the last favor he asked of the Cleveland administration and again he was disappointed.[74] Within his own party, the deceptive magic of Deer Park had failed to work. There was, however, a Republican side to Deer Park that had yet to be explored.

Davis's drive to recover his influence was made all the more urgent by his growing preoccupation with the tariff issue. From 1883 on he worked to prevent his party from committing itself to tariff reform, at first with some success, but after Cleveland's inauguration with a mounting sense of frustration. The reform movement flourished among the Democratic congressional leadership and eventually won the president himself.

"I am not what is called a free trader," Davis once stated.[75] But neither would he admit to being an outright protectionist. He believed, so he said, that the purpose of a tariff was to raise government revenue, not to protect industries, but that the protection incidental to the collection of revenue duties should be distributed as widely as possible among the industries that needed it—and he was certain that

35

coal needed it. This theory of "incidental protection" was very popular among conservative Democrats, who further advocated the exclusive reliance of the federal government on tariff revenues and the reduction or repeal of direct taxes on tobacco or distilled products as a means of cutting down the treasury surplus that plagued the government during this period. In that way the "incidental protection" derived would be as generous as possible.[76] Carter Harrison of Illinois once edified his constituents by explaining incidental protectionism as a belief in a "tariff only for revenue" instead of the classic Democratic position, "tariff for revenue only."[77] That was the theory. In practice, incidental protectionism was indistinguishable from the straight-out Republican variety. Davis's voting record on the "Mongrel Tariff" of 1883 was a case in point. The recommendation of the Tariff Commission appointed by President Arthur, as embodied in both House and Senate bills pending in January 1883, proposed to reduce the bituminous duty from seventy-five to fifty cents per ton. In order to drum up support for an amendment restoring the duty, Davis voted for higher duties on nearly every other article covered by the tariff, or else he refrained from voting at all. As he explained it, "I am not willing in any vote I shall give intentionally to strike down any particular industry."[78] The only significant exception to this rule was his vote for lower duties on steel rails, a vote that said more about his activities as a railroad builder than about his theory of incidental protection.[79] There was little else to distinguish him from such Republican protectionists as Sherman, Aldrich, and Morrill. So far as the duty on coal was concerned, the tactic worked. Davis's amendment passed by a vote of 21-20. Since the narrow majority included—besides himself and Gorman—only two other Democrats, the vote was a forceful comment on the limited economic value of the virtue of party loyalty.[80]

In addition to political theory, Davis summoned history and economics to the defense of the tariff on coal. He cited Washington, Jefferson, Madison, Monroe, J. Q. Adams, Jackson, Henry Clay, Millard Fillmore, Horace Greeley, and

36

James K. Polk among the forerunners of incidental protectionism. He also painted a grim picture of unemployed miners and impoverished operators if Canadian coal should be admitted to the seaboard market.[81] But the argument that he and other coal men voiced with greatest feeling was that their industry was being treated unfairly. The tariff bills of 1872 and 1883 proposed a proportionately greater reduction of the coal duty than of nearly all others; the Morrison tariff bill of 1884 eliminated it altogether.

The fact was that the coal duty, like the duties on wool and sugar, was extremely vulnerable whenever tariff controversy was stirred. These articles were "necessaries of life"; placing them on the free list would be popular not only with the general public but with certain influential manufacturers who otherwise wished the protective system left undisturbed. A politician's advocacy of lower coal duties was therefore not a necessary indication of enthusiasm for a genuine reform across the boards. A posturing statesman like Senator John T. Morgan found it easy to proclaim that the coal interests of Alabama did not want "a tax upon coal . . . to be collected from the shivering poverty of the poor people along the Atlantic seaboard and thrown into our coffers."[82] In truth, Canadian coal posed no threat to Alabama producers; and since the use of relatively smokeless (and duty-free) anthracite coal as domestic fuel was required by law throughout the Northeast, Morgan's concern for the hearthsides of the poor was beside the point. Davis patiently explained this but he lacked the verbal skill to transform it into persuasive argument. Besides, there was a very good case to be made that the *people* as well as the industries of the Pacific coast would benefit from free coal. This argument Davis could meet only by logrolling. "All tariff duties and all taxes, however collected, must bear on somebody and something," he stated. When the West Coast senators had asked that other duties be raised, he had gone along; now they must go along with him. "You tickle me and I will tickle you," snorted Morgan, neatly characterizing a venerable approach to legislation.[83] As far as Davis was concerned, the important thing was that it worked.

With Republican support, he, Gorman, Camden, and the Louisiana sugar senators succeeded in transforming a "manufacturer's bill" into a bill for producers as well.[84] For the Democratic protectionists the Tariff of 1883 was thus a double victory.

Another victory for the Democratic protectionists was the party platform of 1884. Here Davis played a larger role than generally has been recognized. "The conspiracy to set up a tariff straddle" was usually credited to the New York managers of Cleveland's campaign for the nomination; the New Yorkers wanted to paper over tariff divisions lest they complicate the chance for victory in November.[85] Certainly they and their Southern allies were instrumental in persuading the convention to accept the plank that emerged from the platform committee and in snuffing out reformer protests. But it was Davis and his friends who wrote the plank. To be sure, there were "purely political" complications involved. As in former years, Davis rejected the Democracy's New York leadership, perhaps because he distrusted the pragmatism of party leaders there, an attitude which could be turned against as well as for the protectionist cause. Instead, his tastes ran to Ohio or border-state candidates, men of diverse records like Thurman and Bayard, but who were personally accessible to him. Thus in 1884 he supported Bayard, whose record encouraged the reformers, but who, it should be noted, was also a West Virginia Central stockholder.

Indeed, it is difficult to distinguish at some points in Davis's preparations for the national convention his concern for the tariff and his interest in Bayard's success. Probably the former was uppermost in his mind. Throughout the spring he worked to influence the selection of West Virginia delegates to the convention. The result was that only two of the twelve delegates—Davis and one other—were committed to Bayard. But the entire delegation adopted a resolution calling for incidental protection and elected Davis their representative on the platform committee.[86] A week in advance of the convention Davis met in New York with three other Bayard men who happened also to be protectionists (and

West Virginia Central stockholders): Gorman, ex-Senator William H. Barnum of Connecticut, and Senator James A. McPherson of New Jersey.[87] Apparently the four plotted to take the decision on the tariff plank out of the hands of the platform committee and to assign it to a smaller, more manageable group. This is what happened when the full committee met in Chicago on July 8. The vote on the chairmanship between W. R. Morrison and George L. Converse, an Ohio protectionist, ended in a tie, which would not have been likely had not the Maryland delegate, Gorman's man and a devout protectionist, cast his vote for Morrison. When another tie vote the following morning forecast a continuing deadlock, the full committee relinquished its duty and appointed a subcommittee of eight to resolve the difficulty.[88] The subcommittee included in Davis, Converse, and Major E. A. Burke, the Louisiana Machiavel, representatives of coal, wool, and sugar; Ben Butler of Massachusetts, a protectionist of McKinleyan proportions, was delegated to represent the American workingman. Morrison and Henry Watterson, on the reform side of the table, spoke for the rural consumers of the West and South, while J. Sterling Morton and Abram S. Hewitt represented, respectively, the western railroad and eastern manufacturing wings of the reform movement.[89]

After nearly forty-eight hours of "very animated" discussion in Butler's suite in the Palmer House, the subcommittee agreed upon a compromise plank. In truth it was a compromise in name only. While it was aptly characterized as a "meaningless, shiftless evasion," the plank required the reformers to mouth all the articles of incidental protection. It committed the Democracy to a "cautious and conservative" revision of the tariff "in a spirit of fairness to all interests . . . without imposing lower rates of duty than will be ample to cover any increased cost of production which may exist in consequence of the higher rates of wages prevailing in this country." It acknowledged the tariff as "the chief source of Federal revenues" and noted further that "many industries have come to rely on legislation for successful continuation, so that any change of law must be at every step regardful of the labor and capital involved. . . ." Finally, it denounced the internal revenue taxes as a "war tax," though it stopped short of a pledge to repeal them. The protectionists scored a further coup by electing Morrison chairman of the full committee after it had adopted the plank, so that he had to present the document to the convention. It is difficult to see what comfort the reformers took from the "compromise" but Morrison and Watterson loyally defended it. In any case, the convention loved it. Relieved of the prospect of a floor fight on the issue, the delegates approved the platform by a majority of over seven to one.[90]

Returning to West Virginia, Davis drafted one other platform in 1884, this one for the second district congressional convention. His handpicked representative in Congress, William L. Wilson, had not proved satisfactory. He had voted against the protectionist, Randall, in the speakership contest of December 1883 and seemed disposed to favor Morrison's tariff bill. Early in 1884 Davis canvassed district leaders on the possibility of denying Wilson renomination.[91] Now he drafted a resolution binding the convention's nominee "not, directly or indirectly, [to] give support to, but actively oppose, any man or measure which would have an influence tending to put coal, lumber, salt or wool upon the free list, or to discriminate against the industries connected with these articles."[92] Had the resolution been adopted, Wilson could not have accepted the nomination in good faith. But it was not even presented. Apparently Davis backed down in the face of the young congressman's growing popularity in the district and Wilson was accorded the first of six renominations.[93] Davis did not yet abandon all attempts to influence or discipline Wilson, but the stage was already being set for their final, dramatic confrontation ten years later.

The year, 1886, proved to be a turning point for the Democratic protectionists. Events in Congress showed that their influence was diminishing, although Randall was still able to block consideration of the Morrison Bill. Despite the efforts of many politicians in both parties to dodge the question, the tariff emerged as the dominant issue of the 1886 congressional campaign.[94] Thus it was with a renewed sense of urgency that Davis undertook an unusual degree of political activity during the campaign. In July he took over Lewis Baker's old post of national committeeman. Whereas earlier he had preferred the front-porch style of campaigning, highlighted by one or two platform appearances with dignitaries of equal rank, he now took to the stump. Instead of waiting to be asked, he solicited speaking engagements all over West Virginia, winding up with full-dress rallies in Wheeling and Charleston.[95] Overcoming his aversion for William L. Wilson, he asked the congressman if he might join him in his second district campaign.[96] He wrote a formal address—always a strenuous undertaking for him—"principally on Tarriff [sic] and Labor and Capital" and subsidized its circulation in the press of both parties. He even asked politicians if they needed money, a dangerous thing to do in any circumstances and certainly not to be done with no special object in mind.[97]

Precisely what was the object of Davis's unwonted activity in 1886? He did not say, but the evidence suggests that it was something more than an attempt to draw attention to himself and to protectionism in a general way. It is possible that his activities constituted a prelude to another bid to regain his seat in the Senate. We can be sure that he wanted to be on hand when that deliberate body again took up the tariff on coal. Senator Camden was coming up for reelection in January 1887. Davis, of course, did not set out to oppose him. But then he did not have to. The Agrarians having captured the statehouse under Willis Wilson in 1884, it was well understood that Camden would face a strenuous contest when he came up for reelection.

It was thus with every prospect of the sort of stalemate that had failed to materialize in 1883 that Davis took up the party standard and stood forth as a party statesman during the fall campaign. Camden's managers, accompanied by the federal officeholders, went to Charleston in January with a majority of the Democratic legislators in hand. But such were the gains of Republicans and fusionist candidates in the legislature that the statehouse commanded enough insurgent

41

Democrats to prevent his election. Davis was not on the list of preferred compromise candidates that the insurgents put forward. Nevertheless, by the time the list was issued, the capital was buzzing with rumors of a "contingent candidacy of ex-Senator Henry G. Davis," precisely the sort of thing he had failed to bring off in 1883.[98] The rumors were stirred by the prominence of Davis's closest followers in the anti-Camden "kick." C. Wood Dailey, attorney for the West Virginia Central, was in constant attendance in the capitol lobby and in close touch with Secretary of State Walker, the principal statehouse manager. Four South Branch valley legislators, headed by Senator George E. Price, another West Virginia Central lawyer, were among the "twelve apostates."[99] Dailey's name appeared on the bolters' list of compromisers. Elkins was said to be poised to descend on Charleston to swing the Republicans behind Davis when the time was right. Indeed he was planning the trip and put it off only at the last minute.[100] Davis himself went instead and his appearance on the field of battle on February 18 "was the signal for conjectures of every possible nature."[101] The conjectures were promptly denied. Davis's visit to Charleston was connected with two bills before the legislature—a West Virginia Central charter revision and a proposal for expediting land condemnation for railroad construction—connected with his current battle with the B&O. He had hesitated to go to Charleston while the senatorial contest was pending and had planned to send Elkins instead until it became clear that the latter's appearance would set off even wilder speculations. The railroad bills were also Dailey's excuse for being on the scene and were one of the topics of his consultations with Walker.[102]

Nevertheless, it is evident that Davis was quite willing to profit by Camden's misfortune. While it is impossible to determine whether or not he instigated directly the "contingent candidacy," at the very least he allowed Price and Dailey (whose grievance against Camden concerned patronage, not "monopoly") to create it for their own purposes and sat back to see if it would float.[103] The strategy was to stalemate

Camden without alienating him. A victorious candidate would need the Camden bloc of votes plus seven of the insurgents, so the way had to be kept open to both camps. "I do not say that I would decline the honor," Davis explained to a reporter. "But so long as Mr. Camden is a candidate I am entirely out of the race." "I am for Camden," he told Camden. "I do not expect my name to be used in this connection unless by you and your friends."[104] As the contest wore on, Dailey pressed for a more vigorous posture. "I do not think Camden cares enough about the Democratic party to sacrifice himself for it, or cares enough for any friend to step aside for him," he told Davis, and added that this was "in keeping with my views of Mr. C's feeling towards you since the time of Kenna's election...."[105] But Davis declined to press his cause more vigorously. At the same time, he refrained from the sort of statement that would have put an end to the speculation and kept open his channels of communication to both camps. In short, he stood ready in 1887 to answer a "call" from the factionalists on both sides to resume his senatorial duties.

But the call never came. On February 26, 1887, the legislature adjourned with the senatorial deadlock unbroken. Davis had anticipated this possibility and expected Wilson to appoint Judge Okey Johnson, senior justice of the Supreme Court of Appeals and one of the Redeemer-type compromisers on the "kickers' " list, to the Senate vacancy created by the expiration of Camden's term on March 3.[106] More widely it was believed that Secretary of State Henry S. Walker would get the nod.[107] In either case, Walker and Johnson were among those rival factionalists who had shown themselves accessible to Davis on past occasions; both would have debts to pay that might prove useful when a double senatorial vacancy occurred in 1889.[108] Governor Wilson surprised him, however. First of all, he passed over Walker and Johnson and designated Daniel B. Lucas as Camden's successor.[109] Lucas was one of the few West Virginia politicians of his day who was genuinely uncorruptible. "I am almost afraid to tackle Lucas," Dailey had written while pushing the West

Virginia Central bills; "I am afraid he may get to looking into the matter, and make a fight against it."[110] Among Lucas's other peculiarities was a belief in tariff reform of the most radical nature. "The future in West Virginia politics looks dark to me," was Davis's response to his appointment.[111] Wilson's next move came on March 2. He vetoed both of Davis's carefully nurtured railroad bills. "I was very much surprised . . . ," wrote Davis. "It shows that the Governor is hostile to all such enterprises."[112] On March 6 the governor recalled the legislature for April 20, placing a railroad commission at the head of unfinished business but carefully excluding the senatorial matter from the session's purview. Davis recalled Price and Dailey, scheduling a meeting at Deer Park on March 16 to talk over the senatorial question.[113] When they left, he sat down to compose a ringing endorsement of Camden.

The manifesto, an open letter published April 1, said everything Davis might have said two months earlier had it not been for his lingering senatorial hopes. He endorsed Camden as "a liberal progressive Democrat," who had earned re-election if for no other reason than his contribution to the cause of economic development. As for his handling of patronage, "it was but natural for him to take care of his friends."[114] The message was intended to be an invitation to the special session to elect a senator in defiance of Wilson's call. And so it did; after two additional days of balloting, Camden yielded and the place went to Charles James Faulkner, Jr., an ex-Confederate conservative who had the usual compromise credentials.[115]

What is more significant, however, are some passages left out of the published version of Davis's message to the Democracy. "I believe," he wrote, "that, in the consideration of all questions, the welfare of the people of West Virginia, which include [sic] the development of its great resources, should be given the preference over and above advantage or disadvantage that might accrue to individuals or political parties." This required protection for the state's natural resources ("and her manufactures," an interlinear) by "a

44

proper and reasonable tarriff [*sic*]." Otherwise, he concluded, "the interests of the people and state will be better served even by a liberal Republican than by a Free trade anti-improvement Democrat."[116]

Davis's threat to desert his party on the tariff issue, implied in his speeches of five years before, now became explicit in the draft of his April manifesto. He took the first step toward carrying out the threat at Deer Park. Early in August, when it was getting hot in Washington, he invited President Cleveland and his family to come up for the mountain air. Cleveland declined; instead the president stayed home and entertained party and congressional leaders at the "Oak View conferences" near Washington in early September, from which he emerged committed to tariff reform.[117] One who did come to Deer Park, however, was ex-Senator Harrison of Indiana. Davis and Harrison had been good friends since their senatorial days. Indeed Davis seems to have been as close to the frosty Hoosier as anyone outside of Harrison's immediate circle of family and law partners. They had refreshed their acquaintance by yearly rendezvous at Deer Park, but this time there was a difference. For Davis and Elkins now held out to Harrison the prospect of the presidency. Blaine, Elkins told him, might not stand for renomination and if he did, might not get it. In that case, Elkins could think of no one more likely to win the support of the "Blaine Legion" than Harrison. Davis advised his guest not to say or do anything to discourage his Republican friends and added that he would find it difficult to oppose his election. Some of Blaine's biographers have claimed for him the honor of designating Harrison as his legatee. But if we may credit Elkins, who should have known, it was Davis who tapped the Indianian, not Blaine. In any case nothing was settled at the Deer Park conference. Harrison replied to his friends' suggestions with becoming modesty. He did not want to be president and even if he did, did not think his chances all that bright.[118] But the idea had been broached and none of the principals forgot the conversation in the months that followed.

The political careers of Davis and Elkins may be said to have converged at Deer Park in the summer of 1887. Each man was at the nadir of his political career, while their common business interests faced a serious threat in tariff reform. Cooperative action seemed in order. The solution to their dilemma, implied in Davis's unpublished manifesto of the previous spring, pointed to Elkins's election to the Senate seat his father-in-law once held, thus restoring at least *his* political prospects and installing in Washington a senator whose primary allegiance was to coal. This strategy unfolded rapidly in the winter of 1887-1888. By December, when President Cleveland's "Tariff Message" to Congress lent powerful support to the reform movement, Davis was at work among disaffected Democrats, while Elkins kept tabs on the growth of presidential fever at Indianapolis. By February Elkins was ready to resume with Harrison their "several conversations last summer at Deer Park about the presidency."[119]

There was more to the Deer Park strategy than presidential politics, however, although Elkins's initial approaches to Harrison concerned only presidential affairs. Briefly stated, this further logic ran:

1) Given Republican resurgence in West Virginia (48 percent of the vote in the congressional election of 1886), Davis's quiet defection from the Democracy ("passiveness in certain quarters," as Elkins explained it to Harrison)[120] might be sufficient to put the Mountain State's electoral votes in the Republican column in 1888.

2) Given an even more narrow balance of partisan power nationally, West Virginia's electoral votes, though few in number, might be sufficient to provide the margin of Republican presidential success.

3) Both results were needed if Elkins were to go to the Senate when John E. Kenna's term expired in 1889. The route to power in West Virginia, as it had been for Elkins earlier in New Mexico, lay through Washington. If his carpetbag were bulging with federal jobs as well as money when he arrived on the West Virginia scene, he might anticipate a much easier conquest than if he came supplied with money

46

alone. Having gone without their accustomed diet of federal plums during Cleveland's administration, West Virginia Republicans were job-hungry. To satisfy that hunger, Elkins needed the unqualified support of a Republican in the White House. When Blaine took himself out of the running early in 1888, Elkins resumed his courtship of Harrison.

This was the strategy, and it eventually worked, although neither as smoothly nor as swiftly as Davis and Elkins hoped. The path from Deer Park to Washington turned out to be littered with obstacles. There was first of all the problem of Elkins's "domicile." Elkins was only loosely identified with West Virginia at this time and then only through his business ties. Accordingly, he took steps to remedy this. Early in 1888 he bought into the state's leading Republican newspaper, the Wheeling *Intelligencer.* At the same time, the editor, Charles Burdette Hart, joined with Davis to provide "non-political" auspices through which Elkins might be formally introduced to his prospective constituents. Playing on West Virginians' uncritical enthusiasm for anything labeled "development," the two men organized a "Boom Convention" in Wheeling on February 29. Ostensibly called to promote West Virginia's resources and to advertise the state's need for development capital, the convention's real purpose was to provide a bipartisan forum for protectionist propaganda and a platform from which Elkins made his maiden speech in the Mountain State.

"You will fit in very snugly," Hart assured him,[121] and so he did, especially as Elkins incorporated into his speech a brilliant solution to the problem of his residence, or rather his nonresidence. He touched on a theme that was a sore point for many West Virginia patriots—the fact that the tide of capital and immigration, oblivious to the proclaimed advantages of their own treasure house, had bypassed the state for thirty years in favor of the western half of the country. Describing West Virginia as a new frontier, Elkins portrayed himself as a capitalist who had seen the light and abandoned the West for greater economic opportunities in the Mountain State. In the spring Elkins arranged for another "nonpartisan" address, this one at West Virginia University, and also attended to another important detail—the beginning of construction of his new summer home, overlooking the site selected for the new West Virginia Central terminus. Encompassing the village of Leadsville in Randolph County, the place was shortly to be rechristened "Elkins."

Editor Hart was one of many West Virginia Republicans who did not care where Elkins lived, so long as his money and organizational talent were invested in the party's cause. But there were others who were not disarmed by Elkins's explanations. The state's Republican party had leaders of its own who fully expected preferment in their own right if the corner to victory were turned in 1888. Foremost among these were Representative Nathan Goff and former United States Marshal George W. Atkinson. A Union war hero breveted brigadier general at the age of twenty-three, Goff as a state legislator in 1867-1868 had been a member of Davis's team of B&O lobbyists. In 1869 he embarked on a long career in federal office, which culminated in a brief term as secretary of the navy in Hayes's administration. His election to Congress from the first district in 1882, the first major Republican victory since a fusionist win in 1872, signified the party's rebirth in West Virginia. Meanwhile Goff served as a gubernatorial candidate, campaign contributor, and premier Republican orator. "General Goff has long been the idol of the Republican party in West Virginia," wrote Atkinson in 1890. "No man so fully represents its fighting forces as he."[122] Atkinson, the scourge of statemakers during earlier patronage quarrels, matched Goff's record of party service and tenure in federal jobs. Retiring from his latest appointment in 1885, he sat out the Cleveland interval in the practice of law at Wheeling. He was also a veteran Republican editor and, like Goff, a rousing speaker. Individually, these two provided Elkins's most formidable rivals in West Virginia. Had they stood together, he might never have won the prize.

Neither Harrison nor any sensible Republican president is likely to have bulldozed such experienced and popular leaders aside for Elkins. It was thus a mark of the latter's dexterity that he was able to get Goff and Atkinson out of the way in advance. Against his better judgment, Goff became the Republican nominee for governor of West Virginia in 1888. He did not want the prize. Having won and defended his seat in Congress against both Regular and Redeemer Democrats, he was in no hurry to vacate it. Moreover, he was perfectly aware that Elkins intended to supplant him as the party's leading senatorial contender. But as a "popular demand" for his nomination, orchestrated by Hart in the *Intelligencer*, assumed the proportions of a draft following Harrison's nomination, Goff went to Deer Park to discuss the matter. He agreed to make the race on three conditions: that Elkins supplied all the money he needed, that Davis did not oppose him, and that Elkins not "antagonize" him for the senatorship. This last promise was virtually an empty one. Had Goff been elected governor, he would have found it all but impossible to press his senatorial claim. West Virginia had no lieutenant governor, which meant that his resignation to enter the Senate would have entailed a special election, a prospect few Republicans were disposed to contemplate with assurance. Nevertheless, Goff, a devout protectionist, made an excellent gubernatorial canvass, the highlight of which was a series of tariff debates with William L. Wilson. Meanwhile, Atkinson, next in succession, became the Republican first district congressional nominee. If successful, he too would have found it hard to justify resigning. With these two detained in elective office, less influential local leaders might be content with federal plums they had already tasted. All that was needed were Republican wins in state and nation and presidential cooperation. Then Elkins's path to the Senate would be clear.

It was left to the voters to present some further hurdles in Elkins's path. Elkins was indeed instrumental in nominating Harrison for the White House and received for his pains appropriate though vague assurances of presidential gratitude. Davis was also able to deliver a modest improvement in Republican vote totals in the partners' West Virginia mining region. But Harrison narrowly failed to carry the state at large, while close and hotly disputed state elections resulted in Kenna's reelection to the Senate and left Goff in limbo for over a year until a recount under the auspices of the Democratic legislature awarded the gubernatorial chair to his opponent. In these circumstances, Elkins sought admission to Harrison's cabinet, but the president felt unable to oblige (for "geographical and other considerations not involving any lack of fondness or gratitude") until a post of suitable prestige could be found for Goff. Davis spent his Christmas holidays in Indianapolis in 1888, pleading for Elkins's advancement, but without success. It was nearly three years before Harrison unraveled the competing claims for West Virginia. Finally in December 1891 he nominated Goff to a newly created vacancy on the Fourth Circuit United States Court of Appeals, and on the following day, took Elkins into his cabinet as secretary of war. In the meantime, however, Harrison had taken care of Elkins "in other ways."[123]

In supporting the industrialist's bid for Republican supremacy in West Virginia, Harrison stopped short only of moves that could be publicly interpreted as an affront to Goff. During the first weeks of the administration Attorney General W. H. H. Miller, one of Elkins's Indiana enemies, promised Goff the final say in West Virginia patronage, but Harrison promptly overrode him. The first important local appointment made, that of district attorney, went to Elkins's nominee, George C. Sturgiss. Goff and his friends presented another man, Harrison confided in conspiratorial tones, "but I told them they were too late."[124] Other West Virginia appointments reflected Elkins's influence, among them John W. Mason, federal commissioner of internal revenue, A. B. White, state collector of internal revenue, and George M. Bowers, state supervisor of the 1890 census. Even Davis took precedence over Goff when he (Davis) extended his protection to a Democratic treasury employee whose place Goff wanted for one of his own followers. Recognizing "the ex-Senator's kindly feeling toward our party in West Virginia," Secretary of the Treasury William Windom informed Goff that it would not be "good politics" to contravene Davis's wishes.[125] Davis was also allowed to name the Piedmont and Deer Park postmasters, the latter over the protest of a Republican congressman from Maryland. One interesting exception to this pattern, indicating either a conciliatory gesture or unwitting mistake, was the appointment of Charles Goff, the general's younger brother, as treasury agent in the Seal Islands of Alaska, a post of dubious appeal, it would seem, but one where, as noted earlier, Elkins had extremely delicate business arrangements pending at this time. But when young Goff ran afoul of Elkins's seal-fishing company and sided with conservationists who were trying to limit the kill, the administration promptly removed him. Thus long before Elkins's accession to the cabinet, it was clear to West Virginians to whom the Republican future belonged.

Shortly before the president submitted their respective nominations to Congress, Goff sought a meeting with Elkins at Davis's office in Baltimore.[126] It is not known what bargain the two men struck there, but whatever it was, it ended the most formidable opposition to Elkins's entry to West Virginia. Although Goff's name was frequently used to rally future opposition to Elkins, the new judge failed to back his admirers and refrained from active intervention in local Republican affairs. Other West Virginia Republicans fell into line as speedily. Hart in the *Intelligencer* devoted much space to welcoming the Mountain State's new leader and kept West Virginians informed of the progress of construction of his new "summerhouse at Elkins, W. Va., which is also his voting residence."[127] The newspaper also chose an appropriate moment following Elkins's elevation to switch from Blaine to Harrison as its presidential preference in 1892.[128] George W. Atkinson, Goff's successor in Congress, also accepted Elkins's leadership, but declined to abandon Blaine and urged Elkins to follow suit, even if it meant staying out of the cabinet. "Blaine can carry W. Va. in '92," Atkinson argued. "No other candidate can." When Elkins ignored his advice, Atkinson yielded his place on the West Virginia delegation to the 1892 national convention, allowing Hart to lead a solid corps of

51

Harrison voters to Minneapolis.[129] Nathan B. Scott, on the other hand, accepted the Harrison commitment and, as national committeeman and convention delegate, initiated the alliance that would eventually make him second in command in the Elkins organization.[130] Charles Goff, the erstwhile seal protector, found another job in the customs service and then resigned to sell Republican buttons during the 1892 campaign.[131] Those who had earlier come over to Elkins were awaiting "a 'pointer' " from him as to which way to jump in national politics, and, when it came, they jumped.[132] As a result, West Virginia was matched only by Indiana among the states represented in the cabinet in its solid support for the president's renomination. As Hart noted in the *Intelligencer*, Elkins had many reasons to be proud.[133]

West Virginia Republicans accepted Elkins's leadership in other matters with equal dispatch. One important step in his assumption of command was Atkinson's replacement as Republican state chairman by William M. O. Dawson. A veteran legislator and weekly newspaper editor from Preston County, Dawson had welcomed Elkins effusively to West Virginia in 1889.[134] Now he abandoned journalism entirely to devote full attention to politics, for he was a professional's professional. William A. MacCorkle, no mean judge of political flesh, thought him the finest political organizer in West Virginia history, barring only Elkins himself.[135] Dawson's devotion to Elkins and Elkins's reliance on him would have momentous consequences a decade later when Dawson emerged as a political leader in his own right.

Dawson's accomplishments lay in the future, however. For the moment the greatest measure of Elkins's success in his new home was the gubernatorial convention that assembled in Huntington on August 3. Behind the gubernatorial problem lay a good deal of thought and discussion by Elkins and his advisers, very little of which escaped their immediate circle. Apparently the decision was made at a conference with Hart, Mason, and Dawson at Deer Park on July 16, the mantle falling upon Thomas E. Davis, a Grafton banker and former state senator, although the candidate was not unveiled until the eve of the convention.[136] Meanwhile speculation among the faithful centered on Elkins himself; not surprisingly, he declined to run.[137] By some unknown means of suasion, Atkinson was induced to abandon his own gubernatorial hopes and to place Davis in nomination. The convention dutifully accepted him, along with a well-balanced slate of other nominees, but not before the delegates demonstrated their enthusiasm for their new leader. Elkins's keynote address to the convention set off a demonstration that very nearly resulted in his being drafted for the nomination despite himself. He was able to halt the clamor only by promising to consider the matter during a hastily called recess. When calm was restored, he made a graceful speech of declination and regret, pointing out that Democratic objections to his eligibility (based on a constitutional residence requirement of five years), while spurious, might furnish a pretext for once again depriving the party of victory. The explanation was accepted and Davis, who had also sought to decline the honor, was drafted by acclamation.[138] He was a rather weak candidate, which, in combination with his subsequent defeat, lent him something of the appearance of a sacrificial lamb.[139] However, his expendability was a less likely reason for his selection than was his close identification with Goff's losing recount contest before the legislature in 1889-1890. This gave the Republican rank and file a chance to vote for the "vindication" of their old leader without complicating the plans of their new one. It is also likely that Elkins had no desire to share the spotlight with a strong and popular figure like Atkinson, whose ambition might be aroused by the senatorial prize that lay at the end of the campaign trail.

From all accounts, Elkins redoubled his efforts to carry West Virginia in 1892, after having missed victory so narrowly four years before. According to one version of the arrangements, he promised to match dollar for dollar Republican campaign funds from all other sources in return for an undisputed claim on the senatorship in 1893. Scott, who had money and a developing case of senatorial fever of his own, made a $2,000 down payment and by generous contribution exacted the full value of Elkins's promise.[140] How much was collected is uncertain; one admittedly crude measure was Democratic charges, which rose from $100,000 in 1888 to the neighborhood of $400,000 in 1892.[141] However much there was, Dawson saw that the money was well spent. For the first time, he gave the party a thorough modern campaign organization, with lines of responsibility and communications extending from his Wheeling campaign headquarters to every county in the state.[142]

Thus armed and organized, the Republicans took the field confident of certain victory in November. While their fellow partisans in some states were already reeling under the burdens of an uninspiring national ticket, labor unrest, and Populist incursions among the farmers, the West Virginians were undismayed. A decade of steady encroachment on the Democratic majority assured them that 1892 would put them over the top. Their message to the electorate expressed this sense of destiny, stressing their favorite equation of Republicanism with progress in general, protectionism with West Virginia development in particular. As one exuberant orator expressed it: "Look, what the Lord has given you. Coal, iron, lumber, rich valleys. Do you suppose he would have given you all these things if he had thought that you were going to vote the Democratic ticket?"[143] In his speeches, Elkins stated the same theme in quieter tones: "to meet the demands of the times" the Republicans had "made largely a business man's ticket"; without it, West Virginia would never catch up with Ohio and Pennsylvania in population, commerce, mines, railroads, and manufacturing. To help him drive home the point, he invited the leading apostle of protectionism, William McKinley, to join him in a tour of the Ohio valley counties in October.[144]

As the campaign entered the final weeks, however, the confidence of the Republicans began to erode. Their attempt to identify with industrial progress and to turn the state's face northward would pay off in time, but for the moment it failed to ease the many discontents at large in the electorate. The Democrats, in contrast, found a magic formula: race.

West Virginia had not enjoyed a thorough airing of the race issue since the seventies and the Democratic gubernatorial candidate, young MacCorkle of the Kanawha Ring, was perfectly fitted by talent and temperament to remedy the lack. Campaigning in a black slouch hat and red goatee, MacCorkle "appealed to the southern element" by resurrecting the Lodge [Election] "Force" Bill from the congressional boneyard and raising the cry of "Negro domination."[145] The strategy, complained the *Intelligencer*, was simply to crisscross the state with speakers "to shriek 'foace' [*sic*] bill on every hillside and in every hollow and otherwise to stir up all the old prejudices and passions against the Republican party."[146] At first the victims ridiculed the tactic, as well they might in a state where blacks constituted no more than 10 percent of the population. They took to elaborate circumventions of the Lodge bill (which would have set up federal supervision of Southern elections) and past Republican racial policy and embarked on a fruitless hunt for countercharges concerning Democratic breaches of Southern mores.[147] Nothing helped. MacCorkle found the "Force" Bill bogey a perfect medium for rallying the Democracy's mixed bag of high and low tariff men, silver and gold standard men, pro- and anti-Clevelandites. To give the race issue a local as well as a congressional significance, he espied in his rival a threat to the state's system of segregated schools, ignoring the fact that the Republican statemakers had embedded segregation in the constitution thirty years before. The most effective Democratic campaign document was a cartoon that featured a strapping black schoolteacher about to cane a small white boy.[148] Neither ridicule nor imitation could withstand such appeals, and the Democrats carried the state by a margin of 4,200 votes out of 171,000.[149] It was not a large margin, but it was a vast improvement over the cliff-hanger of 1888.

Besides the electoral vote, all four congressmen, and the statehouse, the victory gave the Democrats a healthy majority in the legislature, thus bringing Elkins's senatorial express to an abrupt halt. A promising growth of Democratic factionalism sprouted as Camden, Faulkner, and the

55

governor-elect's Kanawha manager, Joe Chilton, eyed the impending senatorial vacancy. But that was cut down with Senator Kenna, who was "called away suddenly at last" after a lingering illness on the eve of the election. His death opened the way to a peaceful solution, Faulkner claiming reelection, and Camden taking the short term made available by Kenna's demise.[150] Elkins was left with the empty honor of one of the Republican nominations. That was scant compensation for all his careful planning and expense. It brought with it titular recognition of his primacy in the party and that was something at least to show for his pains. But it meant that when the new Democratic Congress convened to consider the tariff, there would be on hand no senator whose first and unyielding allegiance was to coal. Davis was under no illusion about the probable result. On the eve of the election he threw off his "passiveness" in a vain attempt to ingratiate himself with the victorious Democracy. Subsequent overtures to Democratic leaders proved equally futile; only one congressman came to a dinner he staged in February 1893 to honor the state's congressional delegation. Representative William L. Wilson, newly elevated to the chairmanship of the House Committee on Ways and Means, not only spurned Davis, he stripped away the ex-senator's last morsel of Democratic patronage, the Piedmont postmastership, which every president since Grant had let Davis name. Consequently, when Wilson summoned tariff hearings to meet in the fall of 1893, Davis was pessimistic. Even though it would be weeks before Wilson's committee even began to draft the new tariff bill, Davis filed on September 9 a reference to the hearings under the heading, "Bill to remove duty on coal."[151]

While the tariff controversy of the late nineteenth century filled a lengthy page in the nation's history, in many ways it was a personal contest between two West Virginians. An ironic fate had joined Davis and Wilson since the moment of their acquaintance, which began, fittingly enough, when they were political bedfellows, sharing a hotel room at the 1880 Democratic National Convention in Cincinnati. Davis had played an important role in Wilson's initial election to Congress, but their differences emerged as soon as Wilson took his seat in the House. Shortly before the first of the several speakership contests between the protectionist, Samuel Randall, and Democratic tariff reformers (in this instance, John C. Carlisle of Kentucky) in December 1883, Davis summoned Wilson to Baltimore. "He is afraid that the duty . . . on Bituminous Coal will be diminished and that will greatly impair his profits and the value of his property," Wilson confided to his diary. "I told him plainly that I had not yet finally decided for whom I would vote, but that in view of Mr. Randall's record, and his present attitude, I thought that a vote for him would be a dodge of the great issues. . . ." Davis failed to appreciate this logic and threatened the congressman with a speedy retirement. "I fear we shall split," Wilson concluded, and they did.[152] But Davis's fading Democratic authority was too weak to discipline Wilson. For ten years he alternately ignored or courted the congressman, depending upon the prospects of tariff reform. Their last personal confrontation came in Washington on September 19, 1893, in the Ways and Means Committee hearing room. Afterwards Davis took on his opponent in the lobbies of Congress, then girded for a final confrontation in the congressional election of 1894.

Davis and Wilson offered contrasts in personalities as well as in politics. A handsome, small-featured man with the pleasing manner of Old Virginia, Wilson was at home "among the people" at political rallies or gatherings of Confederate veterans. "I am on the other hand not very strong with the politicians and lawyers, so many of whom are candidates in embryo."[153] Despite his success in Congress, he deemed "a literary or rather scholastic life more in accord with my tastes." Following his retirement from Congress, he served a brief term in Cleveland's cabinet, then rejected offers from New York law firms in favor of the presidency of Washington and Lee University in Virginia.[154] Meanwhile his earlier brief presidency of West Virginia University lent him the reputation of a "scholar in politics," which he embellished by writing history and helping to found the Southern Historical Society. None took Wilson more to heart than those whose program he translated into provincial accents—northeastern businessmen who favored tariff reform for the same economic reasons that Davis opposed it. Merchants and manufacturers like Edward Atkinson of Boston and Isidor Strauss of New York were among Wilson's closest friends and advisers. Like Grover Cleveland, another friend and admirer, Wilson believed in Atkinson's bourgeois liberalism in a more disinterested but no less devout fashion. Also like Cleveland, Wilson was honest and courageous, but he lacked the president's oppressive self-righteousness and he was more humane. One of the few West Virginia politicians ever to earn the name of statesman, Wilson was perhaps a fitting but scarcely a deserving victim of the industrialists' brand of politics.

Where Wilson was small and fluent, Davis was large and inarticulate. A trim six-footer who astonished contemporaries by his vigorous pursuit of business and politics into very old age, Davis sported a well-groomed beard and observed a strict Presbyterian Sunday, although in later years he was known to take a glass of wine at dinner. He conducted himself with dignity, evincing the self-assurance that flows from wealth and untroubled purposes, but the effect was bland and, except for the occasional small joke, almost totally devoid of humor. Observers who described Davis wrote of his accomplishments, not his personality. His letters, like his labored public addresses, reflected untutored origins, but they also reflected a basic economy of spirit that reduced words from their original spellings to bony abbreviations without losing a trace of his meaning. A folk song of the period, probably originating among Davis's workers, attributed the same spirit to "Uncle Henry's" outlook on wages.[155] These economical habits revealed themselves in other ways as well. Davis and Elkins gave their names, some money, and their West Virginia houses to found a small college, but Davis shrewdly negotiated with representatives of several faiths before awarding the gift to his own Presbyterians and tried unsuccessfully to get Andrew Carnegie to underwrite part of the cost.[156] On an occasion already noted, his punishment of the editor, Lewis Baker, in 1885 extended to forcing Baker to make over his life insurance to Davis in repayment of earlier loans.[157] Yet Davis seems to have gone about such business pleasantly, without occasioning rancor or the bitter personal antagonisms that haunted Camden and Elkins. Baker remained on friendly terms; Wilson, though cool, was not embittered, nor were others who had plenty of reason to hate the man. Such evidence suggests that Davis added warmth to his parsimony. Or perhaps it merely shows how fully men of the time accepted the prerogatives of Davis's class.

When the two men met in the Ways and Means Committee hearing room on September 19, 1893, Wilson was riding the crest of his career and Davis was fully convinced of his power to bring him down. Their confrontation stretched over a year or more, moving from the committee room—from which Wilson reported out a tariff bill that placed coal on the free list in spite of Davis's dire threats—to the lobbies of the Senate, where Davis and Elkins worked tirelessly through the winter and spring of 1894. Eventually they succeeded in restoring forty cents of the seventy-five cent bituminous duty that Wilson had taken off. The tariff bill that become law in August 1894 was a patchwork, disliked by nearly everyone. Wilson shared with Davis's cousin, Senator Arthur Gorman of Maryland, the doubtful honor of having the new tariff named for him. It would stay on the statute books scarcely three years before the Republicans replaced it with the Dingley tariff (and a seventy-five cent coal duty) in 1897.

Of more lasting impact in West Virginia was the electoral confrontation between Wilson and Davis in the fall of 1894. The election took place against a turbulent background. A deepening economic depression made itself felt in a series of strikes that rocked the industrial centers of the state. Wheeling pottery manufacturers, implementing a policy adopted by their national trade association, announced a 10 percent wage cut in January and made an additional 20 percent cut contingent upon the passage of the Wilson Bill. The resulting pottery workers' strike quickly spread into the northern panhandle's mining and iron and steel industries. A miners' strike began in the New River coalfield in February and spread fitfully during the spring into the Kanawha and Fairmont fields. Governor MacCorkle, dispatching companies of state militia to Fayette County in March in response to pleas from New River coal operators, was surprised to encounter resistance not only from miners but also from local citizens and officials. The same thing happened in June in Benwood, an industrial suburb of Wheeling, when the governor, acting in conjunction with Ohio authorities, sent troops to break up strikers' blockades on the tracks of the B&O. Meanwhile General Jacob Coxey, whom the Wheeling *Intelligencer* regretfully acknowledged as a native West Virginian, sent contingents of his Army of the Unemployed across the state in their historic march on Washington. MacCorkle promised one river-borne group of Coxeyites whiffs of grapeshot if they landed in West Virginia, but the central labor assemblies of Wheeling and Huntington welcomed the marchers with gifts of food and provisions. On May Day city officials and labor representatives feasted a Coxey detachment encamped on Wheeling Island, while respectable burghers shivered in darkened rooms, alarmed for the safety of property.[158] State military authorities, following a national policy initiated by Secretary of War Elkins in 1892,[159] decided to expand the number of troops available in industrial centers and found themselves swamped with applicants. Two new companies were organized at Wheeling in June, but only one could be equipped with the new Gatling guns that had been introduced in the coalfields in March.[160]

By the time that the political season began in earnest, at least seven had died in civil violence in West Virginia and political turbulence was shortly to add to the toll.[161] Senator Camden, beginning his canvass for reelection in the county nominating conventions, initially anticipated trouble only from "the 'Charleston Gang'." But as the season wore on, he found that "strikes, disorganizations and communistic notions are spreading over the land [and] almost every state and section has its Coxey...."[162] Among other local manifestations of the "communistic or populist craze" were Democratic congressional nominations in the first (Wheeling-Clarksburg) and fourth (Huntington-Parkersburg) districts. In the first, a former head of the glassworkers union in Wheeling defeated the Regular incumbent for the nomination; in the fourth, Agrarians from the Ohio and Kanawha valley farm counties forced a second convention and the withdrawal of a conservative candidate in favor of Thomas H. Harvey, a former Greenbacker.[163] But it was ex-Governor E. Willis Wilson who stood out as "the Coxey of West Virginia," in Camden's view. Taking to the stump in May, "Windy" stormed through the state, seeking to rouse farmers and workers against Camden's reelection. Brawling and knife and gun play moved from courthouse to courthouse during the summer as Agrarians and Regulars struggled for control of legislative nominations and the Kanawha Ring fluttered erratically between alliance with the other factions and a senatorial campaign in behalf of its own aspirant, Joe Chilton. United States Marshal S. S. Vinson followed the county convention trail, ostensibly in the interests of law and order but actually to secure pro-Camden nominees.[164] In September his son reported to Camden that "The Chilton faction have become frightened at [E. W.] Wilson's prospects . . . & now say we must all do something to check Wilson & they will heartily cooperate with us toward that end." On the other hand, young Vinson continued, "Some of our most substantial men are taking the Wilson-Communistic fence, while others are afraid to oppose the tide. . . . We are sitting on top of a volcano that is likely to explode at any time—I cannot better explain to you the general discontent than by saying that it is another commune of the French Revolution." Vinson attributed the rebellion to "an anarchistic craze . . . that is growing in volume and force, and bodes no good for either business or politics."[165]

A few days later the volcano exploded when shots rang out at a Wilson rally in Wayne County, leaving one person dead and six wounded. However, it was not the forces of "anarchy," but Marshal Vinson and his deputies who fled across the Kentucky border with a warrant for murder at their heels. Attorney General Richard Olney, forced at last to investigate complaints about Vinson's conduct, removed him from office on October 10 and replaced him with another Camden conservative, A. D. Garden of Wheeling.[166] By this time Camden himself was anxious for peace and quiet. The long tariff wrangle in Congress, climaxed by a Senate inquiry into his dealings in sugar stocks, left him tired and depressed. A brief rest in Florida restored his spirits, but the depth of opposition in West Virginia and the financial demands of Regular candidates and lieutenants exceeded anything he had previously encountered.[167] Accordingly he explored the possibility of bringing William L. Wilson forward as a compromise senatorial candidate. For these political and financial reasons "and other reasons personal to my own comfort," he wrote to John T. McGraw, "if I could get out of being a candidate under creditable and respectable conditions, . . . [I] would gladly do so, if either Mr. Wilson or yourself, or any respectable democrat, will come out as a candidate. Of course I cannot decline to be a candidate with 'Windy' Wilson only in the field. . . ."[168] Congressman Wilson, however, felt honor bound to stand again in the Second Congressional District. On August 30, the second district convention accorded him a tumultuous renomination, whereupon Wilson, also exhausted by the tariff struggle, left to Camden the task of containing his distant Agrarian cousin and departed for a month's vacation.

Rather unwisely William L. Wilson chose to seek his rest in England as the guest of Isidor Strauss, where he was warmly received by what Republicans chose to call his "British constituency." Back in the second district he left determined opponents at work. Camden, John T. McGraw, and other West Virginia protectionists, were ready to regard the congressman as the lesser evil of the two Wilsons and to treat him with the generosity incumbent upon victors. But Davis was not. McGraw and also W. E. Chilton of the Kanawha Ring sought to restrain him, each hinting of the senatorial prize that shimmered on the horizon; "I do not want to see you placed in a false position either now or after the Campaign is concluded," wrote McGraw.[169] Davis was adamant, however. Wilson, he maintained, had once been reasonable in his views, but his views had changed. "He voted for free coal and lumber, and says he will continue the tariff agitation, and he is now doing all in his power to treat unfairly the two great leading and best interests of the people of his district and state." It was "untrue" that he was "actively opposing" Wilson; "He is a Democrat—so am I." But it was Wilson and not himself, Davis argued, who had deserted Democratic principles. "The leaders and founders of the Democratic party, including such men as Madison, Jefferson, Monroe, Jackson, and Adams [Clay and Webster followed but were crossed out] have always consistently been in favor of a tariff for revenue with incidental protection."[170] To underscore his loyalty to Democracy as he construed it, he helped to finance the campaign of John D. Alderson, the Kanawha congressman who "was true & work [sic] for coal duty well & faithful," and urged the C&O and Pocahontas coal interests to do likewise. He also interceded with Elkins to see that Alderson was "treated fairly" by the Republicans.[171] He resented Camden's decision to support William L. Wilson—"Under the circumstances, we would be glad to have you keep out of it," he wrote[172]—but he and Elkins were sufficiently alarmed by E. Willis Wilson's campaign to work for pro-Camden Democratic legislative nominees. However, Davis made certain that the nominees from his region were opposed to *both* Wilsons for senator.

"I am taking no part in his [W. L. Wilson's] canvass, but . . . I have been a Democrat, and expect to vote the Democratic ticket," Davis insisted.[173] Indeed he went to some lengths to keep his active opposition to Wilson secret. When the latter's Republican opponent sought his endorsement, Davis sent him a railroad pass and a statement of his views on the coal duty; otherwise he referred him to his brother, Thomas, and to F. S. Landstreet, another relative and employee. "Colonel Tom" and Landstreet joined C. L. Bretz, the ranking Republican in the companies after Elkins, to lead the open opposition. They concentrated their efforts among the Davis-Elkins employees. Wilson's supporters charged them with a variety of pressures, including a threat to cut wages by 20 percent. Elkins was said to have "admitted reducing wages of mine officials, but said the miners had not been touched because they are already so low that they can scarcely live on what they get."[174] During the last three weeks of the campaign, the top officials of the companies let business slide altogether, devoting their full time to politics. "I surely think we have got Wilson beaten," reported Bretz on the eve of the vote. "There has certainly been a favorable change all along the line of our road."[175]

Davis himself kept carefully in the background. When President M. E. Ingalls of the C&O asked how he could help, Davis put him in touch with Elkins. He also asked Ingalls to "induce Mayer, of the B&O to pass the word quietly along the line. . . ." Here again he was disappointed, for the B&O's most effective political representative, John K. Cowen, its general counsel and an anti-Gorman leader in Maryland, campaigned actively for Wilson.[176] But several of the lumber companies along the West Virginia Central came to Davis's aid. So did his fellow coal producers, who contributed $2,500 in leftover lobbying funds to the anti-Wilson campaign.[177]

All of this may have fallen within the definition of "passiveness" as far as Davis was concerned, but his vendetta against Wilson was a matter of common knowledge. Feeling "very blue" about Wilson's chances, Camden told a Senate colleague that "Davis and Elkins are throwing the whole weight of their railroad and coal mines against him. . . ."[178] For the first time, Davis's subversion of the Democracy became a matter of comment in the Democratic press. Another first was his subjection to the sort of personal abuse that Camden and Elkins had been taking for years. Comment in West Virginia newspapers remained notably subdued, but Democratic correspondents from big-city journals waxed long and loud about Davis's "spirit of parsimony," vindictiveness, and other "notorious" failings.[179] Characteristically, Wilson

64

himself did not indulge in personal attacks on Davis or Elkins, but he boldly invaded their domain for a week of
speeches up and down their railroad, telling the miners that—
the proprietors' claims to the contrary—free coal, along with
"steady work and strong organization," would bring them
"better wages than you men [get] along the West Virginia
Central."[180]

With so much Democratic help, Elkins had no difficulty
mounting an aggressive Republican campaign in the second
district. The national party machinery also contributed powerful support, recognizing that Wilson's defeat "means a great
national reverse to the enemy...."[181] The logical candidate
to oppose Wilson was John W. Mason, who had narrowly
missed defeating him once before. But for some reason
Mason was not "available." Another veteran, George C. Sturgiss, contested the nomination but lost out to a young Phil-
ippi lawyer, Alston G. Dayton. Elkins's hand was not visible
in the contest, but there can be little doubt that he determined the result. Like Dawson's election as state chairman,
Dayton's nomination represented Elkins's policy of bringing
new men with him to power, bypassing the older and more
independent leaders. It was a shrewd policy, but one that left
the seeds of future discord in Sturgiss's stronghold, the "banner" Republican counties of the Monongahela valley. Outside
the district, Elkins supplied campaign funds and made
speeches throughout the state, paying special attention to the
election of legislative candidates.[182] But while his senatorial
candidacy did not go unnoticed, interest remained centered
on the furious Wilson-Dayton campaign.

The extent of the Republican victory in West Virginia
amazed even the party's most optimistic supporters. Instead
of an anticipated 3,000 to 4,000 vote majority, the Republicans swept in by over 12,000 votes, electing all four congressmen and sixty of eighty-four legislative candidates, giving
them—"notwithstanding the democratic gerrymander," Camden noted—a twenty-nine vote majority on joint ballot.[183]
Camden thought the Democratic disaster "so overwhelming

and so unexpected in many quarters that it is ridiculous and amusing. . . . Personally I feel rather relieved with politics a thing of the past for me. . . ."[184] The second district contest proved to be the closest but still Dayton won by 2,000 votes out of 45,000. Nearly half of his margin came from the Elk Garden region; as the victor noted, "The West Virginia Central Country did a magnificent work."[185] Davis was jubilant as he received the congressional returns. "The election is a rebuke to the extremists of the Democratic party," he declared. "The defeat of that class of politicians is a splendid victory, and is right." To his nephew he remarked that, "I hope and believe that the result . . . will be to considerably increase business in the country and we should get our share."[186]

The Wheeling *Intelligencer* proclaimed "United States Senator Stephen B. Elkins" on November 7, 1894. Elkins's leadership, it added, was "gladly accepted and universally acknowledged. . . . As nobody disputed with Mr. Elkins the party leadership when none of the honors of victory were in sight, so now his fair and reasonable claims on the party will not be seriously disputed when the victory has been won and there is a high honor to confer." Editor Hart's memory lengthened somewhat in the days that followed. "Everybody remembers that the coming of Mr. Elkins into West Virginia was regarded by many Republicans with misgiving," he mused; but since Goff was taken care of in 1891, everyone was happy.[187] Not everyone, as it turned out. Senatorial aspirants surfaced in several quarters during the next few weeks. The most formidable was Sturgiss, who angrily disputed Elkins's claim to precedence, insisting that the Republican victory was the result of slow steady growth and the hard work of many people, "not the strong personality of any candidate, the popularity of any so-called leader, nor the work of any committee, nor the size of any alleged barrel on tap. . . ."[188] "Getting angry never has made a United States Senator," Elkins noted drily.[189] But he assembled his forces with his usual care, extracted from Goff a statement of disinterest in the vacancy, and enlisted McGraw, Camden, and

66

Davis to stand guard lest revenge-minded Democratic legislators unite with disgruntled Republicans to snatch away the
prize.[190] The precautions proved unnecessary. By the time
that the Republican caucus opened in Charleston on January 10, the only problem was how to apportion the second-
ing speeches among Sturgiss and the other non-candidates.
Elkins was nominated by acclamation. The Democrats, after
a sharp contest, again put up Camden as their honorary nominee. The official legislative ballot gave Elkins the toga by a
vote of 60 to 29 to 2 for the Populist candidate. "My gratitude," exclaimed the victor, "goes out to you as rivers flow
to the sea."[191]

3

"The Great Cake Walk"

Following the Republican victory of 1894, Camden telegraphed Elkins to ask "where I should send my shoes to him. He answers, 'You bring your shoes and wife up to Elkins and we will have a pleasant time in making an exchange.' "[1] Things were like that in West Virginia politics after 1894, just a matter of fraternal competition among big businessmen. Perhaps the most remarkable aftermath of the 1894 contest was the speed with which ex-Senator Davis recaptured his old place at the head of the West Virginia Democracy. Ironically, it was the further Democratic disintegration occasioned by the free-silver issue and the Bryan campaign that gave Davis his opportunity. While Camden, ex-Governor Fleming, and other prominent Regulars deserted the party on this occasion, Davis swallowed Bryan and his "Chicago Platform" and by doing so was able at a stroke to reverse the direction of his political career and to emerge as the undisputed leader of his party in West Virginia. The move itself was a simple one, but the maneuvers and negotiations preceding it were as intricate as anything Davis had undertaken in his long political career.

Although Davis intervened vigorously in behalf of Arthur Gorman in a losing battle with Maryland Republicans in 1895, he remained quiet in his adopted state after his victory over William L. Wilson.[2] As in the past, one or two newspapers brought up his name in connection with the West Virginia governorship late in 1895. "Although . . . it would be but a fitting recognition of his service to the State to now call him to the executive chair," ran a press release forwarded to one of the journals, his secretary insisted that the gossipers make clear that Davis was not a candidate. Davis himself clamped down even more firmly on the talk. "My inclinations are not in the direction referred to," he told one editor;

he had been "practically offered" the nomination before, "but my time now as then is fully occupied with my different business enterprises."[3] In February 1896 he declined the invitation of state chairman W. E. Chilton to attend the pre-campaign organizational meeting of the state committee. Nor did his brother represent him as he had often done in the past.[4]

Younger and less affluent Democratic politicians could not afford to emulate Davis and Camden, and so they filled the air during 1895 with prescriptions for restoring their shattered party's health. Everyone agreed that what the party needed was unity; "if only the Democrats will quit fighting among themselves . . ." Governor MacCorkle believed, "the party could regain its majority in W. Va."[5] But there was no such happy prospect in sight. No sooner had the tariff issue been declared settled by party spokesmen than the silver issue arose to take its place.

Compared with their brethren of the South and West, West Virginia Democrats were slow in raising the silver banner. Predictably, the first bearer of importance on the scene—in July 1895—was Daniel B. Lucas.[6] A month later, W. H. "Coin" Harvey, a native son and brother of the 1894 congressional candidate, Thomas H. Harvey of Huntington, addressed a silver rally in his hometown.[7] Soon ex-Governor Wilson and other Agrarian veterans were in the field, clamoring for free coinage. However, the party machinery remained in the hands of conservative professionals—Camden's surviving lieutenants in the north,[8] led by John T. McGraw, and the Kanawha Ring in the south, with its base in the state administration. These groups distinctly lacked enthusiasm for the white metal. So did the conservative press. The Wheeling *Register* was openly hostile to free coinage and took up the presidential candidacy of the "Goldbug," William C. Whitney.[9] The Charleston *Gazette*, closely identified with the Kanawhans, was more circumspect. It gave voice to the silverite demands and at the same time brought forth a conservative candidate of its own in the person of Daniel Manning, Cleveland's former secretary of the treasury—only to discover that

69

Manning was dead![10] "There must be a way out of it," sighed Chairman Chilton in private.[11] Chilton pointed to one way out in his call to arms for the 1896 campaign, delivered on the unusually early date of April 19 in the interest of "thorough organization." Democrats, he stated confidently, were divided on the silver question. Therefore it would not be at issue in the campaign. "We are, however, all afraid of the Force Bill, opposed to Republican extravagance, opposed to the McKinley bill, and we want to see the country settle down to business."[12] McGraw's candidate for governor, a Fairmont editor who thought that what West Virginia Democrats needed most was a boss like Gorman, was ready to dispense with issues altogether. He called upon Democrats to "unite as party men for party reasons," even if the platform "declares for Welsh tin money and a tariff on snow, and then go to the polls and vote the ticket straight."[13] In this spirit, the Democratic convention of Ohio County, dominated by Wheeling's equivalent of Tammany Hall, adopted a resolution supporting the national platform, "be that platform what it may," and hastily adjourned.[14]

The practical spirit of the party wheelhorses, and particularly Chilton's call for a campaign on the Lodge Bill, roused Davis from his political slumbers briefly during the spring of 1896. In response to a second appeal from Chilton to aid in the work of organization, he offered a qualified acceptance. He agreed with the chairman's analysis of Democratic strength, but did not like his reference to the tariff. "The State of West Virginia is naturally Democratic, and in my opinion it drawn [sic] from us last year by the attitude of Cleveland and Wilson on the tariff question, especially with reference to coal." In short, the tariff issue should be dropped. He also wanted John Sheridan, a former employee who had since trained with his B&O enemies and William L. Wilson, dismissed as national committeeman. Under these conditions, if Chilton called a meeting later "of the prominent Democrats of the State, with a view to united action and deciding upon policy . . . I will try to attend."[15] He also began to work through Wood Dailey with McGraw, Senator

70

Faulkner, and John A. Robinson of the B&O to head off Lucas's silver movement in the second district.[16] Tentatively he agreed with McGraw to address and preside over the district delegate convention on June 18, but as the strength of the silver forces became apparent, he decided not to expose himself.[17] By the middle of June, some thirty-five county conventions had declared for free silver and the professionals were scurrying to get aboard the bandwagon. Chilton presided over a silver rally in Charleston on June 13; two days later C. C. Watts, the Kanawha Ring's gubernatorial hopeful, came out "in unequivocal terms" for free coinage; McGraw announced his conversion on the eve of the district convention.[18] By declaring for silver and allowing the silverites to write the platforms, the conservatives salvaged their grip on the party machinery. The district conventions bypassed prophets of the silver movement like Lucas, Wilson, and Thomas H. Harvey, and sent a thoroughly conservative delegation to Chicago headed by McGraw.[19] Davis derived some comfort from this development, but otherwise the triumph of the silverites sent him back to his tent.[20]

The nomination of William Jennings Bryan on a radical reform platform seemed to complete Davis's disaffection from the Democracy. To Ingalls of the C&O he expressed a desire to organize a splinter party of "sound money and law and order Democrats . . . and nominate a ticket on a platform of sound, conservative financial views, and of men who respect law and favor individuals and not the Government managing the business of the country."[21] Through Elkins, Ingalls expressed agreement: "He says he will do all he can in West Virginia," a promise followed in short order by the formation of a "bi-partisan" "Railway Men's Sound Money Club" among C&O employees.[22] John Sheridan, on July 12, was the first West Virginia Democrat to make public his opposition to the ticket. Two weeks later a group of salaried retainers of the railroads, together with lesser politicians like Z. Taylor Vinson, the ex-marshal's son, met in Wheeling to organize the West Virginia National Democratic ("Goldbug") party.[23] Bigger fry like Camden and Fleming were more hesitant about an open bolt. "I don't see how either of us can support the Chicago platform and ticket, with its declaration in substance that mobs and strikes are not to be suppressed in addition to free silver," Camden wrote Davis, "but this is confidential and between ourselves until I see you."[24] Eventually Camden and Fleming accepted the leadership of the Gold Democratic forces, contributing funds and dispensing others collected in Baltimore and New York, and ended the campaign by working openly for McKinley, although they endorsed the Democratic state ticket.[25] As the campaign got underway in mid-August, there was every reason to suppose that Davis would join them.

Instead Davis reversed his course completely, embracing the regular Democracy, including Bryan, and campaigning for his party on a scale that exceeded anything he had done since 1886.

Davis backed away from his initial response to the Chicago convention between the end of July and the middle of August, but his correspondence offers disappointingly few clues as to precisely what he was thinking. An important exception, however, is a letter from McGraw, dated July 17, proposing a conference within the next two weeks to talk over "politics within the near future."[26] The reference was to the upcoming state convention, which threatened to produce an explosion between conservatives entirely unrelated to the events at Chicago. Both McGraw and his friends and the Kanawha Ring recognized the need for party unity and tight-knit organization, but the sad fact was that the two groups hated and were unable to trust one another. The feud had been brewing for years, but Camden and Kenna had been around to restrain it earlier. In 1896, however, it burst into the open at the Chicago convention, where McGraw defeated Will Chilton in a sharp contest for national committeeman. Now McGraw was doing all he could to derail Watts's gubernatorial candidacy, with only a moderate hope of success.[27] It is not certain precisely what he wanted Davis to do; probably he recognized the potentially disastrous effect on the

72

party if he pushed his quarrel with the Kanawhans to the limit, and so sought to draw Davis into the field as a means of preserving the balance of power if he yielded to his rivals on the governorship. If that was his program, Davis added a characteristic twist of his own. At the convention on August 12, McGraw withdrew his opposition to Watts and helped to nominate him by acclamation.[28] On August 17, Davis privately gave his blessing to the state nominees, and invited Watts to visit him at Elkins.[29] Three days later, McGraw appeared at a meeting of the State Executive Committee armed with the proxies of Colonel Tom Davis and a neighboring committeeman and defeated Chilton's bid for reelection as state chairman. But instead of one of his own men, he installed a compromise chairman, with a Kanawha secretary and himself as treasurer, and selected a compromise site, Parkersburg, instead of Charleston, as state headquarters.[30]

As the evidence of accommodation suggests, Davis had seized the opportunity to insert himself between the two factions and thereby regained his old status of party leader, this time with two strong organizations at his back. During the campaign, he entertained both Kanawhans and Regulars at Elkins, appeared with both on the stump, and supplied each with campaign funds.[31] The money and harmony he brought to the task provided fuel and lubricant to transform the new Democracy into a powerful machine. In return for this contribution, he secured the commitment of both factions to his election as senator in 1899.

Exactly how and when the bargain was made is unknown. It was not the sort of arrangement that politicians advertised from rooftops or even mentioned in correspondence except in the vaguest possible terms. But the news spread quickly enough among those who made it their business to know and caused Elkins no little embarrassment. By September 22, he was beset by rumors "that in view of Senator Davis being a candidate for the Senate I am not doing anything" to elect Republican legislators. He therefore instructed A. B. White to publish far and wide the news that, irrespective of Davis's plans, "I have done and am going to do all I can to carry the State of West Virginia for the entire ticket, . . ." which was true.[32] Indeed the partners suffered a number of run-ins during the campaign, although they managed to avoid a direct confrontation. Besides making speeches himself, Davis dispatched his brother and Wood Dailey to stump the West Virginia Central region.[33] When Democrats charged that Elkins was bringing the same kind of pressure on their employees both partners had wielded against William L. Wilson two years earlier, Davis publicly extended his protection to Democratic workers and undertook to counter Republican propaganda among the miners and railroad men.[34] Congressman Dayton again sought to enlist his aid, this time against "the spoliation of the rich by the poor driven by adverse times and . . . demagogic appeals." "I have kind feelings for you," Davis answered politely, "and liberal views in politics, [but] I am a Democrat."[35] F. S. Landstreet, who became a Gold Democrat, complained of Davis's activity as bad for business. "You make no reference to Mr. Elkins devoting his entire time, and probably having a dozen men under pay attending to political matters," Davis testily replied. "However, these are subjects that should not come into business, and we better drop them," he added in a statement that reveals how much, in his eyes, conditions had changed since 1894.[36]

At first Davis intended merely to "support our state and local ticket and hesitate on national."[37] On August 18, it was reported that he "declared himself unequivocally and enthusiastically in favor of Bryan and Sewall and of the primitive principals [sic] of the party" in a speech to Randolph and Tucker County Democrats assembled at Elkins.[38] But the initial response to this report was general incredulity. The Wheeling *Register*, which had reversed itself and swallowed Bryan and silver a few weeks earlier, apparently did not credit Davis with an equal agility. It did not print the report of his speech until August 23, and then only in an inconspicuous place in the form of a letter from a Randolph County subscriber. On the same day, Elkins wrote from the

Republican campaign trail that "People are asking about you. The Silver men claim you are for them and the full ticket. Of course I don't make any reply."[39] The "rumor" of Davis's about-face did not reach Baltimore until August 25, when it evoked howls of protest from his business acquaintances there. Some of them coupled polite statements of disbelief with veiled threats of retaliation. Hambleton and Company, private bankers who held West Virginia Central stock and handled market transactions of its bonds, warned Davis that the bonds were already selling at a discount for fear that they would not be redeemed in gold. Gustavus Ober, a banker and stockbroker, feared that the railroad would soon be in receivership "on account of its inability to meet its sacred promise to pay its interest in gold." "Many widows and orphans," Ober added in perfect seriousness, "would pay me visits and upbraid me for investing their means in such a bond. . . ."[40]

Presumably Mr. Ober's brokerage was full of angry widows and orphans that fall, for once having made up his mind, Davis worked for the Democracy with increasing vigor as the campaign warmed. One reason was Bryan's reliance upon the well-worn silver issue instead of the more revolutionary proposals for the regulation of business. "I cannot consistently endorse all that was said and done at Chicago, especially that part of the platform referring to the Courts and Banks," Davis told one silverite, "[but] I have no fears of the coinage of silver."[41] As he noted publicly, he had managed to live with the inflationists of the seventies, especially those who favored silver as their medium. He had voted for the Bland-Allison Act in 1878 and then as in 1896 had tied the coinage issue with the prosperity of the silver industry. In other words, he was willing to look upon silver as a commodity deserving of the same kind of "recognition" that he demanded for coal.[42] Moreover, experience had fitted him with greater political realism than most businessmen could summon in 1896. There was nothing in Bryan's record to justify the opposition's hysteria, he stated, "but if there was [sic], responsibility makes men cautious and conservative"—in short, a lot of politicking lay between the Democratic platform and its enactment.[43] Among other factors that inspired Davis were the eclipse of the tariff issue, which was still very much uppermost in his mind; the opportunity to return favors to southern and western senators who had helped him in 1894; and the identification of the Gold Democratic movement with men like Cleveland and William L. Wilson, which must have dimmed for him much of the original appeal of a bolt.[44] His reservations about Bryan did not vanish entirely. "I do not like all in each candidate," he told his old friend, Thomas F. Bayard, "but as we must take as a whole one or [the] other, I will vote for Bryan."[45]

Publicly, however, Davis ceased to express his misgivings. He disputed Republican predictions of business disaster if Bryan were elected. When the "Commoner" toured West Virginia in October, Davis organized special trains to carry the faithful to hear him and joined him on the platform at Keyser.[46] Although he was "about the only one in this State who is able and willing to contribute," he gave money to the national committee and aided Gorman in Maryland as well.[47] Just as in Maryland the year before, Davis's support of the Democracy had little effect against a national Republican trend, but the election returns offered proof that his return to the fold was in good faith. The Republicans carried West Virginia by roughly the same margin as in 1894, although the Democrats increased their share of the vote by absorbing the Populists. In the second district, however, the Republicans improved upon their 1894 performance, with the sole exception of the West Virginia Central region. In Davis's home territory, the Democracy reversed the district trend and climbed from 45 to 47 percent of the vote, a clear gain since the Populists had never collected more than a handful of votes in the region.[48]

The 2 percent shift of voters was modest enough. But the real measure of Davis's success was not popularity with the voters but with the politicians who controlled the political organizations between which the voters had to choose. In this respect, 1896 proved to be one of the turning points of his career. Two years after having been condemned as a party apostate, Davis heard himself hailed as "an old Democratic warhorse" who had issued forth from "retirement" to represent responsible wealth, honestly earned, in the battle against Mark Hanna and plutocracy.[49] The contrast with other conservatives like Camden and Fleming, who bolted to the Goldbugs, further enhanced his appeal, and the eclipse of the Agrarians, which proved to be one of the permanent, if ironic, results of the campaign, helped to consolidate his position. Following the tactics developed at the delegate conventions in June, the conservatives again allowed the Agrarians to dominate the nominating conventions, insofar as the platforms and honorific positions like Democratic elector were concerned, while reserving to themselves the committees and candidacies.[50] With equal dispatch they brought the Populist party under their thumb; in one instance, it took McGraw less than two hours to get the Populist nomination in the second district for the Democratic congressional nominee.[51]

By November, Davis was in undisputed possession of the party leadership, as the post-election comments of his allies revealed. "I can only regret . . ." wrote McGraw, "that you [sic] friends are not in condition to do as some of them would like to do for you." Had things gone differently, "we would have been able to have rewarded you as your unselfish generousity [sic] deserved."[52] Will Chilton advanced the belief that "a systematic effort might have reversed the complexion of the Legislature on joint ballot" and, at Davis's request, sent along voting statistics that showed that the task might still be completed in 1898. Speaking for his brother and Watts, he added that "our services will always be at your command."[53] Thus for Davis, as for Bryan, 1896 was only the first battle. The critical test of his new authority came at a more congenial season, an off-year election in which the Democracy was unembarrassed by Bryanism and the excitement of a national campaign.

"A well formed Ring embraces members of both parties and the New Mexican one is remarkably well formed," remarked an Elkins associate shortly before Elkins transferred his activities to West Virginia. "They seem to fight when in reality they are pulling together."[54] During the Reconstruction era, Davis had organized a legislative lobby that worked for the B&O as well as for his own enterprises. It was also bipartisan, and included representatives of most factions within each of the two parties.[55] The political system that emerged in West Virginia between 1896 and 1900 was not exactly analogous to the industrialists' earlier achievements, but it was close enough. During 1898 and 1900, Davis, Elkins, and Scott consolidated their power within each political party in West Virginia and at the same time engaged in noisy and expensive two-party competition—within certain limits. The objectives of this bipartisan conservative leadership were less precisely defined than those of the B&O lobby or the Santa Fe ring. Its activities were less the result of conscious conspiracy across party lines—at least none has come to light—than of the several individuals involved simply "doing what came naturally" as businessmen and politicians. And the limits of partisan competition between the conservatives were sometimes overstepped in the excitement of campaigns. But regardless of these differences, the new West Virginia leadership worked in much the same way as had these earlier, more deliberately exploitative political arrangements.

Those Democrats who anticipated an immediate outburst of Republican factionalism upon that party's accession to power were disappointed. C. B. Hart credited the harmonious state of affairs that prevailed in 1895 and 1896 to the peaceful acceptance of Elkins's leadership. Otherwise it "might have been divided and hopeless now instead of united and confident. . . . As it is to-day we are all proud of our new senator and all pressing to the front for another great Republican victory."[56] As this suggests, the uncompleted task of redeeming the state from the Democrats was partly responsible for the tranquillity. But another factor was the care that Elkins took to promote harmony and to avoid giving any

78

Republican group an excuse for offense. On taking his seat in the Fifty-fourth Congress, he set about securing for West Virginia the biggest possible slice in the huge rivers-and-harbors pie with which the Republicans planned to entice Cleveland into one of his apoplectic vetoes. Using this work as his excuse, he remained at Washington throughout the pre-convention period in 1896, ostensibly removed from the arena of state and presidential politics. "After an experience of more than twenty years," he stated,

> I have learned that when the people elect a Senator and confer on him the highest office in their gift they expect him to attend closely to his business, and look with some jealousy upon his attempting to control and dictate in other matters, especially the nomination of Delegates to the National Convention and State officers. You know that I never wanted to appear in the role of a boss. . . .[57]

But while avoiding the appearance of bossism, Elkins managed to enjoy its substance. He did not interfere with George W. Atkinson's gubernatorial aspirations in 1896, but saw to it that Atkinson, in office, took with him to Charleston William M. O. Dawson in the lucrative and politically sensitive post of secretary of state. As to presidential politics, he enhanced the value of West Virginia's twelve votes in the national convention by holding them close to his chest while remaining publicly "not unfriendly" to the leading candidate, McKinley.[58] Accordingly he encouraged the selection of a convention delegation of McKinley admirers but formally uncommitted as to the candidates. And he saw to it that A. B. White headed the delegation, being "some one [who] know[s] my opinions and notions as to what should be done."[59] This strategy did not deceive McKinley, who—to the utter horror of Elkins and his lieutenants—offered a place in his cabinet to Nathan Goff and with it a share in West Virginia's federal patronage. But Goff preferred the security of the bench and turned down the post when the president-elect declined to promise him the first available Supreme Court vacancy.[60] Thereafter McKinley proved entirely adaptable to Elkins's purposes. One of the more revealing appointments was that of George M.

Bowers of Martinsburg as federal commissioner of fisheries. Touted as "a man of wealth [who] has given much of his leisure time to the study of fish culture," Bowers was actually a small-time politician and real estate man. His tenure in office extended through 1913 and dotted West Virginia with federal fish hatcheries, but it doubtless boded no good for the Alaska seals.[61] And so it went on down to the poorly paid but politically useful traveling postal inspectors.[62]

In building his organization, Elkins faced problems engendered by the manner of his entry into West Virginia during the Harrison years. Those local leaders who stood first in Republican ranks at that point had naturally been less than enthusiastic about his bid for power, forcing him both to accommodate them and to appeal over their heads to those Republicans who were less satisfied with the then-existing order of things. Harrison took care of Goff. The vision of another judgeship, barely perceptible on the horizon but sufficient to bring a gleam into Atkinson's eyes, kept this potentially troublesome leader in line for years during and after his gubernatorial term.[63] Scott was another matter. Having reorganized his business interests during the nineties, he was free to devote more time to politics and could have proved dangerous had he not transferred his loyalty completely to Elkins. The whys and wherefores of his decision are not clear, unfortunately, but it is not unlikely that the accommodation of Goff and the shimmer of a second senatorial vacancy on the horizon sufficed to draw him to Elkins's side. In 1896 he held aloof from Elkins's presidential strategy, but he shared Elkins's alarm at McKinley's brief threat to reactivate Goff.[64] Elkins cemented the alliance by backing Scott for West Virginia's biggest federal patronage prize in 1897, the federal commissionership of internal revenue, and for the Senate in 1899.[65] Editor Hart, who showed more independence than Elkins cared for, was shipped off as United States Minister to Colombia, where he remained until the diplomacy of Theodore Roosevelt's Panamanian Revolution necessitated his removal in 1902. The venerable *Intelligencer*, reorganized by Hart's successors as a mature publishing enterprise, drew free from dependence upon Elkins's subsidies, and A. B. White of the Parkersburg *State Journal* became the organization's leading editorial spokesman.[66]

Those West Virginians who had first rallied to Elkins also required his attention as he tightened his hold on the West Virginia G.O.P. While not exactly "outs" in earlier days, the original Elkinsites tended to be more peripheral figures than Goff or Atkinson. Reflecting earlier intra-party struggles, they also tended to be identified with (or to identify themselves with) West Virginia's Republican founding fathers. John W. Mason, upon whom Elkins leaned heavily from 1888 through 1896, had lifted as many G.O.P. lances as either Goff or Atkinson and had also served as a mediator in their quarrels with the statemakers.[67] Yet until Elkins came along Mason had little to show for his pains in the way of offices.[68] Among other early supporters of Elkins, William P. Hubbard of Wheeling was the son of a statemaker; George C. Sturgiss and two other Morgantown lawyers, John M. Hagans and Ralph T. Berkshire, were proteges of Waitman T. Willey, one of the "fathers"; so to a certain extent was Dawson.[69] White, although a newcomer to West Virginia, was the journalistic heir of former Governor W. E. Stevenson.[70]

Some of these men had already shown ideological leanings that would be of future importance. Dawson's record in the 1887 state senate strongly contrasted with Scott's, for example. While the industrialist drifted in and out of the session, failing to vote on over one-third of the roll calls, except to cast a solid negative on Prohibition issues, Dawson compiled a record of consistent support for reform legislation, Prohibition, and, not least in importance, party regularity (at a time, it should be remembered, when some Republicans flirted with intervention in the Democratic senatorial contest of that year). Yet Dawson's organizational skill and faithful service made him a central figure in Elkins's plans. Bowers, census supervisor, fish commissioner, and eventually, congressman, was a member of the 1887 House of Delegates. He voted with Dawson on party issues, against him on railroad regulation, and divided his votes on Prohibition.[71] Another

81

conservative, Representative Dayton, was also the son of a veteran West Virginia Republican. As William L. Wilson had done before him, he managed to establish an independent political base in the polyglot second district. Significantly, Dayton disappeared via the federal judicial route in 1905.[72] Thus in choosing his lieutenants, Elkins took some and left others on the basis of usefulness and reliability, letting ideological and historical chips fall as they might. This pattern had significant implications for the future. For the present, it meant that the early years of the new regime in West Virginia witnessed a growing volume of complaints, centering initially on the distribution of patronage.

Like all intelligent monarchs, Elkins maneuvered to remain above the battle, allowing his ministers to absorb the shock of opposition. The strategy taxed "Smooth Steve's" considerable gifts for tact and diplomacy, but it was successful. Except for Sturgiss's abortive resistance to his senatorial election in 1895, opposition was directed at Dawson, White, or Scott, not at the senator. Clearly this challenged Elkins's authority, but none of the challengers cared to admit it and he was in turn careful to avoid giving grounds for an open confrontation. A trio of Charleston Republicans, William Seymour Edwards, James H. Huling, and John B. Floyd, tried to displace Scott as national committeeman in 1896. Elkins quietly but effectively backed Scott, who retained the office.[73] He backed him again in 1897 when Scott successfully claimed Mason's old job as internal revenue commissioner. At the same time he allowed White to reoccupy his old job as state collector over the protests of Thomas E. Davis. Mason was angry and humiliated; Davis, Dayton, and the other congressman were "utterly stunned" by both developments. But though Elkins was responsible, he managed to shift the blame to McKinley and Mark Hanna and the resentment to Scott and White.[74] To Mason he blandly offered a treasury job with equal pay but subordinate to Commissioner Scott. "Not while I can work enough to support my little family by digging coal!" Mason shot back. But though he knew full well

82

that Elkins approved the arrangement, the senator's low profile forced him to vent his outrage on Scott.[75] Along with Edwards, Huling, Floyd, Thomas E. Davis, and Thomas G. McKell of Fayette County, Mason and Atkinson opposed Scott's senatorial candidacy in 1898.[76] But the anti-organization forces lacked effective leadership. They invoked Goff's name frequently, but he only retreated further into his judicial dignity, leaving both his would-be followers and Elkins wondering where he really stood.[77] Atkinson, who hoped to inherit Goff's mantle, was afraid to grasp it. He antagonized organization insiders by his distribution of state patronage, but otherwise was paralyzed by the inability to decide between pursuing his ambition and the fear of an open clash with Elkins.[78]

Elkins continued to avoid confrontation as nearly as possible during 1898. But unless he were willing—which he was not—to welcome a colleague to Washington like Goff or Atkinson, one with the popular support and the inclination to challenge his hegemony, he had to act forcefully to support his lieutenants. Previously he had intervened only in the guise of peacemaker into the turbulent politics of the Kanawha region, where the Edwards-Huling-Floyd faction maintained a perpetual feud with the Republican version of the Kanawha Ring—the so-called "Hog Combine" entrenched in the Charleston and Kanawha County governments.[79] In February 1898, however, he aligned himself secretly with the "Combine." Acting through Dawson and White, he financed the acquisition of Floyd's newspaper, merged it with another journal to form the Charleston *Mail Tribune,* and placed it under the direction of Dawson, White, E. P. Rucker (currently attorney general and the representative of the N&W region in state politics), and Grant P. Hall, the Kanawha circuit court clerk.[80] Soon afterward, District Attorney Joseph H. Gaines, another Elkins lieutenant based in Charleston, assured the senator that legislative candidates "will be nominated who [are] 'straight,' and friendly to you."[81]

As to the junior senatorship, Elkins allowed Scott and Atkinson to canvass supporters throughout the first half of the year. Then he summoned both, along with Dawson, to Washington on July 14 "to discuss the situation and map out fully a plan of action."[82] From all appearances, Scott, White, and Dawson regarded "Brother Wesley" (Atkinson)—who was, besides being a politician, a pious Methodist and prolific writer of prose tales of idyllic mountain life—as something of a ninny. Whether or not Elkins shared their opinion, he had already committed himself to Scott in advance of the discussion.[83] But Atkinson was a popular figure whom it would be unwise to give cause for grievance, and so he had to be handled with care. Elkins accordingly told him that he "could not afford to take up the case of any one leading candidate against the other." If Atkinson was willing to shoulder the financial burdens of the campaign, Scott would withdraw. Otherwise "it would not be fair to let Scott go forward and elect the Legislature through the State and then not get the Senatorship." This was an impossible proposition from Atkinson's point of view, since he could hardly hope to match Scott's financial resources. The governor therefore wanted to sit on the fence until after the election and then tackle Scott in an open contest. Elkins rejected this approach, pointing out that an open fight might provide an opening for Goff.[84] Unable either to refute the logic of Elkins's arguments or to accept his terms, Atkinson went back to Charleston and sulked, but did nothing to impede Scott's canvass except what damage could be done by whispered complaints that the industrialist was buying the senatorial nomination. Scott thought Atkinson's behavior "mean" but not very dangerous.[85] Elkins, having made it appear as though the aspirants had resolved the issue among themselves, now swung his weight fully behind Scott. The two industrialists agreed to divide the cost of electing the legislature between them, Scott taking the delegates, Elkins the state senators, whose terms extended through the next senatorial election in 1901.[86]

If Atkinson was regarded mainly for his nuisance value, it was quite another thing when it came to Goff. Both Scott and Elkins regarded the judge as the most serious threat to their arrangements. Scott instructed White to "take whatever

grease is necessary with you, and call on me for it afterwards . . ." to prevent nominating conventions in the northern counties from instructing their legislative nominees to
support Goff for the senatorship. If the tactic worked, "I will
bet my existence that Gen. Goff 'will get off the pot.' "[87] It
worked. Later Scott received private assurances that Goff
"was not, and would not be a candidate. . . . Now whether
you can rely on this or not I do not know," he commented;
"I hope though that the Judge has [had] his eyes sufficiently
opened to see that he probably can't get it if he wants it."[88]

By the time Scott turned his full attention to the Democrats, he discovered new complications. On October 2, he
forced Elkins to admit that "Henry G. Davis is a full-fledged
candidate for the U. S. Senate if the Democrats win. . . ."
Combined with what he considered niggardly campaign contributions on Elkins's part, this aroused his suspicions. With
respect to the election of legislators in the West Virginia Central region, he was more than suspicious. "I am satisfied in
my own mind," he told White, that Elkins would not try to
defeat Democratic candidates there and so resolved not to
waste a penny of his own cash in the region until Elkins
showed his true colors.[89] It would seem that Scott misjudged
Elkins in the excitement of the campaign, but he did not
mistake the seriousness of Davis's challenge. After another
foray into Maryland in 1897, Davis was on the field in West
Virginia early in 1898.[90] In January he conferred in Washington with Will Chilton and William A. Ohley of Fairmont, the
current state chairman, who spent the first three months of
the year traveling about the state "on business." The topic of
their discussions was the election of legislators.[91] Officially,
Davis's senatorial candidacy was kept under wraps.[92] But it
was an open secret and his name was frequently connected
with the office, and with the governorship as well, in the
party press.

As in the past, Davis did not leave his press relations to
chance. In May, he, McGraw, and Ohley moved secretly to
acquire control of the Charleston *Gazette.* Easing the current

85

editor, one O'Brien, out of his chair had "to be done adroitly, so as not to let him know our purpose and intentions."[93] Here Elkins was able to lend a hand. Swallowing his distaste for the editor, who as Washington correspondent for another newspaper in 1894 had engaged in especially virulent attacks on protectionists, the senator recommended him for appointment as a paymaster in the army. However, other protectionist senators had longer memories and refused to permit his confirmation. Whereupon Atkinson made him an officer in a volunteer regiment then forming in the state for duty in Cuba.[94] The uproar that followed among Republican patriots created, in McGraw's words, "a delicate and embarrassing situation" until the troops marched off to camp at the end of June. Then Davis re-imported Lewis Baker from Minnesota to take over the *Gazette* in July.[95]

Aside from these preliminaries, Davis left the early organization to the Kanawhans and McGraw. Because of McGraw's subsequent senatorial canvasses and his prominence in the 1898 campaign, the misapprehension arose that it was he and not Davis who was the active senatorial aspirant, an impression fostered by the Republican press who found McGraw a more convenient target.[96] Even Baker was at sea over the exact relationship, but Davis reassured him: "As to Colonel McGraw, we have a friendly and good understanding, and it is not likely that there will be any conflict of Interests."[97] Actually, McGraw was slated for the second district congressional nomination, which he captured with ease at Elkins on August 10.[98] Throughout the campaign, he and Davis worked closely together on both the congressional and legislative fronts. Unlike his Republican rival, Davis did not intervene in the selection of legislative candidates. This went against McGraw's political instincts (and probably his distrust of the Kanawha Ring), but Davis's policy prevailed.[99] Nevertheless, the latter's interests were well looked after in county conventions. S. L. Flournoy, the West Virginia Central's Charleston counsel, appeared on the legislative ticket in Kanawha, while the nominee in Mineral, at McGraw's suggestion, was "Colonel Tom" Davis, who was slated to captain his brother's forces when the legislature convened.[100]

If no other proof of Davis's candidacy were available, the fact that he financed this Democratic campaign more generously than any other save that of 1904 speaks eloquently in itself.[101] The Democracy was also better organized and more harmonious than at any time since the end of Reconstruction. Camden and Fleming did not campaign actively but gave the aspirants their blessings.[102] Other hopeful signs included a series of Democratic victories in municipal elections in the spring.[103] "Things political in this region are moving along smoothly," Davis reported to Camden on the eve of the election. Elsewhere Democrats confidently detected victory in the air.[104] And there was more to support their belief that West Virginia would return to the Democratic fold than just the normal overconfidence of politicians. Thanks to a legislative gerrymander in 1891, the party did not have to win a majority of votes in order to win control of the legislature. There was also the inspiring work of Democratic revival then going on in the neighboring border states of Kentucky and Maryland.[105]

As nearly as can be determined, it was tacitly understood within the Davis-Elkins family that family members belonging to one party would remain "passive" if there were family candidates of the opposite party in the field.[106] But in 1898 this understanding weakened in the heat of partisan rivalry, even in Mineral County, where Colonel Tom Davis was running for the House of Delegates. "The Republicans are working hard to defeat the Colonel," a Democratic employee complained to Davis. Their most effective tactic was to attack the hated company stores, of which the colonel was the manager; Elkins ought to stop this dangerous agitation, the writer contended.[107] But Elkins had complaints of his own about the conduct of Democratic company employees. Davis, upon investigation, found these baseless and reported to Elkins without comment that there was "a considerable stir about the mines" regarding twenty Polish miners recently taken to court for naturalization in the charge of a Republican com-

87

pany lawyer, using excursion tickets on the railroad furnished by another Republican employee.[108] R. F. Whitmer of Philadelphia, who manufactured lumber in Randolph County and had collaborated with Davis and Elkins when they were working together against William L. Wilson in 1894, now found himself not a little confused by the partners' conflicting partisan appeals.[109]

Thus the industrialists did not allow their private relations to interfere with partisan competition in 1898. Even less did they becloud it with issues. The Democrats came down on all sides of the silver issue in their several conventions and platforms. Perhaps Davis's statement—"We all know that when money is scarce it is hard to get"—best conveys the nature of their appeal.[110] At first Elkins believed that "the war would elect the Legislature without any great effort," but his own record of opposition at the outset of the Cuban adventure proved to be a liability. He sought to make up for it with a strident postwar imperialism.[111] Predictably, the Democrats took up both sides of the imperialism issue. Davis unblinkingly denounced Republicans for their monometallic mania, devotion to trusts, and "high protective tariff." Democracy, he stated, stood for a "Tariff for revenue, with incidental protection," civil service reform, the Monroe Doctrine, plus "economical expenditure" and "home rule." McGraw based his campaign for Congress upon his opponent's record of absenteeism.[112] There was little at issue, then, except whether the state's highest political dignity would be conferred upon a Republican manufacturer or a Democratic mine owner. Called to partisan battle on these terms, the electorate returned an eloquent answer. "I never saw such blank indifference in my life," Camden remarked.[113] The politicians themselves, however, approached the election in a state of considerable excitement. A great deal of pride and ambition—not to mention money—rode on the result.

"The Great Cake Walk," as Scott referred to the election,[114] came off as scheduled on November 7, but the outcome remained in doubt for over two months. The Republican majority fell to less than 3,000 votes; that would have been sufficient had not the gerrymander of 1891 proved its effectiveness. With a net deficit of some 2,800 votes in the legislative balloting, the Democrats picked up seven of thirteen Senate seats at stake and thirty-six of seventy-one in the House. On the basis of holdover senators, the G.O.P. retained a majority of seven on joint ballot, but this was pared to five as recounts—financed by Davis and Scott—got underway.[115] Both parties filled the air with claims of victory and charges of fraud as they nervously awaited the outcome of nine additional contests. Since only one of these involved a Democratic senator, the Republicans were at a serious disadvantage. If the Democratic House awarded all disputed seats to Democrats, the Republican overall majority would vanish. "It strikes me," wrote Scott, "that if they organize the House of Delegates that it would hardly be worth while to go any further in the fight, as you know they will unseat a sufficient number there to give them the legislature. . . ."[116]

The one trump card that the Republicans held was Dawson's position as secretary of state, which entitled him to make up the preliminary roll of legislators on the basis of which the two houses would organize. If enough defeated Republicans brought contests or Republican county courts withheld certificates of election from Democratic delegates, Dawson could enroll Republicans for disputed seats in sufficient numbers to enable them to organize the House. But in striving to bring about this result, he and White met with unexpected rebuffs. Obviously beaten Republican candidates refused to bring contests. The Taylor County Court, solidly Republican, declined to withhold the certificate from a Democratic recount winner. In Mineral, where Colonel Tom Davis was elected by nearly two hundred votes, the county chairman icily informed White that "Strange to say, we have in this county a Court that would probably hesitate to do anything of this kind and I do not think I could make them understand the purpose of it." Besides a little matter of ethics, there was the argument that Dawson's strategy would make a mockery of Republican preachments against past Democratic sins like the unseating of Goff in 1890.[117]

Scott was amazed at this development. "It is quite evident to me that the republicans [of] West Virginia are all entirely too d----d pure for this earth," he fumed, "and I think the sooner a few of them die and go to their reward, the better it will be for our party in the State . . ."; "these 'goodey-goodey' fellows" were also scotching another organization proposal, that the Republicans refuse to organize the Senate and so prevent an election until the Democrats came to terms. In the face of such unreasonableness, the candidate could only conclude that "We appear to be doomed by people who wear white robes."[118]

All was not rosy on the Democratic side of the fence, however. McGraw's followers were irritated by the fact that the West Virginia Central counties elected a solid phalanx of Democratic legislators while returning a greater majority for the Republican congressional candidate than they had in 1896. "If ex-Senator Henry G. Davis had an idea that he might drop that 'ex' from his name this time," wrote the *Barbour Democrat,* "he should have used some influence for McGraw along his railroad. . . ."[119] A closer inspection of the vote would have shown the charges to be unfounded, except for Mineral. Colonel Davis ran well ahead of his ticket there, but no more so than did a popular local Republican candidate in normally Democratic Randolph County. In the four-county region as a whole, McGraw captured 46 percent of the vote, Democratic senatorial candidates, 42 percent, and the delegates, paced by Colonel Davis, just under 50 percent. Democratic legislators owed their success, not to Senator Davis's influence—the limit of which had been reached already in 1896—but to the fact that Tucker and Grant counties, which returned their usual Republican majorities were grouped in districts with heavily Democratic Randolph and Hardy.[120] Of course, no one scrutinized the returns in such detail in the post-election excitement, but Davis and McGraw themselves ignored the dispute. Of a conference between them on November 28, Davis reported that

90

"we had a full talk and think we fully understand each other—and will work (as to Senator) together."[121]

Davis and McGraw scheduled another conference for December 7 in Washington, to which the Chiltons and Mac-Corkle were invited.[122] But the Kanawhans were out beating the bushes for additional votes and without their prodding, Davis began to waver about making an open bid for the senatorship. A number of factors explain his hesitation. Early in December rumors began to circulate that Governor Atkinson would call out the militia when the legislature convened. This was promptly denied, but some Republicans openly applauded the idea while Democrats hinted darkly that they would answer as the situation required. In distant metropolitan centers, editors prepared to give full coverage to another outbreak of colorful mountain warfare.[123] Then, too, as Wood Dailey told Davis in something of an understatement,

... there is danger that the management of both [parties] will do something not entirely straight to get the advantage.... Altogether it would be a very disagreeable fight, and the active candidate of the Democratic party, in whose behalf the fight would be made, if successful, would always be charged, or suspected, by some, with having been a party to what would be called "a steal," and to a man like yourself the office under such conditions would not be acceptable.[124]

Davis agreed and on December 7 concluded not to stand for the office. His decision was made public on December 10, on which day McGraw openly entered the race.[125]

Davis's decision appalled the Kanawha Ring. Both Chiltons hurried to Washington but found him immovable.[126] He was still available, but not an active candidate. McGraw would bear the shocks and indignities of leading the fight. Then, "If conditions so shape themselves that I am elected, I of course will serve; but I do not wish to enter into such a contest as I believe will take place at Charleston."[127] He instructed inquiring legislators to keep in touch with the colonel after the legislature convened. "None of us know [sic] what turns things may take at Charleston," he noted.[128] The colonel was also set to work with W. A. Ohley, who, with Davis's approval, approached Dawson early in January with a formula that became known as the "peace protocol." The party managers agreed to "avert chaos" by freezing the membership of both houses, leaving the two most bitterly contested seats vacant until after the senatorial election.[129] This arrangement left the Republicans a majority of three on joint ballot. But, as Ohley noted, with "a solid lining up of the Democrats . . . I am not without hope of electing a Democrat to the U. S. Senate. The Republicans seem hopelessly divided and will not quickly, if at all, get together."[130] It was unlikely that any Republican legislators would flock to the standard of an aggressive partisan leader like McGraw, but Davis was another matter. Joe Chilton had planned to rely on his "known strength with *all the influences* tending to the state's development . . ."; this meant the coal and railroad corporations whose representatives in the "Third House" were always a potent influence at Charleston.[131] Possibly it referred to Elkins as well. In any case, neither Davis nor anyone else had forgotten how he went to the Senate in 1877. It is not improbable that he and his confidants expected a partisan deadlock, followed by his own election to the Senate with Republican support.

Whether or not Davis and Elkins were discussing senatorial matters in the privacy of their neighboring homes in Washington[132] cannot be learned, but Scott's suspicions were once again aroused. His forebodings were not very precise, but he was certain that "several gentlemen [will] rue the day that they ever tried to defeat me by mean dirty little tricks."[133] It appears, however, that once again he underestimated Elkins's fidelity. The senator was determined not to give up the appearance of his neutrality, but behind the scenes he was putting in effective work for Scott. As Scott had predicted, Goff had no taste for an open contest, and issued a formal disavowal of interest in the senatorship on December 26.[134] But Atkinson was still in contention and could provoke the sort of struggle that could leave an opening for Goff, or for that matter, for the Democratic strategists, to exploit. This was what Elkins sought to prevent and he was able to do so.

His secret was the aforementioned carrot that became Elkins's special Atkinson-taming device. Republicans had long
hankered for West Virginia's federal district judgeship, still
held by John J. Jackson, who was appointed by Lincoln in
1861. The problem was that Jackson refused to die or retire.
Nevertheless, Elkins took Atkinson to the White House early
in January to discuss the matter. As Atkinson recalled their
"very satisfactory talk" with McKinley, the president told
him

> ... that if Judge Jackson did not vacate the Bench, one of the
> two District [of Columbia] Judges would, and that during the
> remaining two years of each of our administrations, he was confi-
> dent he could fix me on the bench, in the District—if not in West
> Virginia. . . . On my return home from that trip, I had a fine talk
> with Messrs. Dawson and [U.S. Marshal John K.] Thompson on
> the subject, and we shaped our action accordingly relative to the
> Senatorship. Mr. Dawson can and will explain fully just what was
> done, and how it was done.[135]

Whatever was done, both the Goff and Atkinson supporters
remained divided and leaderless when the Republican senatorial caucus assembled on January 19 and Scott was able to
carry the day.[136]

There remained the danger that not all Republican legislators would accept the caucus decision. McKell threatened
privately to pursue his crusade against Scott "even at the risk
of getting a Democratic Senator" and at least two legislators
from his Kanawha valley neighborhood openly proclaimed
their intention to vote for Goff.[137] But Elkins arrived on the
scene on January 23 to supervise the making of "plans in the
event of a contingency."[138] Thanks to his intervention, all
but one of the malcontents were whipped into line. The joint
ballot on January 26 gave Scott forty-eight votes to forty-six
for McGraw and one for Goff.[139] Thus, instead of a "contingency" developing, tensions relaxed and Republicans of all
persuasions poured out their gratitude to Elkins. "How soon
the atmosphere cleared and order came out of chaos after
Senator Elkins got on the ground at Charleston," cheered the
pro-Goff Morgantown *Post*.[140] " 'All is well that ends

well,' " wrote one Republican to Elkins, "but the situation was critical, a false move or delay, might have lost all & put our State in a chaotic condition & given it a bad name, all is happily averted & Victory is ours, thanks to your successful management."[141] Following the election, Elkins gathered up Scott and his wife and took them back with him to Washington in his palace car. As the new senator entered upon his duties, he speedily forgot all the unkind sentiments he had harbored about his colleague.[142]

"We can win in West Virginia now as long as we all behave ourselves," breathed a Republican businessman after the senatorial crisis of 1898-1899 passed.[143] But Elkins was not yet able to rest on his laurels. A new and fiercer storm appeared on the horizon as the next member of his organization slated for advancement, A. B. White, moved toward the governorship during 1899. Seeking information on the party's health and on his own prospects for reelection, Elkins solicited reports from leaders in every county in May 1899 and again in March 1900. Their replies afford an opportunity to arrive at a preliminary assessment of the nature of Republican factionalism.

With the exception of the Charleston area, reports from urban and industrial counties were optimistic: "The factional spirit that has existed in Huntington for a year or two has about spent its strength . . ."; "everything is very promising here now. A R. R. is being built into our county . . ."; "Oil is being found in larger quantities in almost all directions . . . so you see we are increasing in wealth and Republicanism"; "perfect harmony prevails."[144] Republicans were also optimistic in farm counties where Democratic majorities still obtained or were a thing of recent memory.[145]

The gloomiest reports came from two centers—Kanawha valley counties in the south (Mason, Lincoln, Fayette, and Kanawha), and those northern counties in the Ohio and Monongahela valleys whose farmers and merchants had formed the nucleus of Republican power in West Virginia since 1863. The north was beset by general unhappiness that eventually

94

focused on opposition to White. "In 1898, we lost half of our majority, ... and unless all signs fail, we are in danger of losing the other half next year," reported formerly rock-ribbed Doddridge County. Things were equally bad in neighboring Ritchie and Tyler; in the latter county, gloom was compounded for Elkins supporters by the character of the two leading legislative candidates, one of whom would have to be bought on every question, the other "more objectionable, for the reason that he would not probably agree with the majority on any question, and we could neither persuade nor buy him, so as between the two it would be death, in the event we could succeed in electing either, which does not now look possible." Even along the West Virginia Central, Grant County was full of "soreheads."[146] By the beginning of 1900, the leaders and rank and file of the Morgantown area were in open rebellion against "the Federal Bugaboo and the crack of the ring-leader's whip." John W. Mason, Thomas E. Davis, and George C. Sturgiss were prominent backers of White's opponent for the gubernatorial nomination, Congressman R. H. Freer of Ritchie.[147] Governor Atkinson, as Freer's former law partner and lifelong friend, was suspect as a link between the northern dissidents and their counterparts in the south, although he denied it.[148] Another connection was the Lincoln Club, comprised of Freer followers in Charleston and led by J. H. Huling.[149] By April 1900, Dawson, after four years of missionary work among the fractious Kanawhans, was almost ready to give up. "This is an awful county," he complained to Elkins. "You can't appreciate what I have to contend with."[150] In Fayette, Thomas G. McKell, having failed to enlist Elkins in his vendetta against that "bagful of ignorant egotism," Scott, moved toward a coalition with the Edwards-Huling faction of Charleston, aimed at capturing the region's bloc of seats in the legislature and the third district congressional seat as well.[151] Elkins's lieutenants soon exhausted their patience and longed to cut the opposition down to size. "I am for harmony always," explained Gaines, the organization candidate for Congress in the third district, "but when nothing will do a man but fight, then I say let him have it."[152]

What were the dissidents fighting for? In a word, offices. McKell's quarrel with Scott grew out of the appointment of a hostile postmaster too close to one of his Fayette County coal camps.[153] Similarly, the quarrel in Kanawha centered on a squabble over the Charleston postmastership.[154] The northern leaders included those who were left out in the distribution of patronage during the past five years and who were now determined "to have a say in the selection of men for the ticket." As the Morgantown *Post* explained, ". . . we want the honors distributed evenly."[155] Senator Scott, confronted in Washington by a group of Freer's backers, was "surprised at the bitter feeling some of them manifested against [White], . . ." simply because he had drunk so long and deeply at the patronage well.[156] There were many who had no objection to the way federal plums had been passed out, but who had no desire to see the organization's power extended throughout the state. And the fact that some of the centers of opposition—Charleston, the capital, Morgantown, the university town, and Moundsville, site of the penitentiary—were locations where state officeholders were concentrated indicates that many who enjoyed state patronage were apprehensive about the future.[157]

But the struggle in 1900 was more than just another scramble for places, or the backwash of an earlier scramble, if the rhetoric of the anti-organization forces is to be believed. The rebels clothed themselves in the shiny garments of reform. "It is the people's campaign," proclaimed the *Post*, "this preliminary skirmish" between the "great mass of Republican voters" and a "ring" of professional officeholders.[158] "The State needs broader political lines," declared Freer, "and a few more broadminded leaders and fewer political bosses."[159] A pro-White Grafton writer warned Elkins that "It is common to hear men . . . who before have taken little interest in politics say 'The bosses can make White Collector as often as they wish, but when they try to make him Gov. we will have something to say; and we will teach them that

96

the wishes of the people must be respected.' "[160] C. H. Payne, the leading black politician in the state, reported hearing equally rebellious expressions, not only in the usual listening posts in "hotel lobbies, barber shops, about railroad stations, etc.," but "among those who were at home on the farms and in the workshops throughout the state." "The people," it seemed, were about to rise up against "what they call *the rings*."[161]

This kind of language inevitably suggests the rhetoric of Progressivism as it developed in the state and nation after 1901. And the suggestion is strengthened by the fact that the geographic base of Progressivism as it manifested itself in West Virginia lay in many of the same Kanawha valley and northern Republican strongholds that sheltered the rebels of 1900. Was then the factional disturbance of that year truly a "preliminary skirmish" in a struggle that would recur along "broader political lines" throughout the first decade of the century? The answer must be a weak "perhaps." Although reform rhetoric figured heavily in subsequent intra-party battles, there was little continuity in terms of the individuals and coalitions involved in particular conflicts.[162] Moreover, the men of 1900 advanced no program of political and economic reforms such as characterized later Progressive movements. Yet by harking back to an older, more liberal Republicanism, less closely identified with the interests of corporate enterprise, they aroused a spirit that might have provided a basis for a genuine reform movement in West Virginia later on. But their defeat in 1900 spelled, in effect, the death of West Virginia Progressivism before it was even born. No fusion of reform ideology and traditional leadership ever took place. As a result, such reforms as were enacted, and they were few, were carried out largely under the auspices of the victorious Elkins organization.

The posture of the 1900 dissidents as reformers battling an unpopular machine is, on the whole, unconvincing. The reform program consisted of nothing more than replacing the ins with the outs. The regulars, recognizing this, greeted with contempt the opposition's claim to disinterested motives and popular support. Charlie Elliott, a Republican functionary who traveled about the state "to set up pins" for the organization in county conventions, insisted that "those who are kicking are would[-]be *Bosses,* if they only had the ability."[163] Especially was this true of Morgantown, the financial and journalistic center of the revolt. With some justice, Elliott argued that the anti-organization leaders there—small businessmen like Frank Cox and E. M. Grant, and W. E. Glasscock, circuit court clerk of Monongalia County, behind whom stood Sturgiss—constituted a "Court House ring" that had long been entrenched in local politics and was anxious to expand its base. Elliott also supported Dawson's low opinion of Huling of Kanawha, and discovering that Huling's price was still the Charleston post office, urged Elkins to pay it.[164] "All this talk of the *people* being for [Freer] is sheer jingo politics of the worst sort," scoffed another loyalist. "I will make a wager that Glasscock, Grant & Cox have not talked to one hundred of the dear people."[165] The opposition's claim to popular support was never put to the test, as we shall see. But this did not dampen their penchant for claiming it. "The People are with me," Thomas E. Davis haughtily informed Elkins later in the year. "The fine politicians who run to Washington for places do not represent all W. Va." Noble words, but the setting—Davis's application to succeed White as collector of internal revenue—appears to have had the truer ring.[166]

Progressivism, of course, developed as a movement for economic as well as political reform, an attempt to check the abuses of corporate power, particularly with regard to the exploitation of labor and natural resources. Few of the anti-organization men in 1900 evinced such a desire. In fact, Mason, as a circuit court judge in the Fairmont coalfield, issued a sweeping injunction against United Mine Workers organizers in 1897 and further buttressed free enterprise by advertising the presence of union men through a private network of other conservative lawyers.[167] One exception to this pattern was Atkinson. In 1897 he politely but firmly rebuked Mason's abuse of judicial authority in a public correspond-

98

ence with Samuel Gompers and ordered the attorney general to intervene in the injunction proceedings in the interest of freedom of speech and assembly.[168] In his biennial message to the legislature of 1899, the governor asked for elaboration of the few mine-safety regulations then on the books and deplored the otherwise "total absence of industrial legislation for the welfare and preservation of the life and health of the wage earners ... of West Virginia."[169] Although little of his remedial program was enacted, Atkinson did accomplish something by appointing Isaac V. Barton of Moundsville as his labor commissioner. A tireless and devoted civil servant, Barton became, in effect, a one-man inspectorate and information bureau, constantly pressuring employers and legislators to correct abuses.[170] Barton was prominent among Freer's backers in 1900.[171] Among the others, McKell had rather unorthodox labor relations for a coal operator.[172] On the other hand, he opposed Atkinson's elevation to the bench in place of the ferociously anti-union Judge Jackson because of Jackson's tender regard for the interests of nonresident landholders, of which McKell was one.[173] Few mouthed the articles of West Virginia's faith in development more piously than did Atkinson, and he considered this work of publicizing "the boundless resources" to be the greatest of his public services.[174] The Morgantown *Post*, the most vigorously anti-organization and, later, progressive, journal in the state, received the governor's rhapsodic survey of the industrial future in 1899 with great enthusiasm, though it scarcely noticed his or Barton's pleas in behalf of the workingmen.[175] It is also worth noting that the mine workers lined up with the regulars in Kanawha County and that the slate of four legislative candidates that Dawson designed for the county included two of their spokesmen.[176]

One distinction that can be drawn between the opponents in 1900 is a division between corporate and proprietary business interests. The former lined up solidly behind Elkins and his men. "Of course, we want to serve you in every way we can," wrote H. H. Rogers of Standard Oil, whose South Penn subsidiary was then in process of gaining control over the new Mannington and Sistersville oilfields.[177] White assured the B&O that he would serve it as governor with the same consideration he had shown in twenty-five years as an editor and appointed official.[178] The B&O, C&O, and N&W provided passes for organization workers on Elkins's request, while railroads outside the state sent tokens of gratitude for his services on the Senate Interstate Commerce Committee. "The Burlington will send you $2500.00 perhaps $5000," reported Richard C. Kerens after a fund-raising trip to Chicago. "St. Paul [James J. Hill] will pan out too."[179]

Most of the anti-organization leaders were engaged in industrial enterprises, but on a smaller scale than Elkins, Davis, Camden, or Scott. Besides McKell, W. S. Edwards was a coal operator; J. H. Huling was a lumber manufacturer; in the northern towns, Sturgiss in Morgantown, Mason in Fairmont, Thomas E. Davis in Grafton, Goff in Clarksburg, were all engaged in small-scale coal, oil, railroad, banking, and urban-improvement enterprises.[180] The distinction in size became an important one at a later date, but it had little significance in 1900. Sturgiss, Grant, and Cox, for example, while leading the political revolt in Morgantown, looked to Elkins for guidance and aid in the economic development of their region.[181] Far from feeling threatened by the larger interests at this time, small businessmen very closely identified with them. By the time the smaller men began to have second thoughts in this respect, the moment for successful action had passed.

The one thing that tended to separate the two Republican factions in 1900 was the fact that, as the Wheeling *Register* noted, "the opposition to the ring includes almost all of the old-time leaders of the Republican party, . . . all of whom have been ignored or thrown down by the ring after years of faithful party service."[182] It was not so much a question of age; there was very little difference in this respect between the several antagonists.[183] It was just that the "old-time" leaders had taken up the task of fighting Republican battles at a very young age and now saw the fruits of victory falling to men who had been all but unknown in West Virginia a dozen years before. The dissident leaders of Morgantown could claim with some justice to wear the mantle of the statemakers; others like Atkinson had helped Goff ease the founders of West Virginia Republicanism from power after Reconstruction and still harbored grudges against the "fathers."[184] But all cherished memories of the pre-Elkins era, an era when they had enjoyed more influence and a greater sense of importance than was currently the case. "I helped make and preserve the State of W. Va.," Mason informed Elkins; "for thirty years I have been fighting the battles of Republicanism here, not simply giving a few days during the campaigns, but with me it has been a daily labor. I have spent my time and money in many campaigns where there was not the slightest hope of reward."[185] As fledgling politicians in their twenties, Freer and Atkinson had manned a Republican outpost at Charleston during Reconstruction. "[We] were called upon almost continuously in every campaign to make stump speeches all over the Southern portion of the State," the governor recalled. "He and I have delivered political addresses in more school houses than any other two men in West Virginia in either political party."[186] Significantly, Freer was closely identified with the West Virginia G.A.R., an organization that Elkins had rather hastily joined in 1894 and which was shortly to be investigating rumors that the senator had actually served the Confederacy during his obscure Missouri youth.[187]

Many of the older leaders, Sturgiss and Mason in particular, had welcomed Elkins to West Virginia, but now they faced the disturbing efficiency of his organization in monopolizing and manipulating the party machinery. Even where there was not conflict between the older and newer groups, there was tension. Elkins prevailed upon the older Mineral County leader, F. M. Reynolds, not to oppose White, but as a mutual friend observed, Reynolds badly needed reassurance as to just where he stood in the new order. And no wonder, since Howard Sutherland of Piedmont, currently general land agent for the Davis Coal & Coke Company, was aching "to whip the Reynolds crowd soundly" and forbore only because it was a senatorial year.[188] Nor did the fact that the organization took for granted the huge Republican majorities rolled up in each election in the northern counties help things much. Scott was furious with Elkins in 1898 for pledging $100 to a Moundsville campaigner. "It is ridiculous to give anything to a County that goes from 1800 to 2000 Republican majority," he fumed.[189] The same attitude prevailed when it came time to hand out jobs. "The Republican party is in the majority here," complained the Morgantown *Post*, "and the voters have patiently cast their ballots for the nominees year by year and the party leaders have thanked us with—a smile."[190] The rebels in 1900 hoped to change this.

In the south, the situation, as usual, was more complex. Most Republicans there had converted from Democracy, or come of age, or arrived from other states—all in the course of the region's industrialization. McKell, for example, had expanded his coal operations eastward from an Ohio base. In fact, like Elkins, he still lived outside the state most of the time.[191] But one native, traditionally Republican Kanawha group, the Negroes, shared the nostalgia of the northern leaders for an earlier day. Black politicians were unhappy with the limited recognition they had gotten from the Elkins regime, but their weaker position made them more cautious about treading upon senatorial toes. The West Virginia Colored Republicans Association of Washington was organized by Huntington and Charleston men as one of the first groups to endorse Freer's candidacy. But its president, William T. McKinney, continued to work closely with Elkins and abjured the inflammatory rhetoric adopted by other Freer supporters.[192] So did Payne, who had become the state's first black legislator in 1897. Although he asserted that "a large mass of the rank and file is enthusiastically for Judge Freer," the solution he advanced to Elkins was to withdraw both candidates and name a compromise nominee.[193] Phil Waters, a Charleston informant for Booker T. Washington, stepped forward to second White's nomination after it became inevitable, but his real sentiments were revealed to Washington four years later: "We look upon Elkins as the

102

greatest Senatorial Annanias [sic] of modern times," he reported to Tuskegee. "It is he who has blocked Gov. Atkinson repeatedly."[194] Negro leaders wisely avoided expressing their feelings openly and acted upon them only with the greatest caution. But they were quick to identify the insurgents with "The real founders of the Republican party," the men who had secured their freedom and constitutional rights, not the industrialists and their spokesmen who were now in command.[195]

The foregoing analysis may seem a bit extravagant when the ease with which the anti-organization movement was routed is revealed. But its failure and Elkins's success in consolidating his hold on West Virginia Republicanism meant that subsequent upheavals, however more firmly rooted in Progressive ideology, never threatened to dislodge him, and indeed never attempted to. After 1900, all Republicans, whatever their views on the issues that later arose, acknowledged Elkins as their leader. In fact, it testified to the already impressive extent of Elkins's influence that the insurgents refrained from challenging him openly even now. Publicly, the senator remained neutral and the anti-organization forces were only too happy to take him at his word. "Hurrah for Elkins and Freer," was a slogan heard on many tongues that winter.[196] It was not heard in informed circles, however. The opposition's talk of "bosses," "rings," and "Federal bugaboos" ill-matched its expressions of loyalty to Elkins. "Who are the bosses & what does this mean?" one regular wanted to know; it meant Elkins.[197] "[You] can no more keep out of this 'scrap' than you can fly," White informed the senator. "Freer's candidacy means your defeat if he is successful."[198]

Elkins had no intention of keeping out of it. He had committed himself to White at the very beginning but, as usual, hoped to bring about the desired result through strategy rather than force. As in 1898, he started with Atkinson, whom all of the regulars believed to be behind Freer's candidacy. Once again the prospective judgeship was brought out for Atkinson's benefit and the governor's mouth watered suitably. But he still declined to admit to responsibility for or control over the insurgents or to give his endorsement to White.[199] However, fate—and the insurgents' injudicious choice of a candidate—provided the organization with another trump, which they were ready to play at an appropriate moment. While the Morgantown *Post* ran a temperance column alongside its encomiums of Freer, the candidate himself had an unfortunate history of alcoholism. The disease had ruined his early political career and precipitated a divorce suit, with courtroom revelations of the tragic and shocking sort common in such cases. Later Freer had taken "the cure" and rebuilt his career. But Atkinson—or so the governor later claimed—had tried to talk him out of the gubernatorial race, fearing that the excitement of the contest would tumble him off the wagon.[200] White and his friends were well aware of Freer's history but made no attempt to exploit the issue until it could be more fully documented.[201] The record of Freer's divorce proceedings, which was in circulation among the senators and their lieutenants by February 10, gave them the proof they needed. Although Scott wanted to slip the record to a New York newspaper, it was decided instead to circulate the document privately among party leaders.[202] The mere thought of what the Democrats would do with the record if Freer were nominated was enough to bring Atkinson down off the fence. The governor brought personal pressure upon Freer to withdraw, while further circulation of the record helped quietly to cut away some of the latter's supporters.[203] The whispers served only to stiffen the determination of other "kickers," however, while Freer on February 21 publicly denounced his detractors as "ghouls and hyenas" and threatened to disclose a few things he had "learned in thirty years of public life to the detriment of the men who are hounding me."[204]

Freer's refusal to submit quietly ended Elkins's hesitation about confronting him directly. "There is no kind of doubt about your nomination," he wrote White on February 28. The important thing now was simply to "keep cool, don't get excited, be entirely fair to the opposition. Don't give them

104

ground to complain." "Concede them everything," Scott added, "except when it comes to a vote."[205] Control of the party machinery began to pay off during the first week in March, although, as White admitted, "at great cost of 'ammunition'...."[206] White's followers swept the first five county conventions, all of them in Freer's Fourth Congressional District. The setbacks put the insurgents in an uglier mood than ever and gave force to their utterances about ring rule, to which now was added the charge of character assassination.[207] This was exactly the sort of bad feeling that Elkins had earlier hoped to avoid, but having once grasped the nettle, he and his men proceeded to act vigorously, making plans to fight for the Ohio County and other key delegations during the next two months.[208]

Talk of an open break between the two Republican factions became common as the struggle wore on through March, when the contest was suddenly brought to a close by Freer himself. Late in the month, he had failed to appear at several speaking engagements in the Monongahela valley, where his followers were strongest. If he failed again to show up at a major rally at Kingwood on March 23, Mason admitted to Elkins, "It will be greatly against him. The recent reports circulated against him make people *suspicious* and disposed to *imagine* something wrong."[209] But imagination was not to be needed. Somewhere between Washington and Kingwood, Freer fell off the wagon with a thud that reverberated through the bone-dry Republican heartland. As a result, his campaign collapsed immediately. On March 25, the Morgantown *Post* received his formal letter of withdrawal, offering reasons of health and fear of further "party strife and dissension." His campaign committee dissolved itself and shut down its Morgantown office. It took the leading rebels longer to come over to White but finally they did.[210] While White proceeded to romp toward a unanimous nomination, Elkins set out to heal the wounds that the contest had opened. Within a week, he had enlisted Freer and C. H. Payne "to pour oil" upon "every old soldier and colored man in the city of Huntington," where a critical municipal election took

105

place on April 5. A pocketful of census jobs further helped to smooth ruffled feathers.[211] It took a bit longer to straighten things out in the Kanawha region, where the "kick" was less closely bound up with the gubernatorial fight. Dawson and Elliott worked on Kanawha and Fayette counties throughout April and won a test of strength when delegates to the national convention were chosen on May 8.[212] Subsequently Kanawha nominated a "straight" legislative ticket, although the price tag—$5,000—set Scott and Elkins back a bit. "But I suppose Dawson will explain that in course of time," Scott remarked. Doubtless he did.[213]

The organization's victory was sealed by the gubernatorial convention that assembled in Charleston on July 11. Elkins made his customary keynote address and then turned the gavel over to Freer, who presided over his erstwhile rival's nomination and earned by his good behavior a lower spot on the state ticket, the attorney-general nomination. With one exception, all nominees were chosen by acclamation before the balloting finished.[214] Had the anti-organization men had any issue except rotation in office, they might have rallied after the Freer disaster. As it was, Elkins and his men recovered—and tightened—their grip on the party. It was apparent to all that the senator could return to Washington in 1901 and stay there as long as he liked.

Of course, the Democrats would have something to say about Elkins's reelection, but not much. Davis spent 1899 scouting the prospects for conservative recovery of the national leadership under Gorman. But though he managed to interest Camden and M. E. Ingalls in the matter, the off-year elections and subsequent developments convinced him that the party's prospects were not good and that it was pointless to try to deny Bryan renomination. However, the outbreak of bloodletting among Republicans revived Democratic hopes for carrying West Virginia,[215] with the result that Davis combined with Camden, Ingalls, McGraw, and the Kanawha Ring in a display of conservative power within their party that fully equalled Elkins's Republican achievements. The national convention delegation was a case in point. Headed by Colonel Tom Davis and Joe Chilton, it retained McGraw as national committeeman and made a vigorous fight for Davis's goals of "a conservative platform and a good second man."[216] Disappointed in this, Davis settled down to pro forma support of Bryan. But the state convention on June 6 offered compensation. Playing the role that Elkins would perform a month later at Charleston, Davis delivered the keynote speech and delegated Wood Dailey to write a platform that barely mentioned the issues of 1896. The gubernatorial nomination went to John H. Holt of Huntington, a corporation lawyer closely identified with the C&O, whose candidacy was probably born at a meeting of Davis and Ingalls' West Virginia lieutenants in February.[217] Holt headed what was one of the most conservative tickets ever presented to the voters of West Virginia; McGraw thought it was "the best . . . since the formation of the State."[218] The impotence of the old Agrarian wing of the party was dramatically demonstrated when Daniel B. Lucas abandoned a six-month canvass for the governorship before the convention even brought the matter to a vote.[219]

Thus it was that the West Virginia industrialists brought both political parties securely under their control, control exercised to a remarkable extent by members of the same family. The situation, as in the past, held out to Davis and Elkins possibilities both of collaboration and conflict. Not surprisingly, Davis's correspondence in 1900 is bereft of the attention and funds that he lavished on the senatorial canvass in 1898. But while careful not to complicate Elkins's contest, he tried to uphold the appearance—and as much of the substance as circumstances allowed—of a loyal partisan leader. "You know my relations with Senator Elkins somewhat embarrass me," he informed one party functionary, but he wanted "Democratic principles" to succeed and would "do what I consistently can for the success of the party." He agreed to contribute funds, although not on the scale of 1898, and to make a major address, but stated that business preoccupations made this "the best I can promise to do."[220]

But Davis's fellow Democrats would not leave it at that. Many of them shared his less-than-sanguine views about the party's prospects, which led to a dearth of candidates and funds and a method of dealing with the shortages for which Davis was quite unprepared. He made the mistake of dispatching his brother to look after the second district congressional convention on August 8, and before he knew it, Colonel Tom had been nominated for Congress. The Elkinses were furious at this turn of events. Mrs. Elkins wrote to Congressman Dayton to express their

> ... keen mortification at the treatment accorded us. ... My father assures me it was an entire surprise to him. ... I think that both Pa & uncle Tom were ignorant of the plan to nominate him—and it was so cutely executed, as to come with a surprise, which so flattered and disconcerted uncle Tom that he accepted before realizing that he was defeating his own business partner and niece's husband [i.e., Elkins].[221]

First-district Democrats tried the same tactic a few weeks later with a wealthy Clarksburg banker, but the victim, forewarned by the colonel's example, was quick-witted enough to decline the honor.[222]

Now Davis was in the campaign whether he liked it or not. "While I did not favor [the Colonel's] nomination," he told McGraw, "now that he is in the race, we must elect him." By August 18, he was certain that "Colonel Davis will get a considerable Republican vote, and it looks as if he will be elected."[223] As this suggests, the family arranged a "trade," by which Bretz, Buxton, Landstreet, and the Davis and Elkins sons worked for Republican votes for Colonel Tom for Congress and Democratic votes for Republican legislators. This delicate arrangement was naturally a matter of great secrecy and would probably never have come to light had not the unfortunate lumberman, Whitmer, become confused and accidentally threatened the plotters with exposure on the eve of the election.[224] The effect of the trade showed up in the returns. Colonel Davis, along with Holt, ran substantially ahead of other Democrats in the West Virginia Central region, but the extra margin was not enough to elect them. The

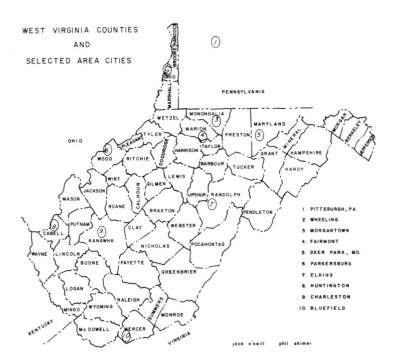

WEST VIRGINIA COUNTIES
AND
SELECTED AREA CITIES

PENNSYLVANIA

OHIO

MARYLAND

HANCOCK

BROOKE

OHIO

MARSHALL

WETZEL

MONONGALIA

MARION

PRESTON

MORGAN

BERKELEY

JEFFERSON

TYLER

PLEASANT

DODDRIDGE

HARRISON

TAYLOR

GRANT

MINERAL

HAMPSHIRE

WOOD

RITCHIE

BARBOUR

TUCKER

HARDY

WIRT

LEWIS

JACKSON

GILMER

CALHOUN

UPSHUR

RANDOLPH

MASON

ROANE

BRAXTON

PENDLETON

PUTNAM

CLAY

WEBSTER

CABELL

KANAWHA

NICHOLAS

POCAHONTAS

WAYNE

LINCOLN

BOONE

FAYETTE

GREENBRIER

LOGAN

RALEIGH

MINGO

WYOMING

SUMMERS

MONROE

KENTUCKY

McDOWELL

MERCER

VIRGINIA

1. PITTSBURGH, PA.
2. WHEELING
3. MORGANTOWN
4. FAIRMONT
5. DEER PARK, MD.
6. PARKERSBURG
7. ELKINS
8. HUNTINGTON
9. CHARLESTON
10. BLUEFIELD

jack o'neill   phil shimer

Republican state ticket swept in by more than 18,000 votes, while McKinley's margin over Bryan in West Virginia was over 21,000.[225] The Mountain State was thus firmly lodged in the Republican column. Camden, as usual, had appropriate words at hand. "The compensation for this overwhelming defeat, if any is necessary [a reference to Bryan]," he wrote to Fleming, "is found in the fact that during the next four years we ought to make lots of money."[226]

But there was more significance to the election of 1900 than most West Virginians realized at the time. It brought to a close a twelve-year period of political suspense. Since 1888 it had been uncertain which way the electorate would swing and which politicians in which party would benefit from its decision. Now the picture was clear. West Virginia, in contrast to the other border states, was indisputably Republican ground. Not just the spokesmen of industrialism, but the industrialists themselves were in secure control of both majority and minority. It remains to be seen how they used their newly consolidated power.

4

The Choice of the People?

"At 3 O'clock P.M. I walked into the place of voting and cast my first Democratic ballot since 1860, . . ." a West Virginia merchant wrote in his diary on election day in 1892. This particular voter persisted in his change of party allegiance and voted, despite misgivings, a straight Democratic ticket again in 1894.[1] Had more West Virginians followed his example, things might have gone differently in the Mountain State. As it was the Republican victories of the nineties brought the Elkins regime to power and enhanced the position of Davis and Camden in the Democracy as well. Thus a first step in understanding the new political order is an understanding of the results at the polls.

West Virginia's voting behavior during the nineties conformed to a broad national trend that, insofar as it is understood by historians, developed under the pressure of economic dislocation against the backdrop of a notable degree of volatility in the electorate in 1890 and 1892.[2] The pivotal vote of 1894 was clearly related to economic distress. Even though the aforementioned merchant, H. J. Mugler of Grafton, embraced the arguments of William L. Wilson and other tariff reformers, he recognized that these fell on stony ground in the hard times of '94. Farmers were concerned with their prices; workingmen wanted not promises but "good wages and plenty work."[3] In this immediate sense, then, the turnover in West Virginia is attributable to impersonal forces affecting the entire nation, forces in which the industrialist-politicians could find little credit or blame.

The same is true for the broader context of the Republican victories. Presidential balloting in West Virginia showed a general Republican trend after 1880 with peaks in 1884—when the Republican share of the vote advanced to 48 percent,

110

compared to 41 percent four years earlier—and 1896, when a smaller spurt put the G.O.P. over the top with 52 percent. Subsequent gains widened the margin to 54 percent in 1900 and 55 in 1904. Voting for state and congressional tickets proceeded in the same fashion, with a few exceptions.[4] Naturally local returns varied more widely from place to place and from time to time than did those of the state at large, but only one of the fifty-five counties (Wyoming) voted in state and national elections in such a way that cannot be related in one way or the other to the general Republican trend. There were two favorite contemporary explanations for this phenomenon. Democrats emphasized the impact of in-migration of white Republican voters from Ohio and Pennsylvania and of black Republicans from the South. Republicans stressed the voters' acceptance of their party as the party of material progress.[5] A closer look at the data suggests that both of these explanations had merit, although neither embraced the whole truth.

It may be doubted that white migration from northern states made much of a difference in West Virginia elections during this period. The proportion of residents born in the Virginias remained roughly the same (85 percent) in 1900 as it had been thirty years before. Apart from Virginia (and it should be noted that those born in western Virginia before 1863 were classed as Virginia natives), Ohio and Pennsylvania furnished by far the largest number of new residents, but the proportion was negligible outside of the Northern Panhandle, where parts of both states lay in the hinterland of Wheeling. On a statewide basis, Ohio- and Pennsylvania-born citizens formed less than 7 percent of the population in 1900, roughly the same proportion as in 1870. The proportion of Pennsylvania-born residents actually declined between 1870 and 1900, as did the number of foreign born.[6] Thus new Republican voters had to come predominantly from West Virginia natives, from local converts and from those who chose the Republican standard as they entered the electorate.

This conclusion is further strengthened by examining each county's voting performance in terms of standard deviations

111

from the statewide Republican mean. On the basis of all counties in West Virginia, the standard deviation for Republican shares of the vote in presidential elections diminished from 13.73 in 1876 to 10.71 in 1900, indicating that the relative performance of individual counties did not vary greatly as the state Republican mean increased. Measuring the individual counties' G.O.P. shares in terms of standard deviations from the state mean at each election indicates that most counties followed the general Republican trend with great consistency, ending up in 1900 with nearly the same proportion of Republicans relative to the state Republican performance as they had had in 1876. Monongalia County, for example, voted 58 percent Republican in 1876, or 1.1 standard deviations above the state Republican mean (42 percent); in 1900, the Republican share was 63 percent, or .9 standard deviations above a mean of 54 percent. For intervening elections, the corresponding figures were 57 percent and 1.2 standard deviations in 1880 (state Republican mean 41 percent), 60 percent and 1.2 in 1884 (48), 61 percent and 1.2 in 1888 (49), 59 percent and 1.2 in 1892 (47), 64 percent and 1.1 in 1896 (52). Greenbrier County voted a similar pattern, except that its Republican shares were smaller, increasing from 27 percent in 1876 to 43 in 1900, and its divergence from the state mean was negative (-1.1 standard deviations in 1876, -1.0 in 1880, and so on). These two plus seventeen other "trend" counties that paralleled the statewide Republican gains while retaining their original partisan allegiance are presented in Table I as "Republican" and "Democratic" counties, respectively. With the Republican districts clustered in the northern third of the state and the Democratic ones in the central and eastern interior, these groupings clearly reflect the impact of statehood and Reconstruction alignments on party choices, but they also reflect subsequent developments that promoted Republican growth in most sections of the state. The third group in Table I comprises fifteen "swing" counties that switched from the Democratic to the Republican column during this period, notably as a result of the G.O.P. surges of 1884 and 1896. This group included in

112

Table I
Republican Shares of the Presidential Vote (%), Trend Counties, 1876-1900

A. Republican Counties (13)[a]

	1876	1880	1884	1888	1892	1896	1900
Preston	64	61	66	67	66	72	73
Upshur	64	56	64	66	64	69	73
Monongalia	58	57	60	61	59	63	64
Marshall	57	57	57	58	53	61	62
Hancock	55	56	58	56	48	58	58
Taylor	53	52	55	56	53	58	59
Ritchie	52	47	55	56	50	57	59

B. Democratic Counties (18)[a]

	1876	1880	1884	1888	1892	1896	1900
Randolph	24	28	33	35	34	42	45
Greenbrier	27	28	35	40	35	40	43
Pocahontas	28	30	36	40	36	39	44
Wayne	28	34	37	41	41	45	46
Braxton	28	32	37	39	35	40	47
Wetzel	29	34	35	37	33	40	43
Pendleton	30	35	41	43	40	41	44
Gilmer	32	34	39	41	40	42	44
Calhoun	33	32	40	40	36	40	42
Monroe	33	39	45	47	44	45	50
Nicholas	34	32	43	42	38	41	44
Summers	36	39	44	48	42	48	49

C. Swing Counties (35)[a]

	1876	1880	1884	1888	1892	1896	1900
Doddridge	46	42	54	55	52	58	60
Mason	49	46	54	53	52	55	56
Harrison	45	38	51	53	51	55	58
Jackson	49	49	51	53	50	52	56
Wood	48	45	50	52	50	54	57
Berkeley	45	44	48	52	51	54	52
Mineral	42	44	47	50	50	53	56
Ohio	46	48	49	49	48	57	56
Brooke	44	45	49	49	48	55	57
Cabell	35	38	43	44	43	50	53
Marion	47	42	49	48	47	50	54
Lewis	41	41	47	48	46	50	53
Barbour	42	40	49	49	49	49	53
Pleasants	43	40	43	46	45	49	52
Wirt	42	40	45	46	45	48	51

[a]Groups' share of total number of males of voting age, 1900.

113

Wood, Cabell, and Ohio the most populous, plus several of the smaller industrial counties along the Ohio River, the remaining farming and mining counties of the Monongahela valley, and the two most populous counties (Berkeley and Mineral) of the Eastern Panhandle.

Taken together, the thirty-four "trend" counties reflect the gradual yet steady changes wrought by the advance of towns, railroads, communications, and industry in northern, central, and western West Virginia. If the political change was a result of migration, Republican recruits and converts here probably came from native rather than interstate migrants, from people who changed their views and allegiances as they changed their addresses from the country and interior districts to the burgeoning railroad and industrial towns. The voters here also responded to such national impulses as the depression of the nineties. Since these voters constituted two-thirds of West Virginia's electorate in 1900, the importance of the relatively gradual and evenly distributed changes they recorded should not be underemphasized. But more dramatic election returns came from the twenty-one counties labeled "deviant" here. It was here that the impact of industrialism—or its absence—was most obvious and that preferred contemporary explanations of the Republican trend found their most plausible support.

Table II displays the Republican performance in presidential elections for the "deviant" counties, again divided into three groups. The five "one-party" counties, all of them in the Eastern Panhandle, offer an interesting comment upon the relationship of economic development and political change in West Virginia. Here the absence of industrialization went hand in hand with the perpetuation of lopsided party alignments dating from the cleavage of Unionist mountain districts and Confederate valleys at the time of the Civil War. The Republicans improved their showing in both of the South Branch valley counties (Hardy and Hampshire), while enlarging their majorities in the mountain counties of Morgan and Grant. The results fell short of the statewide G.O.P.

Table II
Republican Shares of the Presidential Vote (%), Deviant Counties, 1876-1900

A. One-Party Counties (5)[a]

	1876	1880	1884	1888	1892	1896	1900
Hampshire	14	18	19	21	21	26	24
Hardy	14	20	20	27	24	31	32
Jefferson	33	33	31	32	30	34	30
Morgan	55	62	62	61	60	69	64
Grant	66	66	71	73	74	77	78

B. Extractive Counties (17)[a]

	1876	1880	1884	1888	1892	1896	1900
Tyler	55	52	57	58	55	57	57
Fayette	39	40	53	57	51	61	62
McDowell	11	17	48	59	68	73	75
Mercer	18	5	33	50	47	53	56
Tucker	29	35	40	48	48	53	59
Raleigh	37	33	43	46	47	51	55
Logan	8	10	14	20	24	27	30
Mingo[b]						34	38
Webster	12	17	29	31	32	42	41
Wyoming[c]	56	44	48	56	50	53	54

C. Greenbacker Counties (12)[a]

	1876	1880	1884	1888	1892	1896	1900
Clay	45	37	46	52	49	52	55
Kanawha	39	35	59	55	51	59	60
Putnam	35	23	54	50	49	52	56
Lincoln	32	23	39	45	37	49	54
Roane	40	29	45	47	44	46	50
Boone	25	26	43	41	41	45	45

[a] Groups' share of total males of voting age, 1900.
[b] Part of Logan until 1895.
[c] Split congressional and presidential vote, 1870-1890; extractive pattern after 1892.

trend, however, while the Republicans of Jefferson County in the Shenandoah valley suffered a relative decline. Since this easternmost county of West Virginia was also its most "southern" district, one is tempted to conclude that Jefferson Democrats accomplished extralegally the exclusion of Negro voters that Democratic segregationists later tried and failed to adopt on a statewide basis. Be that as it may, the persistence of huge Democratic majorities in these antique and beautiful valleys aroused the contempt of Republican prophets of economic development, who pointed to the correlation of "backwardness" and Democracy to buttress their contention that theirs was the party of the future.[7]

The rigid alignments of the eastern counties suggests that the changes wrought by industrialism acted as solvents on the traditional partisan balances inherited from the homogeneous communities of pre-industrial times. Usually this worked to the advantage of Republicans in West Virginia, but not always. Tyler County, for example, was a farming county on the Ohio River that followed the voting patterns displayed by the Republican trend counties until 1896-1900. Then there occurred a noticeable slowing of the G.O.P. trend that coincided with the boom of the Sistersville oil region. That such occurrences were more common than county-level voting data indicates is suggested by the political complexion of magisterial districts in Marion County. As a unit, Marion was a closely divided "swing" county during the eighties, casting between 48.9 and 50.5 percent of its votes for Republican candidates in 1884. A closer inspection of the vote, however, reveals a high degree of local polarization. Of the county's seven magisterial districts, two were Republican by margins of nearly seven to three, two were Democratic by almost identical proportions. Significantly, the three more evenly divided districts were those bisected by the B&O Railroad, but even here individual precincts tended toward lopsided margins for one party or the other.[8] By the end of the century, however, five of the seven districts tended toward closer party divisions, irrespective of which party had been on top at the start. Of the two exceptions, one was a district not

116

directly touched by the changes of the intervening years (which in Marion included the growth of the Fairmont coalfield, the Mannington oil region, and the commercial center of Fairmont). The second exception, Mannington District, was the one that proved the rule, for here a Republican trend in Democratic precincts outside of the path of oil exploration and development was balanced after 1896 by Democratic growth in the strongly Republican oil region, leaving the district only slightly more divided in 1900 (55 to 45 percent Republican) than it had been in 1884 (52 to 48 percent).[9]

Although in comparison to coal mining development the petroleum industries introduced modest demographic and occupational changes in the counties affected, these were enough to disrupt local political and social arrangements and to set off a series of struggles for local control.[10] These conflicts could take other forms than competition between Democrats and Republicans. One other manifestation in the oil region was a proposal advanced to the legislatures of 1897 and 1899 to create "Augusta County" out of the western parts of Marion, Monongalia, and Harrison, but the established politicians of the counties involved managed to defeat the idea. However, Logan County, where the local leadership was Democratic and thus less subject to the protection of a Republican legislature, was bifurcated in 1895 to create the mining county of Mingo along the Norfolk & Western[11] Another variation was the occasional "county seat war" instigated when newer communities sought the relocation of the courthouse. Davis and Elkins, for example, were involved in a five-year battle to wrest the Randolph County seat for their new town of Elkins from the eighteenth-century town of Beverly. "We might as well have it at Elkins," wrote Elkins, "as we have got to pay 2/3d of the taxes." When the government moved in February 1900, it set up temporary headquarters in the West Virginia Central offices.[12]

Unfortunately for the Democracy, the most intensive growth of new industries took place in that party's sturdy but lightly settled bastions in the southern and eastern

117

interior. Here traditional political arrangements were simply swept aside by the tide of newcomers. By 1900 the process was fairly predictable and attributable, from a Republican standpoint, to the enlightenment that flowed from material gain. "The construction of a railroad in this county is going to give the county to us in a very short time," a Pocahontas County Republican advised Elkins in 1900, when that eastern interior district was on the verge of yielding its Democratic majority along with its hardwoods and spruce.[13] The forecast proved accurate. Four years later the county recorded its first G.O.P. presidential majority since Reconstruction times and by 1908 was electing a full Republican ticket. Meanwhile, the county seat was changed to the new tannery town of Marlinton, founded by nonresident investors and renamed "in spite of the bitter opposition of some of the older citizens, who objected to giving up the descriptive and historic name of Marlin's Bottom."[14]

Democrats found a more plausible excuse for their hardships in the behavior of such interior mining counties as McDowell. There John E. Kenna of the Kanawha Ring had been able to marshal all but six of the county's 304 voters in his congressional campaign of 1878 and fared nearly as well in the presidential years of 1876 and 1880. In 1892 his cohort Governor MacCorkle lost the county by 613 to 1,264. By 1900, McDowell's electorate of 5,000 voters was 40 percent black and 75 percent Republican, and both proportions were increasing. Such statistics, applying with similar though less drastic force to the neighboring mining counties of Mercer, Raleigh, and Fayette, lent weight to the assertions of MacCorkle that the Democracy's mandate had crumbled before a tide of Pennsylvania coal operators and black miners and laborers from the South. But these assertions should be balanced against the performance of other extractive counties (Tucker, for example), where blacks comprised a negligible proportion of the voters and also against the eroding Republican minority noted earlier in Jefferson County, which with McDowell and Fayette constituted the only counties in the state where the black share of the electorate reached as high

118

as 20 percent. If all of them voted (a dubious assumption), eligible blacks accounted for less than 6 percent of West Virginia voters in 1900.[15] Thus the black vote was insufficient in itself to explain the G.O.P.'s success, but its importance in the southern mining counties helps to explain why West Virginia Republicans made it their business to halt the advance of political Jim Crow at the Virginia and Kentucky borders.

Other analysts attributed the voting returns from the extractive regions to the efforts of conservative employers to control the votes of their employees. As one might expect, the evidence on this point is ambiguous and hard to come by. One need hardly credit the votes of Negro Republicans in the Pocahontas and Flat Top coal regions against such race-mongering Democrats as MacCorkle to the manipulations of the mine owners. It was in fact a wealthy mine owner from Philadelphia, L. E. Tierney, who bankrolled MacCorkle's drive against Davis and Camden's "concatenation of organized power" in the north.[16] With respect to the industrialists themselves, we have seen that Davis and Elkins made strenuous efforts to rally their workers and those of neighboring employers against the tariff reformers in 1888-1894 and that they believed, with their critics, that the effort had been successful. On other occasions, Davis expressly or implicitly offered the votes of his workers to a candidate, while his instructions to one mine superintendent in 1898, when his brother was a candidate for the House of Delegates, left little to imagination: "It goes without saying that both he [Colonel Tom] and myself will be obliged to you, and give you the credit for most of the Republican votes he gets in your place. How do you think the vote will be?"[17] But the votes of the workers were not cast *en bloc* or necessarily as the boss thought that they should be. The net local shift (total shift minus statewide average shift) of voters in the West Virginia Central counties with Davis away from the Democrats in 1888 was around 2 percent of the total vote; so was the shift back to the Democrats with him in 1896. Colonel Tom's legislative and congressional candidacies in 1898 and 1900 cut into Republican totals in Mineral County,

119

where he made his home, but this "friends and neighbors" effect might have been registered by any other locally well-known candidate. "The vote in Tucker Co. was, to say the least, most surprising and uncomplimentary," wrote a Davis nephew to Senator Davis in 1900. "The ingratitude of certain persons, to you & uncle Tom, in this election is to be deplored."[18]

The influence of Davis and Elkins was divided when they engaged, as they sometimes did, in partisan competition for their workers' votes. In the cases of Camden and the Watson coal interests in the Fairmont region, voting returns more clearly reflect the employers' preferences. The Marion County precincts of Monongah, a Camden property, and Montana, a joint venture, appeared as separate election districts soon after the opening of the mines to production in 1889 and 1887, respectively, and both strongly reflected the owners' Democratic allegiance through 1892. Table III displays the party shares in 1892 and in four succeeding congressional elections, along with those of Marion County and the state at large. It will be recalled that Camden, for reasons having to do with his battle with the Agrarians and in sharp contrast to Davis, strongly supported the Democratic campaign of 1894 but bolted the national tickets in 1896 and again in 1900. His miners clearly seem to have followed this cue, especially in 1894, but they did not follow his expectations precisely. In 1900, for example, he gave his mine superintendent instructions to distribute local campaign funds equally between the two parties but warned him that "it is very important for the business interests of the county to elect" the Democratic candidate for sheriff over a "dangerous" Republican. The desired ticket-splitting took place at Montana, but at Monongah the offensive Republican ran evenly with McKinley.[19]

All told, the industrialists' political influence over their workers seems to have been somewhat less than they and others thought it to be. But imagination frequently plays a large role in politics. Alleged control over thousands of voters added to the industrialists' reputation for influence and so to their status as party leaders. When the candidates of both parties

Table III
Party Voting in Two Mining Precincts, Congressional Elections, 1892-1900[a]

%	A. Monongah					B. Montana					C. Marion County					D. West Virginia				
	1892	1894	1896	1898	1900	1892	1894	1896	1898	1900	1892	1894	1896	1898	1900	1892	1894	1896	1898	1900
Democratic	75	68	55	57	55	58	56	45	58	44	49	47	49	49	46*	50	45	47	49	46
Republican	25	32	45	43	45	42	44	55	42	56	47	52	51	48	52	47	53	53	50	54
Populist[c]											1	1			2	2	2		b	b
Prohibition											2				2	1		b	b	1

[a] Totals may not equal 100 due to rounding.
[b] Less than .5.
[c] Blank space indicates no candidate stood for this party in this year.

121

bore such leaders' stamp of approval, it hardly mattered which way the miners or anyone else in West Virginia cast their ballots at the polls.

Of course there were more than two political parties in West Virginia, as elsewhere, during this period. The strongest third-party showing was made by the Greenback party of 1878 and 1880 and though Greenback candidates standing alone failed to gather as much as 10 percent of the vote on a statewide basis, fusionist candidates in these and later elections appear to have played an important role in turning dissident Democrats into Republicans and in preventing disgruntled Republicans from straying too far. Thus the third group of "deviant" counties are labeled "Greenbacker." Collectively these six Kanawha valley counties furnished a third of all Greenback votes cast in West Virginia in the three-way presidential and gubernatorial races of 1880. Greenback-Republican fusionist candidates carried Kanawha, Clay, and Putnam counties in the congressional race of 1878, Kanawha and Putnam in 1880, and Putnam again in 1884. The fusionist gains were insufficient to crack the Democratic majorities of the interior counties at this point, but Kanawha and Putnam, the two most populous, were permanently lost to the Democracy from here on, while all six experienced their greatest surge in Republican voting in the presidential election of 1884. So did four of the swing counties where Greenback candidates had earlier run better than in the state at large.

The importance of fusionist arrangements in producing these results is evident in Table IV, which displays the performance in two- and three-party races in the city of Charleston and in two magisterial districts of Kanawha County for state and congressional elections in 1880, 1886, 1894, and 1896.[20]

Not surprisingly, the third-party men fared poorest in Charleston, but fusionists were able to carry the city in 1880 and 1886 by roughly the same proportions as later Republican victories, even when a "straight" Republican lost in a

Table IV
Third Party and Fusionist Voting, Kanawha County, 1880, 1886, 1894, 1896[a]

%	A. Poca District						B. Cabin Creek District						C. Charleston						D. Kanawha County					
	Governor 1880	St. Senate 1880	Congress 1886	St. Senate 1886	Congress 1894	Congress 1896	Governor 1880	St. Senate 1880	Congress 1886	St. Senate 1886	Congress 1894	Congress 1896	Governor 1880	St. Senate 1880	Congress 1886	St. Senate 1886	Congress 1894	Congress 1896	Governor 1880	St. Senate 1880	Congress 1886	St. Senate 1886	Congress 1894	Congress 1896
Democratic	21	23	19	20	21	24	44	46	42	43	32	42	44	46	53	47	42	43	36	39	41	40	36	41
Republican[b]	29		80		78	76	24		55		62	58	41		44		57	57	30		56		61	59
Greenback/ Populist	51				1		32				6		16				1		34				2	
Fusion		77		80				54		57				54		53				61		60		
Prohibition			1						3						4						3			

aTotals may not equal 100 due to rounding.
bBlank space indicates no candidate stood for this party in this contest.

123

direct two-party confrontation, as in the congressional race of 1886. The most striking results, however, lie in a comparison of the voting in Poca District, an agricultural region in the county's western end, with Cabin Creek, the easternmost district containing the center of the Kanawha coalfield. The farming district boasted a Greenback majority in 1880, while in this and the 1886 campaigns fusionists neatly matched the total Greenback and Republican vote. During the nineties this district returned Republican totals proportionate to earlier fusionist strength. Poca returned a single Populist vote in 1894, but two years later experienced a modest shift toward the Democratic ticket headed by Bryan and, locally, by an Agrarian congressional candidate. By contrast, the mining district not only displayed a surprising degree of support for the Greenbackers in 1880, but supplied Populist votes at more than twice the rate of the state in 1894 and restored the Democracy's share of the vote in 1896 to predepression levels. Moreover, these results cannot be attributed to the interior precincts of the sprawling Cabin Creek District; these contained a sparse, mostly Democratic electorate throughout the period, while the third-party men were clustered in precincts with names like Coalburg and Cannelton. Some of the Agrarian architects of Greenback-Republican fusion eventually renounced the third-party heresy and returned to the Democratic fold, while regular politicians competing for the purchase of Populist leaders during the nineties found them quick to respond.[21] But if the Kanawha County returns are a safe indication, their followers did not follow them. The farmers made their way into (or returned to) the ranks of the G.O.P., while the miners entered into a mood of independency that eventually made Kanawha County the most politically volatile in the state and produced a vigorous Socialist movement there and in neighboring mining counties during the early twentieth century.

West Virginians thus responded to a variety of stimuli in making the electoral decisions that made smooth the industrialists' political way, but few of these responses could be

124

thought of as a direct endorsement of their leadership. Perhaps this was the case with those who responded to the pinched wallets of 1894 or the changed outlooks that developed as part of the industrialization process. But the same would scarcely hold true of the "old-line" Republicans and black newcomers whose spokesmen led the anti-organization insurgency of 1900, or of the recruits from the ranks of Greenbackism, or of the workingmen weighing their choices between Elkins's Tweedledum and Davis's Tweedledee. The fact was that neither law nor custom required that the industrialists' leadership bear the stamp of popular referenda. Such matters were decided far from the din of electoral combat, in ways and for reasons that do not lend themselves to precise measurement. Popular appeal was not the least of their political resources, as we shall see. But of far greater significance in establishing their hegemony in West Virginia were their resources of money, retainers, and jobs.

In the political vernacular of the day the most important thing about the West Virginia industrialists was their "barrel" of money. "[T]he 'sinews of war' are the big thing," wrote a Morgantown Republican who would later welcome Elkins to the state. "A few dollars in the proper hand at each poll to get out the voters is all important."[22] It is to be doubted, however, that the tycoons spent the enormous sums usually attributed to them by the opposition press. Davis's correspondence for election years from 1870 to 1900 and for 1904 mentions some $168,000 in political expenditures (money spent, not just promised). Of this total, 1904—when he was running for vice-president on the Democratic national ticket—accounts for $140,000. One has the impression that the cost of earlier campaigns was considerably less than it became after the turn of the century, but only negative evidence supports this impression.[23] Even so, it is clear that the $28,000 traceable to Davis for 1870-1900 represents only a part of his expenditures. Some money obviously went out unrecorded; other letters mentioned money but no sums. Nor does this figure include recorded loans of over $16,000 to

125

prominent Democrats in West Virginia and Maryland. The loans were apt to be called in if the borrower fell out of favor with the senator. Lewis Baker, for example, was forced to sell his newspaper and make over his life insurance to Davis after angering him during the 1884 campaign.[24] Most loans, however, remained on the books and doubtless provided more leverage for the lender than did outright gifts that were more easily forgotten.

As for the other industrialists, Camden seems to have been more free with his money than Davis, but he also went in for loans.[25] Scott was a firm believer in "whatever *grease is necessary*" and instructed his lieutenants to spend freely "if you can do so to advantage." But he preferred to channel funds through third parties and traveled among the faithful with only "a little sugar in my clothes. . . ."[26]

Elkins, too, was reputed to be a big spender and probably was in the campaigns of 1888 and 1892. But two costly defeats followed by economical Republican victories elsewhere in 1893 convinced him "that there has been too much money spent in elections. I am satisfied that where the people are thoroughly aroused, money is not required beyond ordinary expenses of printing tickets, securing speakers, and distributing campaign literature."[27] Apparently he conformed to this belief thereafter, for Scott complained bitterly of Elkins's thrift in subsequent campaigns and told him frankly "that it was ridiculous for a moneyed man like him to expect anybody else to put up the money out of their own pockets."[28]

There were other reasons for economy, too, as is illustrated by the contrast between Davis's recorded campaign contributions of $165 in 1892, when he was at odds with his party on the tariff issue, and $4,300 in 1898, when he got another crack at the senatorship. But even with individual attitudes and fluctuations over time, it is likely that the industrialists provided a large share of party revenues. Davis, Camden, A. B. Fleming, and metropolitan industrialists contacted through them provided upwards of 90 percent of the Democratic state committee's funds in 1904. Four years later they were again on the sidelines with Bryan leading the national ticket and the Kanawha Ring and Lewis Bennett, son of a wealthy West Virginia Confederate and Redeemer, conducting a state campaign based on a demand for Negro disfranchisement. Whereupon the state committee's funds fell to less than a sixth of the 1904 total, while over half of what remained was provided by the Bennett family.[29] The party in power was probably less dependent on the moods of large contributors, however, since it could recruit funds from lesser officeholders and levy contributions from poorer candidates whose prospects stood a better chance at the polls.

How was the money used? This was a delicate question then and one difficult to answer now. Davis hired three lesser Democratic leaders for $100 to $250 each to secure votes for his reelection to the Senate in 1877. How they used the money or got the votes they did not say and he did not ask: "Your success as well as mine," he told one of them, "depends on *keeping our counsels.*"[30] The industrialists generally paid the bills and did not ask too many questions. Indeed Elkins gave explicit instructions: "You know I never want any bills, receipts, items or anything else about any money you spend for me."[31] On one occasion, Davis requested and got an itemized list of expenditures for disbursements by the state committee's Wheeling headquarters in 1904. Since by far the largest sums, accounting for 87 percent of the total, were paid out in lump sums to county chairmen or expended by headquarters workers in unspecified ways, the report is not very illuminating.[32] Presumably most of the money went for printing, rallies, office expenses, travel money for speakers, candidates, and excursions of voters, and all else that came under the heading of "legitimate expenses" attendant to "getting out the vote." But occasionally there is a glimpse of things less legitimate. "If only I had a little whiskey," sighed one Democratic worker to Camden. "I tell you it does more good with our *hill* people than all the speeches that we can get."[33] An upright young lawyer making his first race for the legislature in 1898 found certain features of campaigning "very oppressive,—for instance, the 'bummer' who wants a drink & the influential friend who has ten votes absolutely in his control & desires financial encouragement. . . ."[34] Doubtless less scrupulous candidates spent some of the senators' money in these ways. There is little evidence connecting the leaders directly to vote buying and related crimes. On occasion Davis was urged to buy up blocks of "floaters"; he replied non-commitally or not at all.[35] However, documents circulated privately after the campaign of 1904 point to a special fund of $10,000 created by Davis and Philadelphia and Baltimore businessmen for use in Fayette and McDowell counties, money that was almost certainly intended to be used to buy up black votes in these mining districts. Another $2,900 went to an "Italian organizer" plying the Fairmont coalfield, with smaller amounts going to organizers assigned to German, Polish, Syrian, and unspecified ethnic and labor groups.[36] Scott's tactic of hiring Democrats as Republican workers a day or two before the election amounted to very much the same thing.[37]

None of the industrialists had any apologies to make for the way they used their money. "In politics there are canvassers to be appointed, conveyances to be hired to take the sick and the cripples to the polls, tickets to be bought and distributed &c, and money has to be raised to meet these legitimate expenses," Davis wrote in defense of Camden in 1887.[38] Scott indignantly rejected the charge that he was attempting to buy the Republican senatorial nomination in 1898. "I don't mean to buy it," he explained. "I only want to use whatever funds are necessary in order to protect myself and my friends."[39] Increasing the number of one's "friends" was one of the more telling uses to which the leaders' money could be put. Elkins was correct in believing that the spending of large sums did not insure success at the polls. The Republican defeat in 1892 and the Democratic loss in 1904 testified to this. But decisions affecting the distribution of power within the two party structures were made in caucuses, conventions, and informal conferences—all subject to manipulation with few risks of exposure. The industrialists' money, like their reputed control of the votes of their workers, created a psychology of anticipation by which the mere existence of a senatorial fortune was at least as important in its effects as the actual use of cash. Like money in the bank, the "barrel" earned dividends before being tapped, creating "friends" who would expect to be taken care of later on. The industrialists were often accused of corrupting the political process, but it may be questioned whether they corrupted anyone who was not already corrupt. There were always plenty of lesser lights eager to anticipate or even to go beyond their needs. "The evils of [corrupt] tendencies," wrote Charles Ambler, who had some personal experience in West Virginia politics around the turn of the century, were more common among the smaller fry, "the so-called 'henchmen.' "[40] An example was Congressman Harry Welles Rush of Maryland, who offered his services through Davis to the PRR and whose eagerness to sell them (for $1,000 per year) outpaced the railroad's capacity to use them.[41] On the state level, two of Elkins's Republican lieutenants who sometimes doubled as corporate retainers in the legislative lobbies, Charles D. Elliott of Parkersburg and E. M. Showalter of Fairmont, were such dubious risks that party leaders had to watch carefully to see that the campaign money they handled did not wind up in their own pockets.[42] Another Elliott tactic was to create an atmosphere of panic—"an unnecessary 'splutter' "—in a campaign or lobbying situation in order to loosen the purse strings of his clients.[43] Yet the leaders did not discourage such men—they were too useful. "I hope Elliott is working prudently," Elkins commented on one occasion.[44] But however Elliott worked, he kept on working, enjoying Elkins's confidence and holding a succession of patronage appointments, including a United States marshalship.[45] As Scott put it, "I would not for the world hurt Charlie's feelings, for nobody appreciates his worth to the party more than I do."[46]

Equally vital in taking care of the industrialists' friends was a supply of jobs. The Democrats were at a distinct disadvantage as far as public patronage was concerned. They were out of power at Washington during most of this period, while the constitution of 1872 had pared the number of state officials and lengthened the terms of those that remained. Nor were there large municipal or institutional bureaucracies in West Virginia such as Arthur Gorman exploited in the Baltimore city government and the Chesapeake & Ohio Canal management in Maryland. Camden was able to bolster his influence during the Cleveland administrations with federal jobs, but coming as they did in the midst of famine, the jobs did nearly as much to fuel Democratic factionalism as they did to quiet it. The Republicans were more fortunate. Doubtless as a result of his long experience in territorial and national politics, Elkins moved directly toward control of the job supply when he entered West Virginia in 1888. His dexterous use of federal and then state patronage was a vital element in the growth and consolidation of his regime.

It is open to question whether office hunger was any more acute in West Virginia in the late nineteenth century than it was in most other states. Theodore H. White found the craving there greater in 1960 and attributed the phenomenon to the importance of political jobs in an underdeveloped economy.[47] It is possible that similar factors were at work in earlier times, as the energies and ambition aroused by the desire for material advancement outran the opportunities afforded by the pace and nature of West Virginia's industrialization. When the writer-illustrator "Porte Crayon" (David Hunter Strother) visited the rising town of Charleston in 1871, he found the "Kanawha boom" well underway as far as talk and imagination were concerned. The place was "full of land speculators, schemes, stock jobbers, . . ." Strother recorded in his journal, "moughing [sic] money by thousands and handling it by fractional currency. One indeed has to use a strong magnifier to see the cash used, after having his imagination stimulated by the talk."[48] It was about this time, it will be recalled, that the ambitious lawyers who formed the Kanawha Ring embarked upon their long career on the public payrolls. Had opportunities been more readily available, their energies might have found outlets in private life. It is clear from other comments that the transition period especially intensified competition among lawyers in the more populous districts. "The bar is crowded and the business is small," wrote John M. Hagans in explaining an application for federal office in 1881.[49] George C. Sturgiss gave similar reasons in a similar application a decade before, adding that "the existence of a country attorney of West Va. is of rather a hum drum character, and not ordinarily calculated to develop one into a fully rounded and symetrical [sic] character."[50] "My professional income last year was entirely insufficient," William L. Wilson recorded in his diary in 1881, "and it is now time I should be laying by something for the education of my children."[51] A year later Wilson's hopes were answered by an appointment as president of West Virginia University, from whence Senator Davis launched him on his distinguished congressional career. Meanwhile, the university's first graduate struck out for Washington to look for a federal job, only to come home empty-handed after months of supplication left him homeless, threadbare, and broke.[52]

Whatever the cause of the earlier pressure for places, the pressure continued unabated long after local opportunities improved. Governor MacCorkle received 3,760 applications for the hundred-odd jobs at his disposal in 1893, while his Republican successors were equally swamped.[53] "I had not the remotest idea that every man, woman and child in West Virginia wanted a government position," exclaimed Scott upon assuming his senatorial duties in 1899, "but I believe they do." To accommodate them, he became the Senate's foremost advocate of repealing the civil service laws. "If I had my way," he later remarked, "this Civil Service so-called reform would not last twenty minutes."[54] This spirit was not confined to standpatters, however. "I am perfectly willing to go into the fight and do all I can actively," wrote a Progressive supporter of Theodore Roosevelt in 1912, "but should our side win, then I want something for it. I have always been a firm believer that 'to the victor belongs the spoils,' and consequently am bitterly opposed to Civil Service and constant rotation in office."[55]

It is clear that many people regarded the public payrolls as an informal system of welfare for those who found themselves in need, at least those with the proper party credentials. "John is unfortunate: he is poor and out of work," wrote Labor Commissioner Barton in recommending an applicant for a state position in 1908. Another applicant was "financially embarrassed and is at an age that he is not able to start in life again." An older fellow needed "a job of som sort that I mite maik a living for my family [because] my hilth is poor and I can't work at hard work lik I have all my life." A former minister's friends hoped that a janitorial job would rescue him and his family from the clutches of drink.[56] The applicants continued to include the aspiring as well as the disappointed, however. "I need it—I can fill it," wrote a young Parkersburg lawyer to Elkins, "and I want a chance to *make good* politically." An editor from the same town wanted "any position reasonably lucrative . . . something which has pay rather than honor attached." "If you have nothing better to give me," he told the governor, "how would it suit you to appoint me one of the [university] regents." "I have had a hard time making upward strides," wrote another supplicant, while a crippled man united both the aspiring and deserving themes, basing his petition on the fact of his deformity (plus, of course, his Republicanism) while expressing his belief that "I could save enough money from this office to go into business for myself."[57]

The same themes were voiced by more prominent applicants as well as by the poor and obscure. Ex-Governor Francis H. Pierpont, attributing business reverses to his immersion in politics and to the manipulations of his former mining associate, "that scoundrel [James O.] Watson," was "driven to the necessity of asking Washington for an office" more than once. "If the Pres. cannot grant this favor," he added on one occasion, "perhaps he has some old clothes he could dispense."[58] When Senator Kenna died with his family unprovided for in 1893, his widow received the Charleston postmastership to stave off penury, at least until the Republicans took command.[59] John W. Mason explained his urgent suit for a job to Elkins in 1897 by the fact that his only son was already twelve years old. "I must have him in some good preparatory school for the next 4 or 5 years to get him ready for college in time. For this reason I am exceedingly anxious to spend the next four years at Washington." Mason was willing, he added, "to subject myself to some humiliation" in order to spare his child the social consequences of West Virginia schools.[60] Not all applicants were as needy or persistent as Mason, who sent out a feeler whenever a suitable vacancy occurred.[61] But they represented every shade of local respectability. Elkins's petitioners included a president of the West Virginia Banker's Association and a scion of the Washington family of Charles Town. A West Virginia University professor of Greek, who professed himself "quite without experience in office hunting," wanted the Athens consulship but made do with a job as "state historian," while an engineer who wanted to be state road commissioner ended up on the university faculty.[62] The style of these tonier applications was perfectly captured by a Methodist minister applying in 1908. "I am not a politician seeking a political job as such," he informed the governor, "[but] if you have a place that would not in any way interfere materially with my present 'high calling,' I should be glad to serve."[63] The needier applicants were more direct but the message in most instances was the same. "He wants an office very, very, very bad," Dawson remarked of a Charleston lawyer in 1900. "I can't make it any *badder* than it is; and he wants it instanter . . . a Judgeship, district attorneyship, or a Marshalship, or any old thing."[64]

The power of the senators over patronage had drawbacks as well as advantages, of course. "I do not know what form their resentment will take," Elkins remarked of some disappointed applicants in 1897, "but one cannot be a Senator without being assailed."[65] And the disappointed seekers usually outnumbered the successful ones in West Virginia. Still these resentments were more than balanced by the mood of anticipation and obligation that the industrialists' bushels of plums, like their barrels of money, created. Another important consideration was that opposition to their hegemony

133

usually formed upon no other basis than that of a loose and uncoordinated coalition of disappointed office seekers. Or if it formed on some other basis, it usually descended to that level. The antics of such Democratic Agrarians as Henry S. Walker, who drifted in and out of coalitions formed by and against Camden and between Greenbackism and Democracy, ending up as an applicant—via Davis—for the patronage of the conservative Fleming administration, made it easy to discredit the reformers' motives.[66] Moreover, when enough of the dissidents could be mollified by a judicious disposal of jobs, as we have seen in the case of the Republican revolt against Elkins in 1900, it was easy to inhibit any checks on the senators' power. At the same time, long years of scrambling among the more prominent politicians for the places available created in them a longing for the security that could be provided by an appointment to the bench. In this fashion, the ablest alternative Republican leaders—Goff, Atkinson, and Alston G. Dayton—were removed from the industrialists' path.

As the masters or agents of large corporations, the industrialists enjoyed another supply of patronage, a private one. Its most widespread form was the ubiquitous and controversial railroad pass, which entitled the recipients to free passenger transportation. During his days as a B&O lobbyist, Davis had enjoyed a supply of "blank passes for friends" and continued to act as a broker for local politicians seeking passes from Baltimore until his break with the trunk line in 1887. Later, although less frequently, he continued to perform the same function with friendly carriers like the C&O.[67] He was somewhat more sparing with passes on his own railroads and seized upon the passage of the Interstate Commerce Act of 1887 as an excuse "to get rid of deadheading over our road," whether the deadheads were politicians or not.[68] But after he returned to active support of his party in 1896 Davis issued passes to state and local candidates he approved of and came full circle in 1913, when he issued supplies of blank passes for the use of his grandson, Davis

134

Elkins, then engaged in canvassing the legislature for the family senatorial seat.[69] Camden distributed passes to all legislators and state officials as a matter of course. "Railroads, like individuals," he advised one of his railroad managers, "must have friends to help protect and advance their interests, and I do not think you could make a better investment than to give Sylvester Hardman an annual pass for this year."[70]

How much the passes provided in terms of legislative and political influence is difficult to determine. Unquestionably they were intended to and did create an obligation on the part of the recipients, which added to the permissive climate in which the industrialists pursued their twin careers. But Davis's occasional withdrawal of a pass from an errant legislator indicates that they did not always do the job they were supposed to do.[71] In any event, most West Virginia politicians were determined not to do without them. Frequent attempts to enact an anti-pass law from 1885 on invariably met with failure. Only two of those who received Camden's unsolicited passes returned them. And those who asked for the favors always outnumbered those who got them.[72] As Representative Dayton put it, "I am a good deal like a fish out of water without my B.&O. pass."[73]

Of more varying consequence was the business patronage at the industrialists' disposal. It was hardly a coincidence that most of the top-level officials of the Davis-Elkins enterprises were active in politics. For some of them, F. S. Landstreet, for example, it was a question of emulating their chiefs or being forced to do so in being charged with minor political tasks. Landstreet, a budding business bureaucrat who later made his career with the Western Maryland Railway, bounced back and forth from Democracy to Republicanism and back again as business interests appeared to dictate. Approached to run for the legislature in 1890, he explained that "I would not think of it unless I could be of some use to the firm in the way of legislation."[74] "Colonel" Thomas B. Davis, a silent figure who emerged into the limelight around the turn of the century, apparently had no political aspirations of his

135

own, although he normally sat for his brother on the Democratic state committee. "Thank you, Henry. I owe it principally to you," the Colonel remarked when he was elected to Congress in 1905. As the senator's biographer stated, "This was true."[75] Other officials caught a case of political fever of their own. Howard Sutherland, who eventually succeeded to Scott's seat as West Virginia's first popularly elected United States senator in 1916, had to be called down by Davis for some undisclosed excess of political zeal in 1899.[76] On a smaller scale, James W. Flynn, a subordinate of Sutherland in the Davis-Elkins real estate department from 1890 to 1904, served for sixteen years as Republican county chairman in Preston County, served in the state senate, and acted as manager for statewide campaigns conducted by Elkins, Dawson, Scott, and Davis Elkins.[77] Sometimes employees' careers did not work out so well for the boss. John Sheridan, the first superintendent of the Elk Garden mine, emerged within a decade as a political and business rival of Davis, allied against him with both the B&O and the Cleveland Democracy.[78]

Other business patronage of the West Virginia Central was consciously bestowed on already active politicians or their relatives. This could range from a clerk's post for the son of a West Virginia county politician to managerial positions in the coal companies for the sons of Harrison and Blaine.[79] The position of corporate counsel was held successively in West Virginia by W. C. Clayton, George E. Price, and C. Wood Dailey, all Democratic leaders and legislators from Mineral County, and in Maryland by William Pinckney Whyte, a Baltimore aristocrat whose tenure as United States senator, governor, and attorney general lent a bit of class to the Gorman organization.[80] Davis retained other lawyers on an occasional basis to act as collection agents for H. G. Davis & Brother, his original mercantile firm, and to handle the land transactions attendant to acquiring the mineral properties and railroad rights-of-way upon which the family enterprises were based. Among the earliest recipients of this patronage was an attorney general of West Virginia, Joseph Sprigg, two of the future

Agrarian leaders, Daniel B. Lucas and E. Willis Wilson, and a number of legislators from the nearby South Branch valley.[81] A more significant beneficiary was the Grafton lawyer, John T. McGraw, whom Davis first retained as a collection agent in 1877. A brilliant and unscrupulous political organizer with a taste for land speculation, McGraw's rise in the world illustrated some of the forms the business-political relationship could take. During the seventies and early eighties, McGraw placed himself under Davis's wing but subsequently drew closer to Camden. In part this reflected Davis's declining influence in the Democracy during the Cleveland era. But there was also the fact that McGraw was accumulating timberlands in a part of the state closed off to the West Virginia Central by B&O strategy and by the Camden-Davis-Elkins treaty of 1890. From the standpoint of realizing his land profits, the Camden railroad was a safer bet for McGraw until it plunged with the B&O into a sea of financial troubles during the mid-nineties. Then McGraw returned to his first love, Davis. On February 20, 1896, he and the senator signed a contract for the joint exploitation of the upper Greenbrier valley region, made possible by a connection between the West Virginia Central and the C&O completed in 1901. At the same time, McGraw played a major role in Davis's comeback in Democratic politics at the end of the century.[82]

The other corporate interests active in West Virginia had their politically active retainers, too. Each of the major railroads had a local political troubleshooter, the dean of whom was Randolph Stalnaker, a Camden lieutenant and former state official who served as "special agent" in the B&O's legal department from 1885 to 1915. J. B. Sommerville, the manager of Camden's senatorial canvass in 1887, served the Pennsylvania system during roughly the same period, while the Republicans boasted E. P. Rucker and Isaac T. Mann, the principal legal and political agents for the N&W and Pocahontas coal interests. Reese Blizzard, a Parkersburg lawyer whom Elkins raised to a district attorneyship when the state was divided into two federal judicial districts in 1901, and E. W. Knight, a Democrat whose Charleston law partners were active in Republican politics, served in similar capacities for, respectively, the Western Maryland and Virginian railroads after they entered the state in 1902-1904.[83]

Blizzard provided an interesting example of the retainer's career pattern, for (as Stalnaker had done before him) he climbed via conventional political means from a lowly post in an interior county to an important office before tasting corporate sweets in 1902, when his official duties entailed collaboration with Elkins, Judge Jackson, and the Fairmont Coal Company in routing labor organizers from the Fairmont region by means of an injunction.[84] Thereafter he became one of the corporations' most eager local servitors, seeking retainers from such firms as the Standard Oil Company whenever they were available, yet somehow acquiring a reputation as a thoroughgoing Progressive who favored income redistribution "without revolution or seriously disturbing business."[85] Not all of the retainers were Snopeses, however. John Marshall, Blizzard's law partner and "an able business lawyer" or "a lobbyist for dirty hire," depending upon whether one reads a published assessment or a private one, was the grandson of a statemaker who capped off a Yale education with marriage to the heiress of a Democratic judge. Apparently he was a free-lance retainer, rather than one on regular salary.[86] So were J. W. St. Clair, a veteran Kanawha valley Democrat who handled legal and legislative odd jobs for an assortment of corporate clients, including the C&O and Davis and Elkins,[87] and the aforementioned Republican officials, Charlie Elliott and E. M. Showalter. In addition to these there were dozens of smaller fry who looked after corporate interests on a regular basis in every county that contained a railroad, lumber camp, oil well, or mine. No fewer than eight such corporate counselors could be found among the twenty-six members of the West Virginia Senate in 1903, most of them serving as committee chairmen.[88] As Elliott put it, "The temptations and pit-falls to one of my make up are all around."[89]

The most powerful retainer of them all was Aretas Brooks Fleming of Fairmont. Actually Fleming was a hybrid type, a lawyer who drew $10,000 a year from the Standard Oil Company while holding 11,000 shares of stock in the Fairmont Coal Company founded by his wife's father and brother, James O. and Clarence W. Watson. Born to an extended and prominent Monongahela valley family in 1839, Fleming followed a conventional legal and political career in Marion County, inclining more to the Redeemer than Regular outlook until Camden made him the Democratic candidate for governor in 1888. Meanwhile, the Watsons, with Camden's support, laid the foundations for the firm that became during the next two decades West Virginia's largest coal producer. During his term in the statehouse, Fleming sought and won the confidence of Standard Oil officials as that firm was making its initial leasing and production arrangements in the oil and gas regions opened after 1889. Thereafter he served as an aggressive prosecutor of the legal and political needs of both the Watson and Rockefeller interests, though he claimed to know or care little about the technical aspects of the industries involved.[90] Unless matters were urgent, he usually worked at a distance in political situations, keeping in touch from Fairmont by telephone to appropriate offices in Charleston, Washington, Baltimore, and New York. The closer work was done by lower echelon leaders, who were taken care of by a special fund for "expenses" supplied by the Standard along with Fleming's regular salary.[91] Chiefly these were the Republicans, Elliott and Showalter, and two Democrats, William A. Ohley and O. S. McKinney, who with McGraw and the Kanawhans were the principal architects and beneficiaries of the industrialists' restoration to the Democracy's command. The virtues of such collaborators were fully listed by Fleming in a letter to the B&O's home office in support of McKinney's Democratic candidacy in the First Congressional District in 1902:

> [H]e is one of the stauchest of friends to the railroads, and also of our coal companies. He owns a leading weekly and daily paper in the district, and writes a great deal for his paper. He aided us very much during the labor troubles the past summer; and when a member of the Legislature 4 years ago appointed [as

Speaker] satisfactory committees, aided in the defeat of obnoxious legislation;—in fact, was on the right side of every question.

"If Mr. Stalnaker should be in your office you can inquire of him," Fleming concluded.[92] Such were the just encomiums lavished by and upon individuals who, were they to be encountered by historians among the natives of Portuguese Africa or British India, would properly be labeled members of the *comprador* middle class: in other words, middlemen who helped to make the resources of their homeland available to the invaders who exploited them.

It will become necessary later to distinguish between the corporate "retainers" and the "lieutenants" of the Elkins organization, but before 1903 the aspiring local politician of either party who attached himself to the industrialists could in return for accepting their leadership look forward both to political preferment and economic advancement. As McGraw had done with Davis and Camden, Ohley won Fleming and Watson backing for smaller industrial enterprises of his own, while other collaborators profited from investments in local Standard or Fairmont subsidiaries.[93] Elkins, too, found such transactions useful in binding his subordinates. Beginning around 1900 he placed a series of small investments in coal, railroad, utility, banking, and insurance projects sponsored by such Republican leaders as A. B. White in Parkersburg, Charles W. Swisher in Fairmont, Elliott Northcott in Huntington, Peter Sillman in Charleston, and George C. Sturgiss in Morgantown, while lawyers like Sturgiss, Taylor Vinson of Huntington, and William E. Glasscock of Morgantown were given morsels of legal patronage.[94] Elkins also acted as a contact for local men trying to interest metropolitan capitalists in their ventures, just as Blaine had sometimes done for him and Davis in the past.[95]

By such means Davis was able to complete, and the Elkins organization to perfect, the process of political reorganization that had been underway in West Virginia since the time of the Civil War. In so doing, they were helped by the electoral trends previously discussed, which eroded the character and importance of the preindustrial communities whose local leadership had managed to keep the Democratic industrialists at bay. But the tycoons were by no means idle beneficiaries. An interesting illustration of this point is provided by a comparison of the distribution of campaign funds in two campaigns for which complete reports of disbursements exist. One was the Republican campaign of 1884 in the Second Congressional District where the funds available, in this pre-Elkins era, totaled $3,200 and came entirely from the state and national committees. One thousand dollars of this sum was handled directly by the candidate and his manager. Of the remainder, the district chairman distributed nearly half (46 percent) to party workers in the "one-party" counties of the Eastern Panhandle, where clearly the object was to arouse Republicans "to a sense of their duty" in the party strongholds and to see that the Democracy did not report more than its share of the votes in the homogeneous districts where it held sway. The rest went chiefly to the strongly Republican trend county of Preston (16 percent), the swing county of Berkeley (26 percent), and to Tucker (10 percent), the district's only extractive county.[96] While some attention was paid to transitional districts, the principal object was to "get out" the "normal" Republican vote. The distribution of Davis's and other industrialists' contributions in the Democratic state campaign of 1904 offered an illuminating contrast. Of $137,711 at its disposal, the state committee sent $51,100 to Charleston, where it was distributed in unspecified places and ways under the direction of the Kanawha Ring. Of the remainder, subtracting headquarters expenditures and funds distributed to party workers in unspecified places, $68,126 was sent to individual counties. Of this total, the Eastern Panhandle counties that had supplied such stalwart Democratic voters and leaders during the Gilded Age got only $2,100, or less than 2 percent, while an additional $700 went to their one-party Republican neighbors. The remaining Democratic counties of the central interior got about 5 percent ($6,450), as did the Republican trend counties ($6,200). The bulk of the money went to the swing ($29,878) and extractive ($22,800) counties, to which should be added the $50,000 or so spent in or around Kanawha.[97] In other words the Democratic leaders agreed with Scott that it was "ridiculous" to waste cash on the partisan strongholds. Politicians might talk still of "getting out the vote" but they knew that the critical part of the vote was not gotten but made.

Having inherited a more disciplined and united party in the Republicans, Elkins was in a more advantageous position than his Democratic predecessors, but he did not fail to improve on his legacy. As Davis and Camden had done before him, he recognized the advantage of a loyal press, as his early alliances with Hart of the Wheeling *Intelligencer* and White of the Parkersburg *State Journal* testify. The Charleston *Mail-Tribune*, which came wholly under Dawson's control in 1903, gave the organization an influential voice in southern West Virginia (not to mention the state printing patronage), while Scott bankrolled a journal of his own in Charlie Elliott's Parkersburg *News.*[98] While the local weeklies multiplied with the advance of towns and communications, these and other urban dailies continued to dominate the transmission of political information and views. This much was recognized by the Democratic campaigners of 1904, who divided $805 in "circulation supplements" between twenty-three local journals and apportioned a $3,000-printing kitty between the conservative Wheeling *Register* and O. S. McKinney's Fairmont *Index.*[99]

Perhaps Elkins's single most telling achievement lay in enlisting in his cause the talents of William Mercer Owens Dawson (1856-1916), a man widely regarded as "the most astute politician in the State."[100] A lifelong resident and country editor in staunchly Republican Preston County until Elkins made him G.O.P. state chairman in 1891, Dawson united devoted partisanship with a flair for organization and detail. During his first statewide campaign in 1892, he gave the local party a thoroughly modern organization, appointing workers and captains in every precinct, and committees and chairmen in every county. The whole was responsible to his office in Wheeling or, after 1897, Charleston, which always equipped with a fleet of roving troubleshooters. At one point in the 1892 campaign it was estimated that at least 9,000 Republicans were actively engaged in campaign work.[101] When Dawson resigned as chairman to run for governor in 1904, his methods were continued in operation, as Scott explained to a new committeeman, William E. Glasscock:

> You have five state officers besides the Governor on the ticket. Take these five candidates and take the chairmen of each of the five Congressional districts, making ten in all. Divide the State into ten subdivisions, about five counties to each man to look after. Let that man go directly into every one of these five counties as quickly as he can and organize each voting precinct by appointing a chairman and a secretary. Let that chairman and secretary select three to form an advisory committee to help them in that precinct. Then put each one of them to work and have it arranged so that a week before the election they secure a sufficient number of conveyances to get all their voters to the polls by noon of election day and let the State Committee furnish each one of these precincts with a certain amount of money.

To top off the whole arrangement, Scott contributed a $50 prize to the precinct chairman in each county who reported the highest increase in Republican votes.[102] These methods centralized power and responsibility without sacrificing the widespread rank-and-file participation that was one of the hallmarks of politics in the Gilded Age. Another Dawson innovation was the transformation of the party's legislative caucus, hitherto confined primarily to matters pertaining to senatorial nominations or legislative offices, into a "conference" that managed and expedited legislation. From the time that he and White appeared at Charleston as secretary of state and governor-elect in 1901, it became conventional to speak there (as it did also in Theodore Roosevelt's Washington) of an "administration program," whereby the legislators found themselves dealing with a package of statehouse bills instead of the traditionally vague recommendations of the governor's biennial message.[103]

One such statehouse package of interest in the present context was the series of ten institutional reorganization bills or, less euphemistically, "ripper laws" adopted by a strict party vote in the legislature of 1901. By reconstructing the governing bodies of ten state institutions or supervisory boards, ranging from the home for incurables to the board of health, these bills enlarged Republican membership in these agencies and created eighty-nine new patronage slots. By providing that none of these appointments could be filled before March 10, 1901 (i.e., one week after White took office as governor), the "ripper" threw out all of Atkinson's holdover appointees along with the Democrats.[104]

Thus the organization brought state patronage under its control, an arrangement that White's successor, Governor Dawson, did nothing to disturb. As for the federal plums, White noted during his second term as internal reserve collector in 1898 that "my present Chief [Scott] expects to have a good deal more to say about who my deputies are than my former Chief [John W. Mason]. In fact it goes further even than that...."[105] The distribution of offices bolstered and evened out gaps in the senators' network of local support. The transition from McKinley to Roosevelt in the White House did not disrupt this pattern, nor did competition from the rest of West Virginia's congressional delegation, which was known collectively as "Elkins' Orphans."[106] Thus among twenty-six local figures that Dawson put forward as actual or prospective local contacts for the organization in various counties in 1899, five can be located on lists of postmasters in 1901-1903, along with five others who had the same last names and served in the same localities as those on Dawson's list. At least one other held a state insurance contract.[107] Doubtless others could be accounted for were the search extended to the state and other federal payrolls.

The higher posts served to co-opt or contain potential sources of factionalism, to even out the organization's geographic base, plus of course to take care of the industrialists' friends. The two federal judgeships that became available when the state was divided into northern and southern districts in 1901 and when Judge Jackson at last submitted his resignation in 1905 went, respectively, to Benjamin F. Keller, Rucker's law partner and with him a spokesman for the heavily Republican mining counties along the N&W, and to Congressman Dayton, the most vigorous and independent of the old-line Republicans who rode with Elkins to power on the G.O.P. tide of 1894. Successive appointments as collector took care of Thomas E. Davis and Glasscock, two representatives of the party's traditional Monongahela valley citadels. The attorneys and marshals jobs were distributed among Elliott, Blizzard, Showalter, Northcott, and John K. Thompson, a Putnam County leader whose Republicanism derived from Greenbacker roots. Atkinson also marked time as a federal attorney after he stepped down as governor until Roosevelt made available the long-sought judgeship on the United States Court of Claims in 1905. The two most desirable post offices went to Scott's man in Wheeling and to the Charleston leader of the G.O.P. "Hog Combine."[108]

The patronage, in turn, was fused with Dawson's streamlined party machinery. Scott retained his post as national committeeman until 1912, while as an old-liner grumbled after Dawson stepped up to the governorship in 1905, "The Chairman of the State Committee, Elliott Northcott, is District Attorney; the Secretary is Collector of Internal Revenue, the Treasurer is a U.S. Marshal; another member is a U.S. Congressman."[109] To which list might be added, as the National Civil Service Reform League did in an irritable message to Governor-elect Glasscock in 1908, a clutch of first- and second-class postmasters.[110] Of course, as a celebrated critic of the spoils system, President Roosevelt was keen on keeping federal officials "out of politics," but technicalities could be gotten around in ways such as the one used during the special congressional election occasioned by Dayton's resignation in 1905: in order to evade Roosevelt's restrictions on political activism

...the State Committee did what it had never done before, ...Northcott, Glasscock and Elliott resigned their office as Chairman, Secretary and Treasurer respectively and selected three men that were *not* members of the Committee and placed them in those positions. Understand, — they did not resign from the Committee, but only their positions on said Committee,

which positions they subsequently resumed.[111]

145

Deprived of the cement of state or federal patronage, the Democratic organization of the Elkins era resembled less a machine than a constellation revolving around the industrialists' barrels. Under Davis's patronage, McGraw continued to dominate the other Democratic professionals, continuing as national committeeman through 1912 and rotating in the state chairmanship with Ohley, McKinney, and George I. Neal, the sometime mayor of Huntington. The Eastern Panhandle was represented in party activities by John J. Cornwell of Romney and by "Colonel Tom" Davis, who returned to his familiar post as dean of the state committee after a one-term fling in Congress. In the south, the Kanawhans acquiesced somewhat restively in these arrangements until they discovered a larger barrel attached to Clarence W. Watson in 1910.[112]

In the meantime, Davis and Camden, realizing (as Camden conceded privately to Scott in 1901) that "you Republicans will be in power for a long time to come in West Virginia," shelved their senatorial aspirations and concentrated on national party politics, where they maneuvered to displace the Bryanites from command. One result of the success of this strategy in 1904 was Davis's nomination for the vice-presidency on the ticket headed by Alton B. Parker.[113] Henry Cabot Lodge had the first and best word on that subject when he remarked to Roosevelt that "To nominate a man 81 years old for Vice-President is strange, but I suppose it means money and a desperate bid for West Va."[114] But the development had some noteworthy local complications that will be dealt with later on.

At home, the Democratic industrialists were chiefly concerned with maintaining an appropriate framework of support for their national objectives and with such collaboration as the Republican leadership required in promoting "good government and a continuation of the prosperous conditions that have existed for the past few years. . . ."[115] Davis's collaboration with Elkins, White, and Dawson to that end in their attempts at fiscal and administrative reorganization at Charleston eventually led him into conflict with Camden and

146

Johnson Newlon Camden
1828-1908

Henry Gassaway Davis
1823-1916

Stephen Benton Elkins
1841-1911

Nathan Bay Scott
1841-1924

with Watson and Fleming, just as the same development eventually opened a split between Elkins's "lieutenants" and Fleming's "retainers." But these developments lay unseen in the future as West Virginia welcomed the new century in 1901. Then the industrialists' politico-economic regime bestrode the Mountain State like a colossus, fully earning the term applied to it by the muckraker, David Graham Phillips, in 1905: a bipartisan political "merger" systematically devoted to the needs and interests of the state's most powerful business corporations.[116] In formulating that merger, they had not corrupted West Virginia's political system. If anything, they *created* it in its modern form.

When United Mine Workers organizers came to the assistance of striking coal miners in the Fairmont region in July 1902, they discovered how smoothly and speedily the West Virginia merger could work. Under the prodding of Fleming and with the collaboration of Blizzard, Elliott, Keller, Goff, and Elkins, the aged Jackson issued a blanket injunction that subdued the strikers and placed their leaders under sentence for contempt of court. The time had come, said Jackson, in a ringing declaration of capitalist class-consciousness, to confront "what must soon transpire in this country—the conflict between two elements of society."

Reviewing these proceedings, a West Virginia historian remarks that "When the social, economic, and political fabric was so tightly woven, 'outsiders' were bound to meet formidable resistance at every turn."[117] That depended, however, on just who the outsiders were. The organized power that the coal miners encountered in West Virginia was, if we may depart from the conventional metaphor, only the bottom part of the iceberg. Other outsiders manned the top part, and these might be located in certain metropolitan office buildings, particularly in two that sat conveniently across the street from one another in the Empire City of New York.

147

5

The Boundless Resources

The Washington Building was erected in 1884 as one of New York's first "skyscraper" office blocks. Known familiarly as "No. 1 Broadway," it stood at the foot of the great Manhattan thoroughfare, facing south to the Battery and east across the little park called Bowling Green. Though square and bulky in outline, the building bristled with dormers and turrets; "no long monotonous lines meet the eye," a satisfied observer wrote of its facade. The 348 offices inside housed a variety of tenants, including a notable concentration of coal men. Stephen B. Elkins located his office there soon after the building opened, along with the New York offices of the Davis-Elkins railroads and bituminous firms. Other tenants in 1900 included the Fairmont and Consolidation Coal companies and the Chesapeake & Ohio Coal Agency, a railroad-owned firm that marketed West Virginia's Kanawha and New River coal.

Number 26 Broadway, erected in 1885 diagonally opposite the Washington Building, was as austere in design as most of its neighbors were ornate. Reflecting the celebrated efficiency of Rockefeller operations, this "severe but imposing" tower cost $952,906 and served as international headquarters for the Standard Oil Company. Here amid a privacy much commented upon but rarely disturbed, Rockefellers, Pratts, and Archbolds plotted industrial revolution, while men of inferior fame attended to the routine affairs of the Standard's broad empire. H. H. Rogers, whose Virginian Railroad played a developmental role in West Virginia's Paint Creek and Winding Gulf coalfields comparable to H. M. Flagler's more glamorous conquest of Florida, maintained an office at No. 26. So did Mortimer F. Elliott, the Standard's assistant and then chief legal counsel from 1898 to 1911.[1] Although he was

148

unknown to most West Virginians of the day, Elliott—thanks to the faithful and detailed reports of his local retainer, A. B. Fleming—took a lively and informed interest in their business and political affairs.[2]

We can only speculate about what passed in conversation among the occupants of these two buildings—or those in comparable precincts in Baltimore, Philadelphia, Pittsburgh or Cleveland—as they encountered one another in their metropolitan offices, residences, and clubs. But enough of Elkins's and Fleming's correspondence survives to tell us that as much West Virginia history was made in the confines of Lower Broadway as in any comparable space in the Mountain State. For the men who dominated West Virginia economically and politically at the turn of the century were men of national outlooks and concerns. Elkins, as befitted a chief among princes, buttressed his political and business achievements by social triumphs, gaining admittance to what one historical sociologist calls "the new national upper class."[3] Taking no chances, he sent one of his sons to Harvard, another to Princeton, a third to Yale, while Mrs. Elkins launched their daughter in international society, where she struck up a romance with a relative of the Italian king. "Why should I have another title?" Elkins is said to have remarked in calling a halt to this particular episode. He was already "king of Kingwood and monarch of Morgantown," not to mention a member of "the 'Four Hundred' of the Metropolitan Club" of New York. Mrs. Elkins, yielding to her husband's political judgment in the case of the princely marriage, found consolation in the work of a genealogist who convinced the credulous that the Davis family was descended from a race of ancient Lombard kings.[4]

The other West Virginia leaders were content to live more simply. Davis commuted in his private railroad car between his mountain "cottages" at Deer Park or Elkins and winter quarters in Baltimore or (after 1895) Washington, where he was known for his stag dinners for railroad presidents. For Camden an equally unostentatious track ran between Parkersburg and Flagler's Florida, where he owned an island in

Biscayne Bay. Scott moved in banking and industrial circles in Washington and Cleveland, as well as in Wheeling, and in Denver where he oversaw investments in western mines.[5] But wherever they lived and whatever their social ambitions, all were men whose economic constituencies extended well beyond the borders of their political domain.

Not that the West Virginians were equal to the biggest frogs that splashed in metropolitan ponds. Far from it. In national business circles, their position was not unlike that of their own subordinates in West Virginia. At home they might bestride the narrow world of local business and politics, but abroad they acted as agents and retainers of the true colossi: the Carnegies, Rockefellers, and Morgans who put together the national corporations that exploited the newly integrated nationwide transportation network and market. The West Virginians' chief claim to national prominence was the extent to which, in an age where careers were increasingly specialized, they united business and political leadership roles.

In their business capacities the industrialists acted as the engineers, though hardly the architects, of West Virginia's colonial economy, for as their several local enterprises flourished, they came increasingly under the influence or control of larger corporations based in the metropolitan centers. The enthusiasm with which they embraced this process varied among the individuals concerned, but each at an opportune moment yielded the prerogatives of independence to the higher realities of national economic centralization.

Camden was the first to confront this necessity and embraced it in May 1875 when he exchanged control of the Camden Consolidated Oil Company for stock of the Standard Oil Company. Thereafter he played a vigorous if short-lived role as "Rockefeller's right arm" in the Ohio valley oil industry, guarding a small but strategic flank as the parent firm extended its control over the national market for refinery products.[6] His situation, as Camden outlined it to John D. Rockefeller in 1878 and 1879, was that "The Production of West Va. Oil for refining purposes is between 500 and 600 barrels per day, which it seems to be absolutely necessary that we should take care of, in order to prevent its falling into other hands, or originating other refining interests" in West Virginia or other localities situated to exploit the western markets.[7] By terms of the arrangements whereby Camden entered the Standard combine, the West was now closed to his Parkersburg refinery in deference to Rockefeller facilities at Cleveland and other points, while Parkersburg's eastern and export markets had been turned over to the Baltimore United Oil Company formed from eight Baltimore refineries acquired by Camden under Standard direction in 1876-1877. The difficulty lay in absorbing the disruptive volume of West Virginia crude without: a) buying it at inconveniently high prices or volumes, or b) allowing it to fall in an open market into the hands of "guerilla refineries" that sprung up in the Parkersburg region like "weeds in a garden."

"Looking alone to our Parkersburg interest," Camden conceded, "we could show better results, but [for] the fact that this West Va. oil can exert an unfavorable influence in the Western markets, to the prejudice of the entire home trade interest of S.O. Co. . . ."[8] Although he hoped to salvage something of his Parkersburg firm's original market, Camden eventually accepted Rockefeller's view "that it would be no disadvantage to the general [Standard] interest to reduce our business here to a very low point" and accomplished this purpose by means of a complicated series of transactions involving the extortion of rebates from the B&O and the absorption of bankruptcy of the remaining independent refiners of the Parkersburg area.[9] After 1879, Camden's Parkersburg refinery was confined to a strictly local market, while West Virginia crude producers had no choice but to contract their petroleum for shipment eastward to the Standard's Baltimore refineries. These in turn were later phased out of the export trade in favor of the Pratt and Rogers refineries in New York. To make certain of the Ohio valley flank, and also as a potentially profitable enterprise in its own right, Camden undertook the construction of the Ohio River Railroad from Wheeling to Huntington in 1882-1888, heading a syndicate of Standard and senatorial colleagues that included Oliver H. Payne of Cleveland, S. V. Harkness and Charles Pratt of New York, and James H. Fair of San Francisco, plus E. W. Clark and Company, bankers in Philadelphia and producers of Pocahontas coal. This enterprise gave West Virginia the first north-south rail connection located wholly within the state and was said to have the further advantage of driving from the river the barges that had on occasion provided troublesome links between independent oil producers and refiners in the Ohio valley and the Standard's markets in the West.[10]

Apart from this indirect connection—and of course the collection of dividends from the parent company's stock—Camden's business involvement in the Standard Oil Company came to an end after 1879. So did West Virginia's stake in the refining industry. Even though the state increased its crude production tenfold, the number of refineries fell to five in 1889, while only one (Camden's) remained at the end of the century.[11] The upsurge in oil and natural gas production after 1890 posed no threat to Standard Oil's refining monopoly, since the new Mannington and Sistersville oil fields were exploited chiefly by Rockefeller controlled or dominated firms and the gas wells apportioned among a host of subsidiaries controlled by Standard or George Westinghouse of Pittsburgh.[12] In the meantime, Camden turned his attention to coal and railroad ventures in West Virginia and eastern Kentucky, while his brother-in-law and original partner, William P. Thompson, embarked on the career of a business bureaucrat, ascending first to Cleveland, then to 26 Broadway, finally to the presidency of the National Lead Company.[13]

If refining was of brief duration on the West Virginia manufacturing scene, iron and steel products and the glass industry, both centered in Wheeling and the Northern Panhandle, were of historic importance. Yet here too the process of consolidation and subordination of local enterprises to metropolitan control proceeded apace. In iron and steel the process was incomplete in that sufficient local capital and initiative survived in several family enterprises to provide the basis for one of the smaller integrated steel manufacturers, Wheeling Steel Corporation, organized in 1920. But even in this oldest and best established of Wheeling's industries, the consolidation movement took its toll. "Each time the trail of trusts led back to Wheeling's Industrial District," writes the official historian of Wheeling Steel, "it left a pile of money—in preferred stock or common—but it took one or two steel plants out of local ownership."[14] It occasionally took them out of production as well, as the managers of United States Steel, National Steel, American Can, or whichever, reorganized their facilities in accordance with their calculation of the corporation's national production and marketing concerns.[15]

While the Northern Panhandle perhaps "broke even" in the iron and steel industry, it permanently lost the position of leadership in glassmaking it had held since the time of the Civil War. One of the reasons was the United States Glass Company, a "trust" with few of the virtues that can be summoned to the defense of U.S. Steel or Standard Oil. A combination of Pittsburgh, Wheeling, and Ohio tableware manufacturers organized in 1891, U.S. Glass followed initial success in raising prices and profits with a disastrous attempt to break the American Flint Glass Workers Union's control over worker output. The ensuing four-year strike exhausted the union but also the company, whose factories declined from twenty-five at the beginning of the strike to six in 1900, none of them in Wheeling.[16]

How much Senator Scott had to do with this debacle is uncertain. He combined his Central Glass Company of Wheeling with U.S. Glass in 1892, but retired from the U.S. Glass directorate two years later and seems to have had his Wheeling factory back in independent operation by the end of the century. "I believe in trusts," he was quoted as saying.[17] But even if Scott managed to salvage his own investment, the contrast between his role in the industry and that of Michael J. Owens provides an illuminating comment on the conventionality of the industrialist-politicians' business leadership. A veteran flint glassworker and union organizer who departed

153

Wheeling, apparently because of blacklisting, during the labor troubles that preceded the U.S. Glass Company strike, Owens settled in Toledo. There, in partnership with Edward D. Libbey, a manufacturer whose entrepreneurial skills matched Owens's inventive genius, he founded the firm that would launch a "technological revolution in glassmaking" and with it two great modern corporations, Libbey-Owens-Ford and Owens Illinois. Thus the "Toledo entrepreneurs" solved through technology the productivity problems that U.S. Glass attacked by frontal assault.[18] West Virginia retained its leadership in tableware manufacturing, the smallest and least profitable branch of the industry, but initiative—and profits—in the more heavily-capitalized container and building glass industries shifted to Ohio and Indiana. An interesting footnote to this development is that the technological innovation in glass jar manufacturing comparable to Owens's bottle-making machines was first operated successfully by a Huntington glassmaker in 1892, but the relevant patent soon passed to an Indiana manufacturer by way of the U.S. Glass Company, which sold it for $10,000 in 1898.[19]

The most dramatic local manifestation of the consolidation movement came in the coal and railroad industries at the turn of the century. In 1900 the competitive position of West Virginia shippers never seemed better; in 1901 it collapsed entirely. The reason was the "Community of Interest" among the eastern trunk lines developed under the leadership of the Pennsylvania president, Alexander J. Cassatt. Representing a new breed of professional railroad managers, Cassatt looked with disgust on the carriers' legacy of disunity and combat; rather than participate in such practices as rate wars and the extortion of rebates by large shippers, he had resigned from the Pennsylvania management in 1882. His recall to the presidency in June 1899 thus signalled the acceptance of his terms and the beginning of a new strategy of consolidation among the carriers and the stabilization of rates through intra-industry cooperation.[20] Soon after he took office in Philadelphia, Cassatt approached his strongest competitor, the New York Central, and won its cooperation and also that of

J. P. Morgan, the financier who wielded control of the "anthracite railroads" (Reading, Lackawanna, Lehigh Valley) of the northeast. Beginning in December 1899, the two "strong" carriers, PRR and New York Central, began buying controlling amounts of stock in their "weak" southern competitors, B&O, C&O, N&W. The campaign was not completed, nor made public, until July 1901, when a PRR lieutenant, Leonard F. Loree, took over the B&O presidency.[21]

At the same time, a related consolidation of control developed among major West Virginia coal producers. The C&O already controlled the marketing operations of thirty-two of its coal shippers through the New River Coal Company organized in 1899; after the new C&O management took office in 1900, the railroad extended its control to most major producers in the New River and Kanawha fields through the C&O Coal Agency and put down an attempt to organize an independent marketing agency early in 1901. Meanwhile, Cassatt helped the N&W finance the acquisition of the Pocahontas Coal Company, which by virtue of earlier consolidations controlled most of the 5,000,000-ton output of Mercer and McDowell counties in southern West Virginia.[22] Ex-Senator Camden, having sold or leased his West Virginia railroads to the B&O during 1899-1901, also leased his mines in the Fairmont region to an enlarged Fairmont Coal Company, led by Clarence W. Watson. Early in 1902, Watson, in collaboration with the Hanna Coal Company of Cleveland and the Pittsburgh (Mellon) Coal Company, acquired the largest coal shipping and wholesaling firm in the western "lake" trade, while the Consolidation Coal Company of Baltimore purchased a distributor of similar importance in the New England market. The Consolidation firm itself was taken over in 1902 by a syndicate of B&O and PRR managers. Finally, in January 1903, Consolidation Coal absorbed the Fairmont company, although the latter firm retained its separate identity for operating purposes.[23] As Watson moved to Baltimore to head the management of the combined firms, his second-in-command, a former Camden subordinate, managed the office at No. 1 Broadway.

155

By this time the Standard Oil executives across the street were busy expanding their control and exploitation of the new oil and gas fields by means of Carter and South Penn Oil, Eureka Pipeline, Hope Natural Gas, and other Rockefeller subsidiaries, while Rogers was beginning his singlehanded transformation of a C&O feeder line into the Virginian Railroad, which was scientifically engineered to take advantage of the fall in altitude in moving West Virginia coal from the mountains to Hampton Roads.[24] Since each of the corporations involved transmitted their legal and political requirements in West Virginia via Fleming and a brace of retainers who looked to him for leadership, the effect of the several transactions here summarized was to create a notable degree of unity among the largest business interests of the state. "The Judge [Fleming] is terribly worried over the anti-trust laws, and how to get around them," Camden commented to an official of the B&O. "I look upon the matter a little differently, and am disposed to cut my way through. . . ."[25]

The acquisition of the Davis-Elkins enterprises in January 1902 by a syndicate led by George J. Gould completed the process of consolidation in the Mountain State. Behind this development lay an intricate series of maneuvers. No lovers of competition in the bituminous trade, the senators had long looked forward to the day when the railroads by joint action would stabilize coal freights and prices and help drive price-cutting marginal producers from the trade. Thus they initially welcomed the Community of Interest.[26] But they speedily changed their minds upon finding that they would have to enjoy its benefits on the Community's terms. Four months after taking office in Philadelphia, Cassatt suddenly cancelled the privilege by which the West Virginia Central used PRR coal cars on its line free of charge, thereby putting Davis and Elkins on notice that their strategy of playing the trunk lines off against one another was finished. "We are now between the B&O and PRR systems," Richard C. Kerens remarked when he heard the news; "their interests are united, and the time may come sooner than we expect, when one or both will try to absorb the West Virginia Central."[27]

The prospective completion of the Community of Interest circle by absorption of the Davis-Elkins railroads and mines aroused intense speculation and opposition in West Virginia during the latter part of 1901, but the Wheeling *Intelligencer* assured its readers that Senator Elkins would "do nothing with reference to the West Virginia Central unless the interest of the State are safe-guarded, nor anything but [*sic*] will tend to her aggrandizement and the swifter and more substantial development of her abundant resources."[28] In point of fact, Davis and Elkins considered selling to the Community and demurred only because their uncomfortable position made it difficult to command a top price. The Gould offer to purchase, tendered and accepted within a few weeks at the end of 1901, provided a solution to both the personal and political dilemmas.[29] As Henry Clay Frick later remarked to Rockefeller II, "The West Virginia people did sell their property at a very high figure, even for 'boom' times," while the outbreak of railroad war between Gould and the Pennsylvania reassured apprehensive West Virginians that in their cause was enlisted "the fighting blood of a railroad potentate. . . ."[30]

By this time, however, the Community of Interest leaders knew that Gould's blood told a different tale. The ostensible object of Gould's purchase of the West Virginia Central—and of the Western Maryland and Wheeling & Lake Erie, two other strategically placed roads whose termini lay in West Virginia's Eastern and Northern panhandles—was to join the three with each other and with the Wabash Railroad and other Gould properties in the West and Southwest to form a true transcontinental extending from Baltimore to San Francisco Bay. Behind this strategy, in turn, lay a characteristic maneuver of Andrew Carnegie. Striking a final blow for capitalist competition on the eve of turning his own properties over to Morgan and U.S. Steel, Carnegie signed a contract giving Gould a lucrative share of his company's steel traffic if the Wabash road were extended to Pittsburgh. The Carnegie

157

contract, signed on February 4, 1901, remained legally binding on U.S. Steel when it took over from Carnegie on February 25, but Morgan assured Cassatt that the Community of Interest need have no fear of Wabash competition when "we get into the saddle. . . ."[31]

In the face of Morgan's attitude and of the Community's fierce resistance to the projected Wabash invasion of the East, the latter's strategy swiftly developed into a familiar Gouldian attempt at extortion. The Wabash's projected links through Pittsburgh and across West Virginia to tidewater took on the character of a "strike road," available for sale to the Community of Interest at inflated prices, while the Western Maryland, into which the West Virginia Central and its coal mines were merged in 1905, had its stock heavily watered and made the object of speculation.[32] Cassatt's stubborn refusal to deal with Gould on Gould's terms, a very successful though unpublicized "still hunt" designed to deprive the Gould railroads of freight, the high prices and heavy construction costs incurred by Gould in acquiring and extending his properties, plus the Panic of 1907 combined to disintegrate the Wabash-Western Maryland "system" in March 1908. A reorganized Western Maryland finally completed its extension to the Monongahela near Pittsburgh, after which it became a Rockefeller property (as did, eventually, the Consolidation Coal Company). But the new road did not run through West Virginia as originally planned. The state got only about twenty miles of new railroad construction out of the Gould debacles instead of the projected two hundred or more of 1902. The old West Virginia Central remained a dangling appendage of the Western Maryland, a siphon dipping into the fuel and timber resources of the Mountain State.[33]

How much Davis and Elkins foresaw of this outcome is unclear. They invested some of the proceeds from the sale of their properties in the several Gould syndicates then planning to build through West Virginia, but most of their money went into new enterprises, the Morgantown & Kingwood and Coal & Coke railroads, each so situated with their related coal

158

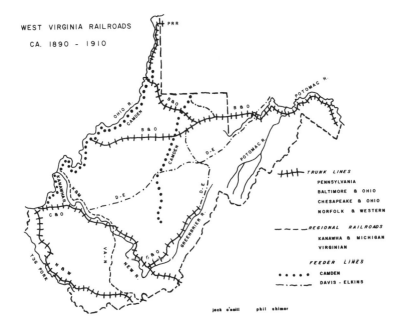

WEST VIRGINIA RAILROADS

CA. 1890 - 1910

PRR

POTOMAC R.

OHIO R.

B & O

B & O

CAMDEN

B & O

CAMDEN

D-E

POTOMAC R.

KANAWHA

K & M

D-E

D-E

GREENBRIER R.

C & O

C & O

T-9 FORK

N & W

N-VA.

NEW R.

TRUNK LINES

PENNSYLVANIA

BALTIMORE & OHIO

CHESAPEAKE & OHIO

NORFOLK & WESTERN

REGIONAL RAILROADS

KANAWHA & MICHIGAN

VIRGINIAN

FEEDER LINES

• • • • • CAMDEN

DAVIS - ELKINS

jack o'neill   phil shimer

companies as to be able to tap the prospective Gould railroads along with the existing B&O and C&O lines.[34] Someone cautioned Davis about the vulnerability of these shorter railroads to trunk line takeovers, but "that depends on circustances [sic]," Davis replied. With characteristically bad grammar but good sense, he added that "one thing is certain big roads has to pay good prices when they buy."[35] It would seem then that the senators were privy to Gould's "strike" strategy but, in any event, their relations with the Wabash managers cooled after one of Gould's subordinates tried to shake *them* down for a commission on the original West Virginia Central sale. By the end of 1903, they were again enjoying pleasant relations and profitable traffic contracts with the Community of Interest roads.[36] As their new enterprises came into production, they moved to a new set of offices at No. 1 Broadway, while their former general manager, F. S. Landstreet, took over the Western Maryland's coal mining headquarters down the hall.

One effect of these reorganizations was an increase in pressure against West Virginia's smaller coal producers similar to the kind that Camden had earlier brought against the Standard's competitors. The traffic agreement concluded by Elkins between the Morgantown & Kingwood and the B&O gave him complete autonomy in the consignment of B&O coal cars delivered to the feeder line; by this means he was able to starve the hitherto leading independent producer of the Morgantown area out of business by the end of 1904. A similar fate befell independent competitors of the Fairmont Coal Company.[37] In the south, Cassatt's control of the N&W and the Pocahontas Coal Company forced the discontinuance of Pocahontas coal deliveries to New York harbor, despite its superior reputation as a marine fuel. Naval vessels were able to follow Pocahontas coal to the N&W terminals in Hampton Roads, but other transatlantic shipping had to make do with Clearfield coal from central Pennsylvania which replaced Pocahontas in the New York market in 1901. It is not surprising then that the combined New York Central and PRR deliveries of coal to the eastern market rose by roughly 10

159

percent during 1902 and 1903, while the B&O-C&O-N&W share declined by a similar amount.[38]

These changes were defended as bringing greater efficiency to the distribution of coal in the eastern region, which was doubtless the case. And since the loss to West Virginia was one of potential rather than actual production, accomplished at the expense of the marginal operators whose price-cutting propensities bedeviled the larger firms, the arrangement can be supported as restrictive of the haphazard and wasteful southern expansion of the coalfields discussed below. But as is usually the case, the process of business "rationalization" was conducted to someone's profit at someone else's loss. In the instance of the New York harbor coal market, the prime beneficiaries were certain Clearfield operators who just happened to have certain connections with certain Pennsylvania Railroad directors. The revelation of these connections by the Interstate Commerce Commission in 1906 was said to have produced in President Cassatt a reaction of pained surprise.[39] It was also a pain to Elkins, whose discriminatory actions became public knowledge at a time when he was helping to steer the Hepburn Railroad Regulation Act through Congress on the carriers' terms. One result was the Hepburn Act's "commodities clause," prohibiting discrimination and collaboration among producers and carriers of the sort just described. By some means of legislative legerdemain not readily discernible, Elkins managed to embrace this amendment as his own and then to postpone its operation until 1910, by which time it had been nullified by the courts.[40] In this as in other instances there was more than a casual connection between the West Virginia industrialists' business and political careers.

"Elkins was a classic example of a man who rose by exploiting political office for private gain," writes a student of his Senate activities.[41] The description is blunt but accurate. Elkins's early accumulations of New Mexico land claims, his success there as a lawyer and banker, his fortunate second marriage to Hallie Davis: all flowed from his successes in politics. His fragmentary correspondence, not to mention the charges of his enemies, contain the hint of many other examples of opportunism, pursued both before and after his success as a railroad builder and producer of coal.[42] Among the other industrialists, Scott's early career was probably bereft of such activities, at least on more than a local scale, as it was also bereft of high public office before 1897. Davis and Camden had fewer opportunities than Elkins, but neither was loath to turn political influence into coin when the chance arose. Camden, for example, could not resist the speculative opportunity presented by the West Virginia-Virginia debt controversy, even though it would have fallen little short of an admission of civic treason had his possession of debt certificates become public knowledge at the time.[43] The same temptation overcame Elkins shortly after he took office, although it is not clear in his case whether he was acting in his own behalf in attempting to secure West Virginia's validation of the certificates or merely for "my friends at the First National Bank [of New York]."[44] Davis nicely expressed the spirit of such temptations when, in connection with a morsel of inside information deriving from a Senate committee assignment, he assured Camden that "We ought to make a large amount on this."[45]

The West Virginia leaders were thus no slower than others of their day who saw their opportunities and took them, but their opportunism is not in itself sufficient to explain their business success or their long-term involvement in politics. They were subject to the array of nonpecuniary stimuli that usually separate the politically active from the quiescent, among businessmen as among other social groups: an inherited bent in Camden's case and perhaps also in the cases of Davis and Elkins; or gradual engagement, as in Scott's long apprenticeship in city, state, and party offices.[46] There was also the rhetorical but rhythmic tug of partisanship and electoral combat and the appeal of social prestige. "Although the party leaders, under Cleveland and Bryan, have made mistakes," Davis commented to Camden in 1898, when no issues worthy of notice separated the combatants in West Virginia,

161

"yet when you compare the principles of the two parties, there appears no doubt to you as well as myself to be much in favor of the Democratic party." Scott made the same comparison and decided, in a moment of Republican gloom, that he might become a Populist "as I would not, I am sure, ever be a Democrat."[47] He also nicely stated the social appeal of high office when he was accused of trying to buy the senatorship and countered with what he believed to be a very effective campaign document—a photograph of his birthplace. "It is a very *dilapidated log cabin,*" he explained. "If ever any poor devil on earth deserves recognition for coming up from the people and being one of the people, I certainly can lay claim to that honor."[48]

Perhaps if we were dealing with more articulate or reflective men, such incentives would come more prominently into view. As the evidence stands, however, those incentives that most readily explain the industrialists' careers are economic ones—certainly this is the case if we speak in terms of the *significance* of their careers as well as of their motivation. And the economic incentives that mattered most were not the casual opportunities for aggrandizement mentioned above. Some of these ended in failure without sidetracking the senators' political or business success.[49] The dominant incentives concerned political objectives that bore or were thought to bear on the growth and survival of their principal business concerns.

The industrialists' most important achievements—important both in terms of the energies invested and the results secured—were not opportunistic but strategic. Camden's political ambitions did not originate with his oil business, but after 1875 his foremost preoccupation was with the public needs of the Standard Oil Company. In and out of the Senate, he sought to protect the firm from congressional scrutiny, to win diplomatic support for the expansion of foreign markets, and to obtain preferential treatment in the writing of tariff schedules. In these concerns he was generally successful and so persistent that some historians have mistaken him for a Standard lobbyist rather than a public official in his

162

own right.[50] Davis and Elkins's concern for the bituminous tariff was an enduring one. Bereft of an official voice in tariff policy between 1883 and 1895, they went to strenuous lengths to regain it, as we have seen. Elkins continued to stand guard over the bituminous duty, while Davis and Camden worked to restore protectionist influence within the national Democracy.[51] Scott's involvement in glassmaking did not lead him to quite so pressing a concern with public policy, although the industry was strenuously (and successfully) protectionist. But he too found influence useful, as when he used his connections to interfere behind the scenes in federal bankruptcy proceedings touching his Colorado investments in 1896.[52]

This concentration on strategic economic objectives in national politics was particularly the case with Elkins, the most successful and influential of the West Virginia tycoons. Throughout his long career as a national party manager, cabinet official, and senator, his attention was centered at Washington, where he handled the political needs of other industries as well as of bituminous coal. His New Mexico friends wanted territorial officials appointed and statehood secured on advantageous terms. Richard C. Kerens needed federal money for Los Angeles harbor. Henry M. Flagler wanted an appropriation for *his* harbor at Miami. The railroads needed congressional authorization for bridges at Saint Louis and Pittsburgh as well as in West Virginia. They also sought his help in circumventing or changing federal regulatory enactments and in resisting the safety legislation sought by the Interstate Commerce Commission and the labor brotherhoods.[53]

In these and other transactions with fellow big businessmen, the spirit was one of mutual benefit and accommodation among members of a self-conscious elite. "Your large holding in the West Virginia coalfields, and in the railroad company moving the coal and coke to tidewater, necessarily gives you a large personal interest in this matter," wrote a financier interested in federal subsidies for shipping. "Any time I can 'throw a stone in your dooryard,' you have only to command me," wrote Flagler, after his Miami appropriation came through.[54] This consciousness does not mean that the tycoons were united in every objective or that they were engaged in a continuous plot. Rather it means that their disagreements and rivalries were bounded by common assumptions and by a sense of solidarity that did not extend to those who stood "outside of our own circle."[55]

Elkins's feeling of capitalist fellowship made him something more than a runner of corporate errands in Washington. He was also a statesman of his class, looking after the broader, long-term interests of corporate capitalism, along with specific clients' immediate needs. One of the lesser-known aspects of his brief term as Secretary of War was a move to relocate federal military forces from the western theaters of Indian warfare to garrisons near the major industrial centers. The move could be justified in terms of cost and efficiency, but it would also "guarantee peace and good order in any of those emergencies which, however improbable, are at all times possible," a reference to the industrial violence of the nineties that was not lost upon the labor organizations who protested Elkins's plan.[56] Later he lent his support to Mark Hanna and his work through the National Civic Federation to promote harmonious reconciliation of industrial conflict, while leaving intact the overlordship of the new national corporations and their chiefs.[57] Meanwhile, as chairman of the Senate Interstate Commerce Committee from 1901 to 1911 and a charter member of the Republican leadership's "Old Guard," he helped to frame a series of measures that met growing demands for railroad regulation while accommodating the trend to consolidation among the carriers.[58] We shall return to these last two subjects later on.

The search for influence at Washington led Elkins by an intricate but unwavering path to the Senate, as it had done Davis and Camden before him. There a voice in the policy decisions affecting their concerns—and the broader processes of national economic growth and integration—might be had at the cost of less time and attention than other offices required, an important consideration for men whose time was money in both the literal and figurative sense. The rules and procedures of the upper house gave it the most abundant of the many instruments of obstruction that characterize the American legislative process, while its prestige opened many doors.[59] Therein lies the paradox of the industrialists' careers for West Virginia history. Their approach to the Senate made of the office what the founding fathers intended it to be: a national office concerned with national policy, whose holders were removed from immediate pressures of parochial concerns. Yet at the same time the office was—again by virtue of the Constitution of 1787—both substance and symbol of an individual state's claim to an equal voice and treatment in the Union's affairs. By virtue of a century of practice and custom, it was also the chief prize of local political competition. In short, to influence national economic policy, Elkins needed a Senate seat. To get a Senate seat, he needed the Republican party leadership in West Virginia. To acquire and hold that leadership, he needed to complete the process of political reorganization and integration that the Democratic industrialists had begun. Thus in their political roles, as in their economic roles, the West Virginia industrialists stood as the agents—and as principal beneficiaries—of the process of national integration that accompanied industrialization. And in both capacities, their work had profound local repercussions.

Irrespective of the controversy that sometimes surrounded their political roles, the industrialists' economic leadership enjoyed a high level of approval among their constituents. "I am glad to see that you are still working to develop the resources of our little mountain state and giving employment to so many of the poor working men," a man from Lost Creek, West Virginia, wrote to Camden in 1889. "May God bless you in all your endeavors to help the poor." "To Mr. Davis, perhaps, more than to any other man, West Virginia owes her progressive material development," ran another encomium. "It is a credit to our state to be represented by Senator Elkins. . . . We hope he may make a million dollars in our county. We will all get a share of it while the develop-

165

ment is going on."[60] The tycoons naturally did nothing to encourage a more realistic appraisal of their efforts, for as Elkins remarked, "It is purely a matter of persistent and well-directed educational work to awaken the people of the country to the necessity of supporting measures that will hasten the development of their resources."[61]

But while the industrialists exploited West Virginia's aspirations for material improvement, they were not themselves responsible for the particularly intense form those aspirations took. The public's craving for all things and persons that came under the heading of "development" were rooted, to apply to the state at large words that Charles Ambler applied to the educational system, in a "poverty complex" and consequent "inferiority complex" that was as old as the state itself.[62] So was the resulting "educational work." The legislature of 1864 created a special office, commissioner of immigration, to alert settlers and investors to the untapped riches of the infant commonwealth. Joseph H. Diss Debar, the first incumbent, produced some 19,000 pieces of promotional literature during the next six years, touting West Virginia as the "Switzerland of America."[63]

Fundamental to Debar's efforts and to other promotional efforts of the statemakers was the belief that "development" of West Virginia's "boundless natural resources" would overcome in time the barriers to prosperity posed by the Appalachian terrain and the attendant difficulties of transport and communications. While getting at the coal, timber, gas, and oil became the first order of business, it was never doubted that the presence of these and other raw materials would eventually lead to the growth of a mature industrial economy comparable if not superior to the one then taking shape in neighboring Ohio and Pennsylvania. "That such a country," exclaimed Debar, "so full of the varied treasures of the forest and the mine . . . should lack inhabitants, or the hum of industry, or show of wealth is an absurdity in the present and an impossibility in the future."[64] The official state seal, another Debar product, gave visual expression to this optimism, featuring a farmer and miner shouldering tools and a railroad viaduct displayed against the backdrop of a mountain sunrise. The "discovery" of Appalachian poverty around the time of the First World War and again in the 1960s, combined with the efforts of local apologists to explain away the embarrassing statistics that "the New York feature story writer and the amateur philanthropist" mined in the hollows and hills,[65] has tended to obscure the fact that West Virginia has always been poor by comparison with its northern and western neighbors and, during the initial decades of statehood, with its southern neighbors as well. But these facts were inescapable to those who scrutinized the census returns in 1880. Despite the completion of the C&O across the southern interior, railroad construction lagged behind the national rate of expansion, with the result that West Virginia had only 691 miles of track in 1880, compared to 352 miles twenty years before. Other indices of stagnation included declining property values and, like other southern states, a smaller share of national per capita and per worker income than had been the case before the Civil War.[66]

"When the war ended, it was confidently expected that West Virginia would advance in population and wealth more rapidly than any other State. But she has not done so," wrote the West Virginia Tax Commission of 1884, which knew by heart the articles of promotionalism. "Situated near the capital of the United States, within the very heart of the population and wealth of this country, with a good climate, richer in minerals than the same area anywhere else, with all her timber and all her coal then untouched, she offered to enterprise and to capital by far the most inviting field on this continent . . . considering our great and peculiar advantages, this State has not progressed one half as much as she ought to have done."[67] The tax commission had a particularly interesting explanation for this state of affairs, as we shall see, but whatever their explanations, most observers agreed that the state's early economic performance was disappointing and that West Virginia in 1880 was not only failing to catch up to its wealthier northern neighbors but in danger of remaining

167

behind Kentucky and, most disappointing of all, behind Virginia too.[68]

For all its failures of deed, the early period had a lasting impact on the rhetorical dimensions of economic development in West Virginia. The fundamental assumption that abundant and cheap resources of fuels and raw materials provided a base for full-scale industrialization was never seriously challenged, nor was the favored prescription for underdevelopment: the promotion of transportation facilities and advertisement to attract the attention of the outside world. Transportation at this point meant railroads. "We must have railroads," cried the Wheeling *Register* in 1881. "We must help our people out of the woods...." The real thing was preferable, but "Better paper railroads than none. Paper railroads always preceded the iron."[69] The coming of a live locomotive belching steam and charging rates laid down in Richmond or Baltimore aroused ambiguous attitudes, as we have seen, but the carrier's role as "the great civilizer" bore fruit in the form of immediate and obvious benefits. A case in point was Buckhannon, the county town of interior Upshur County, penetrated by Camden's West Virginia & Pittsburgh Railroad in 1883. Since the railroad's arrival, the town could boast of a new woolen mill, a handle factory, planing and saw mills, lumberyards, flour mills, and a new hotel. "It is not surprising that the people further on in the interior are longing for the time to come when capital and enterprise shall reach their borders and unlock their doors," enthused the *Register*, "that plenty and prosperity may dwell within their walls."[70]

As the pace of railroad construction doubled during the eighties and proceeded at a nearly equivalent rate during the following decade, the Buckhannon experience was repeated in dozens of West Virginia communities. The Norfolk & Western, crossing the Pocahontas and Tug Fork coalfields along the Virginia and Kentucky borders, and the Kanawha & Michigan, leading northwestward from the Kanawha and New River coalfields to Toledo, gave the state two major new coal carriers by 1890, to which was added in 1905 Rogers's Vir-

168

ginian Railroad, which connected the K&M (now New York
Central) terminus on the Kanawha River to tidewater via the
Paint Creek, Winding Gulf, and Flat Top fields. Under Davis
and Elkins, the West Virginia Central advanced southward
through the coal measures and forests of northeastern West
Virginia, reaching a C&O branch line at the head of the
Greenbrier valley in 1901, while their new Coal & Coke Railroad gave the state its long-awaited central rail route linking
Charleston to the B&O hinterland in 1906. The three trunk
lines (B&O, C&O, N&W)* began double-tracking their main
lines and built or sponsored feeder roads that by the end of
the century had gathered all but nine of the state's fifty-five
counties into a network composing more than 3,100 miles of
track.[71] In Huntington and Bluefield, the C&O and N&W
called into being important new cities, while the smaller
roads created dozens of railroad towns and coal camps bearing such names as Cowen, Watson, and Camden-on-Gauley;
Davis, Elkins, Thomas, Henry, and Junior; Blaine, Harrison,
Windom, Kerens, Bayard, and Gormania; Coalton, Coketon,
Carbon, and Richwood; Quick, Odd, and Bergoo.[72]

Although local investors and governments financed or sub-
scribed to several of the feeder roads, the actual work of
transportation development was generally left to the industrialists and their metropolitan associates. But though ill
equipped with capital, large numbers of West Virginians were
ready to speed the work with enthusiastic words. As the pace
of industrialization picked up, the liturgy of the faith in development also "took off." During the eighties the campaign
to advertise or "boom" the state developed a recurrent

*In technical railroad parlance, a trunk line was an eastern railroad linking
Chicago to an Atlantic seaport. Since the C&O and N&W had not yet reached
Chicago over their own lines, they were technically considered "sub-regional"
systems, but they are included here as "trunk lines" along with those of the
original railroads in that category (B&O, Pennsylvania, New York Central, Erie,
and Grand Trunk) which had West Virginia branches or lines. Had the Gould
railroads projected through the state been completed, the Wabash would have
achieved trunk-line status also. As it was, both it and the Western Maryland remained sub-regional systems and it is under the latter name that the assorted
proposed and existing Gould projects in West Virginia will be grouped.

pattern of ritual—unofficial commissions to promote immigration and investment, special "boom" conventions and editions of local newspapers, and publicly financed exhibits at the endless series of industrial expositions staged in the metropolitan centers—complete with a special language that nearly every aspiring citizen seems to have known by heart. In time "the richest of the States of like size in the Union" became "the wealthiest of American commonwealths"; "our almost fabulous wealth" became "unrivalled abundance."[73] Governor MacCorkle considered it one of the achievements of his administration that he exorcised the word "little" from the traditional nickname, "Little Mountain State." The state was not small, he explained; "It is immense . . . four times larger than Connecticut, eleven times larger than Delaware, and is 9,000 square miles larger than Denmark," to say nothing of Holland, New Jersey, Massachusetts, Rhode Island, and Alsace-Lorraine.[74] Governor Atkinson's optimism in 1899 halted only at West Virginia's imminent commercial conquest of Ohio and Pennsylvania in accordance with the laws of natural selection.[75] "There is not a possible doubt but that in a very few years West Virginia will be ranked as one of the wealthiest states in the Union. It cannot help but be," explained *The West Virginian,* a promotional journal that flourished briefly at Parkersburg at the end of the century. "The coal is of the very best quality. . . . Oil and West Virginia are synonymous. . . . It has other rich mineral deposits. Its great timber belts are too vast to be measured. Its towns are all adapted for large manufactures [*sic*], as fuel and water can be had at their doors at a minimum cost. The soil is rich and fertile. The climate is delightful . . ." and so on. Reciting a similar litany, the Morgantown *Post* in 1900 insisted that "There is no state in the Union that has such a bright outlook for the future as West Virginia."[76] A banker summed it up in verse at the state bankers' convention of 1901:

> West Virginia is a State
> That flows with milk and honey
> Its citizens are up-to-date
> And have the stuff called money.[77]

"To break through the barriers of stagnation in a backward country, to ignite the imaginations of men, and to place their energies in the service of economic development, a stronger medicine is needed than the promise of better allocation of resources or even of the lower price of bread," writes a modern student of economic development. "What is needed to remove the mountains of routine and prejudice is faith—faith, in the words of Saint Simon, that the golden age lies not behind but ahead of mankind." However, "in an advanced country rational arguments in favor of industrialization policies need not be supplemented by a quasi-religious fervor."[78] As the men who linked the wilds of Appalachia to metropolitan centers of finance and industry, the West Virginia industrialists were great expounders of the local development faith. "In regard to senator, I do not wish the office for the mere sake of holding office," Camden wrote to a development-conscious legislator in 1881. "I want to be useful to the State, and I believe I have the power to be of very considerable use . . . in a position where I would be better known and have the influence which official position rightly used gives, and the easy access which it opens up to make the acquaintances of men you want to know. . . ."[79] Wealth was an argument for, not against, political preferment, Davis argued during the senatorial contest of 1887. "Camden has brought two or three millions of dollars into the State, which have been invested in railroads, and scattered among the people, not only developing the state & its resources, but helping to pay the taxes."[80]

But though the industrialists reaped the political dividends attending the development process, they did not allow the fervor of their constituents to cloud their private business judgments. On several occasions, they played upon the hopes and anxieties of local communities to win subscriptions to their railroad projects or to absorb locally initiated projects at minimal cost, although in fact the realities of railroad construction in mountainous country dictated a choice of routes that left few established localities in danger of being passed by.[81] The prevailing attitude also offered them the advantage of discouraging governmental interference with their enterprises or anything else that might, as Davis put it in a somewhat garbled advice to a Wheeling editor, "have a tendency to make capitalists suspicious of our State and prevent money [sic] from giving their [word missing] to assist in developing of same—building railroads &c &c."[82] Camden indignantly thrust aside an Agrarian-inspired legislative investigation of his rebating arrangements with the B&O in 1879 with the claim that his firm was engaged "in building up a large manufacturing interest in West Virginia" where as in truth he was at that moment engaged in shifting West Virginia oil refining to Standard facilities in Baltimore. Later he publicly attributed the fall in employment at his Parkersburg refinery to the legislature's "little side show," although as his biographer noted, this representation "did not tell the whole truth."[83] Davis and Elkins were capable of misleading the boomers just as cynically, a notable instance being the Wheeling Boom Convention of 1888.[84]

In view of their lingering local reputation for disinterested public service, the industrialists' use and abuse of their constituents' trust deserves to be known. But it would be wrong to hold them wholly responsible for West Virginia's eventual economic fate. The tycoons took the place as they found it and shaped it to their needs, assuming as good capitalists are wont to assume that their needs were the same as those of the general welfare. They were fortunate but not to be blamed if resistance to their purposes and assumptions was weak. They merely translated into local reality broader more impersonal forces that ultimately were rooted in the natural environment in West Virginia and in the national economic system within which the state's industrialization took place.

West Virginia's development faith was in effect a primitive version of what specialists would later call the "sector theory" of economic growth. This theory posits a symmetrical process of economic change, by which the growth of primary industry (agriculture, mining, processing) creates the linkages of capital, skills, equipment, and demand that call

172

forth secondary industry (manufacturing), which in turn generates expansion in the service sector (trade, transportation, banking and insurance, private and public services). To be more specific, the boomers anticipated the "leading sector" or "export base" variant of the sector theory, which stresses the importance of an export commodity or product whose earnings outside the territory in question provide the bases of subsequent, more complex growth. Applied to the experience of Great Britain or of the United States as a whole, such a scheme affords a persuasive description of the industrialization process. But it has been justly criticized for overreliance upon the historical examples of the most advanced countries or regions and for failing to account adequately for natural and historical causes of regional differentiation within a given economic system. Among such causes are factors that can create and make permanent so-called "initial advantages" for some parts of a system at the expense of other parts.[85] West Virginia is an excellent case in point.

At the root of West Virginia's economic predicament were natural *dis*advantages from which the state could not have hoped to escape, but some of its obstacles were political in nature. Tariff policy, for example, created and sustained initial advantages for New England textile manufacturers during the nineteenth century, as it did also—thanks to Davis and Elkins—for producers of West Virginia coal. However, the manufacturer-producer compromise that underpinned the "Mongrel Tariff" of 1883 also lowered the duty on aniline dyes made from coal-tar derivatives, a boon to the textile makers that left initial advantage in the coal-based chemical industries in the hands of those German manufacturers who had perfected the commercial aniline processes. One result was that West Virginia's initial manufacturing venture in this field—a firm established at Parkersburg in 1881 with, as fate would have it, some cast-off equipment from Camden's local oil refinery—went speedily out of business, unable to withstand the competition from German imports. Forty years later politics again intervened when the seizure of German patents and the construction of government nitrate plants during World War I gave the Charleston area its modern chemicals industry. But the patents were awarded and government plants sold to metropolitan manufacturers who, having become established in other branches of industrial chemistry, were in a position to react as swiftly as the emergency—and the opportunity—required. The Kanawha valley chemicals complex was thus a branch-plant operation from the outset.[86] Had the tariff decision gone differently, Davis might have lost his New England coal market but he and other West Virginia operators might have gained a large home market for their coal, by-product coke ovens would have replaced the wasteful beehive ovens forty years earlier than they actually did, while local chemical manufacturers could have accumulated the initial advantages that later accrued to firms based in Wilmington, Pittsburgh, Philadelphia, and New York. There is no evidence that the senator was interested or even aware of this possibility. The point is that, while the following account will emphasize natural obstacles to manufacturing development, West Virginia's growth took place in the context of a political economy that allowed men like Davis to identify their private interest with the public welfare and to pursue it successfully by political means, whether or not their identification of public and private goods was correct.

In the actual event, West Virginia failed to develop a mature industrial economy. Like some other parts of the American hinterlands, like southern and eastern Europe, Africa, Latin America, and Asia apart from Japan, the Mountain State instead got "derived" industrialization and a "penetrated" economy characterized by overreliance on primary industry, low or distorted levels of growth in the manufacturing and service sectors, and a high degree of absentee ownership and/or control. In blunter terms, it developed a colonial economy and remained in the industrial age the backwater it had been in preindustrial times. Although this character is more readily grasped from the perspective of later years, it was available to a discerning eye in the statistics gathered by census enumerators at the turn of the century.

174

The most dazzling figures concerned the boundless resources. A distant fourth among coal-producing states with 6,000,000 short tons in 1889, West Virginia a decade later was a close third behind Pennsylvania and Illinois with a tonnage of 20,000,000. It declined from third to fourth place among petroleum producers, but the volume of production increased from 5,000,000 barrels in 1889 to 8,400,000 in 1893 to 13,900,000 in 1899 to 15,100,000 in 1901. The state's natural gas production, substantially a development of the late nineties, was valued at $2,960,000 in 1900, $5,390,000 in 1902, ranking third in both years behind Pennsylvania and Indiana. And the spectacular growth in extractive industry seemed matched by the increasing volume of manufacturing. The value of manufacturing output grew by 93.4 percent during the nineties, compared to a 5.1 percent increase in the decade 1870-1880. Manufacturing employment rose to triple the 1870 figures, representing an 1889-1899 increase of one-third. West Virginia held its own in such traditionally important industries as glassmaking and iron and steel, while adding an important new one in the manufacture of coke.[87]

Yet if these data revealed the quickened pace of West Virginia's growth, others amply illustrated the tributary nature of the industrial economy that emerged. Most revealing was the allocation of the most recently unlocked treasure, natural gas. Half of the natural gas produced in West Virginia in 1900 was exported to other states. Two years later the proportion was 55 percent and was climbing. Among other major gas producers, Pennsylvania and Indiana consumed nearly as much as they produced. Ohio consumed twice as much as it extracted, importing most of the surplus from West Virginia.[88] Apart from the already established pottery, glass, and iron and steel industries of the Northern Panhandle, the chief beneficiaries of this particular "boundless" resource were the manufacturers and consumers of other states. The same was true of the coal and timber, although here West Virginia often handled rudimentary processing before shipment. A federal geologist estimated in 1910 that "more than

50 per cent of the coal mined in the state is shipped away to support manufacturing industries in other states," not including the tonnage first turned into coke at the mines and then shipped.[89] Among the forest industries, the state could boast only six paper and pulp mills in 1900, which together produced 50 tons of fine quality writing paper, 1,500 tons of wrapping paper and 3,500 tons of cardboard. The principal product, 112,000 tons of raw wood pulp, was exported to the paper mills of the northeastern states.[90]

The marginal character of West Virginia manufacturing was disclosed in the position of the state's ten leading industries, which collectively accounted for between 64 and 67 percent of *all* manufacturing investment, employment, wages, and value of production in the state.[91] Four of the ten (coke, leather, lumber, and planing mill products), including two of the four largest employers, were labor-intensive primary industries closely related to the extraction of coal and timber. Only the tanneries involved the import of products for local processing, but the leather produced was then shipped out for final fabrication by the shoe and saddlery manufacturers of the North.

In three other industries (flour milling, machine shop and foundry products, clay products), the state's national rank failed to match their local importance. The exception was pottery, which with brick and tile making fell under the clay products category. West Virginia's fourteen manufacturers made it the eighth ranking state in the Union in pottery production, but as all of these were located in Wheeling or other long-established pottery centers in the Northern Panhandle they were hardly characteristic of the state at large.[92] More revealing was the character of flour industry, which in terms of the value of production was the third ranking industry of the state. Only forty of seven hundred-odd flour or gristmills were engaged exclusively in the production of commercial flour. Of the rest, 139 were partly and 558 fully neighborhood "custom and exchange" gristmills, whose seasonal and casual economic character is further revealed by the fact that the average annual number of workers employed was less than the total number of establishments. West Virginia ranked 25th nationally in the production of flour, with an average daily output of 8 barrels, compared to 234 barrels in Minnesota, 33 in Ohio, 25 in Kentucky, and 18 in Virginia. In terms of the local industry's freight expenditures, a measure of the extent of specialization and export, West Virginia ranked 37th, just behind the Indian Territory.[93]

The three remaining major industries—comprising the first (iron and steel), sixth (railroad car construction and repair shops), and seventh (glass) largest in terms of employment—represented the type of capital-intensive, stable, and profitable manufacturing envisioned by the development faith. Yet here, too, qualifications are in order. Despite the increasing inroads of absentee ownership, iron and steel held its ground compared with earlier periods, both in terms of the number of producers and the state's national rank (eighth). But West Virginia produced none of the industry's bread-and-butter products: steel rails, structural shapes, bars, rods, and armor plate. Instead the local specialities were cheaper producers' goods—barrel hoops and cotton ties—or ingots that could be shipped to fabricators elsewhere. The firms that later came together to form Wheeling Steel specialized in corrugated and galvanized sheet metal.[94] Significantly, the state had no manufacturers of electrical equipment or supplies, nor any of the bicycle, agricultural implement, or metal working machinery producers that provided initial advantage in the important automotive industries of the twentieth century. Nor had it any building glass manufacturers. West Virginia produced only 2 percent of the pressed glass made in the United States, compared to 56 percent of Pennsylvania and the 23 of Ohio. Even in tableware, where West Virginia ranked second only to Pennsylvania, it specialized in the less valuable products. In blown glassware, the average value per dozen pieces of West Virginia products was $0.17 compared to Pennsylvania's $0.31 and Ohio's $0.25. The corresponding figures for cut glassware were $1.23, $5.48 and $43.45.[95]

This left only the railroad shops of Huntington, Bluefield, and Martinsburg to justify all that had gone before in the name of development. Moreover, the most profitable industries, along with *all* manufacturing enterprises, were extremely localized. Wheeling and Benwood, an industrial suburb located immediately south of Wheeling in Marshall County, accounted for 32 percent of West Virginia's manufacturing investment in 1900, 31 percent of the employment, 34 percent of wages, and 37 percent of the value of output. For the four Northern Panhandle counties, the corresponding figures were around 40 percent, for the twelve counties along the Ohio River, 60 percent. As the Census Bureau drily reported, "Manufactures in West Virginia are very largely located in the northern part of the state and along the Ohio River. . . . This localization . . . was shown also at the census of 1860. . . ."[96]

The principal later departure from this pattern was the growth of the chemical industries mentioned above. This development gave the state a more "favorable" industrial structure and in large part accounted for a growth in manufacturing employment that slightly exceeded national growth from 1904 to 1929. However, from 1929 to 1954, West Virginia's growth in manufacturing employment fell behind the national rate by a roughly equivalent amount, one reason being that petrochemicals absorbed most of the expansion in this industry and West Virginia's coal-based manufacturers entered into a period of relative stagnation, then decline. On the whole, Victor R. Fuch's authoritative study of manufacturing growth and locational changes attributes to twentieth century West Virginia the stability vis-a-vis the national performance that characterized its neighbors to the north. The principal difference was that Ohio, Pennsylvania, Maryland, and Delaware already enjoyed a high level of manufacturing development when their rates of expansion fell back toward the national means. West Virginia did not, and at the same time, it lacked the locational pulls that have enabled the states of the South and West dramatically to increase their share of the national manufacturing plant since 1929.[97] In other words, though West Virginia continued to get its share of national growth in manufacturing after 1900, the most dramatic local changes had already occurred. And since the chemical industries also had their antebellum analogs in the Kanawha valley salt and coal oil industries, the pattern of localization of industry within the state was never greatly disturbed.[98] Those parts of the state that benefited most from industrialization were precisely those that had advanced furthest while part of Virginia. Which suggests that—whatever other arguments one might summon to the defense of West Virginia's separate existence—economic development was not one of them. Rather the state developed along lines of initial advantages and disadvantages fully realized under the antebellum regime.

Industrialization brought marked improvements in living standards in West Virginia, increased the speed of movement and communication, and offered residents previously bound to tedious lives in the mountains increased options in places to live and ways to get and spend money. These were dramatic changes but so were those in the rest of the country. By most calculations of progress, West Virginia barely kept up with the national pace of improvement while failing to break out of its marginal and tributary position within the national economic system. Thus in terms of their expectations, the boomers' utopia failed to materialize. What went wrong? Equally to the point, were there alternatives to the disappointing type of growth that took place?

One thing that went wrong was that the West Virginia hills and mountains failed to disappear. The state developed in the context of a continental economic system possessed of abundant land better suited to the intensive and extensive uses of modern urban-industrial society. Thus an historian of the glass industry writes of a bottle factory established by one of the Toledo manufacturers at Fairmont, West Virginia, in 1910, "Wind currents sweeping down the mountain interfered with the furnace drafts, and annual spring floods frequently caused the creek to rise and extinguish all fires at the factory." Although a majority of the company's directors recommended alternative sites in New Jersey, the choice of

179

the Fairmont site and that of another "relatively useless" plant at Clarksburg is attributable to the impulsiveness and obstinacy of Michael J. Owens, who was attracted by the local supplies of cheap natural gas. The same attraction brought West Virginia a more successful Owens plate glass factory near Charleston in 1917 (although not before the Toledo managers of the firm snapped up the gas leaseholds that furnished the fuel supply).[99] But firms whose managers had none of Owens's affection for his native state tended to be more hardheaded. The supplies of energy in which West Virginia abounded, whether derived from fossil fuels or water power, had the long-term effect of liberating manufacturers from the space-intensive industrial buildings of the steam-power era: hence the sprawling factories of present-day suburbia.[100] West Virginia's narrow bottomlands and hollows were ill suited to the extensive use of space, however, while overhead and distribution costs were further increased by a railroad network whose thinness and higher charges reflected the cost of railroad construction in mountain terrain. Davis, for example, engaged in lengthy negotiations with officials of the inappropriately named West Virginia Pulp & Paper Company for a mill site on the West Virginia Central near the point where the railroad tapped the spruce and hardwood forests of Pocahontas and Randolph counties. But the firm eventually chose a site along the C&O main line in Virginia, where its distribution costs would be lower than Davis could promise, just as it had located its initial mill in Maryland along the B&O.[101] Some combinations of fuel and raw materials costs did influence certain industries to settle in West Virginia, the most notable instance being the chemicals producers. In general, however, it was cheaper and more efficient for national corporations to bring the fuels and raw materials to the factories rather than take the factories to West Virginia. Local firms, of course, had to deal with these same disadvantages, to which was added the burden of competition with stronger nonresident rivals.

The barriers to prosperity presented by the terrain will be readily apparent to anyone who compares a modern highway

map of West Virginia or a nineteenth century railroad map—
or, for that matter, a map showing the distribution of Indian
and pioneer settlements in preindustrial times—to a map of
the surrounding lowland states. It is equally apparent why
West Virginians failed to accept the equation between "backwardness" and their hills. For the scenic beauty of the mountains and the peculiar virtues with which mountain men are
often endowed by romance and legend offered a rich sym-
bolic source of native sentiment and pride. It was one thing
to boast that "Mountaineers are always free," quite another
to admit that they are also generally poor. In failing to confront the realities of their environment, the boomers embraced the sentiment of Blake's couplet—

Great things are done when Men & Mountains meet

while rejecting the poet's logic—

This is not done by Jostling in the Street.

In an age when the most profitable industries were becoming increasingly concentrated in the largest metropolitan centers, West Virginia managed to harvest most of the ills of
urbanism with few of its advantages. According to Census
Bureau definitions, it remained a rural state, with only 13
percent of its people in places of 2,500 or more in 1900, 19
percent in 1910. Yet such statistics were misleading. Of
245,000 nonagricultural workers over ten years of age in
West Virginia in 1910, 81,000—or roughly one-third—were
employed as wage earners or salaried personnel in the three
main extractive industries: coal (accounting for 75 percent of
the second figure), forest and lumber products (20 percent)
and oil and gas (5 percent).[102] The great majority of these
can be assumed to have lived in small communities near the
sites of extraction, places that rarely achieved urban status
but which duplicated certain urban conditions. "The only
thing beautiful about Eskdale was its name," recalled a miner
of a coal camp as it appeared in 1912. "It was smoky, sooty,
and grimy. The constant puff of railway locomotives, the
crash and grind of engines, cars, and trains, night and day,
produced an atmosphere similar to that surrounding one of
the great steel centers like Homestead, Youngstown, or Pitts-

181

burgh." The place had less than 2,500 people, but it was hardly the white-picketed, tree-shaded place America thinks of as the old home town. Still "Eskdale was incorporated," that is, it was "private property," not a company town. On neighboring Paint Creek in Kanawha County "No private property existed above Mucklow. The coal corporations owned the creek from the first mine to the last, nearly 20 miles of it and from ridge to ridge." Here one encountered none of the privacy or autonomy of urban workers and consumers. The miner worked for the company, was paid in scrip that could be traded only at the company store, rented a company house and came and went by permission of the company's private police or "mine guards."[103] There was, of course, another view of the matter:

> The Solvay Collieries Company [of Syracuse, New York] owns about four thousand acres of territory in Fayette County, West Virginia, . . . Upon this land is built, building, and under operation, four colliery plants, requiring about five miles of railroad and yards, two steel tipples and conveyors, a large stone power house, about one hundred well built and attractive tenements, school house, church and other structures. At an expense closely approximating one million dollars, the Solvay Collieries Company is maintaining these model plants, and about three hundred operatives, with families, a population approximating 800 souls. Its operatives are happy and contented.

So ran an appeal to Governor "Henry [sic]" Glasscock to protect this splendid property from designs of "an anarchial [sic] or socialistic spirit."[104] Quite apart from the merits of either description, in economic terms the scattering of purchasing power among consumers in hundreds of West Virginia localities deprived local manufacturers and distributors of the economies of scale that an urban home market could provide. Consumers paid the company stores prices that ranged as much as 60 percent higher than competitive prices and in all cases "more than a fair average figure," according to an investigating commission headed in 1912 by the Roman Catholic Bishop of Wheeling, while the operators claimed "but a modest profit" when their overhead "especially freight is taken into account." There was thus much "jostling" in West Virginia, but few of the "great things" associated either with mountains or with city streets.[105]

West Virginia's topographical barriers to economic maturity could not be whistled away by slogans like "The Switzerland of America." But the slogan did contain the germ of an alternative. In White Sulphur and Berkeley Springs and other spas taken from Virginia in 1863, the state possessed at least the beginnings of a resort industry, to which local railroad builders, including Davis, Elkins, and Camden, made modest attempts to add.[106] Unfortunately, if nature outfitted the state as a Switzerland, the practices and attitudes of its developers were better suited to a Silesia. The Kanawha River had turned "from a beautiful, pellucid watercourse into a muddy sewer," complained the Charleston *Gazette* in 1910, but the editor was less concerned with "the sentimental convenient or healthful phase of the question," than with the effect of pollution on navigation or "the higher and greater question of commerce and transportation."[107] Following Theodore Roosevelt's lead, Governor Dawson appointed a three-man Conservation Commission, one member of which was a coal operator and the chairman a professional development publicist, to deal with some of these problems and also to promote "the highest development with the least waste." One of the commission's first acts was to seek the guidance of A. B. Fleming, whose attitude toward nature was fully revealed when local courts prohibited the drainage of sulphurous mine "run off" into the streams. Seeking to remedy this defect in the laws, Fleming was astonished to encounter the opposition of MacCorkle, who not only was "opposed to the pollution of the streams &c &c" but threatened, as a member of the state senate in 1913, to kill Fleming's legislative solution. "I think the riot act should be read to them," Fleming wrote to Clarence Watson, referring to MacCorkle and W. E. Chilton of the Kanawha Ring.[108] It was, and the orange and acrid run-off again flowed freely into the "bounding mountain streams" of America's Switzerland. Some Swit-

183

zerland! It is perhaps revealing of some aspects of the development faith that Joseph Diss Debar, the coiner of the Swiss analogy, ended his career in prison, convicted in New York as a confidence man operating in partnership with a woman who claimed to be the daughter of mad King Ludwig and Lola Montez.[109]

An equally improbable alternative was that of the West Virginia Tax Commission of 1884—or rather one of its three members, James Murray Mason, who was the son of the Virginia senator and Confederate diplomat of the same name. Mason's idea, from which the two other commissioners largely dissociated themselves, was that the disappointing pattern of growth was chiefly the fault of absentee ownership. Nonresident owners extracted and shipped the boundless resources in the most reckless and haphazard way, or else let them lie fallow while pressuring politically for the regressive tax structure and cheap labor that were deemed essential to attract private developmental capital. To correct this pattern, he proposed higher taxes and a tax-based development fund, gathered by the state and distributed by a special development commission. In this way essential overhead would be provided without the drawback of outside control "and the profits, now being reaped by the strangers, [would be] gathered by those who live within our borders, and who are permanently identified with the fortunes of the State."[110]

Mason presented only a sketchy outline of his idea, but it bears an obvious resemblance to the variants of state capitalism that characterized the development of such late-coming industrial revolutionaries as Imperial France, Czarist Russia, or Meiji Japan, variants aptly described in the case of Napoleon III's *Credit Mobilier* as "the socialist garment draped around an essentially capitalist frame."[111] In the West Virginia context, however, the scheme was nothing so much as a throwback to the state-sponsored improvement programs of antebellum times and was thus in accord with Mason's Redeemer antecedents. It was also in accord with his contemporary reputation of being something of a stock jobber, which—at least in connection with the Virginia debt in-

184

trigues—he was.[112] Consequently the scheme attracted little attention at the time. Even if it had, given the levels of planning and equity at which it would probably have been executed in West Virginia, it might have amounted to little more than a consolation fund for those survivors and heirs of the antebellum elite who could not accept their displacement by the new ruling class. Mason's son, "a typical southerner" and the third of the name, manifested a more realistic adjustment when he came to the defense of the labor leaders indicted for treason during the "mine wars" of 1921-1922.[113]

Notwithstanding its improbable character, the Mason proposal raises some interesting questions. Did "the *home* or original owners" of the boundless resources have some sort of superior claim over "strangers" in their exploitation? It was suggested earlier that the antebellum elite accumulated its holdings of western Virginia land through manipulation of the political system in ways that were no more (or less) genteel in their context than the methods for which Mason II expressed aristocratic disdain in 1884.[114] But apart from the sour grapes, were the local disadvantages of absentee ownership outweighed by the national benefits that were gained by the Appalachian region's specialization in extractive industry? A whole school of economists who are devoted to the idea that regional specialization provided the key to successful national growth would answer, "Yes."[115] In any event, the complaint of a colonial economy seems rather archaic. Today we are all colonists in our relationship as employees and consumers to large, anonymous business bureaucracies whose management is divorced from ownership and whose thousands of workers in a hundred locations reflect no allegiance of place. What difference who was colonized first?

It made some difference in terms of those factors of institutionalized advantage that have made Pittsburgh or Wilmington "headquarters cities" long after the locational advantages in the industries concerned have shifted elsewhere. The white collar employment generated by the growth of managerial bureaucracies, with all of the secondary social and economic linkages that flow therefrom, remained in the metropolis,

185

even though the production centers scattered across the nation and, indeed, the globe.[116] For places like West Virginia this entailed a drain of talent and leadership that was not compensated by the rotation of transient managerial personnel. "Wheeling's greatest loss, through the orgy of mergers, was in skilled executives," writes the historian of Wheeling Steel. Each new consolidation sent local business—and civic—leaders to Pittsburgh, Cleveland, or New York.[117] The same phenomenon may be observed in the movement of the most capable Camden or Davis-Elkins subordinates to the metropolitan centers, along with most of the senators' offspring. James A. Moffet, for example, a foreman at Camden's Parkersburg plant, went on to a Cleveland refinery and rose through the Standard Oil hierarchy to a vice-presidency and directorship in 1901, becoming the highest paid employee of the firm outside of the inner circle of founding trustees and their heirs. The migration of human capital for which West Virginia became famous as coalfield refugees moved into the slums of northern cities in the mid-twentieth century would seem to have begun much earlier with the elite.[118] "It's not the people a state loses that matter," writes a modern patriot, "it's who it gets in their place."[119] That may be. But the fact is that West Virginia became known by the natives who left.

Pointing up the contrast between the British plunder of India with the indigenous development of capitalism in Japan, the Marxist scholar, Paul Baran, conceded that resident capitalists were no less exploitative than their imperialist counterparts. The difference was that Japanese wealth stayed home to develop a higher standard of living and the military power that earned Tokyo a place at the worldwide banquet of resources.[120] Such analogies are of limited use in an intranational context, but it is perhaps appropriate to notice one aspect of American capitalism that was often used to justify the corporate elite's hegemony. West Virginia fared poorly in philanthropy. A team of University of Wisconsin scholars who attempted to evaluate statistically the reputation of rich Americans for abundant giving have been unable to discover

186

sufficient data to prove or disprove this claim. It does appear, however, that apart from those few benefactors who gave on the scale of Rockefeller or Carnegie, most philanthropists underwrote projects in their local communities.[121] This was true of Davis, Elkins, Camden, and Scott, who account for all but one of the millionaires attributed to West Virginia by two authoritative lists compiled in 1892 and 1902. The Davis and Elkins College endowment mentioned earlier was valued at $180,000 in 1929, to which should be added the two mansions bequeathed to the institution. Davis also endowed a church and hospital in Elkins and a children's home in Charleston, Camden gave to churches and the YMCA, Scott to a Wheeling hospital. Two emigre industrialists, Earl W. Oglebay of Cleveland and M. L. Benedum of Pittsburgh, also established noteworthy claims on the public gratitude in their native Mountain State.[122] But no tycoon emerged in West Virginia to play the role of Hopkins or Pratt in Baltimore, Carnegie in Pittsburgh, or Mott in Flint. The boundless resources left no great universities or museums or libraries or welfare organizations or other philanthropic monuments to mark the current of the golden stream. Whether the profits from West Virginia fuels helped to erect such monuments elsewhere would be a difficult if not impossible question to answer. Presumably they formed a part of the Rockefeller bounties and perhaps helped to buy the Toledo Museum's splendid collection of antique glass. Philanthropy provides a relatively crude measure of civic responsibility, but such as it is, its weak imprint in West Virginia suggests that the social loss due to absentee ownership was very real.

On the whole, however, it is to be doubted that resident ownership would have eliminated the most glaring evils—the violence, poverty, and human dislocation for which West Virginia became notorious during the twentieth century. These derived from a complex of factors, some of which flowed from the economy's dependence upon the coal industry and the character of that industry, others from the nature of the land and the state's much-touted central location.[123]

Demand for bituminous coal was inelastic both in terms of price and national income. That is to say, a lowering of prices failed to stimulate increased sales during short-run dislocations, and though bituminous production expanded steadily between 1891 and 1910 more or less in tandem with the growth of national income, thereafter it met increasing competition from other fuels in the energy market. Entering around 1910 upon a more erratic version of a boom-and-bust cycle that had always been present, bituminous production expanded steadily to give the industry an annual capacity of 970,000,000 tons by 1923 for a market that had peaked at 579,000,000 tons in 1918. Other conditions that contributed to this imbalance included the growth of "captive mines" operated by large consumers (principally railroads and steel producers), shipping practices by which railroad cars were allotted to operators on the basis of their capacity, and the drastic level of depreciation in an underground mine when it is idled. Moreover, the industry was characterized by a poor performance in increasing productivity, even by comparison with metallic mining industries that worked underground.[124]

Much of coal's overexpansion took place in West Virginia and eastern Kentucky. Southern West Virginia contains the geographic center of the Appalachian coalfields, but the geographic center of actual *production* did not reach there until 1940. With respect to the most lucrative coal markets in the northeastern and Great Lakes industrial regions, the state's location was marginal.[125] In contrast to the older producing regions of Maryland, Pennsylvania, Ohio, Indiana, and Illinois, West Virginia producers had no home market to speak of, especially before the introduction of by-product coke ovens and the coal tar derivatives chemicals industry during World War I. Local operators' shipping costs were higher and their margin of profit lower than was true of their competitors.[126]

Both consolidation and unionization—and the greater stability flowing therefrom—proceeded more rapidly in the older producing states. The United Mine Workers Union was well established in the "Central Competitive Field" of Ohio,

Indiana, Illinois, and western Pennsylvania by 1900, but its success in introducing and stabilizing higher wage rates there was repeatedly undercut by its inability to organize the miners of West Virginia.[127] Similarly, consolidation by 1903 placed control of nearly half of U.S. production in the hands of twenty-five large firms, but only three of these (Fairmont, Western Maryland, Pocahontas) were to be found in West Virginia. Large firms produced less than half of the state's total output, as opposed to two-thirds or more in Ohio and Pennsylvania.[128] At the same time there was a noticeable drift of smaller producers that combination bought or forced out of the northern fields to eastern Kentucky and southern West Virginia. While the Community of Interest was able to slow this trend by promoting further combinations and by refusing cars or loading facilities to new or marginal producers, the *Engineering and Mining Journal* in 1902 correctly predicted its inability to halt it: "our bituminous fields are far too extensive and too widely scattered to make it probable that they can be controlled by a single trust or combination." Thus one of the Clarksburg firms that had been bought out recently by the Fairmont Coal Company appeared in McDowell County on the N&W in February 1902. The movement of Davis and Elkins into central West Virginia after the sale of their original properties was another case in point, as was Camden's entry into eastern Kentucky.[129]

The ease with which West Virginia coal could be mined once the state was penetrated by railroads, plus lower wage scales, compensated the local operators' greater distance from markets, but these factors, in turn, intensified the environmental and human impact of the coal industry. Coal measures lying exposed on the hillsides of the Allegheny plateau could be readily exploited by drift mines instead of the costlier shafts, while the surrounding forests provided abundant lumber for mine timbers and general construction purposes. However, deforestation greatly increased the danger of flooding in the narrow valleys, and the initial assault on the lower and more accessible seams of coal sometimes led to fractures of the measures above, causing wastage or increasing the temptation of strip-mining later on.[130]

At the same time, the remote and thinly populated character of the West Virginia fields virtually dictated the building of company towns to house the work force, while the marginal position of many operators intensified their determination to lower overhead costs at the mines by exploiting these captive communities. The operators of West Virginia, particularly in the southern part of the state, offered savage resistance to unionization, setting off a series of bloody "mine wars" that lasted from 1912 through the 1930s. As for the company houses and stores, census enumerators found in 1909 "not a few" operators who admitted to selling their coal at a loss and making up the difference in their mercantile and real estate profits.[131] By the 1920s some 80 percent of West Virginia's miners lived in company towns, as opposed to 64 percent in Kentucky and 9 percent in Indiana and Illinois. The United States Coal Commission, surveying 708 of these towns in 1922, near the end of a prosperous period, found generally unwholesome living conditions existing in most of them, with the worst examples in West Virginia and eastern Kentucky.[132]

Here and there through the hills were scattered the model communities whose praises were canted in apologists' literature.[133] More common were sylvan Siberias, however, though feudal analogies were more often used to describe them than totalitarian ones. "In the worst of the company-controlled communities," reported the Coal Commission, "the state of disrepair at times runs beyond the power of verbal description or even photographic illustration, since neither words nor pictures can portray the atmosphere of abandoned dejection or reproduce the smells."[134] Again the evil was less glaring where larger and stabler firms controlled. The West Virginia state commission headed by Bishop Donahue in 1912, which "spent most of its time chasing the bogy of socialism," according to a UMW organizer, nonetheless condemned the company towns generally. But it had warm words for the Fairmont (formerly Camden) company town at

190

Monongah, which boasted higher wages, decent housing, competitive stores, and no guards.[135] Davis and Elkins built company towns and stores throughout the West Virginia Central region, but where conditions permitted, as in their town of Elkins, they preferred to confine this sideline to the sale of building lots and the control of hotels and public utilities. Home-owning workers were stabler and better ones, their partner, Kerens, explained.[136] They also inhibited the more ferocious instincts of their subordinates during labor troubles. "I doubt whether it will result in good to at once proceed with the eviction of the tenants," Davis told Landstreet during a strike in 1894. "It appears to me that if I was a tenant, and my goods should be taken out and left in the street, that I would become more desperate than I otherwise would be, and would be more likely to commit unlawful acts. . . ."[137]

Other West Virginia operators more often learned this insight the hard way, if they learned it at all. Moreover, while the larger firms put up a stiff and successful resistance to unionization during the period under study, Elkins had to be talked out of recognizing the UMW by Landstreet in 1901. That the senator's temptation was political in origin is suggested by the fact that the union later scored a peaceful, albeit temporary, advance in northern West Virginia as a by-product of the Davis Elkins-Watson senatorial contest in the election of 1918. This pattern suggests that where firms were larger and their owners more aware of or responsive to local conditions, those conditions were less exploitative.[138] But the difference was only a relative one. Mercantile and real estate profits returned a higher rate on investment to Davis and Elkins than any of their other enterprises, while Davis never forgot that "You can control labor better [at towns like Elkins] than at larger towns."[139] The Fairmont Company's model plant at Monongah produced one of the greatest mine disasters in American history on December 6, 1907, when an explosion claimed 361 lives. And though the company itself admitted that the cost of a "reasonable relief to the sufferers" would run at least to $300,000, no more than a third of this amount was actually paid.[140] When the Austro-Hungarian consul later protested the trifling amounts paid to his nationals among the survivors, Fleming coldly informed him that

> . . . the Company has never contributed anything to persons living here or abroad otherwise than as a gratuity or donation. The Company never for a moment considered that it was legally liable. . . . I think the $2000.00 distributed principally amoung 41 children and 20 widows would be quite a Christmas present.

"I know the Company is not to blame," wrote a native survivor to "my friend Governor Fleming" some years later, "but the manner in which [his son] died, and amid all my troubles, the family was poor they have lived in my [word missing] ever since his death. . . . I paid $92.00 for his head mark, $23.00 in the Bank he owed. I was his surety." The man, a Mr. Snodgrass, wanted further assistance, but whether he got it is unclear. "I am not so vary Stout at present," he added, but "I am trying to make a living by my labor. . . . I will be 81 years of age next Tuesday."[141] It is in such terms as these as well as in the aggregate figures of wages and profits that the industrial fate of West Virginia must be weighed.

To the extent that protectionists were right in claiming that tariff reform would retard the growth of West Virginia mining, the liberal Democrats led by William L. Wilson offered another alternative, although it would have been fatal for them to cast their program in that light. Similarly, the labor organizers offered stability and security at the probable expense of higher costs and thus a smaller share of the market. But so long as the premier article of local patriotism insisted that the rapid development of West Virginia's resources was the key to a prosperous future, neither the liberals nor labor could succeed. All parties involved were the prisoners of a vicious circle. In the broadest terms, West Virginia was the victim of a technological lag between the development of transportation facilities and the development of automated mining equipment and a political lag pending the

192

replacement of laisser-faire attitudes by the acceptance of stabilization under federal auspices at the end of the New Deal. The interval called into being haphazard and wasteful growth and a larger work force than Appalachian conditions could support in the long run. Then after a brief interlude of prosperity during and after World War II, the union and the coal corporations entered into collaboration to liquidate the surplus working population of West Virginia and eastern Kentucky. Those who were young and healthy enough to leave, left. The rest stayed on to rot on the hillsides. The whole long sad story was nobody's fault—and everyone's tragedy.[142]

It was also how the system worked. Confronted by the Appalachian environment, both the developers and their prophets failed to make essential adjustments in their thinking and methods. West Virginia was not the only place this happened. It happened in the Southwest, the Great Plains, the Cotton South, and everywhere that natural and social conditions failed to yield to the capitalist equation of private good and public welfare. Within the capitalist framework, the men of the times could find meaning in the tonnage of coal produced or the prices of town lots, but they lacked the tools to balance these measurements of "progress" by projections of the future's spoiled hopes and wounded pride.

The early twentieth century saw the presentation of two further alternatives, a systematic one and one that accepted the capitalist framework but sought to make some adjustments within it. The Socialist Party appeared in West Virginia in 1904 and increased its share of the presidential vote from a trace of just under 6 percent in 1912. The "Reds" further claimed up to a fifth of the vote in Wheeling and Charleston, elected mayors and other local officials in a few smaller industrial and mining districts, and published at least five newspapers in the largest cities of the state. In 1914 socialist insurgents won control of District 17 of the UMW and held it until John L. Lewis and Van Bittner removed them in 1924. Briefly too the state Federation of Labor affiliated with the party or one of its successors. This pattern of Socialist

193

growth before and during World War I and subsequent decline appears comparable to what took place on the national level: initial success followed by repression and internal fragmentation in the face of the issues generated by war and the Bolshevist Revolution.[143]

That the Socialists would have proved any less aggressive toward nature than their bourgeois contemporaries may be doubted. What they did offer was the prospect of economic planning geared to humane values, which suggests at least the possibility of mitigating the Appalachian tragedy that did occur. Of more immediate impact was their ability to couple a sense of the grievances of miners and other workingmen with a conviction that these grievances flowed from the system rather than from individual failures or short-term circumstances. Whether, given freedom from repression and immunity from world events, the Socialists could have propagated these views among the mass of small proprietors or even among a majority of the propertyless is a moot question. One thing is certain: the aspiring middle class citizens of West Virginia could have profited from the Socialist idea that the disappointment of their economic hopes was an occasion for anger, not for shame.

The alternatives so far discussed would have required for their implementation a greater degree of realism, less materialism, or more radicalism among West Virginians than among the residents of other states. The alternative that came closest to adoption did not. It required only an awareness that the golden age was not materializing, that the boundless resources were being taken out as swiftly and recklessly as possible and that "after they are gone we will have only the worthless lands now yielding them, without the benefits they ought to give us as the golden stream flows out."[144] Such convictions grew in volume and intensity after the turn of the century as aspiring citizens confronted the work of the consolidation movement and were aroused by the "progressive" mood that settled over the nation at large. The development faith was not abandoned, but was merely given a new twist—resentment toward those "outside interests" who were interfering with the growth of a mature economy as God had planned it.[145] But the only outlet for this resentment was through the political institutions of the state, and these were securely under the control of the industrialists. Consequently, the impulse first ran up against a remarkable display of conservative power and then reappeared in milder form on a platform written by Davis and manned by the Elkins political organization. The result was one of the most unusual episodes of West Virginia history, but it featured one essen tial element of continuity. In both its insurgent and authorized versions, the progressive movement in West Virginia failed.

6

Reaction and Reform

As the political fate of West Virginia hung in the balance between 1888 and 1900, the public interest languished. The seven legislative sessions[1] between 1889 and 1899 enacted few items of significant legislation. Partly this was due to the preoccupation of all politicians in both parties with such things as ballot laws, election districts, the creation of new offices—anything that might tip the narrow balance of power their way. Another factor was the development faith, which discouraged interference with the process of industrialization, the source of most of the state's problems. Confronted with an increase in the number of mine inspectors by the legislature of 1897, Governor MacCorkle shrank in distaste. "The greatness of West Virginia is founded upon our coal," he stated. "Can the Legislature of West Virginia afford to do anything that would impede, hamper or hinder the progress of this great industry within the borders of our State? Can we afford, for mere political effect or political place, to interfere with our commercial greatness?"[2] These attitudes were reinforced when needed by the lobbying efforts of the corporate retainers. In response to Governor Wilson's call for reform legislation to the special session of 1890, Camden, the trunk line railroads, and the Pocahontas and Fairmont coal interests, assembled a fleet of persuaders headed by Randolph Stalnaker and J. B. Sommerville.[3] Davis and Elkins, preoccupied with national politics and policies at this point, stood apart from these proceedings, probably because they realized that the legislators would occupy themselves with purely political matters and then adjourn. Camden assured them that this would happen, and it did.[4]

All this was to change by the end of the century. Having achieved their national policy objectives and in the process of placing their enterprises under the control or influence of the metropolitan corporations, the industrialists could afford to pay more attention to local policy matters than they had earlier done. Moreover, this redirection of interest was not wholly a matter of choice. Other pressure groups, notably organized labor, which had acquired some lobbying experience of its own during the intervening decade, were regularly putting forward legislative programs. Not least in importance was the fact that some of the earlier checks to legislative action had weakened. The development faith was as strong as ever, but the seeds of heretical interpretations had been planted by the depression and the trusts. Legislators were still interested in offices and election districts, but the era of political suspense was over. A host of public problems, particularly financial ones, clamored for attention, and the victorious Republicans could no longer escape the responsibility of dealing with them. Those factors made the twenty-fifth session of the West Virginia Legislature in 1901 one of the most critical in the history of the state. Triumphant over rival factionalists in both political parties, the captains of industry now turned their consolidated power to impressive use.

First it is worth examining the sort of government West Virginia enjoyed during the decades preceding the 1901 session. Most revealing were three items in the appropriation bill passed by the legislature of 1893: $25,000 for an exhibit at the Chicago World's Fair, $10,000 for a statue of Senator Kenna, $50,000 for the state university. The first two items were subsequently reduced. Kenna's timely death, it will be recalled, had spared the ruling Democrats another grueling senatorial struggle; thus this otherwise unremarkable lawmaker was to be given West Virginia's niche in Statuary Hall in Washington, but it was decided that $5,000 would do the job. The World's Fair appropriation, in deference to farm county legislators who thought that the developers should themselves pay for showing off their wares, was shaved to $20,000.[5] The university appropriation, the largest in history, emerged unscathed. Indeed, in the most vigorously debated action of the session, the legislature voted an increase in the public school levy. But Governor Fleming found this "inexpedient" and vetoed the bill on his last day in office.[6]

In its way, however, the 1893 session marked a turning point. It enacted few items of what the industrialists termed "hostile legislation," but there were important distinctions in the nature and origin of objectionable bills. Formerly most of the pressure against corporations originated with the Democratic Agrarians. Such men as E. Willis Wilson and Daniel B. Lucas empathized with industrial workers as well as with rural constituents; Wilson had introduced the first comprehensive mine safety and inspection bill in the legislature of 1877, and Lucas rendered an important decision in the miners' behalf after Wilson made him a state supreme court justice in 1890.[7] But the rural backgrounds and old-fashioned style of these leaders made it easy to lump them in Camden's category of "those 'yahoos' who stand in the way of all improvements and decency,"[8] while except for railroad regulation and national issues like the tariff and monetary questions, anticorporation feeling was negative and diffuse, difficult to embody in specific items of legislation. The goals of labor, in contrast, were positive and concrete. Then, too, labor influence was on the upswing as the advance of industrialism increased the number of workingmen, while the Agrarian fortunes were tied to the shrinking rural bases of the Democratic party. That even unsympathetic legislators were disposed to treat this new and expanding constituency gingerly is suggested by the lopsided margins by which the handful of early labor enactments passed. The legislature of 1883, while eschewing anything as precise and comprehensive as Wilson's earlier bill, wrote a rudimentary mine safety law and established the office of mine inspector. Subsequent revisions of the law in 1887 and 1889 increased the number of inspectors, prohibited the employment of children under twelve, and created the office of labor commissioner. The 1887 session also outlawed the use of "scrip" in payment of miners' wages and compulsory trading at company stores. The supreme court subsequently struck down the scrip law, but the

198

legislature of 1891 reenacted it, along with a "screen" law requiring the weighing of coal (upon which basic wages were calculated) before it was sifted. Apart from the Senate's relatively narrow approval of the basic mining law of 1883 and the Scrip Act four years later, the typical votes on such items (18-0, 15-4, 62-3, 44-1, 46-1) gave no hint of the controversy surrounding them.[9] The fact was, of course, that the more "dangerous" or effective proposals were tabled or killed in committees or, in the case of the screen and scrip laws of 1891, confidently sent on to be killed in the courts. Thanks to Lucas and another recently seated justice, however, the Supreme Court of Appeals sustained both laws in a pair of 2-2 decisions in 1892, with Lucas providing a ringing declaration of the state's authority over corporations in each case.[10] Heartened by this development, pro-labor legislators, joined by lobbying delegations from Kanawha valley miners and Wheeling's Ohio Valley Trades and Labor Assembly, advanced another series of bills in 1893, covering the right to organize, compulsory arbitration, the eight-hour day, factory inspection, and a tightening of the child labor and screen and scrip laws.[11]

This time the labor forces met with stiff resistance. The Lucas decision and the spate of labor bills galvanized the mining corporations as the piecemeal legislation of the past had not done. Davis now made up for his earlier inattention. He instructed local legislators on the need for vigilance "in connection with the Labor question of the State . . ." and contributed to the war chest of the Kanawha Coal Exchange, organized by Charleston and New River operators to counter the union lobbyists.[12] Within two weeks—or two days, in some instances—the objectionable bills had been buried, with the exception of one bill raising the number of mine inspectors to three. So was the Chew railroad commission bill, making its sixth appearance since 1885, and other regulatory proposals aimed at railroads and pipelines.[13] "We believe we have effectually stopped legislation of this kind for some time to come," reported the president of the Coal Exchange to Davis.[14] Subsequent events proved the statement correct.

The line between labor and capital appeared in every session of the legislature thereafter, with similar results. The pigeonholed bills of 1893 were reintroduced two years later, to be read, amended, referred back and forth between committees—everything, in fact, but passed, or even (in most cases) voted upon.[15] "Labor asked for little," commented the Wheeling *Register* of this first Republican legislature in twenty-five years; "it got nothing."[16] Just to make certain, Davis dispatched Wood Dailey to Charleston, but Dailey found little to do there so far as labor legislation was concerned, although he and Elkins had to intervene in a quarrel between the C&O and its coal shippers over the railroad's coal marketing practices lest it lead to a dangerous legislative precedent.[17] In 1897, the scrip system (the 1891 law was evaded by using scrip as an advance against wages, i.e., as credit, instead of as currency) and the company stores underwent another vigorous and unsuccessful assault. "I am in constant communication with our friends and doing what I can do to repress this hurtful legislation," Elkins assured ex-Governor Fleming. So was Davis, while Fleming dispatched men of his own to join in the work.[18] Indeed the pressure of the lobbyists became so great that the delegates were forced to erect a barrier around their work space in order "to keep the talent off their backs."[19]

The only objectionable bill to escape in 1897, as in the past, was one adding to the force of mine inspectors, and this had more to do with politics than with the labor question. Although an historian of the West Virginia coal industry cites the multiplication of inspectorships as a barometer of progress, everyone at the time knew that this was merely a device to increase the number of political jobs. Ex-Governor Pierpont labelled the legislation of 1887 "a grim joke gotten up to pacify miners, to give an office, and in no way to offend mine owners."[20] W. H. Toler, union official and Republican delegate from Kanawha County, echoed these sentiments in 1895. When the legislature cut the inspectors' budget after nearly doubling that of the militia and rejecting all other proposals for an improved inspection program, Toler invited

200

it to dispense with the appropriation altogether: "If that item remained in the bill, it should be understood that the money was given as a pension to certain parties, and not for the benefit of the miners." The appropriation remained, but the inspectors were so strapped for funds that one of them applied to Davis for a railroad pass in order to be able to carry out his duties.[21] W. A. Ohley, lobbying for Fleming and the Fairmont interests in 1897, reported that the mine inspection bill had been suitably emasculated, "but it is the intention of the Republican bosses to pass some kind of a mine inspector's bill that will increase the number of inspectors to five—they want the extra offices." At Fleming's request, Governor MacCorkle vetoed the increase, "but that is all the good it did, for they passed it over my veto," as the legislators repassed other vetoed legislation increasing the patronage.[22] Governor Atkinson's appointee as chief mine inspector, J. W. Paul, like Labor Commissioner Barton, met the qualifications and approval of the workingmen.[23] But otherwise the labor program fared no better during his administration than it had before. Despite official backing in Atkinson's message to the legislature of 1899, the lobbyists of the Wheeling Trades Assembly reported home in a mood of bitter dejection. They had received "little or no consideration" at Charleston, they said, and expected none "So long as a majority of legislators were controlled by the corporate influence. . . ." They concluded that "labor must rebuke the corporations at the polls."[24]

In attempting to transfer the legislative struggle over the labor question to the polls, the Wheeling unionists met with limited success. They succeeded in placing one union man, Henry Steck of the cigar makers, on the Ohio County Republican legislative ticket in 1900, but this was nothing new. One place of four was traditionally reserved for a workingman, along with "country," "business," and "professional" slots; Steck's defeated rival for the nomination was a member of the potters' union. Later the Trades Assembly attempted to block the nomination of a Wellsburg glass manufacturer and nonunion employer for the first district state senatorial seat.

201

When the offending candidate made a written agreement with the flint glass workers for a union shop and union wages, the opposition—which in any case constituted less than 20 percent of the Ohio County delegation—relented.[25] There is no evidence that workingmen in other localities sought to follow Wheeling's example, although, as we have seen, Dawson saw that the miners were well represented on the organization's Kanawha County ticket.

It should be noted that Dawson's extensive correspondence with Elkins regarding legislative candidates in several counties dwelt on purely political, rather than economic considerations in selecting them. Not that the organization men were that sympathetic to labor's demands. One of the minor drawbacks of White's gubernatorial candidacy was his anti-union record as a newspaper proprietor. But, as he put it early in the campaign, "I will write Dawson at once to get some labor man to go to work at once. I think that is the proper caper."[26] The idea was to win votes first and worry about what came after, after. The Democratic leaders, on the other hand, were more far-sighted. For Davis and Camden, the first criterion in choosing their gubernatorial nominee was that he should be "an available and strong man . . . who will do justice to corporate interests"; "also Auditor of Legislature is important," Davis added, singling out the official who prepared the budget upon which legislative appropriations were based.[27] Undoubtedly they recognized the value of controlling a few key officials whose exercise of veto, budgetary, and administrative power could blunt the effect of any legislation they disliked. And though Elkins's instructions in composing the Republican state ticket were not explicit, it certainly was safe enough on that score. But there is no evidence on Elkins's motives, other than his political ones, while the Democratic industrialists, like the Wheeling trade unionists, were somewhat less than successful at the polls.

Once the campaign was over, however, both sides squared away for a renewal of the struggle. Barton and Atkinson, although they would remain above the combat in the lobbies and committee rooms, provided a coherent statement of

202

labor objectives in the labor bureau's annual report and the governor's biennial message. "I find that the conditions under which labor is employed have not materially improved in the past two years," the governor stated: "Labor should have some consideration from your honorable body at this time. . . ." Along with the factory inspection, safety and child labor regulations he had requested in 1899, Atkinson asked for expansion of the mine safety and coal weighing laws, and proposed the abolition of company stores.[28] The Wheeling Trades Assembly again appointed a committee of members to lobby for the enactment of this program. They were joined at Charleston by representatives of the mine workers, printers' unions, and railroad brotherhoods, whose objectives included even more controversial proposals for compulsory arbitration, employer's liability ("fellow servants bill"), and anti-blacklisting laws.[29]

An even greater challenge to the ruling industrialist politicians was the current financial position of the state. Whatever Elkins's motives in installing reliable men like White and Dawson in the statehouse and electing legislators pledged to return him to the Senate, an interest or even an awareness of the ordinary governmental problems of the state were probably far from his mind. He had acted mainly on the basis of political calculations. These were still important in view of the legislative and congressional redistricting to be done and the state and federal patronage to be dispensed during the next few weeks, and no doubt these topics along with the threat to corporate interests occupied Elkins and Dawson when they conferred in Washington on January 4.[30] But now that the Republican organization commanded the state government, they had to run it as well as exploit its political potential, and there were indications that this was not going to be an easy task, especially since it was very nearly bankrupt.

One reason for the state's financial crisis was the expansion of public services during the past four years. In part this represented the Republicans' traditionally more positive attitude toward government and also their desire to increase the possibilities of patronage, but the blame was not entirely theirs. The legislature of 1899, which created six new institutions and agencies (for a total of 26 new jobs on the supervisory boards alone) and increased the budgets and services of others, featured, after all, a Democratic House of Delegates. This session also appropriated the first annual budget of over one million dollars, a sum exceeding anticipated revenues by some $200,000, according to the state treasurer.[31] Naturally, spokesmen for the two parties hastened to fix the blame on the opposition. The truth was, however, that financial crises such as the one building in West Virginia occurred all over the nation during this period, as states and municipalities everywhere found the cost and extent of government services on the rise. In an age of rapidly increasing economic activity and population growth, there were simply more cases in the courts, more students in the schools, more doctors, lawyers, dentists, banks, and embalmers to be examined and licensed, more prisoners in the pen.[32]

But another source of West Virginia's financial ills was an extension of the same laisser-faire attitude that hampered the labor reformers into the field of taxation. That low taxation was essential to attract needed capital was a cornerstone of the development faith. How well it was practiced is apparent from receipts from the two principal sources of revenue—railroad and property taxes. Railroad taxes rose from $100,000 a year in 1884 to over $400,000 in 1899, but the increase was deceptive. The valuation of railroad property for taxation purposes slipped steadily downward as mileage increased, from $12,500 per mile in 1890, to $10,700 in 1895, to $8,900 in 1900.[33] Here, as with the labor question, the industrialists did not fail to assist the ideology in its work. Camden discovered that even a hostile governor like Wilson, intent on higher taxation, could be overruled by other officials sitting on the Board of Public Works.[34] When the entire administration was friendly, the limit on what could be done was set only by political expediency. During MacCorkle's term in office, the B&O secured a reduction in valuation of

$250,000 "and the promise of a much larger reduction next year. . . . We would have fared better, but the Board feared that a larger reduction preceding a state election might imperil the success of the party."[35] The absolute fall in total railroad valuations from $22,800,000 in 1894 to $22,300,000 in 1900, despite a 25 percent increase in mileage, indicates that such practices continued under the Republicans. In 1901, a Democratic legislator introduced a resolution calling upon Secretary Dawson to explain this phenomenon, but the resolution disappeared from the House calendar through what was later termed a clerical error.[36]

In the case of the general property tax, abuses owed as much to the system of taxation as to individuals. The tax structure was a patchwork affair, mostly inherited from Virginia—"colonial Virginia," as critics were wont to point out.[37] Its exactions fell mainly upon the owners of real estate and even then in ways that mocked the constitutional requirement for just and uniform taxation. The central feature was a statewide levy laid by the legislature, currently at the rate of twenty-five cents for every one hundred dollars of assessed valuation for general state purposes, plus ten cents for the support of the schools. But assessment was done locally and that only every ten years. By making absurdly low property valuations, the fifty-five counties—and separate assessment districts within the larger counties—competed to see which could pay the smallest share of the uniform state levy, while supporting local government through taxation at a higher rate on the same low valuations. Another archaic feature was the collection of taxes by sheriffs on a commission basis that encouraged them to foster delinquent payments. But here again abuses were most glaring where the influence of the largest corporations was dominant. In fact the average valuation per acre of real property actually declined between 1890 and 1900 in McDowell (N&W, Pocahontas Coal), Wetzel (South Penn Oil), Marion (B&O, South Penn, Fairmont Coal), and Randolph (Davis-Elkins) counties, despite the multi-million dollar industries and numbers of new towns established there during the decade. In highly industrialized

205

Ohio County, however, where corporate political influence was diffused among a large number of firms and balanced by a large and politically sophisticated electorate of small property holders, average valuations increased nearly 50 percent during the same decade and assessments ran closer to real values than anywhere else in the state.[38] But Ohio was the exception. On a statewide basis, the tax rolls in 1901 barely reflected the state's increase in wealth since 1890. In fact, as a proportion of its real wealth, tax receipts were actually in decline. A special reassessment of property authorized in 1899 brought in enough additional money to enable Atkinson's administration to scrape through 1900 in the black. But just barely. The state was so broke by the time the 1901 session convened that the governor was forced to borrow $10,000 on his own signature to finance a West Virginia exhibit at the latest industrial extravaganza, the Pan American Exposition at Buffalo.[39] A situation as bad as that obviously called for solution.

If the legislature stopped short of a general overhaul of the entire system—as every one of its predecessors had done since 1863—it could search for additional sources of revenue within the existing framework. Two such sources suggested themselves. One was the fee system, which siphoned public revenues into the pockets of a few officials. The fees received by the secretaries of state and auditors had grown from $5,000 in 1893 to $12,000 in 1895 to the neighborhood of $25,000 in 1901.[40] And that was only part of the loot. Secretary W. E. Chilton blithely reported in 1895 that some three-hundred-odd corporations had retained him as their attorney "in an individual capacity as a practicing lawyer in no way connected with his office as secretary of state." Small wonder that his successor, Dawson, soon after settling in Charleston hastened to present himself at the bar.[41] Tradition had it that the bulk of the fees found its way into the coffers of the ruling party, a tradition supported by the fact that Dawson, like most of his predecessors, doubled as state chairman of his party. When they were out of power, the Republicans were great advocates of replacing the fee system with salaries;

in power they were less enthusiastic for the change and the Democrats assumed the reform position. But with the treasury *in extremis*, Atkinson now urged his fellow partisans to take the plunge.[42]

The fee system also operated on the county level and here, too, reform proposals coupled the prospect of increased public revenue with a host of political complications. A given official's intake from fees varied according to the locality and office involved. The amounts were generally a closely kept secret, but a survey undertaken by a reformer legislator in 1907 indicates that sheriffs and county clerks held the most lucrative offices, followed by circuit court clerks and county prosecutors. Sheriffs' commissions ranged from upwards of $30,000 annually in populous counties like Ohio and Kanawha to $1,000 in interior Pendleton. County clerks did nearly as well on their commissions on real estate transfers and other services and, with the sheriffs, provided the "sinews of war" for local political organizations in large counties and small.[43] The prosecutors, on the other hand, although they had to meet more rigorous qualifications than other officials, were poorly paid by a combination of salaries and fees that ranged from below $500 in the least populous counties to around $5,000 in Kanawha. This meant that the incumbents were usually drawn from among the less experienced or competent lawyers—"the 'scrub' of the bar," as one reform-minded prosecutor explained—except when "the County court becomes involved in any serious damage suit or other litigation of a serious nature. [Then] it invariably employs some 'able' attorney to assist the prosecuting attorney, and pays to this assistant a large sum for his services in this one case."[44] Thus here was another lucrative, though occasional, source of patronage, one which operated at the state as well as the county level. Over the years such luminaries as E. Willis Wilson, C. C. Watts, and W. M. O. Dawson reaped handsome fees as special attorneys for the state, not to mention less prominent state beneficiaries and the hundreds of local "able" lawyers who must have enjoyed special retainers from the county courts.[45] No matter what the angle of

207

approach, the question of reforming the fee system touched sensitive spots and delicate arrangements high and low.

A second, more extensive source of new revenues was increased taxation of corporations. Currently taxation reached only their undervalued real estate and such personalty as they cared to reveal to the assessors. This meant that the railroads and extractive industries escaped lightly, while such service enterprises as banks, express, telegraph, and insurance companies paid practically nothing at all. The corporation license tax enacted in 1885 increased in yield from $15,000 in 1887 to $140,000 in 1900.[46] But this was due solely to the increase in business activity, not to any intention to divert a part of the corporate harvest to the state. Few Republicans before 1901 advanced the notion of an increase in taxes affecting domestic corporations, since their profits were identified with the progress of development. But out-of-state, or "foreign," corporations were another matter. The legislature of 1899 revealed an ambivalent attitude toward the latter group. The Republican senate passed a bill eliminating a $5,000,000 limit on the capitalization of foreign corporations. Since West Virginia law otherwise placed no limit on corporate size or provided for supervision of corporate activities, this was a frank endeavor to compete with New Jersey and Delaware as a haven for those enterprises which for various reasons found it inconvenient to take out a charter in some less liberal state. The Democratic House, however, saw an opportunity to capitalize on the trust question and rejected the bill.[47] Even without it, the state's corporation laws were so inviting that over two thousand foreign corporations, ranging from the African Village Company—organized to operate same at the Buffalo fair—to the Yakatog Gold Mining Company of Chicago and (hopefully) Alaska, accepted West Virginia's hospitality during the next two years.[48]

Legislators in both parties manifested an opposite attitude in advancing in 1899 a set of proposals that, in the *Intelligencer's* phrase, "would have damaged the reputation of the state, and retarded its progress. . . ." Two such proposals—a bill regulating certain aspects of the insurance business and another taxing the gross receipts of express companies doing business in the state—were enacted. Atkinson vetoed the express company bill, calling it "unconstitutional and discriminatory."[49] And though he pledged at the time to work for increased taxation on *all* foreign corporations, in his 1901 message he turned instead to the removal of the ceiling on capitalization in order to drum up more licensing business. This in itself was harmless insofar as the industrialists' interests were concerned. But the governor tied his proposal to an increase in the license tax on corporations foreign *and* domestic, graduated according to the capitalization and landholdings of the individual firms.[50] In this way the tax question bore directly on Davis and Elkins's legislative plans for their own enterprises. The senators' demands were modest enough—a minor revision of the West Virginia Central charter, an increase in its capitalization, and repeal of a West Virginia law limiting corporate landholdings to 10,000 acres. But their purpose was urgent, for on it rode the success of their current efforts to avoid a forced sale of their properties to the Community of Interest on disadvantageous terms.[51]

Two of the industrialists were thus on the offensive in 1901, but the main emphasis remained defensive. Besides those pressing for labor legislation and higher corporation taxes, danger threatened from a variety of sources during the session. Legislators from the northern Republican counties, many of whom had supported the express company bill and similar items in 1899, were present in their usual strength. Their leaders, although chastened by their experience in 1900, were again scanning the horizon to see whether they would again be "served with cold lunches" at the forthcoming patronage banquet.[52] The urban leaders who promoted reform movements in other states were unlikely to make much of a showing in West Virginia, since Wheeling, the largest city in the state, still numbered less than 40,000 people in 1900.[53] But if it stood alone, Wheeling was nonetheless doing its share and sent to the legislature the president of its newly revitalized Board of Trade, George A. Laughlin. The board itself differed little from other "boom" organizations in West Virginia; its purpose was another thumping of the development drum. But both it and Laughlin were closely related to another movement for municipal regeneration, a "Committee of One Hundred" organized at the same time to rout corruption and the saloon influence from the city government.[54] Thus, as Laughlin stated in his presidential address to the Board of Trade, he represented "a campaign of the people for a new public life—for cleanliness, for decency and for honesty."[55] As the legislature convened in January, the Committee of One Hundred was intervening with great effectiveness in the Wheeling city election, to the dismay of regulars in both parties, while Laughlin brought along to Charleston two bills embodying its primary objectives—the "Laughlin bill," divesting the city council of the power to issue liquor licenses, and the "Wheeling electric bill," authorizing the city to acquire ownership of its public utilities.[56]

In short, the legislature of 1901 was another instance of conditions that *might* have generated a movement for political and economic reform as powerful and creative as those taking shape in western and southern states during the same period. As yet the potential reformers had little in common. In Wheeling, for example, the Trades Assembly explicitly dissociated itself from the middle-class reformers, stating that the latter were interested more in the "effects" of crime and disorder than in the causes to be found in "the accursed competitive system which placed boys and girls of tender age in our factories."[57] But all of them were alienated in one way or another from the existing order that the industrialists had fashioned, and the state's financial crisis, opening up the possibility of assault on corporate privileges along a broad front, offered an opportunity for fusion. An even greater opportunity was the possibility of a constitutional convention. Ever since the Republicans returned to power in 1897, many of them had talked of calling a convention, but the talk had been sternly repressed by the industrialists.[58] Now that they enjoyed an unchallengeable majority in the state, Republicans did not have to be reformers to want an opportunity to rearrange state institutions to suit themselves; moreover, some proposed solutions to the financial problem, such as abolition of the fee system, would necessitate a constitutional change. Accordingly, demands for a convention rose to a higher level than ever before as the legislature convened in January 1901.[59] In any event, many things were possible, and it was bound to be, as the Wheeling *Register* pointed out, "a red hot session from start to finish."[60]

The obvious shortcoming of any reform coalition that the conditions of 1901 might spawn was a lack of power, and that the industrialists had to spare. Perhaps the most striking manifestation thereof was the election of W. G. Wilson, cashier of the largest Davis-Elkins bank, as speaker of the House of Delegates. The disposition of other legislative posts favored reliable, though generally able, Republican members, while the Democratic minority leaders, Delegate John D. Alderson and Senator John J. Cornwell, were conservative veterans long used to taking their cues from Davis.[61]

The party leaders did not rely solely on the institutional channels of power that they commanded. Well in advance of the session, they were manning their defenses in informal ways. "The next Legislature will have to be watched in regard to mining and corporation laws," Camden warned Elkins on December 28; "I want to see you specially before you go to Charleston."[62] Propriety forbade Elkins himself to appear at the capital until his reelection to the Senate had taken place, but he was already discussing with Fleming "the matter of some one to help look after coal matters in the Legislature . . ." and came up with Charlie Elliott and E. M. Showalter, both minor Republican federal officials.[63] On January 4, he met with Dawson and secured the latter's pledge "to look after legislation and matters of general interest . . . during the session." Senator Scott left for Charleston the following night.[64] Among Davis's Democratic lieutenants, W. A. Ohley volunteered "to look out for hostile coal legislation and do what I can to defeat hurtful measures."[65] And that was just the beginning. After the session got underway, the West Virginia Central's expert watchdogs, C. Wood

211

Dailey and F. S. Landstreet, departed for the capital to look after the railroad's private bills but also "to attend to some mining and corporation bills we think very objectionable."[66] The B&O's "special agent," Randolph Stalnaker, together with his C&O counterpart, was already on the ground.[67] In short, the advocates of change would have to cut their way through a formidable bipartisan conservative bulwark.

For all that, the first weeks of the session occasioned some confusion and no little alarm among the conservatives. The record number of bills introduced—over one hundred in the House by the end of the first week—plus the size and determination of the opposing lobbies gave the impression of a concerted attack on corporations where as yet none existed. The Republican leadership in both houses, anxious to concentrate on reapportionment, found itself distracted by the pressure for constitutional revision, and had to create special joint committees to work on both problems.[68] The tax question also created disturbances. On January 17, Delegate Laughlin introduced a bill providing for a small severance tax on natural gas and oil shipped out of the state, which just missed "by a scratch" being reported from committee with the support of the incumbent state treasurer on the same afternoon. At the end of the week, the bill was still in committee, but was believed likely to slip out at any moment under the justification of the need for revenues.[69] Also on the seventeenth, the senate passed the first of the objectionable mining bills, the Ashby bill, requiring more thorough safety regulations; at the same time, another bill providing for the inspection of mine cars ("car branding") to close a loophole in the screen law, escaped from a senate committee, as did another one in the House for the inspection of miners' lamp oil.[70] Fleming, who had earlier sent a reassuring report to his friends at Standard Oil in New York, came down to Charleston to see for himself and informed them on the twenty-second that "matters have taken a turn for the worse."[71] From Washington, Scott urged White and Dawson to convoke the Republican caucus "to weed out those obnoxious and vicious bills that are being introduced at Charles-

212

ton. The railroad corporations and the money interests, which have capital invested in our state are all scared to death."[72]

Part of the trouble was a lack of coordination between the various lobbyists. Dailey, Landstreet, and Elliott, for instance, got their wires crossed as to whether or not Davis wanted the compulsory arbitration bill killed. Dailey thought not; the bill was harmless, he argued, as far as any real authority was concerned. Besides, the railroad lobbyists had made a deal with the brotherhoods, agreeing to the arbitration bill "in order to get rid of the fellow servants bill and some others." There was also the problem of Malcolm Jackson, one of Dawson's Kanawha regulars and chairman of the judiciary committee in the House. Jackson was "very conservative"; both Dailey and Speaker Wilson testified to that. But he was for carrying out the aforesaid agreement and "will have to be convinced he is wrong, or at least shown some reasonable excuse for not carrying out his purpose. In other words we can't say to him we don't want this &c. He's not that kind of timber."[73] Davis nevertheless insisted that nay be said. The bill gave "moral and legal status [to the unions] and forces the operators to indirectly treat with them." Moreover, it opened the way for public inspection of company records.[74] The outcome of the issue therefore remained in doubt. But at least it had been reduced to the problem of mutual accommodation among the interests instead of a confrontation between them and the forces of reform.

Another hassle arose over the principal revenue bill, which was drawn up by Secretary Dawson. The difficulty was not in increasing the corporation license tax—all parties acquiesced in that, provided the landholding restriction was removed—but Davis objected to paying on a scale graduated according to capital stock. Therefore Dailey and Dawson worked out a compromise whereby the burden on domestic corporations would be halved. As for other measures, Dailey wrote, "Will try to keep you posted but find it difficult to keep myself."[75]

Actually, the picture became much clearer by the end of

January. Everyone in the lobbies was finding out where everyone else stood and establishing reliable channels of communication. One result, the *Register* reported, was a diminishing level of noise, although not of activity. "There are many interests represented before the Legislature by special agents, but they are . . . not the old-fashioned, loud-talking, self-obtrusive, all-pervasive lobbyists [of yore]. The men now entrusted with the work are talkers, reasoners, persuaders, making no show of the possession of money."[76] It is difficult to know what accounted for the new style, since the personnel was largely the same as in former days. Perhaps the consolidated political power of their clients made it easier for the lobbyists to get across their point. In any case, evidence of their effectiveness was now to be found in the calenders of the two houses. Most of the regulatory bills remained in committee, with those that had previously escaped bogged down remote from passage. Only one bill had passed one of the two houses, the Ashby mining bill, and Jackson agreed with Dailey that it was "unconstitutional" and would probably die in his committee. Speaker Wilson also assured Dailey that the "danger of vicious legislation" had passed, that "Elliott &c are unduly alarmed. . . ."[77] Still, the legislators were in an unpredictable mood. On January 25, both houses rejected by overwhelming majorities a $25,000 appropriation for the Pan American Exposition and stuck to their decision during three days of vigorous debate. Atkinson was left to pay the funds already expended for the project out of his own pocket, while defenders of the development faith were coldly informed that "the exhibit would be especially to advertise the coal of the state, and that as the coal lands belong largely to wealthy corporations, it would be better to let them pay the expenses of the advertisement."[78] Five days later, the House, again by a substantial majority, passed Laughlin's two Wheeling bills, despite the opposition of a brewer-utilities lobby headed by James K. Hall, Scott's chief Wheeling lieutenant who was also secretary of the Republican state committee. On the thirty-first, the senate advanced mining, insurance,

214

and antitrust bills, in each case ignoring unfavorable committee reports.[79]

The real turning point of the session was reached, however, on February 1, when Senator Elkins arrived in Charleston. One reason for his trip was to regale the Republicans for having returned him to the Senate for another six years; for this purpose Mrs. Elkins, gowned in black chiffon and gold, and a Washington caterer, accompanied him.[80] He was also packing other delectables in the form of jobs. The eventual distribution of patronage included something for everyone; how much was given away in Charleston is not clear. The impression was abroad that "several matters were settled," an impression confirmed by the fact that Elkins called on President McKinley on the day after his return to Washington. The discipline with which the Republican majority responded to the senator's legislative program suggests that many appetites were satisfied by the goodies he brought.[81]

Elkins's legislative program was worked out in a series of informal agreements with legislators and lobbyists, arrived at within the space of four days. It met all the most pressing problems facing his party and his fellow industrialists. On the labor question, he put his stamp of approval on an innocuous compromise of the arbitration bill worked out by Dailey, Jackson, and the railroad lobbyists. Some coal producers, notably Fleming, continued to oppose the bill, while Dailey passed the word to Cornwell in the senate that the Davis-Elkins interests would not be sorry to see it fail there if it passed the House.[82] But no real harm would be done if it had to be passed in order to avoid some more objectionable measure.

Turning to the financial crisis, Elkins's most important move was to separate the need for immediate revenues from the general question of tax reform. He rejected the compromise Dawson bill worked out by Dailey as insufficient to meet the state's current needs. "To this I replied that . . . some of us were not quite so much interested as he in getting the Republican party out of its financial difficulties," Dailey reported to Davis, but the senator had his

215

way.[83] The license tax was restored to its original level for both foreign and domestic corporations, and scaled to the amount of authorized capital, not capital paid in, as Davis had wished. Thus partisan necessity took precedence over the $300 or so that the higher tax would cost the West Virginia Central annually. However, Dailey did manage to wrangle a promise from Dawson and Attorney General Rucker that, if the legislature amended the bill to restore the ceilings on landholding and capitalization, they would help him to kill it. But this precaution proved unnecessary. The Dawson bill was sent back to the House Finance Committee on February 6, promptly reported back in the shape determined by Elkins, and passed by a party vote on February 8. The senate passed it with minor changes on February 15.[84]

On February 5, the morning after Elkins's departure, his solution to the problem of general tax revision was unveiled at Charleston. He proposed a special commission to sit in the interval before the next session and to report to the legislature of 1903 measures to broaden the tax base and to open permanent new sources of revenue. Legislation creating the commission was introduced on February 9 and passed both houses within ten days.[85] The commission proposal, together with the Dawson tax bill, robbed the supporters of the severance, express company, telegraph, and similar corporation taxes of the argument that the financial crisis demanded immediate passage of their bills. And none of the bills passed. Most slept on in the pigeonholes in which they reposed on February 1, or to which they were shortly after remanded.[86] Talk of a constitutional convention also petered out about the time of Elkins's visit. Instead five constitutional amendments, including one that reclaimed the fees of state officials for the treasury and another that made the secretary of state an elected official (both effective as of March 4, 1905), were submitted to the voters as a means of patching up the most glaring deficiencies in the existing document.[87]

The effect of Elkins's visit to Charleston was to freeze the assault on corporate privileges at the level of a scatter-gun effort. Without the unifying effect of the larger fiscal and

216

constitutional issues, the disparate reform elements remained unorganized and ineffective. There remained the danger that some issue or individual would rally and unite the reform forces, and so the lobbyists continued to stand guard. "While I was in the Senate yesterday," reported Showalter to Fleming on February 17, "watching to keep arbitration bill from coming up, Laughlin got up the Car Branding bill S B 70 in the House and had it passed." But this was only a temporary setback. Atkinson, at Showalter's request, vetoed the bill.[88] Why the governor chose this particular moment to desert his erstwhile friend, the workingman, is not clear; it is worth nothing that his thoughts at the time were very much taken up with the judgeship that he wanted so badly.[89]

The incident proved to be an isolated one, illustrating the difficulty of bridging the gap between the groups that might have united for reform under more favorable conditions. During the last few days of the session, the legislature, instead of dishing it out to the corporations, dished it out to the putative reformers. Laughlin's Wheeling electric bill was mutilated in the senate and his liquor license bill rejected outright. The hapless Atkinson had to go down into the lobby himself in order to recover the money he had illegally spent on the Pan American Exposition. Finally the legislators took him off the hook, but the appropriation was couched in humiliating terms that required the governor to account for every penny spent to a special committee. Morgantown, the anti-organization stronghold of 1900, received a double blow when the university's preparatory department was moved out of town and the institution's appropriation made contingent upon the resignation of its president and of George C. Sturgiss from its board of regents.[90] In the same vein was the "ripper" legislation earlier mentioned, replacing Atkinson's and earlier appointees in many state patronage positions with men of the organization stamp. As for labor legislation, the Ashby mining bill was lost along with the car branding bill. Labor did not go away entirely empty-handed. It got a "free employment bureau" (with a budget of $500 a year), a rudimentary factory safety law, and, of course, another mine

217

inspector.[91] By way of contrast, the private legislation sought by Davis and Elkins went through without a hitch.[92]

Quantitative analysis reinforces the impression of ferment yielding to the whip of party discipline during the 1901 legislature. Unfortunately the nature of the session and the record it left for the computer makes it difficult to add much precision to what has already been said beyond the negative conclusion that a reform coalition failed to jell. Few of the controversial measures that so alarmed the industrialists actually made it to the roll call stage. Those that did often passed unanimously or nearly so, reflecting behind-the-scenes agreements carried into effect by the caucus. Other measures were put to a voice vote; this indicates where controversial items were concerned the maneuvers of a small number of expert legislators in a body whose members were more commonly inexperienced and, often near the end of a session, drunk or sleepy as well.[93]

In contrast to Democratic factionalism of prior decades, there was no clear geographic pattern of G.O.P. strife in 1901. The irregular Republican legislators all came from northern West Virginia but from precisely those areas that the Freer insurgency there had least infected. Regulars were proportionately strongest in those counties earlier labelled "Greenbacker," but this had more to say about the Hog Combine of Kanawha County than any vestige of Greenbackism. One group or another had an edge in certain areas but in no instance did the edge approach the regional proportions characteristic of the Democracy's Redeemers and Kanawha Ring. In short, the geographic unity of Republicanism represented the unity of the state at large brought about by industrialism and its penetration of the Appalachian spine. In place of the conflict of "island communities" defined in terms of space, there developed the conflict of classes, interest groups, and ideologies, of the associational (as opposed to ascriptive) groupings characteristic of modern society.[94] Conflict abounded at the turn of the century and grew more intense in the years after 1901. The most important clashes—outs vs.

218

ins, wets vs. drys, town vs. country, small proprietors vs. big business, labor vs. capital—were implied if not expressed in the skirmishes at Charleston. Yet those groups whose interest or urge it was to change things in West Virginia never quite found each other during the session or afterward. By appropriating the fiscal and constitutional crises to its own management, the Elkins organization deprived the disparate malcontents of a meeting place and platform. Without these, a reform movement independent of the organization and its conservative leadership never got underway.

Indeed there might not have been a reform movement at all in West Virginia had not the corporate retainers got out of hand. Something of their habitual arrogance was conveyed when the legislature of 1901 adjourned on February 22, within the constitutional limit of forty-five days. That evening the members of the "Third House" took over the vacant chambers and held a mock session. "Major Ran" Stalnaker held forth in the chair of the senate and a South Penn Oil man presided in the House. The revelers had "a great deal of fun," while "grotesque resolutions and amusing speeches and motions were enjoyed." So ended the interests' skirmish with reform.[95]

But the mirthful hirelings failed to take one important thing into account: what the Elkins organization took away it might also giveth. The industrialists' success in defending their economic order in 1901 was based in part on the development of a retinue of expert lobbyists, but it was also based on party leadership and consequent control of the institutional sources of political power. Governor White naturally pledged in his inaugural "to treat the developing corporations, such as railroads and mining and manufacturing enterprises, [who are] employing labor and building up the State, with the utmost liberality" in searching for a solution to the state's financial ills, but he did not say that he would let the state go bankrupt for the benefit of Standard Oil or Fairmont Coal.[96] Neither did Elkins, whose idea a tax commission was and to whom White first tendered the commission chairmanship. Elkins decided that he was too busy in the senate to serve, whereupon White suggested Davis, who accepted the appointment on April 15.[97] Since Davis was a Democrat, White still needed a Republican chairman. He found him in William P. Hubbard, a Wheeling lawyer and steel manufacturer who had been in and out of Republican politics since Reconstruction days. John H. Holt, White's opponent in 1900 and also a corporation lawyer, became the second minority member. Marshal John K. Thompson represented the Elkins organization on the body, while the fifth member, L. J. Williams, was a Lewisburg banker who had entered the G.O.P. via the Gold Democratic route. Since Thompson and Williams came from rural counties, they were said to represent the farmers of the state.[98] So constituted, this eminently conservative body began the deliberations that produced a platform for progressivism as it existed in West Virginia after 1901.

With the *Report* of the West Virginia Tax Commission issued in November 1902, the local version of progressivism sprang full grown from the head of conservatism. With the keen sense of a well-fed watchdog, A. B. Fleming had sensed something amiss much earlier but F. S. Landstreet, then operating from the Davis-Elkins offices at No. 1 Broadway, sought to reassure him. "I have paid very little attention to this," Landstreet confessed, "for this reason, as you probably know, that Senator Davis is a member of that Board, and has been active in this work, and I have sort of felt as if he would watch the interest of the coal and railroad people in the State...."[99] Fleming's suspicion proved correct, however. Not only had Davis failed to meet the retainers' conception of his duty; so had Governor White. Obtaining an advance copy of the governor's message a few days before its delivery to the legislature of 1903, E. M. Showalter reported to Fleming that "in the main [it] is more unreasonable and extreme than the report of the Tax Commission." Fleming, in turn, promptly telephoned the contents to 26 Broadway in New York and dispatched the usual fleet of Rockefeller and Fairmont lobbyists to Charleston, where they were joined by the railroads' "special agents" led by Ran Stalnaker.[100] With the rallying of the "henchmen," a new and curious era in West Virginia had begun.

Behind the retainers' dread lay not a drastic plan for social upheaval but a modest scheme for fiscal and administrative reorganization. The changes put forward by the Tax Commission, like the commissioners themselves, were nothing if not conservative. Indeed the commission report and the draft bills embodying its proposals were largely the work of C. Wood Dailey, the Davis-Elkins attorney and thus a curious Isaiah for a Bible of reform.[101] Acting at Davis's suggestion, the commission placed itself under the guidance of the business oriented National Civic Federation, and adopted proposals that had already become law under conservative auspices, and without notable controversy, in such states as Indiana, Pennsylvania, and Massachusetts.[102] The central feature of the commission's recommendations was the separation of state and local revenue sources, reserving property taxes to localities and providing for uniform annual assessments under the supervision of a state tax commissioner. The most controversial feature was a small severance tax on coal, oil, and natural gas, but here the commission took special pains in its report to reassure corporate interests; "It would only be natural if those likely to be affected by the imposition of such a tax should be disposed to resist it. It will be impossible for them, however, to say that the amount of the tax here suggested would constitute any serious burden upon those engaged in the development of the resources of the State." This was a judgment with which Davis was in complete agreement. And in order that no one would worry lest the tax become an entering wedge, the commission further proposed to imbed the low ceiling thereon in the state constitution.

As to other forms of corporate taxation, it turned to the familiar device of license taxes, bearing down harder on the owners of saloons and roller-skating rinks than on bankers and mine operators. It expressed complete satisfaction with the present system of railroad taxation, rejecting the notion of taxing railroad earnings then gaining popularity in other

221

states.[103] Governor White, however, having experienced the usual difficulty of extracting revenues from the carriers, added a proposal of his own for a railroad commissioner, embodying the idea in what Elkins later described as "the most modest railroad commission bill ... that was ever drawn."[104] As drafted by the Interstate Commerce Commission at Elkins's request, the railroad bill created authority only to investigate and report, not to regulate. "Publicity is a good regulator," White explained.[105]

Taken as a whole, the organization package amounted to a badly needed modernization of the state's financial and administrative structure, tapping the extractive industries for some of the revenues needed to support the public services (and attendant offices) that industrialization required. There was nothing in the proposals to justify the uproar that followed. But though the changes envisioned were minimal, they *were* changes. To Fleming and others who gave specific local direction to their absentee clients' general will and who did not face the political exigencies confronted by Elkins and his men, the mere suggestion of change was enough to arouse opposition of the most violent and heedless sort.

There was no hint of what was coming in the initial public reception of the Tax Commission report, but its circulation among legislators and other interested parties for two months prior to the legislature's meeting gave the "anti-taxers," as they came to be known, ample time to prepare.[106] Thus Showalter, Stalnaker, Reese Blizzard, Charlie Elliott and others were ready when Governor White submitted his message and the Tax Commission bills to the legislature on January 15, 1903. A week later, White and Dawson initiated a call for the Republican caucus to meet on the evening of January 30, where presumably party loyalists would have been mobilized in support of the administration's reform program. On January 28, however, Senator E. C. Colcord of the Kanawha Hog Combine introduced a resolution calling upon the senate to refuse consideration to the tax bills because "special taxation [of] the product of the coal mines, and the oil and gas wells . . . even were such a law constitutional . . . threaten[s] the continued development of the resources of our State. . . ." The Senate Finance Committee headed by Ira E. Robinson, who was also the Grafton attorney for the B&O, promptly took up the Colcord Resolution and called two sessions of hearings at which Dawson and White's testimony was overriden by the views of sixteen corporation attorneys and lobbyists. When the hearings ended on the morning of the thirtieth, Robinson's committee reported a reworded version of the Colcord Resolution favorably to the senate, which passed it by a vote of 19-7 at two o'clock that afternoon.[107] The administration's senate floor leader, Elliott Northcott, supported by Senators John S. Darst, L. J. Forman, and Harvey Harmer, strived to postpone this development until after the caucus assembly, while F. M. Reynolds, House majority leader in both the 1901 and 1903 sessions, produced a ringing declaration of the House's willingness to consider the Tax Commission report and its request to the governor for a special session to that end.[108] Nevertheless, in the alliterative phrase of Elliott's Parkersburg *News*, "Radicalism in the affairs of State government went down to overwhelming defeat . . . before the sturdy strength of solid, sensible conservatism. . . ."[109] In terms of the subsequent public outcry and the damage done the Republican party, the retainers' course was anything but "sensible," but it certainly was "solid." The Colcord Resolution permanently ended the chances of adopting an integrated reform package such as White and the Tax Commission had designed, while its heavy-handed tone set the character of the controversy that ensued.

Even so, guided by Elkins, White and Chairman Hubbard of the Tax Commission attempted at first to win their case by means of gentle persuasion. In speeches during the spring and summer of 1903, the governor patiently lectured bankers and businessmen on the need for all interests to assume a fair share of the burdens of government, while the commissioners innocently endowed a prize for the best essay on tax reform by a student at the state university.[110] Their patience was rewarded by a further display of intransigence. On June 13,

Fleming assembled in Washington the elite of West Virginia's "henchmen," together with representatives of the Standard, Western Maryland, PRR, N&W, B&O, C&O, and Fairmont and Pocahontas Coal interests. The result of the conference was a purse, initially set at $24,000, to fight the Tax Commission program and an "Anti-Tax Manifesto."[111] This document, which appeared in all state newspapers on August 19 over the signatures of twenty-eight better-known personages (among them Fleming, Rucker, Freer, Alston G. Dayton, J. H. Huling, and the aging Confederate hero, General John MacCausland), disputed the need for tax reform and impugned the motives of the state administration.[112]

With the appearance of the Anti-Tax Manifesto, the reform struggle began in earnest. "I do not want to harm my party or do wrong," White protested to Republican leaders. "But I don't *deserve abuse* & resent it."[113] In this spirit, he and Hubbard took to the stump to rally the public to their program; they were joined by Dawson, ex-Governor Atkinson, and George C. Sturgiss. Thus the quintumvirate of reform leaders, like the anti-taxers, included representatives of both the pro- and anti-organization factions of 1900. In these circumstances, Senator Elkins could hardly be blamed for taking cover in Europe just as soon as the clouds of conflict rolled up on the horizon.[114] However, a new factional pattern emerged during the fall of 1903 as the anti-taxers sought to dispute Dawson's succession to the governorship. To a remarkable extent this Republican development was directed and financed by a Democrat, Fleming, who selected the anti-tax candidate—Charles F. Teter, a protege of Congressman Dayton—and rallied support for him among the major corporations.[115] But Republican disunity also spurred Elkins into action. From here on out, party politics, rather than public or private economic considerations, became the determining factor in the reform movement.

Throughout 1903 and much of 1904, Elkins declined to take a public position on the tax issue; indeed it was not until a month before the 1904 election that he issued a clear-cut statement in favor of tax reform.[116] But on January 18,

1904, he summoned Republican leaders on both sides to Washington and instructed them to resolve their differences. Specifically, he caused the creation of a "Committee of Four" (Hubbard, Sturgiss, Dayton, Blizzard) to work out a compromise version of the Tax Commission bills. A partial reform that preserved the integrity and efficiency of the system designed by the commission was impossible, as Hubbard (and Davis and Dailey) knew.[117] Nevertheless, six months of further private and public squabbling produced a series of "Committee bills," in which the Republican reformers loyally acquiesced.[118] Elkins was less successful in attempting to persuade both gubernatorial candidates to withdraw in favor of a compromise candidate. Instead a bitter factional struggle broke out between the Dawson and Teter forces that continued right up to the eve of the gubernatorial convention on July 12.[119] Dawson, uniting his superb managerial talent and abundant popular support, had by far the best of the preliminaries, but the anti-taxers kept up the suspense down to the wire by threatening to bolt. Instead they submitted peacefully: Dawson was nominated on the first ballot, the compromise tax bills were duly endorsed in the party platform, and on July 16, with Elkins's approval, White called the legislature into special session to enact the bills into law.

Behind Dawson's peaceful and popular victory lay another bit of Elkins's strategy. Fearing the effects of an anti-tax walkout, the senator joined White and Dawson in Wheeling on the eve of the convention and came to terms with the opposition. In return for the peaceful acceptance of Dawson's nomination, the organization pledged to admit anti-tax candidates to the slate of lesser nominees (and thus to the Board of Public Works) and to confine the special session to the compromise (as opposed to the Commission) tax bills. "Thus," Fleming reported to 26 Broadway, "we have on the ticket four conservatives to two radicals." Moreover, he added "confidentially, that I have already been approached by one person who bore me a message from Mr. Dawson, and another from Senator Elkins looking to reconciliation."[120]

225

Nevertheless, the interests and their watchdogs took exception to the fact that White, in his call to the legislature, had neglected to exclude the Tax Commission bills from consideration (a procedure of doubtful constitutionality had he done so) and to the rhetorical radicalism of Dawson's opening campaign statements. They therefore decided to continue the struggle. Meeting in Baltimore on July 23, F. S. Landstreet, presently general manager of the Western Maryland, agreed with Fleming's partner and brother-in-law, Clarence W. Watson, that the Democracy presented the best opportunity for stemming the reform tide in West Virginia. Camden, who had taken little part in earlier developments because of ill health, was informed of the decision and prepared to do his part.[121] Thus, after a breathing space of less than two weeks, the tax reform struggle was renewed on an inter-party basis.

In turning to the Democrats, the anti-tax leaders encountered Davis. It should be noted that Davis was in an anomalous position during the 1904 campaign for more than one reason. As in the past, he had devoted much energy to promoting conservative resurgence in the national Democratic party and, as a tactical device complementing another Gorman-for-President movement, had allowed a gubernatorial boom for himself to grow in West Virginia during 1903 and early 1904.[122] However, instead of nominating Gorman for president, the national conservatives stuck with their New York leadership and named Davis himself for vice-president.

While his nomination did not astonish Davis quite so much as the official version had it, his place on the national ticket entailed a number of difficulties in West Virginia.[123] For one thing, although he took a small part in the national campaign, he felt that his honor—and also his conviction that Democracy could reclaim the border states by running conservative candidates—was at stake in the outcome in West Virginia, and this led him once again into conflict with Elkins. Shortly after Davis's nomination, Elkins agreed to be passive with respect to West Virginia, but the resumption of the tax-reform struggle forced him to take command of the Republican campaign. "If what I hear is correct, which I do not

226

believe," Davis remarked obliquely, "you appear to be taking quite an active part. You will recollect each time you have been a candidate I have taken but little part, either in time or money."[124] But with Republican unity in peril, Elkins could not afford to return the favor, even though he tried to injure Davis's chances as little as possible. A second difficulty concerned attempts to convert the West Virginia Democracy into a "White Man's Party." Along with many others, especially his friends in the Kanawha Ring, Davis believed that a platform calling for Jim Crow laws and Negro disfranchisement offered the party its best hope of recapturing and holding West Virginia. But his position on the national ticket made it inexpedient to advocate openly such measures at this time, as Dailey carefully explained to the Democratic state convention on August 3. "Once in power we can act," Davis privately assured Senator John T. Morgan of Alabama, but for the 1904 campaign the party had to find another issue and this inevitably impaled it on the thorny dilemma of tax reform.[125]

Thus it was that the anti-tax spokesmen encountered opposition from Davis over Democratic strategy in the summer of 1904. This was not because of any genuine commitment to tax reform on Davis's part. From the moment the Tax Commission report became controversial, he had refused to defend it publicly.[126] In January 1904 he reiterated privately his belief that the commission's recommendations were conservative and beneficial, but he discouraged both Elkins and Hubbard from using his views to convert the doubtful.[127] In short, he was perfectly willing to capitalize on Republican division on the tax issue.[128] But he saw no point in the Democracy taking a clear-cut anti-tax position. "I agree with you," he wrote to Camden, "that [a certain anti-taxer] would make a good [gubernatorial] candidate; but I feel that any one of the twenty-eight signers would bring the square issue of tax-reform and anti-tax reform. While we would gain with the corporations, I think we would lose largely with the tax-paying voters." When Camden demurred, Davis pointed out that "The influence of the corporations is now against Dawson"; in that case, why needlessly antagonize the "four or five to one" majority of voters who favored tax reform simply to please those who were already arrayed against the Republicans?[129] But the anti-taxers were adamant; alarmed by the Republican reform rhetoric, they insisted upon a strong Democratic stand against tax reform. To Davis, this meant courting disastrous defeat, but eventually he had to compromise. John J. Cornwell, a rural conservative close to Davis but also an anti-tax leader on the stump and in the legislature, became the Democratic nominee. The platform, written by Dailey, was a straddle. Indeed it so closely resembled Elkins's first draft of a compromise Republican platform that the senator hastened to assure Republicans that he had not written it, but rather that the coincidence proved the wisdom of the safe way.[130] The Democratic platform, which the anti-taxers ignored, did not prevent Republicans from taunting Davis for suffering this repudiation of his work on the Tax Commission. Davis ignored the taunts and, maintaining his silence on the tax issue, financed the Democratic campaign to the extent of $140,000. With Landstreet, he joined in raising additional money from "the railroad people," while Fleming contributed "several thousand dollars from New York."[131]

Inspired by its most capacious war chest in years, the Democracy plunged heedlessly into its worst defeat in West Virginia since the election of 1864—on the national ticket. In the gubernatorial race, however, Dawson ran over 10,000 votes and five percentage points behind President Roosevelt. In Kanawha County, where Dawson had somehow finagled an enduring alliance with the Hog Combine, the conservative defection affected the local ticket as well as the governorship. Thus the Kanawha Ring was able to elect some of its members to local and legislative offices for the first time in a decade, a fact that Davis noted pointedly in later inquiries about the $50,000 he had sent Kanawha Democrats during the campaign.[132] If Dawson's rejection by some G.O.P. voters was painful, it did not keep him from office. Davis's embarrassment was much more complete. The thundering loss of the national ticket, the cost of the campaign, and a blunt discussion of his advanced age in the national media did not cure him of his itch for political endeavors, as we shall see. But combined with the apparently hopeless cause of West Virginia Democracy against even a divided G.O.P., these factors sent Davis to the sidelines, where one of his first acts was to recall a $4,000 loan from W. E. Chilton of the Kanawha Ring.

Although he won the "vindication" of his brother in the special congressional election of 1905 and supplied occasional advice and money to loyalists like John T. McGraw, Davis's role as a major actor in West Virginia politics ended in 1904. So did Camden's, whose death in January 1907 left Fleming, Watson, and the irrepressible Kanawhans in command of the Democratic helm.[133] Four years later the Democracy held its deferred Jim Crow campaign, but this species of reactionism fared no better with the voters than the anti-tax movement had done. So long as the G.O.P. maintained some semblance of unity, West Virginia was safe Republican ground.

Despite the beating they took in 1904, the anti-tax forces seem to have learned nothing from their defeat. In the months that followed Dawson's victory, the organization leaders again sought to come to terms. Charlie Elliott, having done his Republican duty after Dawson's nomination, was once again "in a position to know about these things & to help friends, to help stear [sic] the ship & smooth over the rough places." Accordingly he warned Fleming to be reasonable, to ignore those who were

> ... making an effort to scare the business interests in regard to Dawson & the coming Legislature. I want to assure you that the business interests are in more danger from these alarmists than from the Administration ... for these same interests to go into another looseing [sic] fight would certainly cause feeling to rise, that would be hard to keep in check no matter what the attitude of those who are supposed to be leaders [i.e., White, Dawson and the senators] might be.[134]

After further discussions with White and Dawson a few days later, Elliott again reported that

... both are willing to consult and work along conservative lines.... We must keep in mind that Dawson will be Governor for the next four years, that he knows how to give and take blows and that he won out in two fights against the most powerful forces that any candidate ever had to contend with ... conservative action will prevail. ...

"provided," he added, "an uncalled for war is not started, based on unfounded rumors."[135]

One indication of the administration's conciliatory spirit that later came to light was a deal by which Dawson agreed— or appeared to agree—to forego the severance tax opposed by Standard Oil. A reassessment bill designed to implement the fiscal modifications adopted at the special session of 1904 was foremost on the agenda. Otherwise, the chief administration revenue measure was a new "Dawson bill" reducing license taxes of foreign corporations and raising those on domestic ones. While it required some sacrifices on the part of the interests, this bill actually marked a retreat from the Tax Commission program toward the stop-gap measures first advanced in 1899, as did a related item raising the tax on liquor licenses yet another time. "I am worrying a little bit about what I shall say and how I shall say some things," White wrote Elkins in regard to his annual message, "but agree with you that it is the best policy to be conservative."[136] The resulting biennial message, which White and Dawson submitted to Elkins and Scott for approval before its delivery on January 12, reiterated the spirit of moderation, as even the Fairmont *Times* admitted, despite White's call for tax and railroad enactments considerably more radical than the administration was in fact willing to support.[137]

Why, then, did "our friends who control the great interests of the State" (as Elkins described them)[138] go ahead and start "an uncalled for war?" The reason is not altogether clear. There were a number of legislators who were more strongly committed to reform and were ready with bills of their own embodying the severance tax and other Tax Commission proposals. There was also another large labor lobby on the scene. Under these circumstances, Fleming dispersed the usual corps of lobbyists; perhaps the persuaders got out of hand.[139] It is also possible that by this time the corporations were the prisoners of those Republicans who had backed them, and hence the wrong man, in 1904, and who now stood to lose out entirely in the new distribution of patronage unless they impressed the senators with a show of force. Whatever the causes, the war broke out. This time the attack shifted from mere legislative obstruction to personal assaults designed to discredit White and Dawson in the eyes of their followers. The first bombshell was the "Elliott letter," mysteriously acquired and published on January 28 by an anti-tax journal in Charleston, in which the honest corruptionist, Charlie Elliott, frankly described certain legislators as "grafters" and implicated Dawson and Secretary of State-elect Charles W. Swisher, at this point the administration's senate floor leader, in behind-the-scenes arrangements with Standard Oil. From here on one sensational revelation followed another as the two sides hurled charges and demanded investigations. The Elliott letter turned out to be genuine but the writer was unable to recall precisely what he had meant by "grafter" or "tractable" or to shed further light on the administration's relations with the oil men. The Republican majority in the legislature speedily dropped this inquiry when it threatened to implicate "certain witnesses" who were alleged to have brought Dawson and the oil men together, namely Senators Elkins and Scott.[140] Meanwhile White accused Senator Charles T. Caldwell of Parkersburg, one of the "tractable" legislators mentioned by Elliott, of bribery in connection with one of the licensing bills, whereupon Caldwell, backed by Blizzard, asserted that White and Dawson had enjoyed since 1901 an arrangement by which the governor got a share of the secretary of state's fees. The senate refused to entertain the charges against Caldwell, who in turn refused to answer the summons of a House investigating committee that White asked to probe the "fee-splitting" charge.[141] As metropolitan newspapers broadcast the uproar over the country, the administration program foundered, the real progressives threatened to get out of hand, and Elkins descended to Charleston to try and salvage some shred of Republican discipline.[142] To Fleming he issued an appeal that measured the full extent of his exasperation. "Matters are in bad shape at Charleston, there is too much fighting and division," he wrote. "We are doing everything we can to deal justly with the great interests of the State but the people representing them seem to concede nothing in the world."[143] The appeal went unheeded, however. Even though Dawson helped to kill a severance tax bill advanced by rebel Republicans and White vetoed another "objectionable" item, the retainers defeated a key provision in the administration's reassessment bill. Thus one of the closing days of the session featured a shouting match in the capitol lobby between Governor-elect Dawson and a lobbyist from Fairmont Coal.[144] Finally, after being held over long enough to patch up at least an appropriation bill, the legislature of 1905 performed what one newspaper justly described as its finest service. It adjourned.[145]

7

Years of Jubilee

As the muckraker, David Graham Phillips, was casting about in the spring of 1905 for material for his forthcoming assault on United States senators, he came up with the ringing progressive phrases of Governor Dawson's inaugural and used them to frame his indictment of "Elkins-Davis 'merged' politics" in West Virginia.[1] If in nothing else, the "progressive movement" in the Mountain State was rich in irony. Yet while Phillips assuredly had his facts garbled, his comments were not wholly misplaced. By occupying the principal reform platform, the Elkins organization deprived more thoroughgoing reformers of a rallying place, while the Elkins men themselves tended to be intimidated by the type of opposition they met. After 1905 the organization's energy tended to be directed primarily toward political survival. Whether these tendencies derived from the leaders' limited commitment to change or were forced upon them by circumstances, the results were modest reform achievements and an intensification of Republican factionalism during the second half of the decade.

Each session of the legislature after 1905 saw the introduction by progressive Republicans of severance tax bills or equivalent methods of taxing the boundless resources, along with primary election bills, antitrust and regulatory measures, prohibition amendments, pure food and drug bills, curbs against lobbying, and so on through the full range of progressive ideas. The labor reformers also presented their demands for improved working conditions and an employers' liability law. Most of these measures won verbal support at one time or another from Governor Dawson, but his deeds were much more ambiguous. Shortly after assuming office, he added by executive order to Tax Commissioner Charles W. Dillon (whose office was established by the 1904 laws) mineral and petroleum leaseholds to the property rolls, but this marked the forward advance of the tax reform movement.[2] Subsequently, Dawson pressed for further rationalization of the new system and for its extension to the county level, but the structural changes, such as they were, ended in 1905.

One reason is that the reforms already enacted, particularly the annual reassessments under the commissioner's supervision (and that of local boards of equalization established in 1909), eased the state's revenue crisis. What remained to be done existed in the realm of platform pledges and fiscal justice rather than of necessity.[3] Yet other reasons had to do with practical politics. The legislature of 1907, for example, charged with the duty of returning Elkins to Washington for a third term, saw a change in the practice of using the Republican caucus to carry out the governor's published demands. Senator L. J. Forman of Grant County, a persistent and hardworking advocate of the severance tax and other progressive measures, presented himself as a candidate for the senate presidency and through it control of the committees and procedural machinery that had previously stifled administration bills, but he was unable to secure the organization's backing. Instead the post went with Dawson's support to Joseph H. McDermott, a Morgantown gas producer close to Standard Oil and to Secretary of State Swisher. Swisher, in turn, was able to assure his fellow Fairmonter, A. B. Fleming, that "There is not any chance of any vicious legislation along any line. You may rest assured of this." The assurance proved correct.[4]

A similar moderation was evinced in the election year of 1908, when Dawson called a special session of the legislature to complete the work on his reassessment program. In 1909, however, he presented a full schedule of "radical" fiscal, regulatory, and labor demands, which Swisher, McDermott, and the retainers as handily strangled. The chief product of the 1909 session was a "Board of Control," another salaried commission given supervisory powers over the business affairs of state institutions, to which body Dawson was appointed in

234

1913.[5] Withal, those conservatives who harkened more to words than to actions rejoiced when Dawson stepped down in tandem with Theodore Roosevelt on March 4, 1909. Those who looked at the record, however, had to conclude that the governor's "radicalism" had been badly misunderstood.[6]

But the trend toward moderation failed to halt Republican bloodletting. Instead all parties concerned continued to press for personal vindication and the upper hand over their enemies, straining Senator Elkins's celebrated tact to the limit. When the Roosevelt administration declined to discipline Blizzard and the other federal officeholders for their roles in the lobbies at Charleston in 1905, White and Dawson worked to force their tormentors to repeat the fee splitting charges under oath. Blizzard and Caldwell in turn declined to withdraw the charges but also to testify, thus initiating a legal battle over the investigating committee's subpoena power that dragged on until the end of 1906. Elkins and Scott sought to act as peacemakers, but both sides refused to budge. "I have kept still and been as sweet as I could under a torrent of lies and slanders and abuse from these people," Dawson retorted to Elkins's plea, but no longer. "If I had been the leader of the party I would have done otherwise; but you are the leader and I did not want to embarrass you." Now it was up to Elkins to call the conservative regulars to heel.[7] Instead the senator sought to mollify all of his followers. Blizzard and his sidekicks kept their federal jobs, Dawson had a free hand at the statehouse, Hubbard and Sturgiss got the first and second district congressional seats, respectively, in the election of 1906. These arrangements papered over the breach sufficiently to permit Elkins a tranquil canvass for reelection.[8] But his refusal to back his most trusted lieutenants and their program was the first step in a series of events that was leading to rival statehouse and senatorial factions of the organization at the time of the senator's death.

In the interim a new and more violent quarrel broke out over the choice of Dawson's successor. Dawson's preferred heir—and apparently Elkins's first choice also—was Elliott Northcott of Huntington, currently state chairman, district

235

attorney, and a loyal supporter of tax reform since the inception of the program in 1903. But Northcott steadfastly refused to run. So did Dillon and ex-Governor White. Instead Northcott wanted and got a diplomatic appointment. White took Dillon's place as tax commissioner in 1907. Dillon returned to "a very lucrative law practice." The organization's gubernatorial mantle fell upon Swisher, who, as Dawson explained, may have trained with the corporations in the capitol lobby but at least had supported the administration as a member of the Board of Public Works.[9] This turn of events appalled the progressives among the organization's backers. "It is hard to get needed legislation when the governor is behind it and in sympathy," Forman complained. With Swisher as governor the reform movement would collapse:

> He may sustain the Governor in all his contests before the Board of Public Works. He is shrewd enough to see the advantage this action will give him. I observed his conduct during the last session of the Legislature and he was not in favor with [sic] tax reform. When the question came up of taxing oil and gas he was against it. . . . He was against investigating the mine explosions until it was too late to gain definite knowledge. He played his part well, claimed to be with the administration and yet did ten times more harm so far as needed legislation as if he had been openly opposed to it.[10]

Through the summer and fall of 1907, Forman prodded Sturgiss and other reform leaders to "take this responsibility" and produce a more acceptable man. All replies were rebuffs, however, and not always gentle ones.[11] "Men who realize the tremendous sacrifice of Governor Dawson in the interest of the people, shrink at trying to make the race for Governor," one of Dawson's appointees explained. Though none of the organization men had lost their thirst for public service, neither did any wish to confront "the array of legal talent and the unlimited funds" with which White and Dawson had had to contend since 1903.[12] Given the option of taking on *both* standpatters and the Elkins organization, the progressives were themselves intimidated. "The only question is, shall we take half a loaf or no bread?" stated one of Forman's contacts. "The rest of us . . . are more or less discouraged. . . . It may be that some light will come out of this darkness, but I am frank in saying I do not know where it is to come from."[13]

Certainly no light was to be expected from the anti-organization candidate in 1908. Arnold C. Scherr, elected state auditor as an anti-tax member of the slate nominated with Dawson in 1904, was an old-line Republican who nursed a smoldering resentment of Elkins and his men. The most he would promise in his gubernatorial campaign was a "pure" and "economical" administration, "free from ring rule." This was sufficient to attract to his candidacy a mixed bag of conservatives and opportunists, most prominently Elliott, Blizzard, and Freer.[14] Given a choice of rue and water, some progressives came over to Scherr on the grounds that he at least was honest and independent. Others took to the fence.[15] But though it engaged few of the issues that divided West Virginia Republicans in 1908, the Swisher-Scherr contest managed to arouse all the frustration and bitterness. With the organization's usual efficiency behind him, Swisher won most of the preconvention battles. However, when the state committee awarded credentials to Swisher's men in the cases of several contested county delegations to the nominating convention on July 8, the Scherrites made good on their threat to bolt. The result was two Republican tickets, two platforms with promises of reform occupied by candidates who offered meagre prospects of change. The principal difference was that the Scherr platform held Elkins, Scott, Dawson, and "machine domination" "largely responsible" for this "deplorable" state of affairs.[16]

Since the G.O.P. faced an enemy in 1908 that was fully determined to disfranchise its 20,000 black supporters, the party split was deplorable indeed. Again Elkins assumed the role of a peacemaker. Assembling the party leaders in conference at Hot Springs, Virginia, after tempers had cooled, he persuaded Scherr and Swisher to withdraw and placed their mantle on William E. Glasscock, whom the reassembled gubernatorial convention duly nominated in September. Glass-

237

cock had worked for Freer in 1900, for Dawson in 1904, and as a state committeeman had sided with Scherr without joining his walkout.[17] He was thus an acceptable compromise candidate. His election in November saved the party from long-range disaster, but it marked the beginning of the end for the Elkins regime.

All of the contradictions of the Elkins era came to the surface during the administration of Governor Glasscock. The governor, like his predecessors, was a contradiction himself. There was little in his record to peg him as a reformer. At the time of his election, he was correctly identified "as part of Mr. Elkins' personal machine, one of his federal officeholders and his personal attorney in Monongalia County. . . ."[18] Yet Glasscock brought to the statehouse commitments that eventually made him the most "progressive" of all the organization reformers. One of these commitments was a faith in West Virginia's development, and alarm at the drain of its resources, particularly in the case of natural gas. Accordingly he took charge of the demand for severance taxes, aimed it at the gas producers and—aided by a new wave of Standard Oil consolidations and pipeline installations linking the West Virginia fields to yet more metropolitan centers—brought it to its highest pitch of intensity in the winter of 1909-1910. It was generally conceded in the press (and by the gas producers) that, had Glasscock summoned a special legislative session at this point, the "gas tax" stood an excellent chance of enactment.[19]

Glasscock was also a devoted partisan and hoped to put an end to the factional struggles that wracked the West Virginia G.O.P. One of his prescriptions was the institution of primaries in place of caucuses and conventions and, though he was sensitive to the fears of other partisans that primaries might work to the benefit of disruptive minorities or the Democrats, he eventually inclined to the far-reaching Oregon model as the best solution for local Republican ills.[20] He also called for redemption of Republican platform pledges on prohibition, either by adopting the local-option law demanded

238

by the increasingly powerful Anti-Saloon League or by the submission of a prohibition amendment. After seeing each of these items separately butchered in the legislature of 1909, he searched for a means to secure their adoption, considering a special session and the appointment of multifactional drafting commissions as White had done in the tax matter in 1901. Eventually he decided to present them along with the gas tax to the next regular session after due publicizing of the reform package during the legislative campaign of 1910.[21] The decision was a plausible one, but by the time the 1911 session convened to hear Glasscock's proposals, the chance for their adoption had passed.

Notwithstanding the circumstances of his election, Glasscock was also determined to establish his independence from Elkins. Although relations between the two men remained cordial throughout 1909 and 1910, the governor moved quickly with Dawson and Representatives Hubbard and Sturgiss to establish a channel of communications to the White House free of senatorial eavesdropping. President Taft, however, gave Glasscock encouraging words and the federal appointments to Elkins and Scott.[22] Two of the first to go were Elliott and Blizzard, apparently in punishment for their role in the Scherr insurgency, but this was Scott's doing, not Glasscock's. Indeed Elliott shortly turned up in Charleston as commander of the West Virginia National Guard by virtue of Glasscock's appointment, thus completing the circle of organization veterans now within the "progressive" statehouse combination. "Perhaps Scott is right," remarked the marshal-turned-general; "two terms of any good thing ought to satisfy the most ravenous. However, when I retire their [sic] will be other graves on which to strew flowers."[23] Indeed one of the first graves marked for strewing was that of the "assistant Senator," Scott. In January 1910, Hubbard announced his candidacy for the upcoming senatorial vacancy and, with the support of Dawson, Sturgiss, and Elliott, challenged Scott to a series of county primaries for control of legislative nominations. Scott accepted and, as both sides won or lost depending upon the disposition of local county

239

organizations, both began to cry foul.²⁴ "Mr. Dawson and Mr. Hubbard are resorting to the most contemptible politics that were ever practiced in this State," Scott complained to Glasscock in April. He might lose the battle, but "never, as long as I have life in me or a dollar in the world, will I hesitate to punish those who are trying to disrupt the party for purely personal and selfish motives." While Glasscock stood publicly apart from Hubbard's candidacy, he gave it quiet encouragement and coldly informed Scott that "I am not afraid of either you or your money or both. . . ."²⁵ Thus as the canvass progressed, it assumed the bitter proportions of 1904 and 1908, except that this time the issues were joined in dozens of local contests instead of a single statewide campaign.

Elkins not surprisingly found this trend of events perturbing, but being less directly concerned with the outcome than Scott, managed to keep his cool. Sensitive to Glasscock's assertion of independence, he gave the governor a free hand in the distribution of state patronage and gently advanced suggested appointments which the governor as gently rebuffed.²⁶ He also chimed in with an endorsement—albeit a heavily qualified one—of Glasscock's severance tax program. He also favored, or so he said, a public service commission and "some sort of primary," although not one of the "disastrous" sort that would abridge the "sacred right" of legislatures to elect United States senators.²⁷ Altogether he urged Glasscock gently but persistently to slow down. "Things should be moving on conservative lines," he wrote in 1909. "We are at a point now where we want to make a good impression on capital and the business interests of the State."²⁸

Tariff and railroad matters in Congress greatly complicated Elkins's position by requiring his attention in Washington throughout 1909 and 1910, while Glasscock was careful to keep out of his reach. The governor assured Elkins that the drive against Scott would not affect the senior Senate seat, but Davis Elkins was not so certain. "They don't like to fight you both at the same time," he reported to his father from

Glasscock's home city of Morgantown in April 1910; "therefore, they pick out Scott and take you the next time, no matter what they promise. . . . Governor Glasscock is a good friend of all of us, and I like him, but he is influenced a great deal by a set of men that are not such good friends."[29] With mounting anxiety, Elkins warned the organization reformers that the drive against Scott would alter the balance of Republican power and that the conservatives, "Scherr, Stalnaker, Teter, Blizzard and that crowd would feel they were in the saddle." Glasscock ignored the warnings, however, and without exactly rejecting Elkins's appeals for a conference in Washington or at some neutral site in Virginia somehow managed never to be able to come.[30]

Throughout the summer of 1910, Elkins and Glasscock worked separately to contain the effects of the Scott-Hubbard contests. Increasingly it became apparent to each that the problem was less one of advancing conservative or progressive viewpoints than of simply holding the party together by the best means available. But by the time that Glasscock was ready to admit that "I do need some help," he was informed that Elkins could no longer see him.[31] Exhausted by the struggle over the Mann-Elkins Act in Congress, the senator failed to respond to a prolonged summer rest in the Virginia mountains. In August he took to his bed with what was first diagnosed as a touch of malaria. Although the precise state of his health remained a closely kept secret, it was known in informed circles by November that Elkins had cancer of the stomach and was slowly starving to death in his luxurious West Virginia home. "I am sorry the Republicans of the State did not appreciate the gravity of the situation more during the campaign," Glasscock later reflected; he had tried to warn them "in a confidential way that the probabilities were that this Legislature would have to elect two United States Senators."[32] But the warning went unheeded and when the end came it was as a Democratic rather than a Republican legislature was preparing to convene. "Poor Elkins died last night," wrote New Mexico's congressional delegate to Thomas B. Catron on January 5. "What a loss to the contry [*sic*] and to West Virginia people." In tribute to the leader's memory, Glasscock appointed Davis Elkins to hold his father's seat in the senate until a Democratic successor was named.[33]

Had the captain gone down with the ship or the ship with the captain? Elkins's active participation in the 1910 campaign might have made some difference, but it probably would not have altered the outcome. Revolving around dozens of local legislative or congressional contests, the campaign of 1910 unleashed a bewildering variety of conflicts, as Glasscock discovered when he sought to patch things together in the fall. Rarely did these have the character of a direct progressive-conservative confrontation. Such was initially the case in Monongalia County, for example, where progressive and labor insurgents attempted to prevent the renomination of Senator McDermott, but this quarrel subsequently became entangled with a factional struggle in Marion, also in McDermott's district, which centered on the Fairmont and Mannington post offices.[34] In Clay County "dry" insurgents sent a separate ticket into the field against a regular organization whose leaders were "wet"; in Mercer, the drys were the regulars and the wets in revolt.[35] The impact of social change cast its shadow in Wetzel—one of the oil counties—where old-line Republicans refused "to be dictated to by new comers" on the county committee, and in Barbour, where the county court "after this county had been dry for a quarter of a century" was alleged to have "gone into an agreement with the liquor people, for money consideration, to grant licenses at the mining towns."[36] Scott's supporters were boycotting the Hog Combine's pro-Hubbard ticket in Kanawha, while Hubbard men fielded a second Republican ticket in the fifth senatorial district.[37] The age and complexity of the split in Mason County was well represented by the meaningless names of the factions: Ninnyhammer and Ninnysquaw. In 1910 one was wet, the other dry; one controlled the county committee and election officials, the other declined to recognize them, but these were only the temporal manifestations of a local feud "so broad and [with] so many ramifications" that one of the combatants found it "impossible to discuss them at length in an ordinary letter."[38] Where conservatives were in control the question was "whether the decisions of the party tribunals . . . are binding and shall be respected"; where they were in revolt, "Some of our mutual friends should have thought of these matters before they followed off ideas foreign to the Republican party."[39]

Altogether there was very little of "the old time party loyalty," as Charlie Elliott complained of the Mason County squabblers, among Republican politicians in West Virginia in 1910.[40] Through the autumn Glasscock and Elliott worked industriously to heal the breaches and reduced the number of insurgent local tickets to four by election day. Elsewhere the various factions accepted Glasscock's arbitration, settled in the courts or by primaries or, in Clay where the regulars refused to call the primary a primary, by "Arbitration by the People."[41] But as Glasscock perceived, arrangements among leaders were no guarantee "so far as the individual voters are concerned." Under the circumstances it was difficult to know how the voters would react to the turmoil. Sturgiss sensed "a spirit of indifference" combined with "unrest." "This State is Republican," wrote Glasscock in a postelection analysis. Had not so many voters stayed home from the polls "the results would have been different." Presumably the electorate reflected the manifold irritants of its chiefs, but "In addition to that many people had become thoroughly disgusted with our methods and they were determined to have a housecleaning."[42]

If the voters expected a clean sweep to come from the Democrats, however, they were in for a surprise. The West Virginia Legislature of 1911 did not enact a severance tax or a public service commission law. Nor did it enact a primary law, even though Governor Glasscock recalled it for that specific purpose later in the year. It did submit a prohibition amendment which the voters approved in a referendum held at the general election of 1912. Otherwise it was distinguished by two developments, both of which drew national attention to Charleston. One was the bolt of fifteen Republican state senators to Ohio, where they fled beyond the reach of the sergeant at arms. As organized and approved by Governor Glasscock, the purpose of the hegira was to prevent the Democrats from organizing both houses of the legislature and so passing their own versions of legislative and congressional apportionment bills.[43]

The session's second achievement lay in its choice of United States senators. The prospect of two senatorial vacancies attracted a number of Democratic hopefuls, among them ex-Senator Davis, who moved quickly to cash in his fifteen-year-old chips from the Kanawha Ring. Along with many others, Davis got a brush-off.[44] The Kanawhans had found a more generous patron in Clarence W. Watson, who got the two-year vacancy created by the death of Senator Elkins, while William E. Chilton claimed a full term as the successor of Scott. Unlike the industrialists who preceded him in the office, Watson had no record of party leadership or service and had not given even pro forma support to the national Democracy during the three campaigns when it was led by Bryan. The Kanawhans had enlisted his money in the 1910 campaign but not as a senatorial candidate "under any circumstances," or so Watson had stated in the spring.[45] Now the consummation of the apparent bargain set off an uproar that persisted throughout Watson's two years in office. "There is but one plausible excuse that any member of the Legislature can give for supporting either Chilton or Watson," wrote an angry progressive Democrat, "and that is, that he was paid for it." "What [were] the issues that caused the demand for the change of parties?" asked another; was it a demand for more United States senators of the Watson type? "I feel very sure that not a single Democrat could be elected from these counties next year, if he ran on a Watson platform," wrote an editor whose Republican district had returned twelve of thirteen Democratic legislative candidates in 1910. "Anti-Watson sentiment is so strong in this section that no one can possibly be mistaken in the matter."[46]

As a result of these feelings, bipartisan demands for an investigation of bribery charges circulated in Charleston for more than a year,[47] but other Democrats were ready with apologies of the usual type. "Watson is no accident," explained a Parkersburg banker. "Great concerns like the Consolidated [sic] Coal Company don't make Presidents of pygmies, and with his strong character, his great organizing ability, and his close touch with people who do things, I verily believe he can do as much for the development and building up of our State as any one we could have selected...."[48] There was no bribery involved in his deal with Watson, Senator Chilton later explained. "Other candidates combined their strength. Why should not we?" The enemies of "Watsonism," he added, were really the foes of West Virginia's prosperity.

> I was born in the mountains of West Virginia, and so was Watson. We came from the people, who have made these mountains famous—who have conquered the difficulties and overcome the obstacles in the way of civilization, progress, and development. Whenever one of the boys from the mountains breaks into the Senate, there are always those ready to charge fraud and corruption.[49]

The most revealing comments of all in 1911 came from a future Democratic governor, John J. Cornwell. After his defeat as the anti-tax gubernatorial candidate in 1904, Cornwell sought and eventually won a share of the party leadership with Watson as the spokesman of Bryanite and working class Democrats and so presided over the West Virginia Democracy's transition from its "Bourbon" to "liberal" phases. In reality, however, Cornwell was an intelligent *comprador* who maintained metropolitan financial and industrial connections of his own independently of the usual Watson-Fleming connection. "It is useless to conceal the fact or ignore it that Mr. Watson's candidacy is going to precipitate a tremendous row in this State whether he is elected or not," Cornwell explained to B&O officials and to Rockefeller bankers in New York. "Out of this Senatorship wrangle will come a new and vicious assault on the corporations in this State and somebody in whom the people have confidence must stand out to again meet it and do the best they can to stem the onslaught . . . "; "my strength in the Party is largely with the more radical element," he later added,

> . . . which is hostile to [Watson] and would not be reconciled to him or his election no matter what I might say or do. I have striven very earnestly to control this element and direct it along more conservative lines of thought and action, for it is, numerically, in the majority in the State. To have espoused Mr. Watson's candidacy would have alienated this large and influential element from myself and done him no good.[50]

In other words, the industrialists may have called the *compradors* into being in West Virginia; but "the boys from the mountains" were now ready to rule on their own.

The roles of Senator Watson and Governor Cornwell would be played among West Virginia Republicans by Senator Davis Elkins and Governor (and later Senator) Henry D. Hatfield. The younger Elkins rapidly moved to take charge of the conservative wing of the party during the two years after his father's death, but his success was incomplete despite Scott's support of Elkins and the assistance of his Democratic cousins and grandfather. The conservatives of southern West Virginia presented a rival candidate in the person of a Bluefield banker and coal producer, Isaac T. Mann. Thus the second Elkins era opened in 1913 as the first one had in 1887 with a grueling senatorial struggle, ending in a compromise by which the G.O.P. dusted off its ill and aging former leader, Judge Nathan Goff, and sent him at last to Washington. The younger Elkins was forced to wait for a term to don the toga but eventually won it by defeating Clarence Watson in the general election of 1918.[51]

In the meantime, the old Elkins organization channeled its reformist urge into national politics. Having failed to secure the adoption of a general primary law in 1911, Glasscock secured one for state and local Republican nominations by action of the state committee in 1912. Then the reformers allowed its fruits to go by default to Hatfield in the gubernatorial primary, while they used the old bureaucratic machinery to swing the state firmly behind Theodore Roosevelt's campaign against Taft.[52] Glasscock himself helped to launch the Roosevelt candidacy by joining with six other Republican governors to provide the ring into which the ex-president tossed his hat in February 1912. Then the governor summoned West Virginia's Roosevelt supporters to an organizing session at Parkersburg on February 28, where they selected Dawson to lead them.[53] Beginning in mid-April, when Glasscock and Davis Elkins exchanged telegrams accusing one another of fraudulent intent in the Monongalia County convention, the Roosevelt forces swept a series of county primaries and conventions climaxed on April 26, when the Hog Combine presented Dawson with a thumping Roosevelt victory in Kanawha. The state delegate convention in May, described by the Wheeling *Intelligencer* as the "worst bossed" in recent history, also selected a solid Roosevelt delegation to the national convention, where the delegates displaced Scott—now standing for Taft and the forces of "law and order"—from the national committee after six consecutive terms.[54]

Following Taft's nomination in June, Dawson, White, Hubbard, Glasscock, Charlie Elliott, and Grant P. Hall of the Kanawha Combine turned to organizing the West Virginia branch of Roosevelt's Progressive party, establishing what surely must have been one of the more distinctive herds of Bull Moose to be found anywhere in 1912. They dissuaded their followers from launching state and local Progressive tickets, however, citing the threat of Negro disfranchisement if the Democrats won.[55] Consequently Wilson won the state's electoral votes, while control of the legislature and congressional delegation returned to the Republicans, along with the governorship. With this outcome the unity and insurgency of the Progressives quickly subsided. William Seymour Edwards, a Charleston businessman and Scott's successor as national committeeman, was the principal Progressive entry into the senatorial lists in 1913, but White, Hubbard, and Dawson arranged themselves in available poses in the wings.[56] When less prominent Progressives sought to float a statewide third-party movement in 1914, the veteran leaders gave them meagre encouragement, apart from Elliott.[57] The others returned to the regular fold, but while some of them (Dawson and White, for example) also returned to the state or federal payrolls, the old group never again functioned as an effective political combination. It was perhaps fitting that the man who in many ways symbolized the Elkins organization's chequered career, General Charles D. Elliott, rode out of West Virginia history on horseback at the head of Governor Hatfield's inaugural parade on March 4, 1913. Hatfield, who a scant month later was to order the state militia under different leadership into the coalfields, travelled behind in a car.[58]

West Virginians are fond of the idea that their state, by virtue of its geographic position, is "a crossroads of the nation." "The most Northern of the Southern, the most Southern of the Northern . . ." and so on around the compass is a favorite slogan. The Progressive era suggests that a location on the frontiers of the East, South, and Middle West could combine the worst as well as the best of the three sections in the Mountain State. For West Virginia produced a hybrid reform movement. In its objectives, it was comparable to those eastern states where fiscal and administrative reorganization were carried out under conservative auspices without much disturbing the political status quo. In its political turbulence, it resembled those southern and western states were insurgent Progressives transformed the majority party into an engine of political and economic change.[59] In its achievements the movement was unequal to either model, as those contemporaries who were interested in wide-ranging changes were fully aware.

Writing as a young professor in 1905, Charles H. Ambler commented wistfully in another context about "the tradition of all mountainous countries for slowness to adopt reforms."[60] Looking back from the perspective of later years, he concluded that West Virginia, while conservative, was "not

248

averse to change." The changes adopted during the decade after 1903 included many of the administrative and electoral reforms associated with the progressive movement in other states. Yet "These changes and tendencies did not entitle West Virginia to rank among the 'progressive' states of the Union." For one thing, Ambler noted, there was a persistent tendency at Charleston to shape reforms to suit one essential local condition: an increase in the number of political jobs.[61] As for tax reform, the measures adopted failed to alter the pattern of regressive taxation. And even these, W. P. Hubbard noted dejectedly in 1913, tended to be abandoned in favor of stopgap measures under pressure of a continuing need for revenues.[62]

Even had the Tax Commission program been adopted *in toto,* this alone would not have made West Virginia "one of the most progressive states of the Union," as one enthusiast has written.[63] But it would have made a difference in the answer to what was perhaps the central question of the era that drew to a close in 1913: Who would control the boundless resources? The defeat of severance taxes spelled a definitive answer: West Virginia's resources had been and would continue to be exploited, not developed, chiefly for the benefit of nonresident corporations, with such public advantages and disadvantages as private exploitation might provide. No finer testimony on this point exists than that provided by ex-Governor Fleming at the end of the tax reform period in 1909. Queried by Philadelphia capitalists about the prospects for free enterprise in West Virginia, the stalwart retainer replied in glowing terms:

> Any person who will take the code of West Virginia or the statutes enacted by the legislatures, even during the recent period of crusade against corporations in the United States, will find that this hostility has not reached the West Virginia legislatures, and I can say has not reached the people generally. . . . I represent as General Counsel the Standard Oil interests in the state, and some of the largest coal interests, and generally appear before one or more of the committees every session of the legislature to discuss and object to some anti-corporation legislation proposed. We have

always succeeded in defeating everything to which we objected, and that too without the use of money.

"If there is a state in the Union from which I would expect fair treatment to corporations," Fleming concluded, "it would be West Virginia. Corporations have no right to complain of their treatment in this state."[64]

If the first phase of industrialization determined the control of West Virginia's resources, the problem of industrial relations remained to be dealt with. The Progressive era saw an increase in the number of politicians who seemed attentive to the demands of the workingmen and a dearth of legislation shaped to their needs. A Republican legislator explained to Fleming how this was so:

> As you will remember, in order to placate the labor interests, certain of their bills were allowed to pass the House. In permitting their passage, we knew full well there would be no time for them to be considered in the Senate. Consequently, the House, and especially some of its officers, received credit for being very favorable to labor interests, and I have received assurance from numerous [labor] organizations that I would be consulted on all matters which may have a political aspect.[65]

Similarly Governor Dawson won favor with the coal miners by publicizing peonage charges initiated by the Italian Embassy against two southern West Virginia coal camps and by making the first official criticisms of the system of private guards and detectives that made detention of unwilling workers possible. He also consorted with union leaders and appointed a commission to recommend a revision of the mining laws to the legislature of 1907.[66] But the resulting changes were carried out chiefly "according to the ideas of the coal barons," or so stated a Charleston labor newspaper. Fleming put it more bluntly in alerting the Consolidation Coal Company: "Legislature passed the mining bill we desired. Defeated labor bills."[67] Later in the year when the devastating explosion at the Fairmont Coal Company's Monongah mine occurred on the eve of the governor's special session, coal operators from all over the state rushed into emergency meetings in fear of "further mining laws . . . making the matter of

250

mining a burden." Dawson excluded the matter from his call to the session, however, and privately let it be known that "He [would] oppose any radical coal legislation" until the memory of Monongah's victims had cooled.[68] Both White and Dawson continued in the office of chief mine inspector James W. Paul, originally an Atkinson appointee, whose independence and vigor made him, among other things, a "crank" on the subject of mine explosions.[69] When Paul moved on to the Federal Bureau of Mines at the end of his third term, the operators prepared a bill to abolish his office and to turn over its duties to a three-man commission dominated by them. Instead Glasscock appointed as Paul's successor John R. Laing, a former (and future) operator himself, in whom the other producers found themselves "very much pleased. . . ."[70] Meanwhile the number of mine inspectors grew from five in 1901 to seven in 1907 to fifteen in 1915.[71]

The same period saw a deterioration of labor relations in the coalfields. Ignoring their defeat in the Fairmont field in 1902, the United Mine Workers spent "about $1,000,000" trying to solve its "West Virginia problem" during the succeeding decade.[72] Yet the union's position steadily deteriorated as some of the smaller operators of the Kanawha valley sought to roll back an earlier union advance. Here, instead of the smoothly efficient politico-legal bulwark manned by Fleming, the organizers encountered the deadly private violence of a different type of retainer, the most notorious of whom came from the Baldwin-Felts Detective Agency of Roanoke, Virginia. When newly consolidated operators in the Cabin Creek and Paint Creek districts of Kanawha County refused to renew UMW contracts that expired in March 1912, a general conflict broke out between the miners and the guards. Though the miners lacked the machine guns and other modern equipment supplied the detectives, both sides were armed and both were implicated in the bloodshed, although by the light of modern labor relations standards, the miners endured extreme provocations before taking their weapons off the wall. Governor Glasscock ordered the militia to Cabin Creek in July, denounced the mine guards and

251

appointed an investigating commission, which, in turn, denounced the guards *and* the UMW. A cycle that would become disturbingly familiar in twentieth-century West Virginia had begun.[73]

The man who succeeded Elkins to the Republican party leadership was to preside over the new age with the same conservative realism that had characterized the senator's approach to reform. Governor Henry Drury Hatfield was a practicing physician who combined a medical education in Louisville and New York with a background as colorfully West Virginian as any old-line Republican could have asked for. A member of the state's most celebrated mountain clan, the doctor was a nephew of Anderson Hatfield, better known to lovers of feud lore as "Devil Anse." He belonged to a more respectable branch of the Hatfields, however. His father had moved his children out of the feud region to escape the violence and to provide for their education, while Henry eschewed the clan's traditional Democracy for the Republicanism of McCoys. Even so, this background might have proved fatal in West Virginia politics twenty years earlier. The "ignorant" and "improvident" mountaineers of the interior had constituted a serious source of embarrassment to pioneer votaries of the development faith, and the first "New York journalists" to earn the wrath of local patriots had been those who broadcast the stories of the feuds.[74] Now with Hatfield's native Tug Fork valley pitted with hundreds of coal mines, the doctor impressed Wheelingites as "an interesting and picturesque candidate" as he made his first northern West Virginia campaign trip in the gubernatorial race of 1912.[75]

Notwithstanding his antecedents, Hatfield was no backwoodsman when it came to politics. Having returned to West Virginia as a company doctor for the N&W, he quickly secured an appointment from Governor White as director of one of the miners' hospitals established by the legislature of 1899. Later he served as county commissioner and state senator in the McDowell County organization headed by E. P.

Rucker and became its foremost representative in state political circles following Rucker's death in 1908.[76] It was at this point that he came to the attention of Elkins. Perhaps the senator was attracted by the "Hatfield bill," which Elkins endorsed as the most conservative of the primary election measures introduced in the legislature of 1909.[77] Perhaps, too, Hatfield offered a solution to another practical problem: how to accommodate in a Republican organization led by northern West Virginians the "clamorous" demands for political recognition that assailed Elkins from the burgeoning south.[78] During the Democratic era, heavy majorities from the southern counties had provided Greenbrier valley Redeemers and the Kanawha Ring with leverage against Camden and Davis. Now the region was just as strongly Republican and its leaders, like the Kanawhans, enjoyed connections with the dominant metropolitan mining and railroad corporations independently of the organization command. Yet all but a few of Republican party and public officials still came from the north, a situation that, as I. T. Mann's senatorial challenge to Davis Elkins in 1913 indicated, southerners were determined to change. Possibly Elkins saw in Hatfield a man to guard the southern flank of the kingdom. In any event, he liked what he saw. As the party crisis approached in 1910, he urged Glasscock to "get closer to Senator Hatfield. You may need the benefit of his judgment and advice. He is a strong man...."[79]

Given the dynastic instincts of his own offspring, it is doubtful that Elkins intended Hatfield as his successor, but that is in fact what the doctor became. To an electorate weary of the noisy and unproductive factional squabbling of the past four years, Hatfield projected the image of fresh leadership, untrammeled by previous factional involvements, yet devoted to Republican success. Taking advantage of the organization reformers' preoccupation with presidential politics in 1912, he trounced Swisher and Dillon in the gubernatorial primary and swept on to victory with a Republican legislature in the fall.[80] Continuing to hold himself aloof from factional struggles during senatorial combat in 1913, he pledged a religious observance of the spoils systems and unveiled his own reform program under the label of "constructive socialism." Under his leadership, the legislatures of 1913 and 1915 established a public service commission, primary elections, and an optional workmen's compensation scheme, thus bringing to an end the era of reform.[81] Concurrently, Hatfield sent troops into the Kanawha coalfields, proclaimed martial law shortly after taking office, and hounded the real socialists by suppressing their newspapers and jailing Socialist party organizers as "criminals" and "carpetbagger[s] from some other State."[82] He also laid the foundations of a new Republican organization that would endure until the 1950s. In all of these endeavors, Hatfield was doubtless aided by the lack of competition for G.O.P. leadership, with the federal patronage and one of the senatorships in the hands of Democrats and the other on loan to old Judge Goff. He was also aided by Walter S. Hallanan, a young Huntington newspaperman who came to Charleston as Hatfield's private secretary and remained in a series of state and federal appointments to become the Dawson of the modern Republican age.[83] Meanwhile congressional investigators and other "outsiders" probed the coalfield disturbances and initiated the local elite into a new series of embarrassing encounters with visiting journalists and "pseudophilanthropists."[84] Thus Hatfield's inauguration in the fiftieth year of West Virginia statehood made the year 1913 a turning point as well as an anniversary.

The omens pointed to the future in 1913. The anniversary year saw violence in the coalfields, record-breaking floods in the valleys, the consolidation of the colonial political economy under a new generation of leaders. Each of these occurrences pointed in the direction of modern "Appalachia." At the time, however, most articulate citizens were less interested in portents of the future than in mellowing their view of the past.

Conceding the ambiguous character of the statehood era as it had actually taken place, the historian Ambler lamented the fact that circumstances had deprived West Virginia of the heroic men and events upon which might have been founded "a wholesome state pride."[85] But the jubilee years showed that where pride was lacking, braggadocio and romance could supply. The first of several sentimental occasions took place in October 1909, when Governor Glasscock dedicated a monument at Point Pleasant—the site of an episode of Indian warfare that had somehow become the first battle of the American Revolution—with a stirring address about West Virginia's manufacturing potential.[86] In May 1910 old Governor Pierpont was dredged up from the obscurity to which his political enemies had consigned him and installed next to John E. Kenna in Statuary Hall in the United States Capitol.[87] That fall another unveiling took place on the capitol lawn in Charleston, where that scion of the antebellum elite, Stonewall Jackson, having "died as he was born, a Virginian," was now mounted in bronze as West Virginia's most eminent native son. Less than two decades before a commemoration of Stonewall's birthday under MacCorkle's auspices had scandalized West Virginia Republicans. Now the only untoward incident occurred when the National Guard contingent carrying the national colors was somehow mustered into the parade behind Virginia Military Institute cadets. Even the once-despised mountaineer was rejuvenated and a stone figure clad in skins and grasping a mountain rifle was set in place beside Stonewall on the capitol lawn.[88] As the real life backwoodsmen passed from ignominy to legend, sending their sons to the coal mines, their grandsons to the shipyards of Baltimore and the factories of Detroit, editors along the main streets of West Virginia towns learned how to enliven their conservative catechisms with a syrup of hillbilly humor, creating a form of cornpone Babbitry that still sells well in local markets and is occasionally peddled abroad.

The biggest blowout of all was the official semicentennial celebration at Wheeling on June 19-20, 1913. Three years in the planning, the event was threatened by some last minute hitches. The city of the statemakers had not only to adorn itself for the occasion but to clean itself up after the spring inundations, while there was some apprehension that the keynote speaker, Governor Hatfield, would be detained in Charleston by the "mine war." Also the organizers forgot to include Senator Goff in the ceremony or even to invite him, and when someone finally recalled his existence, the indignant old gentleman refused to come.[89] Otherwise everything came off splendidly. Official delegations from Washington and Richmond beefed up the array of local dignitaries. Hatfield made his address and the Semi-Centennial Commission released an official "Jubilee Song," both of which conveyed pretty much the same message. Additional commemorative exercises included a banquet, a ball, an airplane show, and some motorcycle races.[90]

Presiding over the Wheeling affair was the chairman of the Semi-Centennial Commission, ex-Senator Henry G. Davis. At the price of being hailed as "West Virginia's Grand Old Man," a tribute for which he had no fondness, Davis witnessed his own apotheosis as a visible saint of the development faith and heard his praises canted in verse:

> No other state can boast of such a peer
> Hale, staunch and wholesome in his ninetieth year.
> He looms as a connecting-link in time
> . . . .
> Before the locomotive raced the rail;
> Before the harnessed lightning pierced the vale;
> Before a thousand things of wondrous make—
> He lived, and gave his being for their sake.

All that remained to be done, his biographer later suggested, was to erect Davis's statue on the capitol lawn in Charleston, but almost as soon as the statue was raised, the capitol building burned down and was rebuilt in another location. Stonewall and the other statuary went along, but Davis and his horse stayed behind in downtown Charleston, across the street from a bank. Perhaps his statue was superfluous, in any case. For as a contemporary remarked shortly before Davis's death in 1916, "What Henry Gassaway Davis has done for West Virginia and her people will be a standing monument to his memory for centuries to come."[91]

Appendix

The following letters reveal cash contributions or loans by Davis to other politicians. They are designated as follows: [box] : [volume] , [page] . Except where noted, all references are to Davis Papers, series I. Letterbook volumes are unnumbered in this series; numbers assigned to them here refer to the chronological order in each box. (1870) 1:1, 199, 202; 2:1, 488; 3:1, 409; 27:2, 9, 14; (1872) 1:1, 239, 261-264, 271; (1874) 1:1, 345, 351, 361, 363, 366, 370-371, 375-378, 383, 385; (1876) 3:1, 167, 191, 228, 251, 262, 292-294, 296-297, 304, 306, 351, 365, 370; (1878) 1:2, 100, 102, 104-105, 124; (1880) 1:2, 381-382, 384, 386-387, 391, 401-403, 406, 414; (1882) 2:1, 222, 227; (1884) 2:1, 351, 374, 424, 426, 432, 438, 445; 3:2, 299, 435; (1886) 27:2, 54, 63, 67, 70; (1888) 4:1, 663, 694; 27:2, 142, 159, 164, 172; (1890) 4:3, 496, 686; 27:2, 285, 287; (1892) 27:3, 509, 511, 513; (1894) 7:1, 218, 305, 432, 467, 488, 531; (1896) 8:3, 273, 317, 325, 362, 533; (1898) 10:4, 186, 249, 393, 410, 417, 468, 516-517; 27:3, 681 687, 690, 692, n.p. (October 25-November 28, 1898); (1900) 12:1, 288, 579, 594, 616, 684; 12:2, 36, 137; (1904) see above, p. 228, n. 131; (off-years, chiefly to Maryland and Ohio) 4:3, 700; 8:1, 373, 589-590; 8:2, 156, 161; 8:3, 315; 11:3, 91, 309; 27:2, 27-28, 325-326; 27:3, 637, 642, and Murray Vandiver to HGD, October 18, 1897, in Correspondence, Personal.

Notes

NOTES TO CHAPTER 1

1. The historiography of Virginia sectionalism and the West Virginia statehood movement is still dominated by Charles H. Ambler. Of special importance are his *Sectionalism in Virginia, 1776-1861* (Chicago, 1910); "The Cleavage between Eastern and Western Virginia," *The American Historical Review*, 15 (July 1910), 726-780; *Francis H. Pierpont, Union War Governor of Virginia and Father of West Virginia* (Chapel Hill, 1937); *West Virginia, The Mountain State* (New York, first ed. 1933; rev. ed. 1940); "The Makers of West Virginia," *West Virginia History*, 2 (July 1941), 267-278. An important revisionist work is Richard O. Curry, *A House Divided, Statehood Politics and the Copperhead Movement in West Virginia* (Pittsburgh, 1964). Other studies include James M. Callahan, *Semi-Centennial History of West Virginia* (Morgantown, W.Va., 1913); J. A. C. Chandler, *Representation in Virginia* (Johns Hopkins University Studies in Historical and Political Science (Baltimore, 1896)); Granville D. Hall, *The Rending of Virginia* (Chicago, 1901); Theodore F. Lang, *Loyal West Virginia from 1861 to 1865* (Baltimore, 1895); James C. McGregor, *The Disruption of Virginia* (New York, 1922); George E. Moore, *A Banner in the Hills, West Virginia's Statehood* (New York, 1963); Henry T. Shanks, *The Secession Movement in Virginia, 1847-1861* (Richmond, Va., 1934); Edward C. Smith, *The Borderland in the Civil War* (New York, 1927); and Theodore M. Whitfield, *Slavery Agitation in Virginia, 1829-1832* (Johns Hopkins University Studies in Historical and Political Science (Baltimore, 1930)). Three important documentary sources are Virgil A. Lewis, *How West Virginia Was Made. Proceedings of the First Convention of the People of Northwestern Virginia at Wheeling, May 13, 14, and 15, 1861 and the Journal of the Second Convention ...* (Charleston, W.Va., 1912).

2. John C. Campbell, *The Southern Highlander and His Homeland* (New York, 1921; reprinted Lexington, Ky., 1969), and Harry M. Caudill, *Night Comes to the Cumberlands* (Boston, 1963), are works that expressed and influenced the key periods of twentieth-century interest in Appalachia. Thomas R. Ford et al., *The Southern Appalachian Region, A Survey* (Lexington, Ky., 1962), is an important anthology of scholarly viewpoints, while David S. Walls and John B. Stephenson,

259

Appalachia in the Sixties, Decade of Reawakening (Lexington, Ky., 1972), collects varied samples of recent commentary; see also *Appalachian Bibliography* (2 vols., Morgantown, W.Va., 1972).

3. John A. Williams, "The New Dominion and the Old: Ante-Bellum and Statehood Politics as the Background of West Virginia's 'Bourbon Democracy,' " *West Virginia History* 32:4 (July 1972), 350-352.

4. See Chapter 5.

5. H. G. Davis to Lewis Baker, November 4, 1870, Henry Gassaway Davis Papers, West Virginia Collection, West Virginia University Library (hereafter identified as WVU).

6. These leaders' early careers are treated in Festus P. Summers, *Johnson Newlon Camden: A Study in Individualism* (New York, 1937), a scholarly work, and Charles M. Pepper, *The Life and Times of Henry Gassaway Davis* (New York, 1920), an authorized biography.

7. A somewhat garbled version of Elkins's early career may be found in Oscar D. Lambert, *Stephen Benton Elkins: American Foursquare* (Pittsburgh, 1955).

8. Williams, "The New Dominion and the Old," 317-407.

9. Important sources of biographical information on West Virginia leaders are George W. Atkinson and Alvaro F. Gibbens, *Prominent Men of West Virginia* (Wheeling, W.Va., 1890); George W. Atkinson, *Bench and Bar of West Virginia* (Charleston, W.Va., 1919); James M. Callahan, *History of West Virginia Old and New* (3 vols., Chicago, 1923); and William A. MacCorkle, *Recollections of Fifty Years of West Virginia* (New York, 1928).

10. Summers, *Camden*, 229.

11. MacCorkle, *Recollections*, 49-50, 227, 616-618.

12. *Ibid.*, 469.

13. William N. Chambers and Walter D. Burnham, *The American Party System, Stages of Political Development* (New York, 1967), especially the essays by Paul Goodman, Richard P. McCormick, Eric L. McKitrick, and Samuel P. Hays, proved helpful in formulating this hypothesis.

14. New York *Times*, October 18, 1876.

15. George W. Atkinson to Waitman T. Willey, April 14, 27, 1876, Waitman T. Willey Papers, WVU.

16. MacCorkle, *Recollections*, 453.

17. David Graham Phillips, *The Treason of the Senate*, George E. Mowry and Judson A. Grenier, eds. (Chicago, 1954), 149-153.

18. Ambler, *West Virginia* (edn. 1940), 459-460.

NOTES TO CHAPTER 2

1. "Notes for a speech, 1888," one copy in correspondence, dated "Sept. 1888," another in scrapbook, Davis Papers.

2. *Congressional Record*, 47th Congress, 2nd session, 1796.

3. Wheeling *Register*, September 3, 1882.

4. *Congressional Record*, 47th Congress, 2nd session, 2605-2608.

5. *The Coal Trade*, 5 (1878), 29.

6. *Congressional Globe*, 42nd Congress, 2nd session, 3398ff., 4088.

7. *Congressional Record*, 43rd Congress, 2nd session, 2065.

8. *The Coal Trade*, 12 (1885), 71, 13 (1886), 22, 72, 14 (1887), 16, 18 (1891), 88.

9. *Ibid.*, 8 (1881), 16, 11 (1884), 12 (1885), 16; "Memorandum," dated 1893, Correspondence, series VI, Davis Papers.

10. Rendig Fels, *American Business Cycles, 1865-1897* (Chapel Hill, 1959), 124-130; *The Coal Trade*, 10 (1883), 30, 11 (1884), 14, 13 (1886), 22, 14 (1887), 32; Galloway C. Morris, "A Few Statistics of the Bituminous Coal Trade of the United States," pamphlet (Philadelphia, 1894), 3-14.

11. H. G. Davis to G. H. Watrous, February 10, 1886, Davis Papers.

12. Thus Cumberland producers sold only 125,000 tons of the nearly 1,000,000 sold as marine fuel in New York harbor in 1887; the rest came from Clearfield. Later Pocahontas coal made inroads into this market, but only because of its greater efficiency for marine purposes. (*The Coal Trade*, 15 [1888], 66; Joseph T. Lambie, *From Mine to Market. The History of Coal Transportation on the Norfolk and Western Railway* [New York, 1954], 44-45.)

13. H. G. Davis to J. T. Furber, February 9, 1885, March 2, 1886, Davis to G. H. Watrous, February 23, 1886, Davis to W. H. Barnum, June 2, 1886, Davis Papers.

14. Morris, "The duty on coal," 7, 12.

15. *The Coal Trade*, 15 (1888), 12, 81.

16. New York *Tribune*, December 9, 1882, March 19, 1883; Summers, *Wilson*, 49-50, 163, 166; H. Wayne Morgan, *From Hayes to McKinley, National Party Politics, 1877-1896* (Syracuse, 1969), 168-170.

17. H. G. Davis to John C. Scott & Sons, November 18, 1882; Davis to Elkins, May 11, 1883; Davis to Abram H. Hewitt, March 6, 1885; Davis to W. H. Barnum, June 7, 1887; Davis to Messrs. Mayer, Lee, and Loveridge, November 30, 1887, and correspondence with Galloway C. Morriss, 1887-1893, in Davis Papers, series I; "Articles of Agreement of the Seaboard Steam Coal Association," n.d. [February 1, 1889?], *ibid.*, series VI.

18. American Coal Trade Committee, Secretary's Record (C. M. Hendley letterbook), minutes and letters, December 1893-April 1894, *passim;* Davis to L. N. Lovell, January 25, June 21, 1894; Davis to Kerens, February 6, 1894; Davis to M. E. Ingalls, February 22, 1894; Davis to Elkins, April 28, 1894, Davis Papers.

19. Elkins to Davis, December 19, 1893, February 10, 15, 21, 1894, Stephen B. Elkins Papers, WVU; J. N. Camden to Columbus Sehon,

February 26, 1894; Elkins to Camden, March 2, 1894, Camden Papers; Gorman to Davis, April 23, 1894, Davis Papers.
20. S. B. Elkins to H. G. Davis, September 23, 1893, Elkins Papers; Mark D. Hirsch, *William C. Whitney, Modern Warwick* (New York, 1948), 416-417.
21. "Relating to Manassas Road and Coal," September 24, 1881, Davis Papers.
22. This was the burden of Alexander Shaw's complaint in *Alexander Shaw vs. Henry G. Davis et al.*, 78 Md. 308 (1893), typescript of testimony, West Virginia University Library, 2-5, 170, 179-185. Elkins made the same observation after Shaw was forced out of the company. (Elkins to Davis, April 28, 1899, Davis Papers.) See also Davis to Messrs. Garrett and Keyser, February 21, 1881; George W. Harrison to Elkins, August 6, 1885, Elkins Papers.
23. Elkins to Davis, February 1, 1890, Davis Papers.
24. Edward Hungerford, *The Story of the Baltimore & Ohio Railroad, 1827-1927* (2 vols., New York, 1928), 2:160-168.
25. Davis to Robert Garrett, October 13, 1885, March 29, 1887, "Memo. for discussion of points of difference, . . ." March 29, 1886, "Interviews with Mr. Garrett," n.d. [1885-1886]; Davis to G. B. Roberts, March 2, 1887, Hambleton & Co., "Weekly Letter," July 16, 1887; Davis to A. P. Gorman, October 14, 1887, Davis Papers.
26. Unidentified clipping, August 15, 1888, scrapbook, Davis Papers. The annual surveys of *The Coal Trade* break down Davis-Elkins tidewater shipments according to carrier, beginning with 18 (1891), 37.
27. Memorandum of agreement, April 10, 1891, Davis Papers. For lawsuits see 65 *Md.* 198, 73 *Md.* 557, 78 *Md.* 308, and 37 *W. Va.* 342.
28. "Purchase of Shaw Stock. Account date February 10th, 1894," R. C. Kerens to Davis, June 17, 1895, Davis Papers.
29. Summers, *Camden*, 173-198, 201-211.
30. *Ibid.*, 318-376; Camden to G. B. Roberts, September 23, 1885, Camden Papers.
31. Summers, *Camden*, 391-401; Camden to W. P. Thompson, January 8, 1885; Camden to J. D. Rockefeller, March 9, 1885; Camden to Davis, September 27, 1889, September 28, 1889; Davis to Camden, October 12, 1889; J. K. Cowen to Camden, September 28, 1889; Camden to Cowen, April 2, 1890; Elkins to Camden, May 29, 1890; Camden to A. B. Fleming, October 7, 1890; Fleming to Camden, December 23, 1890; H. G. Davis & Bro. to Camden, January 17, 1891, Camden Papers; Elkins to Davis, November 2, 1893, Davis Papers.
32. Davis to Keyser Bros. & Co., April 12, 1886, Davis Papers.
33. *The Coal Trade*, 15 (1888), 38-40; *Poor's Manual of the Railroads in the United States*, 19 (1886), cx, 36 (1903), 165.
34. Oscar D. Lambert, *Stephen Benton Elkins, American Four-*

square (Pittsburgh, 1955), 1-23, 29-34; Chicago *Herald*, March 12, 1892, clipping, scrapbook, Elkins Papers; Ralph Emerson Twitchell, *The Leading Facts of New Mexican History* (6 vols., Cedar Rapids, Iowa, 1912), 2:401-402; Howard R. Lamar, *The Far Southwest, A Territorial History, 1846-1912* (New Haven, 1966), 137-151.

35. Howard R. Lamar, "Political Patterns in New Mexico and Utah Territories," *Utah Historical Quarterly*, 27 (October 1960), 366-372; *The Far Southwest*, 49-52, 139-146; Jim Berry Pearson, *The Maxwell Land Grant* (Norman, Okla., 1961), 13-14, 49-65.

36. See unidentified clipping, 1891 n.d., scrapbook, and Elkins's correspondence with Henry L. Waldo, another Missouri friend who became the leading Democratic member of the Santa Fe Ring (Waldo to Elkins, February 25, 1864, September 8, 1865, February 18, May 9, 1866, Elkins Papers). See also Lamar, *The Far Southwest*, 133-138, 166.

37. William A. Kelleher, *The Fabulous Frontier, Twelve New Mexico Items* (Santa Fe, 1945), 98-99; Lamar, *The Far Southwest*, 137-139; C. P. [Otero] to Lyman Trumbull, April 22, 1869; William Breeden to Elkins, May 31, 1874; A. G. Hoyt to Elkins, June 6, 1874; Elkins to Catron, August 15, 1879, Elkins Papers.

38. Lamar, *The Far Southwest*, 144-146; *Congressional Record*, 44th Congress, 2nd session, 1396-1402.

39. *Congressional Record*, 43rd Congress, 1st session, 4138; *ibid.*, 43rd Congress, 2nd session, 1690-1692, 2238-2239.

40. Twitchell, *New Mexican History*, 2:407; Lamar, *The Far Southwest*, 166-167; *House Reports*, 54th Congress, 1st session, report 2259, p. 1. Robert W. Larson, who presents the most thorough investigation of the matter, credits the handshake story even though it rests on an anecdote told forty years later by the then delegate-elect from Colorado (*New Mexico's Quest for Statehood, 1846-1912* [Albuquerque, N.M., 1968], 116-134).

41. Catron to Carey, July 8, 1892, Thomas B. Catron Papers, University of New Mexico Library, Albuquerque, box 404. Catron revived the statehood project after the Land Claims Court established in 1889 began the work of settling New Mexico's land grant tangle and became one of the state's first senators upon its admission to the Union in 1912. (See other statehood documents in *ibid.*, box 404, and Catron to Elkins, August 15, 1892, box 401.)

42. The amendment in question is discussed in *Congressional Records*, 43rd Congress, 2nd session, 1670-1691, and Hereford's vote in *ibid.*, 2239. On Blaine's role, see Larson, *New Mexico's Quest for Statehood*, 128, 131; on the unresolved status of the grants in 1875, see Pearson, *The Maxwell Land Grant*, 60-66, and Lamar, *The Far Southwest*, 144-145, 149-151, 182-185, 192. Elkins married Hallie Davis in

Baltimore on April 14, 1875; after a European honeymoon, the Elkinses set up joint housekeeping with Senator and Mrs. Davis (Davis to J. G. Bassett, October 11, 1875, Davis Papers).

43. W. W. MacFarland to Collis P. Huntington, February 11, 1878, Chicago *Herald,* March 12, 1892, and various other clippings, scrapbook, Elkins Papers; Pearson, *The Maxwell Land Grant,* 72-73, 76, 88-91, 210; U.S. Congress, *House Reports,* 48th Congress, 1st session, vol. 7, report 2165, p. 15. Stephen W. Dorsey later charged that Elkins offered him immunity from prosecution in the Star Route trials (New York *World,* June 11, 1884, clipping, Elkins scrapbook); for limited evidence connecting Elkins with Star Route affairs, see G. E. Spencer to Elkins, October 28, 30, November 14, 1881; Huntington to T. J. Brady, September 13, 1880; Jefferson to Elkins, November 16, 1881, Elkins Papers. During the airing of the scandal, Elkins transferred his holdings in the Davis enterprises to his wife for undisclosed reasons. (*Shaw vs. Davis,* transcript, 453, 456.)

44. Lambert, *Elkins,* 50, 66-69; Davis to Alexander Shaw, April 21, 1880, Davis Papers.

45. Wheeling *Intelligencer,* February 22, 1890; San Francisco *Chronicle,* February 27, March 1, 1890, June 16, 1891; New York *Times,* May 1, 2, June 16, 1891; *North American Commercial Company vs. United States,* 171 U.S. 110 (1898); *United States vs. North American Commercial Company,* 74 Fed. 145 (1896); Charles C. Tansill, *The Foreign Policy of Thomas F. Bayard, 1885-1897* (New York, 1940), 491-507.

46. Wheeling *Register,* June 8, 1884. For Elkins's continuing interest in New Mexico matters, especially involving land, see New York *Times,* June 29, 1884, St. Louis *Globe-Democrat,* 1891 n.d., clippings, scrapbook, Elkins Papers; Elkins to Eugene Hale, December 17, 1885; Benjamin Harrison to Elkins, June 5, 1886, and correspondence and contracts involving Ortiz Mine, Bosque del Apache, Mora, Cerillos, and Mesita Juana de Lopez grants, 1886-1891, *ibid.;* J. N. Camden to Elkins, January 27, 1892, Camden Papers; Wheeling *Register,* March 28, 1896, February 2, 1901.

47. Blaine to Elkins, June 13, 1884, Elkins Papers.

48. David Saville Muzzey, *James G. Blaine, A Political Idol of other Days* (New York, 1934), 7, 233. (Hereafter cited as Muzzey, *Blaine.*)

49. Blaine to Elkins, November n.d., 1881, January 23, May 14, 1882, February n.d., 1883, Elkins Papers.

50. Theodore Clarke Smith, *The Life and Letters of James Abram Garfield* (2 vols., New Haven, 1925), 2:947. (Hereafter cited as Smith, *Garfield.*)

51. Blaine to Elkins, June 13, 1884, Elkins Papers.

52. Blaine to Elkins, October 19, 1884, Elkins Papers; Muzzey, *Blaine*, 319.

53. Blaine to Elkins, November 17, 1879, Elkins Papers.

54. Smith, *Garfield*, 2:1086; J. C. Parker to Garfield, January 1, 1881; Henry L. Waldo to Garfield, January 11, 1881, copies in Elkins Papers.

55. Clipping, 1884 n.d., scrapbook, Elkins Papers.

56. Blaine to Elkins, August 10, 1881, Elkins Papers.

57. Blaine to Elkins, March 15, June 30, 1887, Elkins Papers.

58. J. S. Clarkson to Elkins, February 2, 1887, Elkins Papers; Harry Thurston Peck, *Twenty Years of the Republic*, 1885-1905 (New York, 1917), 151-152.

59. B. F. Jones to Elkins, October 22, 1887, Elkins Papers.

60. Pepper, *Davis*, 152-161; Davis to J. W. Garrett, February 24, 1877, Garrett Family Papers, Library of Congress, box 130; Elkins to John W. Mason, August 13, 1883, John W. Mason Papers, WVU; St. Louis *Commercial Gazette*, August 8, 1884, clipping, scrapbook, Elkins Papers; G. F. Muller, "Deer Park, Oakland, 1894," pamphlet, Davis Papers.

61. Pepper, *Davis*, 141, quoting Davis's journal, which is no longer available.

62. Davis to Baker, June 11, 1884; Davis to Editor, *Register*, June 20, 1884, Davis Papers; Wheeling *Register*, June 19, 21, 23, 1884.

63. Baltimore *Sun*, August 14, 1884.

64. Quoted in Pepper, *Davis*, 141.

65. Davis to W. H. Barnum, August 20, September 15, October 11, December 2, 1884; Davis to D. H. Leonard, September 19, October 24, 1884; Davis to "Dear Judge," October 11, 1884, Davis Papers.

66. Grover Cleveland to Davis, September 24, 1884; Davis to Cleveland, September 29, 1884; Davis to Gorman, October 12, 1884; Gorman to Davis, October 28, 1884, Davis Papers.

67. W. P. Thompson to Davis, November 28, 1884; and letters from Davis to Camden, Leonard, and Bayard, December 1884, Davis Papers; Summers, *Camden*, 265-267.

68. Davis to Camden, March 19, 1885, Camden Papers.

69. Davis to Camden, March 9, May 11, and letters to Okey Johnson, James M. Jackson, E. Boyd Faulkner, and Bayard, February-September 1885, Davis Papers.

70. Davis to Bayard, September 12, 1885, Davis Papers.

71. Allen Nevins, *Grover Cleveland, A Study in Courage* (New York, 1932), 305-306 (hereafter cited as Nevins, *Cleveland*); Pepper, *Davis*, 159-160.

72. Pepper, *Davis*, 164.

73. Pepper, *Davis*, 142. Pepper quotes a journal entry of Janu-

ary 28, 1887: "I was in Washington yesterday; had by appointment a long talk with President Cleveland. I suggested special message to Congress urging tariff legislation and reduction of revenue. He received the suggestion kindly, and I think will act upon it." Cleveland's papers reveal no evidence of the meeting, but it probably represented an attempt by Davis to enlist the president's aid to head off the more dangerous threat of congressional tariff reform. As we shall see, he was disappointed.

74. Davis to Cleveland, March 18, 1887, Davis to Windom, April 11, 1887, Davis Papers; Windom to Davis, February 5, 1887, Grover Cleveland Papers, Library of Congress (microfilm copy, Yale University Library), reel 45.

75. *Congressional Record,* 43rd Congress, 2nd session, 2065.

76. The theory is stated by Samuel J. Randall of Pennsylvania in New York *Tribune,* November 18, 1882.

77. Chicago *Tribune,* July 4, 1884.

78. *Congressional Record,* 47th Congress, 2nd session, 1796.

79. *Ibid.,* 1548.

80. *Ibid.,* 2215. This was the key vote in committee of the whole; the vote on passage was 24-19 (p. 2622). Camden was absent but paired for the amendment.

81. *Ibid.,* 1767-1768.

82. *Ibid.,* 2606.

83. *Ibid.,* 2605.

84. On manufacturer-producer conflict within the protectionist camp, see remarks of Senators Bayard, Morrill and Davis (*ibid.,* 2337-2338) and Sherman (*ibid.,* 2201-2202; New York *Tribune,* March 19, 1883).

85. New York *Tribune,* June 19, July 3, 4, 1884; Chicago *Tribune,* July 8, 1884.

86. Davis to Bayard, July 15, 1884; and letters to Baker, Camden, B. F. Martin, W. F. Dyer, and H. D. Colston, March-April 1884, Davis Papers; Wheeling *Register,* April 16, 17, 1884.

87. Chicago *Tribune,* July 2, 1884.

88. *Ibid.,* July 9, 1884; on the Maryland delegate, C. J. M. Gwynn, see Davis to W. L. Wilson, May 26, 1888, Davis Papers.

89. Chicago *Tribune,* July 10, 1884; Pepper, *Davis,* 139.

90. Democratic National Convention, *Official Proceedings* (New York, 1884), 198 (see also 47, 153, 193, 195); Chicago *Tribune,* July 11, 1896.

91. Davis to Joseph Sprigg, February 26, 1884; Davis to W. F. Dyer, March 1, 1884, Davis Papers; see also Summers, *Wilson,* 53-54.

92. Draft resolution, 1884 n.d. [July 16], Davis Papers.

93. Summers, *Wilson,* 57-58.

94. *Ibid.*, 64-68; Nevins, *Cleveland*, 285-290.
95. Davis to Randolph Stalnaker, June 18, 1886; Davis to J. B. Taney, June 25, 1886; Davis to D. H. Leonard, July 14, 1886, Davis Papers.
96. Davis to W. L. Wilson, September 4, 8, 24, 25, 1886, Davis Papers.
97. Davis to C. P. Snyder, September 24, 1886; and letters to D. H. Leonard, Robert White, J. B. Taney, R. G. Barr, J. A. Naylor, G. E. Price, and George Baylor, September-October 1886, Davis Papers.
98. Summers, *Camden*, 294-297; Wheeling *Register*, January 19, 20, February 4, 1887.
99. *Ibid.*, January 27, 1887.
100. *Ibid.*, January 19, 1887; Price to Davis, February 8, 1887; Davis to Dailey, February 12, 1887, Davis Papers.
101. Wheeling *Register*, February 18, 19, 1887.
102. Price to Davis, January 18, 1887; and correspondence of Davis, Price, and Dailey, February 3-March 1, 1887, Davis Papers.
103. Dailey to Davis, February 15, 1887, Davis Papers, suggests that Davis was well informed about his lieutenants' plans to bolt Camden; but cf. Davis to Camden November 15, 1886, January 8, 10, February 22, 1887; Davis to Price, February 22, 1887; *ibid.*, and Wheeling *Register*, February 11, 1887.
104. *Ibid.*, January 28, 1887; Davis to Camden, January 30, 1887, Davis Papers.
105. Dailey to Davis, February 12, 15, 1887, Davis Papers.
106. Davis to Okey Johnson, February 28, 1887, Davis Papers.
107. Wheeling *Register*, February 26, 1887.
108. Davis to [Okey Johnson], August 7, 1884, February 24, 1885, December 11, 1886, Davis Papers.
109. Wheeling *Register*, March 6, 1887.
110. Dailey to Davis, February 12, 1887. Cf. A. H. Kunst to J. N. Camden, January 18, 1892, Camden Papers, on Lucas's refusal to accept passes.
111. Davis to Okey Johnson, February 28, 1887, Davis Papers.
112. Wheeling *Register*, March 3, 1887; Davis to J. J. Chipley, March 7, 1887, Davis Papers.
113. Davis to Dailey, March 9, 1887, Davis Papers.
114. Wheeling *Register*, April 1, 1887.
115. Wheeling *Register*, May 5, 6, 1887.
116. "Draft of a letter to *Register,*" March 27, 1887, Davis Papers.
117. Davis to Daniel S. Lamont, August 5, 9, 10, 1887, Cleveland Papers, reels 114, 151; New York *Herald*, September 7, 10, 1887; Nevins, *Cleveland*, 312-313, 372-373.
118. Harry J. Sievers, *Benjamin Harrison, Hoosier Statesman, From*
267

the Civil War to the White House, 1865-1888 (New York, 1959), 310-312 (hereafter cited as Sievers, *Harrison*). Elkins refers to the conversations in Elkins to Benjamin Harrison, February 11, 1889, Harrison Papers; and Davis's role in initiating them in Elkins to Davis, October 28, 1889, Elkins Papers.

119. Elkins to Harrison, February 11, 1888, Benjamin Harrison Papers, Library of Congress (microfilm copy, Yale University Library), reel 8. Elkins's drive to the Senate and its implication for national and state politics are described and documented more fully in the following articles: John A. Williams, "New York's First Senator from West Virginia: How Stephen B. Elkins Found a New Political Home," *West Virginia History* 31:4 (July 1970), 76-87; "Stephen B. Elkins and the Benjamin Harrison Campaign and Cabinet, 1887-1891," *Indiana Magazine of History* 48:1 (March 1972), 1-23; "The Final Confrontation of Henry G. Davis and William L. Wilson in the Election Campaign of 1894," *West Virginia History* 32:1 (October 1970), 1-9; and "The Bituminous Coal Lobby and the Wilson-Gorman Tariff of 1894," *Maryland Historical Magazine* 68:3 (Fall 1973), 273-287. Except where otherwise noted, the following discussion is drawn from these accounts.

120. Elkins to Harrison, August 4, 1888, Harrison Papers, reel 10.

121. Hart to Elkins, February 6, 1888, Elkins Papers.

122. Gerald Wayne Smith, *Nathan Goff, Jr., A Biography* (Charleston, West Virginia, 1959), 22-154 (hereafter cited as Smith, *Goff*); Atkinson and Gibbens, *Prominent Men of West Virginia*, 226.

123. Harrison to Elkins, February 22, 1889, Elkins Papers.

124. Harrison to Elkins, April 5, 1889, Elkins Papers.

125. Davis to Windom, April 11, 1889, Davis Papers; Windom to Goff, July 5, 1889, Nathan Goff, Jr., Papers, West Virginia University.

126. Davis to Elkins, 1891 n.d. [November 26 or 27], Davis Papers.

127. Wheeling *Intelligencer*, June 24, July 22, 1890, August 25, 1892. Hart claimed that Elkins had registered to vote in West Virginia in 1885, a dubious assertion in view of the facts that West Virginia had no voter registration laws between 1872 and 1901 and that as late as 1890 Blaine was urging Elkins to vote in West Virginia so as to make his claim to residence there more plausible. (Blaine to Elkins, 1890 n.d. [February ?], Elkins Papers.)

128. Wheeling *Intelligencer*, February 8, 1892.

129. Atkinson to Elkins, September 16, 1891, Elkins Papers; Wheeling *Intelligencer*, March 15, 1892.

130. *Ibid.*, April 19, 21, May 4, 6, 1892.

131. *Ibid.*, August 25, 1892.

132. G. C. Sturgiss to Elkins, September 3, 1891, Elkins Papers; cf. comments by John W. Mason and other West Virginia federal officials in Wheeling *Intelligencer*, December 18, 1891.

133. Washington *Post,* June 5, 1892; Wheeling *Intelligencer,* June 10, 11, 18, 1892; New York *Herald,* June 11, 1892.
134. *Preston County Journal,* March 28, 1889, clipping, William M. O. Dawson Papers, WVU; Wheeling *Intelligencer,* May 23, 1892. On the importance of Dawson's elevation to the chairmanship to Elkins's leadership, see George C. Sturgiss to Elkins, September 3, 1891, Elkins Papers.
135. MacCorkle, *Recollections,* 447-449.
136. Washington *Post,* July 20, 22, 1892; Wheeling *Intelligencer,* July 20, 21, 1892.
137. Wheeling *Intelligencer,* July 22, 1892.
138. *Ibid.,* August 2, 3, 4, 1892.
139. Romney *Hampshire Review,* October 6, 1892; New York *Herald,* November 6, 1892.
140. Smith, *Goff,* 263.
141. *Ibid.,* 166-167; Washington *Post,* November 2, 1892.
142. *Ibid.,* November 1, 1892.
143. Wheeling *Intelligencer,* September 20, 1892.
144. *Ibid.,* September 17, October 19, November 4, 1892.
145. Washington *Post,* August 2, 1892; Wheeling *Intelligencer,* August 8, September 2, 1892; MacCorkle, *Recollections,* 474-478.
146. Wheeling *Intelligencer,* October 17, 1892.
147. *Ibid.,* September 22, October 24, November 2, 4, 1892.
148. Wheeling *Intelligencer,* October 6, 1892; Baltimore *Sun,* November 5, 1892; Washington *Post,* November 7, 1892.
149. Wheeling *Intelligencer,* December 12, 1892.
150. *Ibid.,* January 4, 10-12, 16-20, 25, 1893; Summers, *Camden,* 452-463.
151. Memorandum, September 9, 1893, Davis Papers.
152. Diary, November 27, 1883, William L. Wilson Papers, private possession (microfilm copy, WVU).
153. Diary, September 3, 1887, Wilson Papers.
154. Diary, March 4, 1888, Wilson Papers; Summers, *Wilson.*
155. "The Coal and Coke Railroad," Archive of Folk Song, Library of Congress, accession number 3571 B 1, sung by Addison Boserman, collected by Gordon Barnes, Tygart Valley Homesteads, Elkins, W.Va., April 1939.
156. Davis to Robert Bridges, October 22, 1894, Davis Papers; Carnegie to Elkins, January 20, 1900, Elkins Papers.
157. Davis to Baker, July 11, 1885; Davis to R. G. Barr, October 5, 1885, Davis Papers. Yet Baker returned to West Virginia on Davis's summons in 1898 (see Chapter 4).
158. Wheeling *Intelligencer,* May 2, 3, 7, 12, June 1, 1894.
159. On Elkins's role in the policy, see Washington *Star,* Decem-

ber 5, 1892; and numerous newspaper clippings, December 1892-January 1893, scrapbook, Elkins Papers.

160. Wheeling *Intelligencer*, June 21, 1894.

161. *Ibid.*, June 4, 1894.

162. J. N. Camden to John H. Holt, July 1, 1894, Camden Papers.

163. Wheeling *Register*, August 18, 22, October 3, 1894; Wheeling *Intelligencer*, August 20, 22, October 3, 1894.

164. Camden to John H. Holt, July 1, 1894; L. E. Tierney to John D. Alderson, June 3, 1894, Camden Papers; Wheeling *Intelligencer*, May 19, 23, 28, June 18, 19-25, July 14, 21, 23, 31, August 1, 17, 18, 20, 23, 25, 29, September 5, 1894; Wheeling *Register*, July 3, 5, 16, 23, August 2, 6, September 22, 1894.

165. Vinson to Camden, September n.d., 1894, Camden Papers.

166. Wheeling *Register*, September 6, 7, 1894; Wheeling *Intelligencer*, September 6-8, October 10, 11, 1894.

167. Camden to C. K. Newlon, August 3, 1894; Camden to A. B. Fleming, August 20, 1894; Camden to S. S. Vinson, August 31, 1894, Camden Papers.

168. Camden to McGraw, September 1, 1894, Camden Papers.

169. McGraw to Davis, September 18, 1894, Davis Papers.

170. Davis to McGraw, October 31, 1894, Davis Papers.

171. Davis to Alderson, September 21, October 6, 1894; Davis to M. E. Ingalls, September 22, 1894; Davis to W. C. Bullitt, September 22, 1894; Davis to W. E. Chilton, October 15, 1894, Davis Papers. Indicative of the times was the fact that many Kanawha coal operators had shorter memories and resisted Davis's appeals because Alderson had "made a speech to the miners, which was in bad taste, and did harm to them." (Davis to Alderson, October 6, 1894, Davis Papers.)

172. Davis to Camden, September 12, 1894, Davis Papers.

173. Davis to G. W. Tippett, October 8, 1894, Davis Papers.

174. Wheeling *Register*, September 22, October 3, 11, 1894; Baltimore *Sun*, October 15, 1894.

175. Bretz to Davis, November 3, 1894; T. B. Davis to Davis, November 3, 1892 [*sic*]; Landstreet to Davis, November 8, 1894, Davis Papers.

176. Davis to Ingalls, October 6, 8, 1894, Davis Papers; Summers, *Wilson*, 219.

177. Wheeling *Register*, October 3, 1894; Davis to E. R. Ladew and J. J. Hetzel, November 9, 1894; W. Del. Walbridge to Davis, December 6, 1894; Davis to Walbridge, December 14, 1894, Davis Papers.

178. Camden to James K. Jones, September 29, 1894, Camden Papers.

179. Romney *Hampshire Review*, October 24, 1894; Wheeling *Reg-*

ister, October 24, 1894; R. C. Kerens to Davis, November 3, 1894, Davis Papers.
180. Wheeling *Register,* October 20, 1894.
181. T. F. McKee to A. G. Dayton, September 10, 1894, Alston G. Dayton Papers, WVU.
182. Elkins to Mason, October 27, 1894, Mason Papers; Elkins to A. B. White, October 28, 31, 1894, A. B. White Papers, WVU.
183. Wheeling *Register,* November 21, 1894; Camden to W. P. Thompson, November 8, 1894, Camden Papers.
184. Camden to W. P. Thompson, November 8, 1894, Camden Papers.
185. Dayton to S. B. Husselman, November 15, 1894, Dayton Papers.
186. Davis to E. R. Ladew and J. J. Hetzel, November 9, 1894; Davis to H. G. Buxton, November 10, 1894, Davis Papers.
187. Wheeling *Intelligencer,* November 7, 13, 24, 1894.
188. Wheeling *Register,* January 5, 1895.
189. Elkins to A. B. White, December 19, 1894, White Papers.
190. Elkins to Dayton, November 13, 15, 1894, Dayton Papers; Elkins to Mason, November 16, December 14, 1894, Mason Papers; Elkins to White, December 17, 19, 26, 1894, White Papers; John T. McGraw to Davis, December 6, 15, 1894; Davis to Lloyd Hansford, December 28, 1894, Davis Papers; T. H. Norton to C. B. Hart, January 8, 1895, Elkins Papers; Wheeling *Intelligencer,* January 3, 5, 1895.
191. *Ibid.,* January 9, 11, 12, 17, 18, 24, 1895.

NOTES TO CHAPTER 3

1. Camden to W. P. Thompson, November 8, 1894, Camden Papers.
2. Davis to M. E. Ingalls, September 18, 1895; and correspondence of G. S. Hamill, Hopewell Hebb, R. M. G. Brown, C. L. Bretz, C. H. Hilleary, and Owen Riordan, September-October, 1895, Davis Papers.
3. Memorandum, enclosed in C. S. Cobb to Huntington *Herald,* November 2, 1895; Davis to D. W. Gall, December 29, 1895, Davis Papers.
4. Davis to Chilton, February 8, 1896; Wheeling *Register,* February 26, 1896.
5. *Ibid.,* December 16, 1895.
6. *Ibid.,* June 29, July 7, 1895.
7. *Ibid.,* August 12, 1895.
8. W. A. Ohley and A. G. Garden, two important party functionaries in the north, were severely injured in a train wreck near Wheeling on September 27, 1895. Ohley eventually recovered, but Garden died (*Ibid.,* September 28, 1895; Wheeling *Intelligencer,* February 22, 1896).

9. Wheeling *Register*, May 15, 23, June 29, July 9, August 16, 1895, February 13, April 7, 23, 1896.

10. Quoted in Wheeling *Intelligencer*, February 29, May 1, 1896.

11. Chilton to A. B. Fleming, April 21, 1896, A. B. Fleming Papers, WVU.

12. Wheeling *Register*, April 20, 1896.

13. Wheeling *Intelligencer*, September 7, 1895, and February 27, 1896; quoting C. L. Smith in the *Fairmont Index*.

14. Wheeling *Register*, June 9, 1896.

15. Chilton to Davis, April 21, 1896; Davis to Chilton, April 27, 1896, Davis Papers.

16. Dailey to Davis, May 1, 1896, Davis Papers; Wheeling *Register*, May 20, 1896.

17. Davis to McGraw, May 28, 1896, Davis Papers.

18. Wheeling *Intelligencer*, June 11, 1896; Wheeling *Register*, May 28, June 14, 16, 18, 1896.

19. *Ibid.*, June 18, 1896; Wheeling *Intelligencer*, June 22, 1896.

20. Davis to Camden, June 25, 1896; McGraw to Davis, June 26, 1896, Davis Papers.

21. Davis to Ingalls, July 17, 1896, Davis Papers.

22. Elkins to Davis, July 28, 1896, Davis Papers; Wheeling *Intelligencer*, August 17, 1896.

23. Summers, *Camden*, 511; Wheeling *Intelligencer*, July 12, 1896.

24. Camden to Davis, August 18, 1896, Davis Papers.

25. Camden to Fleming, September 15, November 1, 1896, Fleming Papers; Wheeling *Register*, September 22, October 3, 10, 31, 1896. For Republican acknowledgment of the G.O.P.'s debt to Camden, see George W. Atkinson to A. B. White, April 2, 1897, White Papers.

26. McGraw to Davis, July 17, 1896, Davis Papers.

27. Wheeling *Intelligencer*, June 6, 27, July 7, August 11, 1896; Wheeling *Register*, July 6, 7, 1896. On the genesis of the feud see McGraw to Davis, July 13, 1892, Davis Papers; Summers, *Camden*, 454-463; and MacCorkle, *Recollections*, 462.

28. Wheeling *Intelligencer*, August 13, 1896.

29. Davis to Watts, August 17, 1896; and letters of the same date to T. S. Reilly, V. A. Lewis, W. H. Boggs, and J. H. Holt, Davis Papers.

30. Wheeling *Intelligencer*, August 21, 22, 1896.

31. Wheeling *Register*, September 11, 1896; Davis to McGraw, September 15, October 7, 17, 1896; Davis to Chilton, September 18, 24, 1896; Chilton to Davis, November 1, 1896, with marginal notation by Davis, Davis Papers.

32. Elkins to White, September 22, 1896, White Papers.

33. Wheeling *Register*, August 30, September 12, 1896; Dailey to Davis, October [27?], 1896, Davis Papers.

34. Wheeling *Register,* October 3, 1896; George A. Meyer to Davis, October 12, 13, 1896, Davis Papers.
35. Dayton to Davis, September 5, 1896; Davis to Dayton, September 11, 1896, Davis Papers.
36. Davis to Landstreet, October 24, 1896, Davis Papers.
37. Davis to Camden, August 21, 1896, Camden Papers.
38. Wheeling *Register,* August 23, 1896.
39. Elkins to Davis, August 23, 1896, Davis Papers.
40. Hambleton & Company to Davis, August 25, 1896; Gustavus Ober to Davis, August 25, 1896, Davis Papers.
41. Davis to George Baylor, September 4, 1896, Davis Papers.
42. Wheeling *Register,* September 11, 1896; cf. Davis to George Baylor, September 4, 1896, and his remarks on the Bland-Allison bill of 1878, in *Congressional Record,* 45th Congress, 2nd session, 926.
43. Davis to Editor, Wheeling *Register,* September 22, 1896.
44. Davis to W. G. Brown, August 29, 1896; Brown to Davis, September 1, 1896; Davis to James K. Jones, September 24, 1896, Davis Papers.
45. Davis to Bayard, October 5, 1896, Davis Papers.
46. Wheeling *Register,* September 22, October 1, 3, 1896.
47. Davis to James K. Jones, September 24, 1896, Davis Papers.
48. Mineral, Grant, Tucker, and Randolph counties experienced a net shift (total shift minus statewide average shift) of plus 2.1 percent in their Democratic vote in 1896 (Wheeling *Register,* November 20, 1894, October 24, 1898, and untitled pamphlet, n.d. [1894], scrapbook, Elkins Papers, giving congressional voting data for 1894 and 1896).
49. Wheeling *Register,* October 3, 1896.
50. Wheeling *Intelligencer,* August 12, 1896; Wheeling *Register,* August 16, 1896. The exception was E. Willis Wilson, congressional nominee in the third (Kanawha) district.
51. *Ibid.,* August 6, 7, 13, October 8, 9, 14, 24, 1896; McGraw to Davis, October 11, 1896, Davis Papers.
52. McGraw to Davis, November 6, 1896, Davis Papers.
53. Davis to Chilton, November 7, 1896; Chilton to Davis, November 10, 1896, [W. E. Chilton?]; "Majorities, Members of the Legislature," memorandum, n.d. [1896], Davis Papers.
54. Quoted in Lamar, *The Far Southwest,* 148.
55. See correspondence of Nathan Goff, John J. Jacobs, George J. Koonce, and James H. Ferguson, 1868-1870, Davis Papers.
56. Wheeling *Intelligencer,* April 3, 1896.
57. Elkins to White, May 5, 1896, White Papers.
58. Wheeling *Intelligencer,* April 27, May 8, 1896; Elkins to John W. Mason, March 25, April 15, May 6, 1896, Mason Papers.

59. Elkins to White, April 13, May 5, 18, June 8, 1896, White Papers.
60. C. H. Grosvenor to John W. Mason, March 18, May 18, 1896; McKinley to Mason, April 20, 25, 1896, Mason Papers; Wheeling *Intelligencer*, January 13, 14, February 8, 1897.
61. Wheeling *Register*, February 2, 15, 1898.
62. See the letters of inspectors E. S. Allen and S. T. Hooten to Elkins during the critical months of March and April, 1900, Elkins Papers.
63. See note 135.
64. Wheeling *Register*, August 16, 1894; correspondence of Scott, Hart, Mason, Elkins, and C. H. Grosvenor, March-May 1896, Mason Papers; Scott to Elkins, December 5, 1896, Elkins Papers.
65. Scott to Mason, November 14, 18, 1896, January 25, 1897; R. C. Campbell to Mason, January 6, 1896, Mason Papers.
66. Elkins to White, May 18, 1896, White Papers; Wheeling *Register*, March 30, 1902.
67. John M. Hagans to Mason, October 21, 1872; Goff to Mason, July 27, 1876, July 9, 22, 1882; A. W. Campbell to Mason, March 2, 1881; Francis H. Pierpont to Mason, July 26, 1882; W. H. H. Flick to Mason, July 27, 1882; Atkinson to Mason, March 8, 1884, Mason Papers.
68. Atkinson and Gibbens, *Prominent Men of West Virginia*, 389; New York *World*, March 19, 1889, Mason Papers, clippings file, series I, box 7, folder 1.
69. Atkinson and Gibbens, *Prominent Men of West Virginia*, 253-254, 359, 774-775, 778; Hagans to Elkins, December 25, 1888; Hubbard to Elkins, December 31, 1888, Elkins Papers; Hubbard to Mason, January 13, 1889; Sturgiss to Mason, January 21, 28, 1889, Mason Papers; New York *Tribune*, January 10, 1889; Dawson to Waitman T. Willey, January 15, 1878, September 23, 1880, Willey Papers.
70. Atkinson and Gibbens, *Prominent Men of West Virginia*, 691.
71. For location of relevant roll calls and method of evaluating legislators' performance, see Williams, "The New Dominion and the Old," Appendix, 402-407.
72. Dayton to Mason, March 11, 1898, Mason Papers; Washington *Post*, March 7, 1905.
73. Wheeling *Intelligencer*, May 18, 20, 21, 1896.
74. Elkins to Mason, January 25, February 22, March 11, 18, April 9, 14, 16, May 1, 1897; Mason to Scott, January 26, 1897; White to Mason, January 28, February 27, May 22, 1897; Dayton to Mason, February 26, May 19, 1897; Thomas E. Davis to Mason, May 21, June 14, 1897, Mason Papers; Elkins to White, June 18, 20, 1897, White Papers.
75. Mason to Elkins, April 15, 17, May 2, 1897, Mason Papers.

76. Scott to Mason, January 12, 1898; Mason to Scott, January 15, 1898; Atkinson to Mason, August 22, 1898, Mason Papers; McKell to C. H. Grosvenor, November 17, 1898, Elkins Papers; Scott to White, December 28, 31, 1898, White Papers.

77. Goff to Mason, June 9, 1898; Atkinson to Mason, August 22, November 22, 1898, Mason Papers.

78. Atkinson to White, April 7, 1898, White Papers; Atkinson to Mason, August 22, November 22, 1898, Mason Papers; see also notes 30-32 and 82.

79. For a characteristic outbreak of the feud, see Wheeling *Register*, February 2-9, 1898.

80. Wheeling *Register*, February 18, 1898; Scott to White, July 29, August 23, 1898; J. J. Peterson (editor) to the Board of Directors and Stockholders of The Tribune Company, January 31, 1899, White Papers.

81. Gaines to Elkins, June 11, 1898, Elkins Papers.

82. Scott to White, July 8, 1898; Elkins to White, July 14, 1898, White Papers.

83. Elkins to White, July 8, 1898; Scott to White, July 8, 1898, White Papers; cf. Dawson to White, January 11, 1898 (copy), and Elkins to Mason, February 7, 1898, Mason Papers.

84. Elkins to White, July 18, 1898, White Papers.

85. Scott to White, August 8, 1898, White Papers; Atkinson to Mason, August 13, 22, 1898, Mason Papers.

86. Scott to White, October 5, 1898, White Papers.

87. Scott to White, July 29, 30, 1898, White Papers.

88. Scott to White, October 3, 1898, White Papers.

89. Scott to White, September 30, October 3, 5, 1898, White Papers.

90. Davis to Arthur Gorman, September 18, 1897; Murray Vandiver to Davis, October 18, 1897, Davis Papers.

91. Chilton to Davis, January 19, 1898; Davis to Chilton, January 21, 1898; Ohley to Davis, January 21, 1898, Davis Papers; Wheeling *Register*, January 9, March 14, 1898.

92. Davis to G. W. Tippett, January 31, 1898, Davis Papers.

93. McGraw to Davis, May 6, 1898, Davis Papers.

94. Wheeling *Register*, May 18, 19, 24, 26, June 16, 1898; Wheeling *Intelligencer*, May 25, 1898.

95. McGraw to Davis, June 21, 1898; Davis to McGraw, April 13, May 13, June 23, 1898; Davis to Baker, June 11, July 11, 15, 1898; Baker to Davis, July 23, 1898, Davis Papers; Wheeling *Register*, June 21, 24, 26, 1898.

96. Turner, "Life of John T. McGraw," 151-153.

97. Davis to Baker, October 28, 1898, Davis Papers.

98. Wheeling *Register*, August 11, 1898.

99. Davis to McGraw, September 7, 1898, Davis Papers.

100. McGraw to Davis, September 5, 1898, Davis Papers; Wheeling *Register*, August 8, September 19, 1898.

101. See below, pp. 126-128, and Appendix.

102. Fleming to John K. Cowen, September 15, 1898, Fleming Papers; Summers, *Camden*, 515-516.

103. Wheeling *Register*, April 9, 1898.

104. Davis to Camden, November 1, 1898, Davis Papers; Wheeling *Register*, October 31, 1898; John W. Davis to Julia McDonald, November 4, 1898, John W. Davis Papers, Yale University Library.

105. Davis to Camden, September 25, 1897, Davis Papers; John R. Lambert, *Arthur Pue Gorman* (Baton Rouge, 1953), 259-263; *Appleton's Annual Cyclopaedia*, 38 (1898), 356-357; C. Vann Woodward, *Origins of the New South, 1877-1913 (A History of the South, 7* [Baton Rouge, 1951]), 377-379.

106. In 1900, Elkins assured Camden that "we did not intend to put up a candidate if the Colonel ran. . . ." for the state senate. (Elkins to Camden, July 29, 1900, Camden Papers.) See also Davis to Elkins, July 29, 1904, Davis Papers.

107. H. G. Buxton to Davis, October 31, 1898, Davis Papers.

108. Davis to Elkins, November 4, 1898, Davis Papers.

109. R. F. Whitmer to Elkins, October 14, 1898, Elkins Papers; Whitmer to Davis, September 27, October 29, 1898; Davis to Whitmer, October 31, 1898; Davis to McGraw, October 31, 1898, Davis Papers.

110. Wheeling *Register*, October 12, 1898.

111. Elkins to White, July 18, 1898, White Papers; Wheeling *Register*, March 18, April 5, 13, 14, 16, 17, August 8, November 4, 1898; Wheeling *Intelligencer*, May 26, July 11, October 29, 1898. Elkins announced his about-face after a two-month silence on July 11, shortly after the only other West Virginian in Congress to vote against the war was denied renomination.

112. Wheeling *Intelligencer*, July 22, August 11, September 30, October 15, 1898; Wheeling *Register*, August 22, October 6, 12, 1898; "Remarks of Temporary Chairman Elkins Convention," [August 10, 1898], Davis Papers. Davis had 20,000 copies of his principal speech circulated throughout the state.

113. Quoted in Summers, *Camden*, 515.

114. Scott to White, October 31, 1898, White Papers.

115. Wheeling *Intelligencer*, November 15, 1898; Wheeling *Register*, November 11-16, 1898; Scott to White, November 16, 1898; Davis to Ohley, November 16, 1898, Davis Papers.

116. Scott to White, November 14, 1898, White Papers; Mason to Atkinson, December 5, 1898; Dawson to Mason, December 6, 1898, Mason Papers.

117. Wheeling *Register,* November 16, December 2, 1898; Wheeling *Intelligencer,* November 17-19, 21, 1898, January 2, 1899; F. C. Reynolds to A. B. White, November 12, 1898, White Papers. Eventually, the Taylor County Court complied with Dawson's request.

118. Scott to White, December 3, 1898, White Papers.

119. Quoted in Wheeling *Register,* November 21, 1898.

120. Based on unofficial legislative returns in Wheeling *Intelligencer,* November 11, 1898, and official congressional returns in Wheeling *Register,* October 26, 1900.

121. Davis to W. A. Ohley, November 28, 1898, Davis Papers.

122. Davis to McGraw, November 30, December 3, 1898; Davis to Joseph E. Chilton, December 2, 1898, Davis Papers.

123. Wheeling *Register,* December 5, 12, 1898; Wheeling *Intelligencer,* December 6, 1898, January 13, 1899.

124. Dailey to Davis, December 9, 1898, Davis Papers.

125. Wheeling *Register,* December 10, 1898; H. G. Armstrong to Davis, December 16, 1898, Davis Papers.

126. Joseph E. Chilton to Davis, December 9, 1898; Davis to Chilton, December 12, 1898; Davis to McGraw, December 19, 1898, Davis Papers.

127. Davis to G. C. Burgess, December 20, 1898, Davis Papers.

128. Davis to George Koonce, January 7, 1899; see also letters to J. W. St. Clair, R. F. Kidd, A. S. Johnston, G. W. Tippett, C. L. Bretz, and J. A. Cunningham, December 13, 1898-January 4, 1899, *ibid.*

129. Ohley to Davis, January 3, 1899; Davis to Ohley, January 5, 1899, Davis Papers; Wheeling *Intelligencer,* January 6, 24, 25, 1899.

130. Ohley to Davis, January 17, 1899, Davis Papers.

131. Chilton to Davis, December 9, 1898, Davis Papers. For the role of corporation lobbyists in carrying out the peace protocol, see John W. Davis to John J. Davis, January 14, 1899, John W. Davis Papers.

132. *Boyd's Directory of the District of Columbia, 1897* (Washington, 1897), 253, 1101. Davis moved to Washington from Baltimore in 1895; he also maintained an office there, although the principal business offices remained in Baltimore and New York.

133. Scott to White, January 5, 1899, White Papers.

134. Goff to John W. Mason, December 21, 1898; E. M. Grant to Mason, January 19, 1899, "Copy of a telegram sent to E. M. Grant, January 19, 1899," Mason Papers; Morgantown *Post,* January 5, 1899.

135. Atkinson to Elkins, July 4, 1899, Elkins Papers; cf. Atkinson to John W. Mason, February 5, 1899, Mason Papers.

136. Wheeling *Intelligencer,* January 20, 1899.

137. McKell to C. H. Grosvenor, November 17, 1898, Elkins Papers; Wheeling *Intelligencer,* January 23, 1899.

138. *Ibid.,* January 23, 25, 1899.

277

139. *Ibid.*, January 26, 1899.
140. Morgantown *Post*, February 2, 1899.
141. Arnold C. Scherr to Elkins, January 26, 1899, Elkins Papers.
142. Wheeling *Register*, January 26, 1899.
143. T. G. Pownall to Elkins, February 6, 1899, Elkins Papers.
144. H. M. Adams to Elkins, May 18, 1899; T. K. Scott to Elkins, May 23, 1899; H. R. Thompson to Elkins, June 5, 1899; M. F. Matheny to Elkins, May 19, 1899, Elkins Papers.
145. Reese Blizzard to Elkins, May 30, 1899; A. M. Miller to Elkins, n.d., 1899; A. S. Veach to Elkins, May 29, 1899, Elkins Papers.
146. M. H. Willis to Elkins, May 17, 1899; C. E. Haddox to Elkins, May 29, 1899; C. L. Hall to Elkins, May 24, 1899; O. W. O. Hardman to Elkins, April 23, 1900, Elkins Papers.
147. Morgantown *Post*, March 3, 1900; see also *ibid.*, November 23, December 14, 1899, January 18, February 8, 22, 1900; Wheeling *Intelligencer*, February 8, 1900.
148. He was also suspected of flirting with Goff. (J. K. Thompson to A. B. White, November 15, 1899, White Papers.)
149. Wheeling *Intelligencer*, February 3, 1900.
150. Dawson to Elkins, April 23, 1900; and letters of Samuel Dixon, O. A. Petty, and J. J. Haptonstall, May-June 1899, Elkins Papers.
151. McKell to Elkins, January 4, 1900; Huling to Elkins, April 6, 1900; Dawson to Elkins, April 12, 1900, Elkins Papers.
152. Gaines to Elkins, April 25, 1900, Elkins Papers.
153. McKell to C. H. Grosvenor, January 8, 1900; C. C. McIntosh to Elkins, April 30, 1900, Elkins Papers.
154. C. D. Elliott to Elkins, April 29, 1900, Elkins Papers.
155. Morgantown *Post*, March 1, 1900.
156. Scott to White, February 8, 1900, White Papers.
157. Gaines to Elkins, March 17, 1900, Elkins Papers; W. J. Burley to White, November 4, 24, 1899; Scott to White, November 16, 1899; White to Scott, January 25, 1900, White Papers.
158. Morgantown *Post*, February 8, 1900.
159. *Ibid.*, March 1, 1900.
160. T. F. Lanham to Elkins, March 19, 1900, Elkins Papers.
161. Payne to Elkins, March 10, 1900, Elkins Papers.
162. The sixteen counties that gave the Progressive party a plurality or majority (between 40 and 59 percent) of its presidential vote in 1912 included Grant, Upshur, Monongalia, Preston, Taylor, Tyler, and Ritchie—northern counties that had voted Republican in every presidential election since 1864 (there were eleven such counties altogether); plus Kanawha, Putnam, Fayette, Mason, and Raleigh in the Kanawha region. (Robinson, *Party Vote*, 367-371.) A less striking but similar

pattern is shown by the gubernatorial ballot at the 1904 state Republican convention. (Morgantown *Post,* July 13, 1904.)

163. Elliott to Elkins, March 12, 1900, Elkins Papers; Scott to White, June 4, 1900, White Papers.

164. Dawson to Elkins, April 13, 1900; Elliott to Elkins, April 29, 1900, Elkins Papers.

165. Unidentified correspondent to Elkins, February 15, 1900, Elkins Papers.

166. T. E. Davis to Elkins, n.d. [post-July], 1900, Elkins Papers.

167. Mason to Camden, July 31, 1897; Mason to Henry D. Hatfield, July 1, 1913, Mason Papers.

168. Wheeling *Intelligencer,* August 4, 12, 1897.

169. *Ibid.,* January 12, 1899.

170. *Ibid.,* January 12, 1899, October 5, 1900; Wheeling *Register,* June 10, 1901.

171. Morgantown *Post,* February 15, 1900.

172. See W. C. Scott to C. W. Osenton, November 20, 1898, and various unidentified clippings, 1898-1902, C. W. Osenton Papers, in Landsdowne Family Papers, University of Kentucky Library (microfilm copy, WVU), for McKell's collaboration with the United Mine Workers in Fayette County politics and his assistance to striking coal miners during a labor dispute in 1902.

173. McKell to C. H. Grosvenor, January 2, 8, 1900, Elkins Papers.

174. Wheeling *Register,* January 12, 1899; Atkinson to Elkins, April 29, 1900, Elkins Papers.

175. Morgantown *Post,* January 19, 1899.

176. S. C. Harless to Elkins, April 20, 1900; Dawson to Elkins, April 23, 1900, Elkins Papers.

177. Rogers to Elkins, April 25, 1900, Elkins Papers.

178. White to Scott, January 20, 1900, White Papers.

179. Dawson to White, n.d., 1900; M. C. Jameson to Dawson, February 10, 1900; John Cummins to White, February 14, 1900, White Papers; G. C. Stevens to Elkins, August 20, 1900; Kerens to Elkins, October 12, 1900, Elkins Papers.

180. On Huling, see J. C. Cannon to Elkins, November 22, 1895, *ibid.;* on Edwards, Wheeling *Intelligencer,* January 27, 1895, Mac-Corkle, *Recollections,* 407; J. W. Mason to Elkins, March 22, 1900, Elkins Papers; Smith, *Goff,* 209-220; on Davis, Atkinson and Gibbens, *Prominent Men of West Virginia,* 529-530; Sturgiss, *ibid.,* 775.

181. Sturgiss to Elkins, April 15, 1900; Grant to Elkins, April 20, 1900, Elkins Papers.

182. Wheeling *Register,* January 1, 1900.

183. Scott, Sturgiss, Elkins, Goff, Mason, Davis, and Atkinson were all between fifty-five and sixty in 1900; Dawson was forty-seven, White,

forty-four, Glasscock, thirty-eight. See biographical sketches in Atkinson and Gibbens, *Prominent Men of West Virginia*, and Phil Conley, ed., *The West Virginia Encyclopedia* (Charleston, W.Va., 1929).

184. Ambler, *Pierpont*, 360-361.
185. Mason to Elkins, April 17, May 2, 1897, Mason Papers.
186. Atkinson to Elkins, March 28, 1900, Elkins Papers.
187. T. E. Pittman [War Department Auditor] to Elkins, April 26, 1902, Elkins Papers, provided proof that Elkins had served fifty-three days in the Enrolled Missouri Militia.
188. Elkins to White, January 30, 1900, White Papers; T. G. Pownall to Elkins, February 15, 1900; Sutherland to Elkins, February 19, 1900, Elkins Papers.
189. Scott to White, October 3, 1898, White Papers.
190. Morgantown *Post*, March 1, 1900.
191. McKell lodged his complaints against Scott with his Ohio congressman, C. H. Grosvenor; however, one of his biggest grievances was that he had not been given full credit for converting Fayette County to Republicanism. (McKell to Grosvenor, November 12, 1898, Elkins Papers.)
192. Morgantown *Post*, November 2, 1899; McKinney to Elkins, March 23, 26, 1900; H. A. Robinson to Elkins, April 20, 1900, Elkins Papers.
193. Payne to Elkins, March 10, 1900, Elkins Papers.
194. Waters to Washington, February 13, 1904, Booker T. Washington Papers, Library of Congress. Waters believed that Atkinson's unwillingness to challenge Elkins proved that the governor was "greater and stronger than his party." (Waters to Washington, April 26, 1904, *ibid.*)
195. J. B. Poindexter to Editor, March 14, 1900, Parkersburg *State Journal*, quoted in Morgantown *Post*, March 22, 1900.
196. Wheeling *Intelligencer*, January 16, 1900; Morgantown *Post*, February 8, 15, 1900; H. C. Lockney to Elkins, January 31, 1900, Elkins Papers.
197. Unidentified correspondent to Elkins, February 15, 1900, Elkins Papers.
198. White to Elkins, January 18, 1900, White Papers.
199. Elkins to White, November 15, 1899; Scott to White, November 16, 23, 30, 1899, White Papers.
200. Atkinson to Elkins, March 28, 1900, Elkins Papers.
201. Dawson to White, December 26, 1899, White Papers.
202. Scott to White, February 10, 1900, White Papers.
203. Dawson to White, February 17, 1900; Elkins to White, February 28, 1900, White Papers. But Atkinson still wanted to be promised the judgeship.

204. Quoted in Morgantown *Post*, March 1, 1900. A milder version of Freer's remarks appears in Wheeling *Intelligencer*, February 21, 1900.

205. Elkins to White, February 28, 1900; Scott to White, February 28, 1900, White Papers.

206. White to Elkins, March 4, 1900, Elkins Papers.

207. Morgantown *Post*, February 28, March 12, 1900.

208. Scott to White, February 8, 1900, White Papers; and Wheeling *Intelligencer*, March 14, 1900.

209. Mason to Elkins, March 23, 1900, Elkins Papers.

210. Wheeling *Intelligencer*, March 23-24, 26, 1900; Morgantown *Post*, March 29, 1900; W. E. Glasscock to White, June 28, 1900, White Papers.

211. E. M. Campbell to Elkins, March 31, 1900; G. A. Poffenberger to Elkins, April 17, 1900; E. M. Grant to Elkins, April 20, 1900, Elkins Papers.

212. Wheeling *Intelligencer*, May 9, 1900.

213. Scott to White, June 4, 1900, White Papers. For the spadework in Kanawha, see letters to Elkins from Dawson, Elliott, and Gaines, March-April 1900, Elkins Papers.

214. Wheeling *Register*, July 12, 1900.

215. Davis to J. T. McGraw, November 30, 1899; Davis to G. W. Tippett, December 4, 1899; and letters to Camden, Ingalls, Tippett, and J. R. McLean, May-September 1899, Davis Papers; Davis to Camden, April 9, 1900, Camden Papers.

216. Davis to McGraw, May 23, 29, June 16, 25, 1900, Davis Papers; Wheeling *Register*, May 17, July 3-6, 1900.

217. Wheeling *Intelligencer*, June 7-9, 1900; see also correspondence of Davis, McGraw, and H. C. Simms, February 12, 14-16, 23, 1900, Davis Papers.

218. McGraw to Davis, August 31, 1900, Davis Papers.

219. Wheeling *Register*, June 8, 19, 1900.

220. Davis to J. H. Miller, July 9, August 2, 1900, Davis Papers; cf. Elkins to J. N. Camden, July 8, 1900, Camden Papers.

221. Wheeling *Register*, August 9, 1900; Hallie Davis Elkins to Dayton, August 9, 1900, Dayton Papers.

222. Wheeling *Register*, August 29, 31, September 1, 6, 7, 1900.

223. Davis to McGraw, August 12, 1900; Davis to W. A. Ohley, August 18, 1900, Davis Papers.

224. H. G. Buxton to Davis, September 24, 1900; Davis to F. S. Landstreet, October 29, 30, 1900; Landstreet to Davis, October 30, 1900; Davis to J. H. Markwood, October 29, 1900, Davis Papers.

225. Wheeling *Intelligencer*, November 24, 1900.

226. Camden to Fleming, November 7, 1900, Fleming Papers.

NOTES TO CHAPTER 4

1. Diary of Henri Jean Mugler, November 8, 1892, November 6, 1894, WVU. Mugler was an Alsatian immigrant who settled in Grafton before the Civil War and fought in both the Union and Confederate armies.

2. V. O. Key, Jr., "A Theory of Critical Elections," *Journal of Politics*, 17 (1955), 3-18; Carl Degler, "American Political Parties and the Rise of the City: An Interpretation," *Journal of American History*, 51 (1964), 42-50; Samuel P. Hays, "New Possibilities for American Political History: The Social Analysis of Political Life," in S. M. Kipset and Richard Hofstadter (eds.), *Sociology and History: Methods* (New York, 1968), 195.

3. Diary of Henri Jean Mugler, November 10, 13, 1894.

4. These and subsequent analyses of electoral data, except where otherwise noted, are based on presidential voting returns listed in W. Dean Burnham, *Presidential Ballots, 1836-1892* (Baltimore, 1955), 854-863, and Eugene E. Robinson, *The Party Vote, 1896-1932* (Stanford, 1934), 367-417 and on gubernatorial and congressional voting returns supplied by the Inter-University Consortium for Political Research, Ann Arbor, Michigan.

5. MacCorkle, *Recollections*, 479; S. Myers, *Myers History of West Virginia* (2 vols., n.p., 1915), 352; Wheeling *Register*, December 2, 1886; Wheeling *Intelligencer*, December 30, 1892. For Wyoming County's behavior see Table II, note (c).

6. *Ninth Census of the United States* (1870), *Population and Social Statistics* (Washington, 1872) 1:376; *Thirteenth Census of the United States* (1910), *Population* (Washington, 1913), 3:1027.

7. Wheeling *Intelligencer*, December 30, 1892.

8. Precinct level voting returns are given in an unidentified clipping, 1880 n.d. Fleming Papers, and in the Fairmont *Index* for October 24, 1884, November 12, 1886, November 9, 1888, November 31, 1890, and November 25, 1892. Precinct boundaries changed as new ones were added, but those of the magisterial districts, which in West Virginia generally conform to topographical features such as watersheds, did not.

9. Based on unidentified clippings for 1894 and 1896, scrapbooks, Elkins Papers, and Fairmont *Free Press*, November 11, 1898, November 9, 1900. On the location of oil activity in and around Mannington, see Eugene D. Thoenen, *History of the Oil and Gas Industry in West Virginia* (Charleston, W.Va., 1964), 201-203, 211.

10. *Ibid.*, 153-157, 167-175.

11. Wheeling *Intelligencer*, January 18, 22, 30, 1895, January 29, February 2-5, 8, 11, 1897.

12. Elkins to Davis, May 23, 1897; Davis to R. F. Whitmer, Septem-

ber 24, 1898; Davis to John J. Davis, December 31, 1898, Davis Papers; Wheeling *Register*, February 17, 21, 1900.
13. N. C. McNeil to Elkins, March 30, 1900, Elkins Papers.
14. James M. Callahan, *History of West Virginia Old and New* (3 vols.; Chicago, 1923), 1:440.
15. *Thirteenth Census of the United States* (1910) *Population*, 3:1027.
16. MacCorkle, *Recollections*, 467.
17. Davis to O. Tibbets, October 21, 1898, Davis Papers. For other examples, see Davis to D. W. Gall, August 29, 1890; Davis to John H. Hurst, August 2, 1895; Davis to C. S. Hamill, November 1, 1895, *ibid*. The last two instances concern Maryland elections.
18. H. G. Buxton to Davis, November 8, 1900, Davis Papers.
19. Camden to J. A. Fickinger, October 11, 1900, Camden Papers. For the sources of voting data, see notes 8 and 9.
20. Charleston *State*, October 19, 1880; Charleston *State Tribune*, November 6, 1886; unidentified clippings, 1894 and 1896, scrapbooks, Elkins Papers.
21. Wheeling *Register*, August 6, 7, 1896; on the fusionist leader, Henry S. Walker and the Populists, see note 66. Robert S. Carr, the fusionist senate candidate whose victory in 1886 is portrayed in Table IV, later became a member of the Kanawha Ring. (Wheeling *Intelligencer*, February 5, 8, 1890; Charleston *Labor Argus*, May 13, 1909.)
22. John M. Hagans to John W. Mason, September 14, 1882, Mason Papers.
23. David J. Rothman, *Politics and Power, The United States Senate, 1869-1901* (Cambridge, Mass., 1966), 186, reports the same impression. For references on Davis's expenditures, see Appendix.
24. Davis to Lewis Baker, March 9, April 2, June 18, July 11, 1885; Davis to R. G. Barr, October 5, 1895, Davis Papers; cf. Davis to Henry S. Walker, March 7, 1877, October 12, 1877; and Davis to John W. Avirett, December 20, 1895, *ibid.*, for other editors whose loans were called in or renewed, respectively.
25. Summers, *Camden*, 146-147, 157, 220, 264-265, 296-297, 426-427, 450, 489, 519, 559; J. H. Ferguson to Camden, September 10, 1882; R. J. McCandlish to Camden, December 11, 1885, Camden Papers.
26. Scott to A. B. White, July 29, October 7, 1898, White Papers.
27. Elkins to White, November 30, 1893, White Papers.
28. Scott to White, September 30, October 3, 5, 1898, White Papers.
29. Affidavits of Louis Bennett and W. W. Beall, November 30, December 1, 1908, Louis Bennett Papers, WVU.
30. Davis to W. W. Arnett, November 21, December 12, 22, 28,

1876, January 29, February 6, 1877; Davis to A. W. Knotts, November 29, 1876, February 6, 1877; Davis to T. B. Kline, December 12, 1876, Davis Papers.
    31. Elkins to A. B. White, January 7, 1899, White Papers.
    32. "Report of T. S. Riley, Treasurer, . . ." Davis Papers.
    33. J. V. Cunningham to Camden, September 22, 1894, Camden Papers.
    34. John W. Davis to Julia McDonald, November 6, 1898, John W. Davis Papers, Yale University Library, box 5.
    35. D. W. Gall to Davis, August 28, 1890; Davis to Gall, August 29, 1890; J. W. Miller to Davis, September 18, 1900, Davis Papers.
    36. O. S. McKinney to Thomas B. Davis, October 20, 1904 (copy); John T. McGraw to Davis, May 11, 1905; unidentified correspondent to F. S. Landstreet, 1905 n.d., Davis Papers.
    37. Scott to A. B. White, October 31, 1898, White Papers.
    38. "Draft of a letter to Register, . . ." March 27, 1887, Davis Papers. Apparently Davis thought better of publishing this inside view of the matter, for the passage was stricken out of the letter before it was printed.
    39. Scott to A. B. White, August 8, 1898, White Papers.
    40. Ambler, *West Virginia* (1940 edn.), 456.
    41. Harry Welles Rush to Davis, March 4, 1892; Davis to Frank Thomson, March 7, 15, 28, 1892; Davis to Rush, August 12, 1892, January 31, 1896, Davis Papers.
    42. W. M. O. Dawson to John W. Mason, November 16, 1896; Alston G. Dayton to Mason, June 19, 1900, Mason Papers; N. B. Scott to A. B. White, December 28, 1898, White Papers.
    43. Scott to White, February 28, 1900, White Papers; Dailey to Davis, January 28, 1901, Davis Papers.
    44. Elkins to White, December 26, 1894, White Papers.
    45. See Chapter 7.
    46. Scott to White, June 4, 1900, White Papers.
    47. Theodore H. White, *The Making of the President 1960* (New York, 1961), 99.
    48. Cecil D. Eby, Jr., " 'Porte Crayon' and the Local Color Movement in West Virginia," *West Virginia History*, 201 (April 1959), 156.
    49. Hagans to Waitman T. Willey, March 21, 1881, Willey Papers.
    50. Sturgiss to Willey, February 7, 1871, Willey Papers.
    51. William L. Wilson, Diary, January 15, 1881; see also December 21, 1881, February 19, 1882, *ibid.*
    52. M. M. Dent to Waitman T. Willey, February 9, 1871, Willey Papers.
    53. MacCorkle, *Recollections*, 480.
    54. Scott to A. B. White, February 18, 1899, White Papers; Scott to

W. E. Glasscock, September 6, 1904, William E. Glasscock Papers, WVU.

55. C. A. Swearingen to Glasscock, February 10, 1912, Glasscock Papers.

56. I. V. Barton to Glasscock, December 22, 1908; S. A. Hale to Glasscock, December 28, 1908; C. L. Duckworth to Glasscock, September 29, 1909; M. Withrow to Glasscock, December 18, 1908; G. C. Sturgiss to Glasscock, January 8, 1909, Glasscock Papers.

57. York Coleman to S. B. Elkins, January 21, 1908 [sic]; Elkins to Glasscock, January 27, 1909; Pressley W. Morris to Glasscock, March 12, April 5, 1909; W. S. Brown to Glasscock, January 1, 1908 [sic]; C. L. Duckworth to Glasscock, September 29, 1909, Glasscock Papers.

58. Pierpont to Waitman T. Willey, January 4, 1871, March 3, 1881, Willey Papers.

59. Wheeling *Intelligencer*, May 4, 1893; Wheeling *Register*, January 1, 1898.

60. Mason to Elkins, July 3, 1897, Mason Papers.

61. Mason to William McKinley, January 13, 1901, Mason Papers; Mason to W. E. Glasscock, January 4, 1911, November 20, 1912, Glasscock Papers.

62. Henry S. Green to Alston G. Dayton, January 14, 1905, Dayton Papers; W. M. O. Dawson to Granville D. Hall, February 9, 1914, Hall Papers; A. D. Williams to L. J. Forman, May 25, 1907, L. J. Forman Papers, WVU.

63. D. L. Ash to W. E. Glasscock, December 18, 1908, Glasscock Papers.

64. Dawson to Elkins, April 23, 1900, Elkins Papers. The applicant got a consulship in Mexico.

65. Elkins to A. B. White, June 20, 1897, White Papers.

66. Summers, *Camden*, 143, 151, 160-161; Wheeling *Intelligencer*, September 2, 1891; Davis to A. B. Fleming, January 7, 1890, Davis Papers.

67. Davis to John King, June 15, August 12, 1868; Davis to William Keyser, July 20, September 12, 1874, June 17, December 13, 1876; Davis to Samuel Spencer, January 5, 10, 1882, December 8, 1883; Davis to D. C. Gallaher, September 20, 1884; Davis to M. E. Ingalls, January 3, 1899, Davis Papers.

68. Davis to Thomas B. Davis, April 1, 1887, Davis Papers.

69. Davis Elkins to Davis, December 7, 1912; Richard Elkins to Davis, January 15, 1913, Davis Papers.

70. A. H. Kunst to Camden, January 18, 1892; Camden to G. W. Thompson, January 4, 1894; Camden to Kunst, December 11, 1894, Camden Papers. Hardman was a state legislator; Camden also supplied

an annual carload of free coal to federal district Judge John J. Jackson. (Glenn F. Massey, "Legislators, Lobbyists and Loopholes: Coal Mining Legislation in West Virginia, 1875-1901," *West Virginia History*, 32:3 [April 1971], 169.)

71. Davis to Benjamin Wilson, August 20, 1884; Davis to J. A. Cunningham, March 19, 1900, Davis Papers.

72. Wheeling *Register*, February 18, 1887; Morgantown *Post*, February 5, 7, 1903; A. H. Kunst to Camden, January 18, 1892; A. S. Johnston to Camden, January 6, 1893, Camden Papers.

73. Dayton to G. M. Shriver, August 6, 1903, Dayton Papers.

74. Landstreet to Davis, April 11, 1890, Davis Papers.

75. Pepper, *Davis*, 225.

76. Sutherland to Davis, June 2, 1899, Davis Papers.

77. Callahan, *History of West Virginia Old and New*, 2:591.

78. Davis to Sheridan, January 14, 1882; H. G. Buxton to Davis, February 25, 1893; Davis to Wilson G. Bissell, April 18, 1893, Davis Papers; Wheeling *Register*, February 6, 1902.

79. Camden to Davis, December 3, 1900; Davis to Emmons Blaine, January 19, 24, 1884, January 25, 1889; Davis to J. R. McKee, January 19, 1889, Davis Papers.

80. Davis to Clayton, July 29, 1881; Davis to Whyte, December 20, 1880, Davis Papers; Atkinson and Gibbens, *Prominent Men of West Virginia*, 66, 68, 803; Lambert, *Gorman*, 33-34, 36-37, 112, 133.

81. Davis to Sprigg, February 1, December 19, 1882; Davis to Lucas, September 21, 1878; Davis to Wilson, December 2, 1880; Davis to George F. Moffett, August 11, 1881; and similar correspondence with J. F. Hardin, B. L. Butcher, Benjamin F. Martin, Robert White, J. V. Cunningham, John Brannon, and Samuel Young, Davis Papers.

82. William Patrick Turner, Jr., "From Bourbon to Liberal, The Life and Times of John T. McGraw, 1856-1920," Ph.D. dissertation, West Virginia University, 1960, 6-7, 9-18, 35-37, 40-41, 56, 60-66, 70, 72, 74-77, 92, 96, 98-107; Memorandum of agreement, February 20, 1896, Davis Papers.

83. Biographical data for the individuals involved was found in Atkinson and Gibbens, *Prominent Men of West Virginia;* Callahan, *History of West Virginia Old and New*, vols. II and III; Atkinson, *Bench and Bar;* and Conley (ed.), *West Virginia Encyclopedia*.

84. Edward M. Steel, "Mother Jones in the Fairmont Field, 1902," *Journal of American History*, 57:2 (September 1970), 290-307. A. B. White included a rumor that Blizzard had accepted money from the Fairmont company in the course of exercising his duties as marshal during the strike in a letter to Theodore Roosevelt in 1905, but struck the reference out before sending the letter (White to Roosevelt, February 7, 1905, White Papers).

85. Callahan, *History of West Virginia Old and New*, 3:5; cf. Blizzard to A. B. Fleming, January 13, 1904, January 30, February 21, 1907, Fleming Papers.

86. Callahan, *History of West Virginia Old and New*, 2:190; A. B. White to W. E. Glasscock, March 20, 1909, Glasscock Papers.

87. American Coal Trade Committee, Secretary's Record, 38-39 (January 31, 1894), Davis Papers; Massey, "Coal Mining Legislation in West Virginia," 159.

88. Romney *Independent*, February 18, 1903, clipping, scrapbooks, White Papers. Where it is possible to check this allegation, it proved correct, as in the case of Senator Ira E. Robinson, later state supreme court justice and gubernatorial candidate (Robinson to G. Ricket, February 25, 1907, Ira E. Robinson Papers, WVU).

89. Elliott to John W. Mason, March 20, 1901, Mason Papers.

90. Thoenen, *History of the Oil and Gas Industry*, 219-220; Steel, "Mother Jones into the Fairmont Field," 292; "Statement of Stock Values and Distribution, Watson Interests, 1900"; M. F. Elliott to Fleming, December 5, 1906; George Chesebro to Fleming, June 3, 1907, Fleming Papers.

91. Fleming to M. F. Elliott, February 28, 1913, Fleming Papers, mentions the special expenses fund.

92. Fleming to H. L. Bond, October 30, 1902, Fleming Papers.

93. "List of Stockholders of Fairmont Development Company, May 1, 1905," Ohley to Fleming, January 18, 1907, Fleming Papers; see also p. 290, note 23.

94. Davis to Sturgiss, March 11, 1893, Davis Papers; Elkins to White, February 9, 1900, White Papers; T. W. Peyton to Elkins, April 7, 1901; White to Elkins, December 12, 19, 1901, April 5, 1902; Sturgiss to Elkins, November 12, 1902; W. E. Sadler to Elkins, February 7, 1907; Vinson to Elkins, April 29, 1899, Elkins Papers; Glasscock to Frank Cox, March 31, 1905, Glasscock Papers; Morgantown *Post*, March 6, 1903.

95. Elkins to White, June 3, 1895, White Papers.

96. "Campaign funds 1884," found in last three pages of unlabeled notebook, Mason Papers, box 1; see also David H. Cox to Mason, September 5, 1882, and other correspondence, 1882-1884, and entries in William L. Wilson, Diary, for the campaign season in election years.

97. "Report of T. S. Riley, Treasurer, . . ." Davis Papers.

98. Scott to Elliott, March 14, 1904 (copy), White Papers; Morgantown *Post*, January 10, 1903.

99. "Report of T. S. Riley, Treasurer, . . ." Davis Papers.

100. W. E. Glasscock to Edwin W. Sims, March 6, 1912, Glasscock Papers.

101. Washington *Post*, November 1, 1892.

102. Scott to Glasscock, September 27, 1904; H. F. Ashby to Glasscock, November 28, 1904; Elliott Northcott to Glasscock, December 2, 1904, Glasscock Papers.

103. Wheeling *Intelligencer,* January 28, 1895; see also pp. 211-219 below.

104. Wheeling *Register,* February 19, May 8, 1901; *West Virginia House Journal* (1901), 280-288; *West Virginia Acts* (1901), chs. 48-53, 55-58.

105. White to Mason, May 19, 1898, Mason Papers.

106. MacCorkle, *Recollections,* 447-448.

107. Dawson to C. H. Livingston, March 17, 1899, Elkins Papers; *Official Register of the United States* (1901) 2:399-420, (1903) 2:392-408.

108. *Ibid.,* (1901) 1:298, 1308, (1903) 1:249-250, 1369, (1905) 1:236, 1406; Wheeling *Register,* June 18, 1901, February 12, 22, 1902; Fairmont *Times,* January 28, 1905; Dawson to Glasscock, March 27, 1905; White to Glasscock, January 19, 1909, Glasscock Papers. For routine contemporary use of the term "Hog Combine," see Scott and White, August 24, 1903; E. S. Boggs to White, 1903 August n.d., White Papers.

109. A. C. Scherr to F. M. Reynolds, August 26, 1905, Francis M. Reynolds Papers, WVU.

110. Charles B. Marble to Glasscock, December 29, 1908, Glasscock Papers.

111. Scherr to Reynolds, August 26, 1905, Reynolds Papers.

112. Correspondence of Davis and Camden, John T. McGraw, O. S. McKinney, and John J. Cornwell. 1901-1910, Davis Papers; see also pp. 244-245 below.

113. Camden to Scott, April 6, 1901, Camden Papers; Davis to Camden, November 6, 1902, Davis Papers; R. M. G. Brown to Alston G. Dayton, August 27, 1903, Dayton Papers; Pepper, *Davis,* 167-179.

114. Lodge to Roosevelt, July 12, 1904, in Lodge, ed., *Selections from the Correspondence of Theodore Roosevelt and Henry Cabot Lodge* (2 vols., New York, 1925), 2:88.

115. Camden to Scott, April 6, 1901, Camden Papers.

116. Phillips, *The Treason of the Senate,* George A. Mowry and Judson A. Grinier, eds. (Chicago, 1954), 149-153.

117. Steel, "Mother Jones in the Fairmont Field," 300, 307.

NOTES TO CHAPTER 5

1. *Trow's New York City Directory* (1889), 57, 61, 561; ——— (1904), 228, 266, 307, 380-381, 393, 398, 1442; ——— (1911), 300, 345, 429, 449, 877, 1647, 1678; *Directory of Directors in the City of New York* (1901), 511, 542, 370; ——— (1909), 358, 809; Moses King, *King's Handbook of New York City* (New York, 1893), 141-142, 821;

John A. Kouwenhoven, *The Columbia Historical Portrait of New York* (Garden City, N.J., 1953), 395.

2. Ralph W. and Muriel E. Hidy, *History of the Standard Oil Company* (New Jersey); I: *Pioneering in Big Business, 1882-1911* (New York, 1955), 68-69, 335-336, 639-641. In order to avoid confusion with the West Virginia politician, C. D. Elliott, M. F. Elliott's name is used infrequently in the pages that follow but his influence can be traced in detail in the Fleming Papers, as the references will suggest. According to the Hidys, Elliott did not believe in engaging politically active lawyers as local counsel. If this was true, West Virginia was clearly an exception.

3. E. Digby Baltzell, *The Protestant Establishment: Aristocracy and Caste in America* (Vintage edn., 1966), 3-142.

4. These episodes can be followed in Lambert, *Elkins*, 281-283, and in the scrapbooks, Elkins Papers (e.g. Washington *Post*, August 5, 1909). See also Social Register Association, *Social Register, New York*, 9:1 (November 1894), 103; 19:1 (November 1904), 156.

5. Pepper, *Davis*, 163, 181, 279-299; Summers, *Camden*, 567-569; Scott to Elkins, December 5, 16, 1896, Elkins Papers; George C. Shinn to White, September 14, 1903, White Papers.

6. This topic is treated at length in Summers, *Camden*, 168-211, upon which, unless otherwise noted, the following account is based.

7. Camden to Rockefeller, January 1, 1878, Camden Papers.

8. Camden to John D. Rockefeller, June 2, 1879, Camden Papers.

9. Camden to Rockefeller, November 2, 1878, June 2, 1879, Camden Papers.

10. Summers, *Camden*, 344-360; Ambler, *History of Transportation in the Ohio Valley*, 271-272.

11. *Twelfth Census of the United States* (1900), *Manufactures, Part IV* (Washington, 1902), 10:684.

12. Thoenen, *History of West Virginia Oil and Gas Industry*, 218-226.

13. Summers, *Camden*, 211, 361-414, 550-556; Thompson to Camden, October 10, 1890, Camden Papers.

14. Earl Chapin May, *From Principio to Wheeling, 1715-1945. A Pageant of Iron and Steel* (New York, 1945), 200-227.

15. Wheeling *Register*, March 27, 1902.

16. New York *Times*, February 9, September 14, 1891, January 6, 1892; Warren C. Scoville, *Revolution in Glassmaking: Entrepreneurship and Technological Change in the American Industry, 1880-1920* (Cambridge, Mass., 1948), 22, 88-89.

17. Wheeling *Register*, August 16, 1894; New York *Times*, October 28, 1900. Scott to C. H. Livingston, March 21, 1900, Elkins Papers, indicates by the letterhead that Central Glass Company was operating,

although the census official in charge of surveying glass manufacturing reported no U.S. Glass Company plants in West Virginia (Shirley P. Austin, "Glass," in *Twelfth Census of the United States* (1900), *Manufactures, Part III* [Washington, 1902], 9:977-978. See also, Phil Conley, ed., *The West Virginia Encyclopedia* [Charleston, W.Va., 1929], 133-285.) It should be pointed out that Scott's business career, in contrast to the other industrialists, must be followed on the basis of fragmentary evidence.

18. Warren C. Scoville, *Revolution in Glassmaking*, 22, 92-93, 277-311.

19. Richard H. Slavin, *The Pressed and Blown Glassware Industry (West Virginia University Business and Economic Studies*, 8 [Morgantown, W.Va., 1963]), 1-5; Scoville, *Revolution in Glassmaking*, 155, n. 26, 323-324.

20. George H. Burgess and Miles C. Kennedy, *Centennial History of the Pennsylvania Railroad Company, 1846-1946* (Philadelphia, 1949), 455-459.

21. *Ibid.*, 459-462; U.S. Senate, Committee on Interstate Commerce, *Railroad Combination in the Eastern Region, Part I (Before 1920)*, Senate Report 1182, 76th Congress, 3rd session (Washington, 1940), 16-26. (Hereafter cited as *Senate Report on Railroad Combination.*)

22. *Engineering and Mining Journal*, 67 (February 11, 1899), 186; 68 (September 23, 1899), 380; (October 7, 1899), 437-438; 69 (January 6, 1900), 21; 70 (December 22, 1900), 741; *The Coal Trade*, 27 (1901), 39; 28 (1902), 6-7; *Coal & Coke*, 8 (January 11, 1901), 13; 8 (May 15, 1901), 12; Lambie, *From Mine to Market*, 238-240.

23. Summers, *Camden*, 521-546; Wheeling *Register*, October 23, 1900, June 29, 1901, March 22, 1902, January 7, 10, 1903; *Coal & Coke*, 10 (March 1, 1902), 8; "In the matter of the relation of common carriers subject to the act to regulate commerce to coal and oil and the transformation thereof" (docket 869 [1906] Records of the Interstate Commerce Commission, National Archives, record group 134), volume 22, file 38 ("Property owned by Consolidation Coal Company"), volume 23, file 38 ("Fairmont Coal Company, ownership of stock, July 1, 1903"), file 41 ("Consolidation Coal Company, ownership of stock, July 1, 1903"). Hereafter these records will be cited as follows: ICC Records, Coal and Oil Investigation, [volume number]: [page or file reference].

24. *Trow's New York City Directory* (1904), 266, 398, (1911) 300, 449, 1647, 1678; Thoenen, *History of the Oil and Gas Industry*, 218-227; *The Coal Trade*, 33.

25. Camden to H. L. Bond, October 15, 1900, Camden Papers.

26. Davis to Andrew Carnegie, December 14, 1899, Davis Papers; Carnegie to Elkins, January 20, 1900, Elkins Papers.

27. Samuel Rea to Davis, March 22, 1900; Kerens to Davis, April 14, 1900; Davis to Cassatt, April 19, 1900; Cassatt to Davis, April 20, 1900, Davis Papers.

28. John E. Day to C. H. Livingstone, January 14, 1902, with enclosed clipping, Elkins Papers.

29. Elkins to Davis, November 14, 19, 20, 25, December 2, 1901; Davis to Gould, January 23, 1902, Davis Papers; *Railway Age*, 33 (February 7, 1902), 186.

30. H. C. Frick to John D. Rockefeller, Jr., January 18, 1904 (copy), in *Senate Report on Railroad Combination* (subpoenaed from files of the President's Office, Pennsylvania Railroad Company, and printed as exhibit C-301), 305; Morgantown *Post*, December 25, 1902, June 8, 1903.

31. *Senate Report on Railroad Combination*, 27-33; Morgan to A. J. Cassatt, March 2, 1901 (copy), exhibit C-243, in *ibid.*, 277.

32. *Ibid.*, 33-41; Harold A. Williams, *The Western Maryland Railway Story. A Chronicle of the First Century, 1852-1952* (Baltimore, 1952), 89-101.

33. *Senate Report on Railroad Combination*, 56-59; Williams, *The Western Maryland Railway Story*, 110-129.

34. Davis to Joseph Ramsey, February 7, May 2, 1902, February 13, 1903; Davis to Elkins, March 21, 1902; Elkins to Davis, July 25, 1902, May 9, 1904; Davis to C. Wood Dailey, May 19, 23, 1904, Davis Papers; Wheeling *Register*, December 21, 1902, March 13, 1903; Morgantown *Post*, July 10, 25, 1902; George C. Sturgiss to Elkins, November 12, 1902, Elkins Papers.

35. Davis to Elkins, August 25, 1902, Elkins Papers; see also Elkins to James Stillman, April 2, 1908, Frank A. Vanderlip Papers, Columbia University Library.

36. Joseph Ramsey to Elkins, May 19, 1903, December 21, 1904; Elkins to Davis, May 22, 1903, June 18, 1904, January 7, 1905; W. H. Bower to Davis, March 2, 1904; Davis to Oscar Murray, September 22, 1903, March 14, 1904; Davis to Ramsey, March 17, 1904, May 5, 1905, Davis Papers; Murray to Elkins, December 18, 1903; George F. Randolph to Elkins, February 11, 1904; J. H. Wheelwright to Elkins, June 16, 1904, Elkins Papers.

37. Oscar Murray to Elkins, December 18, 1903, Elkins Papers; ICC Records, Coal and Oil Investigation, 1:369-372, 380-386, 401-408, 882-888, 1023, 3:1394-1476, 5:2681-2684; Wheeling *Register*, December 23, 1902, January 18, October 17, November 20, 1903; Fairmont *Times*, January 14, 30, 1903, March 25, 1903; *Coal & Coke*, 10 (January 1, 1903), 12.

38. *Ibid.*, 28 (1901), 59-60; 31 (1904), 26-27, 41, 51; Lambie, *From Mine to Market*, 223-226, 240, 252-253; ICC Records, Coal and Oil Investigation, 1:3-12, 32-35, 54, 21:15.

39. ICC Records, Coal and Oil Investigation, 2:756-767; *The Coal Trade*, 34 (1907), 137-138; Cassatt to Martin A. Knapp, December 3, 1906, correspondence file 103809, Records of the Interstate Commerce Commission, National Archives. Coal industry sources made these charges as early as 1903 (*Engineering and Mining Journal*, 75 [January 3, 1903], 49; Morgantown *Post*, August 10, 1904). Cf. Minutes of the Pennsylvania Railroad Company Board of Directors, May 9, 1900, exhibit C-138 in *Senate Report on Railroad Combination*, 211, and John P. Green, Memorandum as to the sale of Chesapeake and Ohio Stock to the New York Central Interests, April 5, 1909, exhibit C-103 in *ibid.*, 182-183. As for the railroad itself, PRR freight revenues per ton mile rose from 0.473 cents in 1899 to a peak of 0.605 cents in 1903 and 1904; for passenger revenue per ton mile, the figures were 1.945, 2.028, and 2.000, respectively. (Burgess and Kennedy, *Centennial History of the PRR*, 461.)

40. Elkins to James Stillman, April 1, 1908, Vanderlip Papers; Unidentified clipping, April 3, 1908, scrapbooks, Elkins Papers; Thomas Le Duc, "Carriers, Courts and the Commodities Clause," *Business History Review* 39 (1965), 57-73. Kolko, unaware that Elkins himself conceivably faced prosecution under the commodity clause, assumes that it reflects his interest as a coal producer (*Railroads and Regulation*, 163-164). On Elkins's lengthy promotion of a Commerce Court, see *ibid.*, 198-201, and Elkins to Richard Olney, January 22, 27, February 6, 1902, Richard Olney Papers, Library of Congress, volume 93. Also instructive is the haste with which Elkins settled the car assignment dispute when it became public during the Hepburn Act debate (Alston G. Dayton, Memorandum of Arbitration, March 30, 1906, ICC Records, Coal and Oil Investigation, 23:66).

41. Kolko, *Railroads and Regulation*, 91.

42. For example, the Alaska fur seal venture described on p. 33. See also G. E. Spencer to Elkins, October 28, 30, November 14, 1881; Jefferson Chandler to Elkins, November 16, 1881; New York *World*, June 11, 1884; New York *Times*, December 18, 1891, clippings, scrapbooks, Elkins Papers.

43. The certificates were issued unilaterally by Virginia in 1891 to cover West Virginia's share of the commonwealth's antebellum debt. The instruments soon passed into the hands of speculators at prices as low as six cents on the dollar, who then launched repeated endeavors to collect on them from West Virginia, who insisted that Virginia assigned it too high a share of the debt. The numbers of West Virginia politicians involved in this matter between 1871 and 1909, which Virginia finally

took to the Supreme Court, were probably legion. Some of them acted in a disinterested fashion, hoping to save the state the enormous burden of interest that it eventually had to pay. This was in fact Camden's explanation of his interest in the debt. (Camden to W. M. O. Dawson, November 29, 1907, Camden Papers.) For his actual role as speculator, see Summers, *Camden,* 423-443.

44. Elkins to John W. Mason, March 11, April 29, 1896; H. C. Fahnestock to Elkins, April 28, 1896, Mason Papers. Elkins was endeavoring to get Mason to run the political interference for a settlement. Mason's reply (March 13, 1896, *ibid.*) indicates what a hot political potato it was. For Elkins's public denial of his involvement, see Wheeling *Register,* January 27, 1895; and Elkins to A. B. White, February 1, 1895, White Papers. For his continuing involvement, see H. C. Fahnestock to Elkins, November 9, 1898, January 11, 1899, Elkins Papers.

45. Davis to Camden, March 30, 1874, Davis Papers.

46. Camden's background is described in Chapter 1, note 27. Davis's uncle, Peter Gorman, was a Democratic leader in Maryland (John R. Lambert, Jr., *Arthur Poe Gorman* [Baton Rouge, 1953], 3-7), while Elkins's middle name, "Benton," suggests that political leaders were held in high esteem among his Missouri family. For Scott's background, see Atkinson and Gibbens, *Prominent Men of West Virginia,* 515.

47. Davis to Camden, November 1, 1898, Davis Papers; Scott to A. B. White, February 28, 1900, White Papers.

48. Scott to A. B. White, August 8, 1898, White Papers.

49. For example, Camden died before a Virginia Debt settlement was reached; the opportunity referred to in note 45, the prospect of federal aid for West Virginia railroads, also fizzled.

50. Camden to John D. Rockefeller, June 23, 1879; H. M. Flagler to Camden, March 10, 1882; William Rockefeller to Camden, March 17, 1882; W. P. Thompson to Camden, March 16, April 6, 1894; Camden to L. A. Cole, June 21, 1894, Camden Papers; Hidy and Hidy, *Pioneering in Big Business,* 211-213.

51. Lambert, *Elkins,* 297-307; Davis to Alston G. Dayton, January 5, 1897, Davis Papers; Wheeling *Register,* November 15, 1902, January 13, 14, 1903.

52. Slavin, *The Pressed and Blown Glassware Industry,* 11; Scoville, *Revolution in Glassmaking,* 240-245; Scott to Elkins, December 5, 16, 1896, Elkins Papers. Again, however, the evidence is far less definitive with respect to Scott. His engagingly cynical letters to A. B. White and Elkins often reflect the attitudes of one whose basic attraction to politics is that of the sportsman.

53. Eugene Hale to Elkins, December 17, 1885, February 24, 1887;

John J. Ingalls to Elkins, February 24, 1887; Hoke Smith, Memorandum on Mesita de Juana Lopez land grant, May 13, 1893; John K. Cowen to Elkins, April 6, 1894; E. R. Bacon to Elkins, June 9, 1897; Flagler to Elkins, January 5, 1899; John K. Cowen to Elkins, April 13, 23, 1900; J. N. Camden to Elkins, April 6, 1900; Matthew Quay to Elkins, January 4, 1903, Elkins Papers; Thomas B. Catron to Elkins, August 15, 1892, Catron Papers; Wheeling *Register*, March 28, 1896. Cf. Davis to Arthur Gorman, March 3, 1891, February 8, 1893; John P. Green to Davis, January 22, 1892; Davis to A. J. Cassatt, May 25, 1892; W. J. Sewell to Davis, 1893 n.d., Davis Papers; H. B. Plant to Camden, September 1, 1894, Camden Papers; Elkins to James Stillman, April 1, 1908, Vanderlip Papers.

54. John J. McCook to Elkins, December 19, 1899; Flagler to Elkins, January 5, 1899, Elkins Papers.

55. Davis to Camden, May 13, 1893, Camden Papers.

56. Wheeling *Intelligencer*, April 25, 1892; and numerous clippings, March-December 1892, scrapbooks, Elkins Papers; Lambert, *Elkins*, 145-146.

57. Hanna to Elkins, September 12, 1902, Elkins Papers; cf. James Weinstein, *The Corporate Ideal in the Liberal State, 1900-1918* (Boston, 1968), 3-39.

58. Kolko, *Railroads and Regulation*, 90-98, 139-144, 151-152, 190-198. In general Kolko is right for the wrong reasons, that is, Elkins's pro-railroad course cannot be explained by his personal economic interests alone, as Kolko attempts to do.

59. This view of the Senate is informed by general reading in the sources and literature of the period, and especially by Rothman, *Politics and Power*, 11-108, 159-240.

60. M. H. Davis to Camden, July 22, 1889, Camden Papers; Atkinson and Gibbens, *Prominent Men of West Virginia*, 187; Morgantown *Post*, December 6, 1900.

61. Morgantown *Post*, September 5, 1901.

62. Ambler, *History of Education in West Virginia*, 207.

63. Roberta Stevenson Turney, "The Encouragement of Immigration in West Virginia, 1863-1871," *West Virginia History*, 12:1 (October 1950), 47-49, 52-59; Debar to Waitman T. Willey, December 9, 1874, February 3, 1875, Willey Papers.

64. J. H. Diss Debar, *The West Virginia Handbook and Immigrant's Guide* (Parkersburg, W.Va., 1870), 11.

65. Conley, *History of the West Virginia Coal Industry*, 84-85.

66. *Poor's Manual of Railroads*, 34 (1901), vi; Ambler, *West Virginia* (1940 edn.), 467; Richard A. Easterlin, "Interregional Differences in Per Capita Income, Population, and Total Income, 1840-1950," in National Bureau for Economic Research, Conference on Research in

Income and Wealth, *Trends in the American Economy in the Nineteenth Century* (Princeton, 1960), 97-100 (Tables A-1, A-2).

67. West Virginia Tax Commission, *Preliminary Report* (Wheeling, W.Va., 1884), 4.

68. Wheeling *Register*, August 15, 1881.

69. *Ibid.*, November 10, 1881.

70. *Ibid.*, August 17, 1884.

71. Ambler, *West Virginia* (1940 edn.), 478-481.

72. Hamill Kenny, *West Virginia Place Names* (Piedmont, W.Va., 1945), 98, 107, 148, 181, 200, 261, 277, 299, 306, 339, 347, 624.

73. Wheeling *Register*, November 19, 1882; *ibid.*, December 13, 1882, quoting Parkersburg *Sentinel;* Morgantown *Post*, December 21, 1899; Wheeling *Intelligencer*, September 25, 1900.

74. MacCorkle, *Recollections*, 482-483.

75. Wheeling *Intelligencer*, January 12, 1899; see also Atkinson to John W. Mason, November 22, 1900, Mason Papers.

76. *The West Virginian* (1900), 7; Morgantown *Post*, May 22, 1900. Cf. *The Virginias* (February 1885), 23.

77. Wheeling *Register*, May 19, 1901.

78. Alexander Gershenkron, *Economic Backwardness in Historical Perspective. A Book of Essays* (Cambridge, Mass., 1962), 24-25.

79. Quoted in Summers, *Camden*, 338.

80. "Draft of a letter to Register," March 27, 1887, Davis Papers; and Wheeling *Register*, April 1, 1887.

81. West Virginia Tax Commission, *Second Report, State Development* (Wheeling, W.Va., 1884), 3-6; Summers, *Camden*, 317, 327, 340, 344, 346; *Coal & Coke*, 10 (January 1, 1903), 17; Wheeling *Register*, January 9, 1903; Morgantown *Post*, January 2, 1904.

82. Davis to Lewis Baker, February 24, 1882, Davis Papers.

83. Summers, *Camden*, 222, 250.

84. See Chapter 2, note 121.

85. Gershenkron, *Economic Backwardness in Historical Perspective*, 6-9; Harvey S. Perloff, Edgar S. Dunn, Jr., Eric E. Lampard, and Richard F. Muth, *Regions, Resources, and Economic Growth* (Baltimore, 1960), 58-62.

86. William Haynes, *This Chemical Age* (New York, 1942), 82-90; Elizabeth J. Goodall, "The Charleston Industrial Area: Development, 1797-1937," *West Virginia History*, 30:1 (October 1968), 391-397; Conley, *West Virginia Encyclopedia*, 139-143, 405; Haynes, *Chemical Pioneers. The Founders of the American Chemical Industry* (2 vols., New York, 1939), 138-139, 194-195. The Standard Oil official who interested himself in the Parkersburg aniline firm was not Camden, but James A. Moffet, his superintendent, who is mentioned on p. 186.

87. *Twelfth Census of the United States (1900). Special Reports:*

Mines and Quarries (Washington, 1902), 680, 725, 768-769; *Manufactures, Part II* (Washington, 1902), 8:939. (All subsequent references to the Twelfth Census in this chapter will be as follows: [Subtitle], [Part, if any], [Volume, if any] : [page].)

88. *Mines and Quarries*, 769, 772.

89. Unidentified clipping, February 13, 1911, scrapbooks, Glasscock Papers.

90. *Manufactures*, III, 9:1029.

91. *Manufactures*, II, 8:940-941.

92. *Manufactures*, I, 7:362-365.

93. *Manufactures*, I, 7:206-209; III, 9:358-359.

94. *Manufactures*, IV, 10:22, 60-65; May, *From Principio to Wheeling*, 212-213, 222-223.

95. *Manufactures*, III, 9:954-958, 975-978; cf. Slavin, "The Pressed and Blown Glassware Industry," 1-10.

96. *Manufactures*, II, 8:939, 943, 948-949.

97. Victor R. Fuchs, *Changes in the Location of Manufacturing in the United States since 1929* (New Haven, 1962), 23, 71-74, 95, 439.

98. Goodall, "The Charleston Industrial Area," 358-364.

99. Scoville, *Revolution in Glassmaking*, 114, 127-128, 169, 296.

100. Blake McKelvey, *The Urbanization of America, 1860-1915* (New Brunswick, N.J., 1963), 234-239; Raymond E. Murphy, *The American City: An Urban Geography* (New York, 1966), 317-367.

101. John G. Luke to Davis, March 2, 1899, Davis Papers. The pulp mill was probably in turn responsible for a rayon factory that later located in the same Virginia town.

102. *Thirteenth Census of the United States (1910) Population*, 3:1032, 4:529-530.

103. Fred Mooney, *Struggle in the Coal Fields: The Autobiography of Fred Mooney*, edited by J. W. Hess (Morgantown, W.Va., 1967), 10-15, 22-27. Mooney's ms. autobiography was written "in the late 1920s or in the 1930s" (p. ix).

104. J. C. Rawn to Glasscock, April 29, 1912, Glasscock Papers.

105. "Report of the Mining Commission Appointed by Governor Glasscock on the 28th Day of August, 1912," in *West Virginia House Journal* (1913), 96-118, also printed separately (Charleston, W.Va., 1912). Cited hereafter as "Donahue Commission Report." Cf. Allen Pred, *The Spatial Dynamics of U.S. Urban-Industrial Growth: Interpretative and Theoretical Essays* (Cambridge, Mass., 1966), 12-85, on urban locational pulls on industry.

106. Davis's greatest success was Deer Park, Maryland (see Chapter 2); neither Davis, W.Va., nor Elkins, W.Va., enjoyed success as a resort, although attempts were made to duplicate Deer Park at Elkins by luring prominent politicians to build summer residences there (R. C. Kerens to

Davis, September 30, 1889, Davis Papers; Benjamin Harrison to Elkins, June 16, 1894, Elkins Papers). See also Summers, *Camden*, 412, 507-508, and Percival Reniers, *The Springs of Virginia: Life, Love and Death at the Waters* (Chapel Hill, 1941).

107. Charleston *Gazette*, May 5, 1910; cf. "Resolution of the Williamson [W.Va.] Board of Trade," in E. F. Randolph to W. E. Glasscock, January 11, 1911, Glasscock Papers.

108. Hu Maxwell to Fleming, November 11, 1908; J. M. McKinley to Fleming, January 11, 1913; Fleming to C. W. Watson, February 1, 1913, Fleming Papers.

109. Wheeling *Register*, April 1, 13, June 10, 1888; see also *National Cyclopedia of American Biography*, 33:413 (biographical entry of M. V. Davis, prosecutor in the case).

110. West Virginia Tax Commission, *Preliminary Report* (Wheeling, W.Va., 1884), 5, 11-37; ———, *Second Report, State Development*, 9-10, 19-21.

111. Gershenkron, *Economic Backwardness in Historical Perspective*, 24.

112. For a sample of Mason's extensive involvement in the debt speculation, see Mason to Davis, April 14, 1881, September 12, 1889, March 31, April 19, 1892, Davis Papers; Mason to Waitman T. Willey, November 22, 1883, Willey Papers; Mason to Camden, April 19, 1894, Camden Papers; Wheeling *Intelligencer*, March 21, 1910.

113. Mooney, *Struggle in the Coal Fields*, 120-121.

114. West Virginia Tax Commission (1884), *Preliminary Report*, 32-33; *Second Report*, 7-8, 21-23.

115. Douglas C. North, *Growth and Welfare in the American Past: A New Economic History* (Englewood Cliffs, N.J., 1966), 75, 148, 165 and exchanges of Albert Fishlow and Robert W. Fogel in Ralph I Andreano (ed.), *New Views on American Economic Development* (Cambridge, Mass., 1965), 187-224; Perloff et al., *Regions, Resources, and Economic Growth*, 55-58.

116. Pred, *Spatial Dynamics of Urban-Industrial Growth*, 15-16, 25, 59-61, 79-83.

117. May, *From Principio to Wheeling*, 207.

118. Hidy and Hidy, *Pioneering in Big Business*, 317. Other examples were Jere H. Wheelwright of Camden and later Fairmont Coal (Summers, *Camden*, 504) and W. P. Thompson and F. S. Landstreet mentioned before. Of the Camden, Davis, and Elkins progeny who can be located in the *Social Register*, 1920-1930, only one, John T. Davis, is given a West Virginia address. Johnson N. Camden, Jr., served briefly as a United States senator from Kentucky, then retired to breed horses near Frankfort (*Biographical Directory of Congress*, 675). The others migrated to Washington, Baltimore, and New York. Cf. the careers of John W. Davis (no relation), Earl W. Oglebay, and Cyrus Vance.

119. Jim Comstock, "Welcome, Sharon," in Otto Whittaker, ed., *Best of Hillbilly* (Pocket Books, edn., New York, 1968), 101. Cf. Alex Campbell, "John D. Rockefeller IV, Youth Power and Dreams of Glory," *New Republic*, 159 (December 7, 1968), 16-19.

120. Paul A. Baran, *The Political Economy of Growth* (New York, 1957), 144-162.

121. Merle Curti, "American Philanthropy and the National Character," *American Quarterly* 10 (Winter, 1958), 420-437; ———, Judith Green, Roderick Nash, "Anatomy of Giving: Millionaires in the late Nineteenth Century; *ibid.*, 15 (Fall, 1963), 416-435 (reprinted in Lipset and Hofstadter (eds.), *Sociology and History*, 216-292).

122. Davis to Robert Bridges, October 22, 1894, Davis Papers; Andrew Carnegie to Elkins, January 20, 1900, Elkins Papers; Wheeling *Daily News*, December 7, 1911; Conley (ed.), *West Virginia Encyclopedia*, 198-202; Thoenen, *History of the Oil and Gas Industry*, 223. The lists of millionaires are reprinted, with a discussion of their authenticity, in Sidney Ratner, *New Light on the Great American Fortunes: American Millionaires of 1892 and 1902* (New York, 1953). Many years earlier, Davis had considered donating $5,000 anonymously to West Virginia public schools, but the letter and check are marked "reconsidered and not sent." (Davis to B. W. Byrne, January 15, 1874, Davis Papers.)

123. Much of the following discussion is based on Homer L. Morris, *The Plight of the Bituminous Coal Miner* (Philadelphia, 1934), which contains a useful digest of the 1925 report of the United States Coal Commission as well as a later social and economic survey; Harold Barger and Sam H. Schurr, *The Mining Industries, 1899-1939, A Study of Output, Employment, and Productivity* (New York, 1944), a N.B.E.R. study; Conley, *History of the West Virginia Coal Industry*, an apologetic account; "Donahue Commission Report"; James H. Thompson, *Significant Trends in the West Virginia Coal Industry, 1900-1957* (West Virginia University Business and Economic Studies, vol. 6 [Morgantown, 1958]), a useful brief survey; and Harry M. Caudill, *Night Comes to the Cumberlands: A Biography of a Depressed Area* (Boston, 1963), a moving first-hand account primarily concerned with eastern Kentucky. J. W. Hess provides a valuable bibliography in Mooney, *Struggle in the Coal Fields*, 174-180. Of the industry serials consulted, *The Coal Trade* is more oriented toward the anthracite industry but contains annual compilations of bituminous data; *Coal and Coke* appears at times to have reflected the viewpoints of smaller operators; *Engineering and Mining Journal* is comprehensive, and from a journalistic standpoint, more professional.

124. Morris, *Plight of the Bituminous Miner*, 1-11.

125. Raymond E. Murphy and Hugh E. Spittal, "Movements in the

Center of Coal Mining in the Appalachian Plateaus," *Geographical Review*, 35 (1945), 624-633.

126. Bluefield *Telegraph*, January 3, 1911, and other clippings, scrapbooks, Glasscock Papers.

127. Hess, Introduction in Mooney, *Struggle in the Coal Fields*, vii-ix, and 169, note 1.

128. *The Coal Trade*, 31 (1904), frontispiece, n.p.

129. *Engineering and Mining Journal* 69 (December 1, 1900) 650, 72 (January 11, 1902), 258, (February 15, 1902), 258, 74 (March 21, 1903), 460; *The Coal Trade*, 29 (1902), 69, 31 (1903), 30, 34 (1907), 33, 136.

130. Caudill, *Night Comes to the Cumberlands*, 306-317; 86.8 percent of West Virginia coal came from drift mines in 1909, compared to 51.1 percent in Pennsylvania, 52.3 percent in Ohio, 1.0 percent in Illinois (*Thirteenth Census of the United States* [1910] *Mines and Quarries* [Washington, 1913], 9:213-214).

131. *Ibid.*, 9:205.

132. Quoted in Morris, *Plight of the Bituminous Miner*, 85-87.

133. For example, Conley, *History of the West Virginia Coal Industry*, 72-81.

134. Quoted in Morris, *Plight of the Bituminous Miner*, 85.

135. Mooney, *Struggle in the Coal Fields*, 20; "Donahue Commission Report," 110.

136. R. C. Kerens to Davis, March 28, 1895, Davis Papers. However, for further building of company houses elsewhere, see Davis to F. S. Landstreet, October 12, 1892, *ibid.*, and Wheeling *Register*, January 23, 30, February 6, 20, 1898.

137. Davis to Landstreet, May 8, 1894, Davis Papers.

138. Landstreet to Elkins, November 30, 1901, Elkins Papers; Mooney, *Struggle in the Coal Fields*, 59-60; cf. "Donahue Commission Report," 109, on the civic activities of Charles A. Cabell, an operator who lived in his camp at Decota, Kanawha County.

139. "Cost of Elkins property, Hon. S. B. Elkins in account with H. G. Davis & Bro., September 1, 1890"; Edward A. Warner to Davis, October 5, 1893; Landstreet to Davis, October 10, 1895; H. A. Mayer to Davis, October 24, November 25, December 24, 1896; Davis to Elkins, June 16, 20, 1898; John T. Davis to Davis, January 3, 1900; Davis to Joseph Ramsey, February 13, 1903, Davis Papers. Although the senators realized at least a 200 percent profit from the sale of lots at Elkins, their utilities firm there paid an annual dividend of only 2 percent compared to 10 percent from the stores and houses in other towns.

140. A. B. Fleming to G. W. Fleming, December 14, 1907, Memorandum, "Explosion at Monongah, 1907, Name of Person Killed . . . Amount Paid," Fleming Papers. The second document

records "donations" totalling $38,725 to the families of 135 victims who lived nearby. Assuming that equivalent amounts (which ranged individually from $50 to $450, depending on the number of survivors) were paid to nonresident survivors of the 224 remaining victims, the total would top $100,000. However, Fleming's correspondence with foreign consuls (see note 141) indicates that much smaller amounts were paid to such people, perhaps as low as $100 per victim.

141. Fleming to Imperial & Royal Austro-Hungarian Consul, December 30, 1909; ——— Snodgrass to Fleming, November 23, 1911, Fleming Papers.

142. Three books stand out in the voluminous literature on contemporary Appalachia: Caudill, *Night Comes to the Cumberlands*, and Todd Gitlin and Nanci Hollander, *Uptown: Poor Whites in Chicago* (New York, 1970); Thomas R. Ford (ed.), *The Southern Appalachian Region: A Survey* (Lexington, Ky., 1962).

143. Charleston *Labor Argus*, September 1, September 29, 1910, January 13, 26, April 20, 27, June 1, 1911 (founded in 1905, this weekly changed from a nonpartisan to "a red hot revolutionary rag" in 1910 and became the official Socialist party organ at Charleston in January 1911); Mooney, *Struggle in the Coal Fields*, x, 39-54, 127-128, 172-173, notes 1-4; James Weinstein, *The Decline of Socialism, in America 1912-1925* (New York, 1967), 34, 102, 116-117, 284, 287, 309; Irving Bernstein, *The Lean Years: A History of the American Worker, 1920-1933* (Boston, 1960), 381-385; Frederick A. Barkey, "The Socialist Party in West Virginia from 1898 to 1920: A Study in Working Class Radicalism" (Ph.D. thesis, University of Pittsburgh, 1971).

144. E. A. Bennett to A. B. White, March 19, 1901, White Papers. Bennett, a merchant and former mayor of Huntington, had dissented from much of James Murray Mason's equivalent indictment as chairman of the West Virginia Tax Commission of 1884.

145. For expressions of this sentiment, see Wheeling *Register*, March 27, 1902, January 15, 1903; Morgantown *Post*, December 25, 1902, May 4, 1903, March 25, 26, 30, 1904.

NOTES TO CHAPTER 6

1. The number includes six regular biennial sessions plus the special session of 1890. Officially there were more, since occasionally, as in 1891 and 1893, the legislators failed to complete their work within the constitutional period of forty-five days and were held over in special session until appropriations bills were passed.

2. Quoted in Massey, "Coal Mining Legislation in West Virginia," 164.

3. Camden to John K. Cowen, December 17, 30, 1890; M. E. Ingalls

to Camden, December 26, 31, 1889; E. W. Clark to Camden, December 28, 31, 1889, Camden Papers.

4. Camden to Davis, January 18, 1890, Davis Papers; Davis to Elkins, February 4, 1890, Elkins Papers.

5. Wheeling *Intelligencer*, February 13, 21, 23, 1893; *West Virginia Acts* (1893, regular), ch. 12.

6. Wheeling *Intelligencer*, February 9, 10, 16, 25, March 2, 3, 1893.

7. Massey, "Coal Mining Legislation in West Virginia," 135-137, 159-162.

8. Camden to J. A. Fickinger, October 2, 1895, Camden Papers.

9. Massey, "Coal Mining Legislation in West Virginia," 141-159; *West Virginia Acts* (1883), ch. 70, (1887) chs. 11, 50, 53, (1889) ch. 15, (1891) chs. 76, 82. Davis wanted to fight *any* enactment in 1887, but C. Wood Dailey, on the scene in Charleston, advised that it was pointless to do so under the circumstances. (Dailey to Davis, February 15, 1887, Davis Papers.)

10. *State vs. Peel Splint Coal Co.*, 36 W.Va., 802.

11. Wheeling *Intelligencer*, January 17, 19, 21, 1893.

12. Davis to J. B. Finley, January 27, 1893; F. L. Garrison to Davis, February 11, 1893, Davis Papers.

13. Finley to Davis, January 23, 1893, *ibid.;* Wheeling *Intelligencer*, January 21, 25, February 2, 11, 15, 24, 1893.

14. Evan Powell to Davis, February 11, 1893, Davis Papers.

15. Wheeling *Intelligencer*, January 16-19, 22, 26, 29, 31, February 2, 4, 6, 11, 18, 21, 22, 1895, referring to House Bills 56, 76, 79, 88, 90, 110, 153, 203.

16. Wheeling *Register*, February 25, 1895.

17. Dailey to Davis, February 1, 18, 1895, Davis Papers; Wheeling *Intelligencer,* January 19, 21, 25, 30, February 1, 9, 1895.

18. Elkins to A. B. Fleming, February 2, 1897; E. M. Showalter to Fleming, January 26, 1897, Fleming Papers; Davis to T. P. R. Brown and Lloyd Hansford, February 1, 1897; Davis to Hansford, February 10, 1897, Davis Papers.

19. Wheeling *Intelligencer*, February 5, 6, 8, 1897.

20. Conley, *History of the West Virginia Coal Industry,* 9-27; Ambler, *Pierpont,* 357.

21. Wheeling *Intelligencer,* February 22, 1895; D. M. Harr to Davis, September 12, 1895, Davis Papers.

22. Ohley to Fleming, February 9, 1897; MacCorkle to A. B. Fleming, March 1, 1897, Fleming Papers; Wheeling *Intelligencer,* February 11, 16, 20, 26, 28, 1897.

23. *Ibid.,* January 16, February 1, 1897.

24. *Ibid.,* February 27, 1899.

25. *Ibid.,* September 3, 7-10, 1900. In the November vote, Steck

301

fared neither better nor worse than any other Republican candidate, including the senatorial nominee, in any part of the city. (*Ibid.*, November 20, 1900.)

26. White to N. B. Scott, January 23, 1900, White Papers.
27. Davis to Camden, December 4, 1899, Davis Papers; April 9, 1900, Camden Papers; Camden to J. A. Fickinger, October 11, 1900, *ibid.*
28. Wheeling *Register*, January 9, 1901.
29. Wheeling *Intelligencer*, November 26, December 10, 1900; Wheeling *Register*, January 13, 17, 1901.
30. Elkins to A. B. White, January 4, 1901, White Papers, box 9.
31. Wheeling *Intelligencer*, March 4, 7, 9, 12, 1899; *West Virginia Acts* (1899), chs. 9, 16, 20, 24, 57, 58, 60, 63.
32. National Civic Federation, *National Conference on Taxation . . . May 23-24, 1901* (Buffalo, 1901), 6-8.
33. W. P. Hubbard, "Development of Taxation and Finance," in Callahan, *Semi-Centennial History*, 502; West Virginia Commission on Taxation and Municipal Charters, *Preliminary and Final Report* (n.p. [Charleston, W.Va.], 1902), 5 (hereafter cited as *Tax Commission Report*); *Poor's Manual of Railroads*, 34 (1901), vi.
34. J. N. Camden to W. T. Thompson, September 15, 1889, Camden Papers.
35. John A. Robinson to C. K. Lord, September 5, 1894, Camden Papers.
36. *Tax Commission Report*, 5; Wheeling *Register*, January 16, 25, 1901.
37. The following analysis is based on *Tax Commission Report*, 11-45; see also Elmer Guy Hendershot, "Tax Reforms in West Virginia during the Administration of Governor Albert Blakeslee White, 1901-1905," M.A. thesis, West Virginia University, 1949, vii-ix.
38. *Tax Commission Report*, 6-14.
39. Wheeling *Register*, January 26, 1901.
40. Wheeling *Intelligencer*, February 16, 1893, February 20, 1895; Wheeling *Register*, January 11, 1901.
41. Wheeling *Intelligencer*, February 20, 1895; Charleston *Gazette-Mail*, December 20, 1959, clipping, Dawson Papers.
42. Wheeling *Intelligencer*, January 23, 1891; Wheeling *Register*, January 9, 11, 17, 1901.
43. T. H. Landham to L. J. Forman, January 27, 1907, and Forman correspondence with county officials, January 1907, Forman Papers, box 10; John Wallace to W. E. Glasscock, October 23, 1910, Glasscock Papers.
44. H. Roy Waugh to L. J. Forman, January 19, 1907, Forman Papers.

45. *West Virginia House Journal* (1887 Regular), 516, 521-522, (1887 Special), 77-78, 80, 83, 89-90; Wheeling *Intelligencer*, March 11, 1891, February 13, 1895; Charleston, *Gazette-Mail*, December 20, 1959, clipping, Dawson Papers.

46. Hubbard, "Taxation and Finance," 502.

47. Wheeling *Intelligencer*, March 7, 1899.

48. *West Virginia Acts* (1901), Appendix, 507-778.

49. Wheeling *Intelligencer*, February 27, March 2, 1899.

50. Wheeling *Register*, January 9, 1901.

51. For details, see Elkins to Davis, January 31, 1899; C. M. Hendley to W. P. Whyte, February 10, 1899; Davis to T. B. Kennedy, February 14, 1899; J. T. Harris to Davis, March 11, 1899; Hendley to C. Wood Dailey, January 4, 1901, Davis Papers.

52. Morgantown *Post*, December 13, 1900.

53. *Twelfth Census of the United States* (1900): *Population Part I* (Washington, 1902), 1:411.

54. Wheeling *Intelligencer*, September 1, 3, 19, 25, November 22-24, December 1, 17, 24, 1900.

55. Wheeling *Intelligencer*, December 1, 1900.

56. Wheeling *Register*, January 22, 24, 25, 1901.

57. Wheeling *Intelligencer*, November 26, 1900.

58. A. E. Kenney to Davis, April 21, 1897, Davis Papers; A. B. Fleming to R. E. Fast, May 24, 1897; Elkins to Fleming, December 15, 1897, Fleming Papers.

59. Wheeling *Register*, January 11, 1901.

60. *Ibid.*, January 10, 1901.

61. On the organization of the legislature, see *ibid.*, January 8-10, 1901. On Wilson, see N. B. Scott to A. B. White, July 8, 1898; Elkins to White, July 8, 1898, White Papers. On the Democratic leaders, J. D. Alderson to Davis, September 24, 1894; Davis to Alderson, January 6, 1895; J. J. Cornwell to Davis, January 27, 1900; Davis to Cornwell, February 20, 1901, Davis Papers.

62. Camden to Elkins, December 28, 1900, Camden Papers.

63. Elkins to Fleming, December 28, 1900, Fleming Papers.

64. Elkins to White, January 4, 1901, White Papers.

65. Ohley to Davis, January 7, 1901, Davis Papers.

66. Davis to Dailey, January 24, 1901, Davis Papers.

67. Dailey to Davis, February 15, 1901, Davis Papers.

68. Wheeling *Register*, January 15, 16, 17, 20, 24, 1901.

69. *Ibid.*, January 18, 22, 1901. The emphasis in the bill was on exports, which indicates, though there is no other evidence to support the conclusion, that the Wheeling boomers were among the first to identify development with nonexport of natural resources.

70. Wheeling *Register*, January 8, 19, 1901.

71. M. F. Elliott to Fleming, January 24, 1901, Fleming Papers.
72. Scott to White, January 24, 1901, White Papers.
73. Dailey to Davis, January 28, 1901, Davis Papers. Cf. Camden's attitude; when Jackson was later mentioned as a possible appointee to West Virginia's new federal judgeship, Camden opposed him on the ground that his stand on the arbitration bill made him a threat to West Virginia's development. (Camden to Scott, April 6, 1901, Camden Papers.)
74. Davis to Dailey, January 30, 1901, Davis Papers.
75. Dailey to Davis, January 29, February 13, 1901; Davis to Dailey, January 31, 1901, Davis Papers.
76. Wheeling *Register*, January 29, 1901. However, all was not orderly. Dawson and Charlie Elliott, working hand in hand on corporation matters, were vigorously competing as agents of rival school book companies. Dawson to A. B. White, January 28, 1901, White Papers.
77. Dailey to Davis, January 28, 1901, Davis Papers.
78. Wheeling *Register*, January 26, 27, 28, 1901.
79. *Ibid.*, January 31, February 1, 1901.
80. *Ibid.*, February 3, 1901.
81. *Ibid.*, February 3, 1901. One who dined well was the labor delegate from Wheeling, Henry Steck (*Official Register of the United States* [1901], 1:298).
82. Dailey to Davis, February 13, 1901, Davis Papers. (Dailey's reports, especially this one, are the source of information on Elkins's activities in Charleston, unless otherwise cited.) The arbitration bill never passed, even though the railroad brotherhoods withdrew their fellow servants bill according to agreement. (Wheeling *Register*, February 23, 1901.)
83. Dailey to Davis, February 13, 1901, Davis Papers.
84. Wheeling *Register*, February 7, 8, 9, 16, 1901.
85. *Ibid.*, February 10, 12, 21, 1901.
86. *Ibid.*, February 8, 9, 1901.
87. *Ibid.*, February 5, 6, 12, 15, 19, 22, 1901.
88. Showalter to A. B. Fleming, February 17, 22, 1901, Fleming Papers; Wheeling *Register*, February 22, 1901.
89. Elkins to A. B. White, February 17, 1901; Atkinson to White, February 22, 1901, White Papers. Laughlin angrily rejected the stated reason for the veto, that the title was defective, pointing out that the title had been on the lawbooks since 1883. But he failed to win enough votes to repass the bill. (Wheeling *Register*, February 25, 1901.)
90. *Ibid.*, February 5, 6, 8, 12, 21, 22, 23, 1901. Morgantown *Post*, February 14, 21, 28, March 7, 1901. The university president's sins consisted principally of his attempts to modernize the school. The worst grievances were his practice of hiring faculty members from

outside of the state, thus reducing patronage, and sending them on "junkets" to professional meetings. (Ambler, *History of Education,* 333-339.)

91. Wheeling *Register,* February 11, 13, 14, 16, 19, 23, 25, 1901.

92. Except for increasing the authorized capital, the legislature did not revise the West Virginia Central charter. However, it passed another law "extending the time in which railroad companies, organized since June 1, 1880, may complete their railroads and put them in operation," thus indirectly confirming the generous territorial rights granted to the road by earlier sessions. (Wheeling *Register,* February 18, 1901.) Besides railroad legislation, the senators also secured a charter for their town of Elkins, enabling them to suppress a breakaway suburb, and a provision in a general banking law allowing them to use railroad bonds as bank assets. (See W. C. Russell to Davis, February 4, 1899; Davis to C. W. Dailey, January 24, 1901; Dailey to Davis, February 15, 1901, Davis Papers; *West Virginia Acts* (1901), chs. 85, 108, 113, 151.)

93. The employment bureau bill, for example, passed unanimously, while Laughlin's last-minute maneuver to pass the car branding bill entailed a voice vote. For the problem that drunk or incompetent legislators presented to legislative leaders, see M. S. Hodges to W. E. Glasscock, February 21, 1911, Glasscock Papers. Guttman scale analysis yields few useful attitude scales for the 1901 legislature. Cluster-bloc analysis shows greater cohesion among both Republicans and Democrats compared with the 1887 legislature; greater unity among Republicans than Democrats in 1901; an increase in Republican cohesion following Elkins's visit to Charleston of February 2-4, 1901; and the most persistent Republican "irregulars" grouped in clusters of two to five men each. For a discussion of quantitative methods used, see Williams, "The Old Dominion and the New," Appendix, 402-406.

94. Robert Wiebe, *The Search for Order 1877-1920* (New York, 1967), 11-75.

95. Wheeling *Register,* February 23, 1901.

96. Wheeling *Register,* March 5, 1901.

97. White to Elkins, March 14, 19, 28, 1901; Elkins to White, March 15, 30, 1901; Davis to White, April 15, 1901, White Papers; White to Davis, April 12, 17, 1901, Davis Papers.

98. Holt to White, April 5, 1901; Thompson to White, April 15, 1901; Hubbard to White, April 29, 1901, White Papers.

99. Landstreet to Fleming, September 11, 1901, Fleming Papers.

100. Showalter to Fleming, January 11, 1903; M. F. Elliott to Fleming, January 14, 1903, Fleming Papers; Fairmont *Times,* January 10, 1903; Wheeling *Register,* January 15, 17, 20, 21, 1903; Morgantown *Post,* January-February, 1903, *passim.*

101. Davis to C. W. Dailey, May 1, July 22, 1902; and other letters

of Davis, Dailey, and W. P. Hubbard, July 1901-September 1902, Davis Papers.

102. Davis to A. B. White, April 15, 1901, White Papers; National Civic Federation, *National Conference on Taxation*, 14-15, 56-57, 84-89, 95-96, 101-111, 116-127.

103. *Tax Commission Report*, 2-56, esp. 35, 43-44; Hendershot, "Tax Reforms in West Virginia," 53-54; Davis to C. W. Dailey, July 22, 1902, Davis Papers. For a convenient summary of the report, see Ambler, *West Virginia* (1940 edn.), 496.

104. Elkins to A. B. Fleming, February 17, 1905, Fleming Papers.

105. Elkins to Edward A. Moseley, September 3, 1902, correspondence file 59782, Records of the Interstate Commerce Commission. This letter is a request for railroad mileage and tax information of the type subsequently included in the *Tax Commission Report*. On December 26, 1901, Elkins wrote the ICC stating his desire to discuss "the subject of [national?] legislation relative to interstate commerce as soon as he can" and on February 10, 1903, wrote to acknowledge "draft of bill to establish commission in W. Va." These letters have not been found but their "purport" is described on correspondence file cards 56637 and 62240, respectively, *ibid*. For White's comment, see Wheeling *Register*, January 15, 1903.

106. *Ibid.*, November 23, 29, 1902.

107. Fairmont *Times*, January 31, 1903, and numerous clippings, scrapbooks, White Papers. Unless otherwise cited this account rests on the voluminous collection of West Virginia newspaper clippings in the White scrapbooks, especially upon the Wheeling *News* and *Intelligencer* and the Parkersburg *News*. The Wheeling *News* owned by George A. Laughlin during the Progressive era, the *Intelligencer* by H. C. Ogden, an Elkins ally who endorsed reform (Ogden to Elkins, November 7, 1906, Elkins Papers), and the Parkersburg *News* was edited successively by or under the direction of Charles D. Elliott and Reese Blizzard.

108. Copy of House resolution, 1903 n.d., White Papers.

109. January 31, 1903.

110. Wheeling *Register*, April 27, 1903; Morgantown *Post*, June 8, 1903.

111. W. A. Ohley to Fleming, June 8, 1903; Memorandum, "Resolved: That the oil, gas, coal and railroad interests, . . ." n.d., 1903; Randolph Stalnaker to Fleming, August 26, 1903, Fleming Papers. Among those present on June 13 were Elliott, Ohley, Stalnaker, former Attorney General Rucker, and District Attorney Reese Blizzard, who represented the West Virginia Central in its new Wabash-Western Maryland connection. Although Davis and Elkins's new enterprises were related to the Wabash, they were not represented at the meeting.

112. Ohley to A. B. Fleming, July 17, 1903, Fleming Papers; Fairmont *Times*, August 19, 1903.
113. Marginal comment on copy 3 of a pamphlet in the White Papers, box 11. White privately printed the pamphlet to circulate among key party leaders certain letters exchanged by him and Dayton after the appearance of the manifesto. Most copies were returned to White, who yielded to Elkins's wishes (Elkins to White, October 14, 1903, *ibid.*) and did not make them public.
114. W. M. O. Dawson to Elkins, May 17, 1903, Elkins Papers.
115. J. Worthington to Fleming, August 14, 1903; W. A. Ohley to Fleming, October 7, 1903, Fleming Papers; R. M. G. Brown to Alston G. Dayton, August 27, 1903, Dayton Papers.
116. Wheeling *Register*, October 5, 1903; Wheeling *Intelligencer*, June 18, October 13, 1904; Morgantown *Post*, July 28, 1904.
117. Davis to Hubbard, January 30, March 1, 1904; Dailey to Hubbard, February 1, March 7, 1904; Hubbard to Davis, February 15, 1904; Dailey to Davis, February 18, March 7, 1904, Davis Papers.
118. Blizzard to Fleming, January 13, 1904, Fleming Papers.
119. On Elkins's role in the compromise, Elkins to White, January 19, 1904; and other Elkins-White correspondence, January-June 1904, White Papers.
120. Fleming to Dayton, July 18, 1904; Fleming to M. F. Elliott, July 18, 1904, Fleming Papers.
121. Watson to Fleming, July 23, 1904, Fleming Papers.
122. See Elkins to Davis, November 6, 1903; Davis to Elkins, November 7, 1903; and correspondence of Davis and Camden, John T. McGraw, John J. Cornwell, O. S. McKinney, J. W. Avirett, and Holly Armstrong, December 1903-June 1904, Davis Papers; see also, Fairmont *Times*, January 4-July 13, 1904, *passim*.
123. Cf. Davis to W. S. Pierce, July 11, 1904; and Davis to Camden, July 14, 1904, Davis Papers.
124. Davis to Elkins, July 29, 1904, Davis Papers.
125. Davis to Morgan, August 12, 1904, Davis Papers; cf. Dailey's speeches on race at the delegate convention before Davis's nomination and at the gubernatorial convention afterwards. (Fairmont *Times*, April 20, August 4-5, 1904.)
126. Davis to Hubbard, August 1, 1903; C. S. Robb to Hubbard, September 17, 1903; Davis to W. M. O. Dawson, November 12, 1903; Davis to Parkersburg *News*, June 8, 1904, Davis Papers.
127. Davis to Hubbard, January 30, February 17, 1904, Davis Papers.
128. For example, see Dailey to Davis, August 26, 1904, Davis Papers, regarding the use of the partial reform laws just enacted as anti-Republican propaganda. Dailey was uncertain as yet whether the

laws should be described as too much or too little, but thought the idea worth keeping in mind.

129. Davis to Camden, July 26, 29, 1904, Davis Papers.
130. Fairmont *Times*, August 1, 4, 5, 1904; Elkins to A. B. White, August 5, 1904, White Papers.
131. Davis to W. F. Sheehan, August 31, 1904; Fleming to Davis, November 4, 1904, "Report of T. S. Riley, Treasurer,..." Davis Papers.
132. Davis to W. E. Chilton, November 14, 1904; Davis to O. S. McKinney, November 19, 1904, Davis Papers.
133. Davis to W. E. Chilton, February 25, 1905, Davis Papers; Camden to Davis, August 13, October 7, 1906; Camden to John T. McGraw, September 12, 1906, Camden Papers.
134. Elliott to Fleming, December 3, 1904, Fleming Papers.
135. Elliott to Fleming, December 8, 1904, Fleming Papers.
136. White to Elkins, December 23, 1904, White Papers.
137. Washington *Post*, January 13, 24, 25, 1905; Fairmont *Times*, January 14, 1905.
138. Elkins to White, December 20, 1904, White Papers.
139. Fairmont *Times*, January 11-14, 16, 18, 19, 26, 1905; Washington *Post*, January 17, 20, 1905; W. A. Ohley to Fleming, January 18, 1905, Fleming Papers.
140. Washington *Post*, January 29-February 13, 1905. Elliott himself was not responsible for the expose; the resulting publicity almost cost him his job as U.S. marshal. The newspaperman who acquired it said he found it in a Charleston hotel room.
141. The most interesting of the four separate official inquiries that followed was that of the Seaman Committee, detailed to investigate an accusation that White and Dawson were guilty of "fee-splitting." A two-year court battle failed to force the accusers to appear at the hearings and repeat their statements, and so the statehouse leaders were exonerated on the main charge. But Dawson was forced to admit to a damaging connection with a ring of Charleston lawyers who attempted to shake down the foreign corporations expected to benefit from lower license taxes. (Fairmont *Times*, February 10, 1905; West Virginia Legislature, House, *Report of the Committee appointed . . . on February 24, 1905* [Charleston, W.Va., 1907], 3-6, 18-20, 32-35.) Elkins did everything in his power to suppress the investigation, but White insisted on vindication. (Elkins to White, February 23, October 27, 1905; and other letters, November 1905, White Papers.)
142. Washington *Post*, February 10, 12, 14-19, 21-24, 1905.
143. Elkins to Fleming, February 17, 1905, Fleming Papers.
144. Fairmont *Times*, February 24, 1905. At issue was a provision

of the reassessment bill (needed to put the partial tax reforms of 1904 into effect) calling for the assessment of coal leases at their real value.
145. Fairmont *Times,* March 2, 3, 1905.

NOTES TO CHAPTER 7

1. Phillips, *Treason of the Senate,* 149-153.
2. Morgantown *Post,* April 3, 1905; W. A. Ohley to M. F. Elliott, April 19, 1905 (copy), Fleming Papers. Ohley noted, however, that while Dawson and his tax commissioners were determined to tax the leaseholds, they were "possibly inclined to accept very low valuations, at least for this year. . . ."
3. W. M. O. Dawson to Granville D. Hall, July 20, 1905, Hall Papers.
4. A. J. Welton to Forman, January 18, 1907; G. C. Baker to Forman, February 13, 1907, Forman Papers; Fleming to Swisher, January 25, 1907; Swisher to Fleming, January 29, 1907, Fleming Papers.
5. Neil Robinson, "To the Coal Operators of West Virginia," circular, February 3, 1909; McDermott to Fleming, February 16, 1909; M. F. Elliott to Fleming, February 5, 15, 17, 1909, Fleming Papers; Conley (ed.), *West Virginia Encyclopedia,* 84-85.
6. N. E. Whitaker to A. B. Fleming, February 25, 1909; J. C. McKinley to Fleming, January 2, 1908, Fleming Papers.
7. Fairmont *Times,* February 6, 26, 28, 1905; Morgantown *Post,* April 7, 1905; White to Theodore Roosevelt, February 7, 1905; Dawson to Elkins, November 4, 1905 (copy), White Papers; Dawson to Granville D. Hall, July 20, 1905, Hall Papers.
8. I. V. Barton of Elkins, September 26, 1906; G. W. Atkinson to Elkins, September 24, 1906, January 16, 1907, Elkins Papers.
9. C. E. Haddox to L. J. Forman, September 21, 28, 1907, Forman Papers.
10. Forman to C. E. Haddox, September 25, 1907, Forman Papers.
11. Forman to George C. Sturgiss, August 10, 1907; Forman to W. P. Hubbard, October 7, 1907; and draft letter to "Dear Sir," 1907 n.d. [August ?], Forman Papers.
12. C. E. Haddox to Forman, September 21, 28, 1907, Forman Papers.
13. C. E. Haddox to Forman, September 28, 1907; Forman to Solomon Clark, March 4, 1908; F. C. Leftwich to Forman, March 13, 1908, Forman Papers.
14. Wheeling *Intelligencer,* June 12, 16, 1908; A. C. Scherr to S. B. Elkins, October 29, 1907, Elkins Papers; Harry Scherr to Don Blagg, August 25, 1958, "Notes of Proceedings, Court House Convention, July 8, 1908," in William M. O. Dawson Papers, WVU.
15. L. J. Forman to Swisher, March 11, 1908; Forman to Scherr, March 11, 1908, Forman Papers.

16. Wheeling *Intelligencer*, June 19, July 8-11, 1908; O. H. Booton to Don Blagg, July 7, 1960; Blagg to Booton, July 18, 1960, "Notes of Proceedings, Court House Convention, July 8, 1908," Dawson Papers.

17. Harry Scherr to Don Blagg, August 25, 1958, Dawson Papers; G. W. Atkinson to Glasscock, September 28, 1908, and various clippings, August-September 1908, scrapbooks, Glasscock Papers. Unless otherwise noted, this account of the Glasscock administration rests on the clipping files in the Glasscock scrapbooks.

18. G. W. McClintic to Glasscock, September 23, 1908, Glasscock Papers.

19. C. A. Swearingen to Glasscock, December 26, 1908, Glasscock Papers; M. F. Elliott to A. B. Fleming, September 8, 1909; Fleming to Neil Robinson, September 15, 1909, Fleming Papers.

20. Harvey W. Harmer to Glasscock, December 30, 1908; Glasscock to Harmer, January 1, 1909; Glasscock to John T. Cooper, December 31, 1908; W. P. Hubbard to Glasscock, March 8, 1909; Glasscock to John W. Mason, September 27, 1910; Jonathan Bourne to Glasscock, February 2, 1911, Glasscock Papers.

21. Glasscock to S. B. Elkins, February 21, 1909, Elkins Papers; Howard Sutherland to Glasscock, May 20, 1910, Glasscock Papers.

22. Sturgiss to Glasscock, March 19, 27, 1909; Glasscock to Sturgiss, March 23, 1909; John W. Mason to Glasscock, April 12, 1909; Glasscock to Mason, April 14, 1909, Glasscock Papers.

23. Elliott to Glasscock, March 12, 20, 1909, Glasscock Papers.

24. W. P. Hubbard, "To the Republicans of West Virginia," circulars, January 19, May 5, 1910; W. P. Hubbard Association of Monongalia County, circular, May 20, 1910; Edwin R. Kingsley to Glasscock, May 3, 6, 1910; Glasscock to Kingsley, May 5, 1910; C. D. Elliott to Glasscock, May 3, 1910; H. Roy Waugh to Glasscock, May 14, 18, 1910; Glasscock to Waugh, May 17, 1910; Joseph H. McDermott to Glasscock, May 17, 1910; Glasscock to McDermott, May 24, 1910; John L. Steele to Glasscock, May 23, 1910; Stephen F. Glasscock to Glasscock, May 24, 1910; Glasscock to Stephen F. Glasscock, May 26, 1910, Glasscock Papers. Glasscock seems to have tried to remain neutral, but the fact that many of his appointees and most of the legislative candidates he favored were ranged against Scott made it difficult for Scott to accept his behavior as neutral.

25. Scott to Glasscock, April 20, 1910; Glasscock to Scott, April 22, 1910, Glasscock Papers.

26. Elkins to Glasscock, May 3, 22, June 19, August 21, 1909, Glasscock Papers; Glasscock to Elkins, May 20, 23, June 23, August 23, 1909, Elkins Papers. So far as it is discernible, Glasscock did not appoint anyone Elkins recommended, but Elkins did not insist except in

the case of assessment officials in Monongalia County, where he had important coal and railroad investments.

27. Elkins to Glasscock, December 19, 1908, January 29, February 2, 16, 1909, Glasscock Papers.

28. Elkins to Glasscock, January 29, February 2, 1909, Glasscock Papers.

29. Stephen F. Glasscock to S. B. Elkins, February 3, 1910; S. B. Elkins to W. E. Glasscock, March 15, April 7, 8, 1910; Davis Elkins to S. B. Elkins, April 7, 1910, Elkins Papers.

30. Elkins to Glasscock, March 15, May 6, July 7, August 25, 26, 1910, Glasscock Papers; Glasscock to Elkins, May 9, July 11, August 30, 1910, Elkins Papers.

31. Glasscock to C. F. Snyder, October 11, 1910; Snyder to Glasscock, October 9, 20, November 2, 1910, Glasscock Papers.

32. Lambert, *Elkins*, 324-328; C. F. Snyder to Glasscock, January 3, 1911; Glasscock to John W. Mason, January 6, 1911, Glasscock Papers.

33. William H. Andrews to Catron, January 5, 1911, Catron Papers, box 801; H. R. Warfield to Glasscock, January 6, 1911; C. F. Snyder to Glasscock, January 24, 1911, Glasscock Papers.

34. S. B. Elkins to Glasscock, April 7, 1910; Davis Elkins to Glasscock, May 12, 1910, Elkins Papers; McDermott to Glasscock, May 17, October 10, 1910, January 19, 24, 1911; Glasscock to Robert R. Green, October 22, 1910; Green to Glasscock, October 24, 1910; Ellis A. Yost to Glasscock, October 31, 1910; Glasscock to Yost, November 2, 1910, Glasscock Papers. The split was also entangled with the Prohibition question since McDermott was identified as a lobbyist for the distillers.

35. S. J. Bowman to L. J. Forman, March 12, 1908, Forman Papers; T. O. Horan to Glasscock, September 24, 1910; James Reed to Glasscock, September 24, 1910; Glasscock to N. B. Scott, October 6, 1910; Hugh Ike Shott to Glasscock, September 24, 1910; S. M. Smith to Glasscock, October 5, 1910; Isaac T. Mann to Glasscock, October 8, 1910, Glasscock Papers.

36. J. W. McIntire to Glasscock, September 21, 1910; Fred O. Blue to Glasscock, May 13, 1909, Glasscock Papers; Blue to L. J. Forman, October 13, 1910, Forman Papers.

37. Scott to Glasscock, October 1, 8, 1910; Glasscock to Scott, October 6, 1910, Glasscock Papers.

38. C. D. Elliott to Glasscock, September 22, 27, 1910; George Poffenbarger to Glasscock, September 23, 1910; O. M. Pullen to Glasscock, September 24, 1910; H. A. Barbee to Glasscock, September 24, 1910; Barbee to Owen Shinn, January 17, 1911, Glasscock Papers.

39. George Poffenbarger to Glasscock, September 23, 1910; M. T. Roach to Glasscock, September 24, 1910, Glasscock Papers.

40. Elliott to Glasscock, September 27, 1910, Glasscock Papers.

41. H. M. Young to James Reed, September 28, 1910; and Glasscock's correspondence with politicians in nearly every county in the state, September-November 1910, Glasscock Papers.

42. Sturgiss to Glasscock, September 19, 1910; Glasscock to George Poffenbarger, September 26, 1910; Glasscock to M. L. Brown, November 14, 1910, Glasscock Papers.

43. Glasscock to A. B. White, Glasscock to George C. Sturgiss, and other telegrams sent to Republican leaders and officeholders, all January 14, 1911; N. B. Scott to Glasscock, January 15, 21, 1911; W. P. Hubbard to Glasscock, February 28, 1911, Glasscock Papers. Hubbard was the only leader to withhold his approval of this strategy, although he waited six weeks to tell Glasscock that he feared that the bolt made for "an opportunity for trades and bargains which would not enure to the advantage of some things in which you and I believe."

44. W. A. MacCorkle to Davis, November 17, 1910; Davis to MacCorkle, December 1, 1910, Davis Papers. As in the past, however, Davis intrigued for Republican votes in case a Democratic deadlock gave him an opening (Howard Sutherland to Davis, January 15, 1911, *ibid.*).

45. Watson to John J. Cornwell, May 26, 1910, John J. Cornwell Papers, WVU.

46. R. W. Baker to John J. Cornwell, November 30, 1910; J. H. Crosier to Cornwell, January 26, 1911; S. P. Smith to Cornwell, March 9, 1911, Cornwell Papers.

47. G. W. Atkinson to W. E. Glasscock, February 8, 1911; Glasscock to Richard R. McMahon, February 1, 1912, Glasscock Papers; A. B. Fleming to Watson, May 20, 1911, Fleming Papers.

48. E. M. Gilkeson to John J. Cornwell, March 7, 1911, Cornwell Papers.

49. Charleston *Gazette*, September 19, 1911.

50. Cornwell to H. L. Bond, November 21, 29, 30, 1910, January 6, 1911; Frank A. Vanderlip to Cornwell, December 20, 1910, January 26, 1911, Cornwell Papers. Cornwell's original letters to Vanderlip (dated December 17 and January 20) cannot be found in the Vanderlip Papers at Columbia University, but that Cornwell expressed the same views to Vanderlip that he did to Bond may be inferred from Vanderlip's congratulatory remarks "on having come so successfully through so difficult a situation." Cornwell's business relationship with Vanderlip and other Rockefeller banking and industrial associates is illustrated in later correspondence (1917-1921) at Columbia, as well as by numerous items in the Cornwell Papers, WVU.

51. W. S. Laidley to John W. Mason, November 8, 1912; Mann to

Mason, November 16, 1912, Mason Papers; H. G. Davis to R. C. Kerens, January 13, 1913; Davis to W. G. Wilson, February 12, 1913; Davis Elkins to N. B. Scott, January 15, 1913 (copy), Davis Papers; see also note 56.

52. Wheeling *Intelligencer*, June 5, 7, 1912. Hatfield's defeated rivals were Swisher and Dillon.

53. H. S. Hadley to Glasscock, February 5, 1912; Roosevelt to Glasscock, March 2, 1912, Glasscock Papers; Wheeling *Register*, March 1, 1912.

54. W. S. Edwards to Glasscock, March 9, 1912; Glasscock to Davis Elkins, April 16, 1912; Davis Elkins to Glasscock, April 17, 1912; W. H. Morgan to Glasscock, April 23, 1912, Glasscock Papers; Wheeling *Intelligencer*, April 8, 9, 27, May 16, 18, June 18, 24, 1912.

55. Parkersburg *Sentinel*, July 6, 1912, and other clippings, scrapbooks, Glasscock Papers; Glasscock to Stephen F. Glasscock, July 1, 1912; Glasscock to White, July 12, 1912; Everett Leftwich to Glasscock, July 18, 1912; Glasscock to Robert R. McCormick, July 25, 1912; Glasscock to Joseph R. Sanders, July 27, 1912; Glasscock to Joseph M. Dixon, September 28, 1912; Glasscock to E. F. Baldwin, October 28, 1912, *ibid.*

56. Glasscock to Edwards, November 14, 1912; Glasscock to William Allen White, December 2, 1912, Glasscock Papers; Glasscock to John W. Mason, November 29, 1912; Hubbard to Mason, December 6, 1912, Mason Papers; Davis Elkins to N. B. Scott, January 15, 1911 (copy), Davis Papers; *West Virginia House Journal* (1913), 326, 348-349, 374-375, 408, 441-442, 476-477, 502-503, 522-523, 553-554, 577-578, 603-604, 619-620, 649-650, 690-691, 728-729.

57. B. Randolph Bias to Glasscock, October 17, 1912; Glasscock to Bias, December 2, 1912, Glasscock Papers; S. G. Smith to Harvey W. Harmer, September 5, 1914; Elliott to Harmer, September 17, 1914, Harvey W. Harmer Papers, WVU.

58. Wheeling *Dailey News*, March 4, 1913.

59. Useful comparisons can be made in Richard C. Abrams, *Conservatism in the Progressive Era: Massachusetts Politics, 1900-1912* (Cambridge, Mass., 1964); Winston Allen Flint, *The Progressive Movement in Vermont* (Washington, 1941); Hoyt L. Warner, *Progressivism in Ohio, 1897-1917* (Columbus, 1964); Herbert F. Margulies, *The Decline of the Progressive Movement in Wisconsin 1890-1920* (Madison, 1968); Sheldon Hackrey, *Populism to Progressivism in Alabama* (Princeton, 1969); Albert D. Kirwan, *Revolt of the Rednecks, Mississippi Politics, 1876-1925* (Lexington, Ky., 1951).

60. Ambler, "Disfranchisement in West Virginia," 180; see also his *West Virginia* (1933 edn.), 431.

61. Ambler, *West Virginia* (1940 edn.), 491-500.

313

62. Hubbard, "Development of Taxation and Finance," 508-516.
63. Hendershot, "Tax Reform in West Virginia," 16.
64. A. B. Fleming to Messrs. Chandler and Bros., May 20, 1909, Fleming Papers.
65. F. P. Moats to Fleming, March 1, 1904, Fleming Papers.
66. Charleston *Labor Argus*, January 31, February 7, 1907; E. W. Knight to A. B. Fleming, September 18, 30, October 15, 1907, Fleming Papers; Charleston *Sunday Gazette-Mail*, December 20, 1959, clipping, Dawson Papers.
67. Charleston *Labor Argus*, February 21, 28, 1907; Fleming to L. L. Malone, February 23, 1907, Fleming Papers.
68. G. H. Caperton to A. B. Fleming, December 17, 1907; Joseph H. McDermott to Fleming, Neil Robinson to Fleming, January 15, 19, 1908, January 11, 1908; W. A. Ohley to Fleming, January 15, 29, 1908; L. L. Malone to Fleming, January 24, 1908; Fleming to Ohley, February 19, 1908, Fleming Papers.
69. New River Operators Association to James W. Paul, October 18, 1907 (copy); W. N. Page to A. B. Fleming, December 14, 1907, Fleming Papers.
70. W. A. Ohley to A. B. Fleming, November 16, 1908; James Martin to Fleming, August 11, 1913; Fleming to Martin, August 14, 1913, Fleming Papers; Frank E. Parsons to Glasscock, February 18, 1909; J. A. Springer to Glasscock, February 22, 1909; C. H. Boswell to Glasscock, August 16, 1912, Glasscock Papers.
71. Conley, *History of the West Virginia Coal Industry*, 9-27.
72. Ambler-Summers, *West Virginia*, 447.
73. Mooney, *Struggle in the Coal Fields*, 31-38; Glasscock to Roy Smith, July 12, 1912; George C. Baker to Glasscock, September 23, 1912; Joseph M. Sanders to Glasscock, November 8, 1912; various clippings, June-November 1912, scrapbooks, Glasscock Papers; "Donahue Commission Report," 97-117.
74. For example, Theodore F. Lang, *Loyal West Virginia from 1861 to 1865* (Baltimore, 1895), 8-9; Wheeling *Register*, February 2, 4, 1888; Wheeling *Intelligencer*, February 20, 1890, and George W. Atkinson, *After the Moonshiners* (Wheeling, W.Va., 1881). On the feuds, see Jean Thomas, *Big Sandy* (New York, 1940), 176-244; and Virgil Carrington Jones, *The Hatfields and the McCoys* (Chapel Hill, 1948).
75. Wheeling *Intelligencer*, May 4, 8, 1912.
76. Charleston *Gazette*, January 3, 1960, clipping, Henry Drury Hatfield Papers, WVU; Hatfield to White, July 7, August 3, November 6, 1901, June 5, 1902, August 4, 1904, White Papers.
77. Elkins to Glasscock, February 16, 1909, Glasscock Papers. Hatfield's primary would not have applied above the county level. For a

progressive view of his bill, see B. Randolph Bias to Glasscock, February 12, 1909, *ibid.*

78. Elkins to Glasscock, December 18, 1908, Elkins Papers; March 20, 1909, Glasscock Papers.

79. Elkins to Glasscock, July 7, 1910, Elkins Papers; cf. *idem*, April 14, 1910, for Elkins's intervention in Hatfield's behalf in a matter concerning taxes in the N&W region.

80. Wheeling *Intelligencer*, June 5, August 11, 1912; Hatfield to W. E. Glasscock, July 24, November 26, 1912, Glasscock Papers.

81. Hatfield to W. E. Glasscock, December 6, 1912, Glasscock Papers; Wheeling *Daily News*, March 4, 1913; Carolyn Kerr, "A Political Biography of Henry D. Hatfield," *West Virginia History*, 28:1, 2 (October 1966, January 1967), 35-63, 137-170.

82. Kyle McCormick, "The National Guard of West Virginia during the Strike Period of 1912-1913," *West Virginia History*, 22:1 (October 1960), 34-35; James Weinstein, *The Decline of Socialism in America, 1912-1925* (New York, 1967), 34; Hatfield to John W. Mason, July 12, 1913, Mason Papers.

83. Hatfield-Hallanan correspondence, 1916-1953, Hatfield Papers, box 6.

84. Conley, *History of the West Virginia Coal Industry*, 84-85.

85. Ambler, *West Virginia* (1933 edn.), 357-364, 444.

86. Wheeling *Register*, October 10, 1909, and other clippings, scrapbooks, Glasscock Papers.

87. Ambler, *Francis H. Pierpont*, 361-362.

88. Wheeling *Register*, September 28, 1910; cf. Wheeling *Intelligencer*, May 11, 1893. For a melding of Stonewall with the mountaineer stereotype, see W. E. Blackhurst, *Sawdust in Your Eyes* (Parsons, W.Va., 1963), vi.

89. W. E. Glasscock to B. W. Peterson, November 21, 1910, Glasscock Papers; Stuart F. Reed to John W. Mason, June 11, 1913; Goff to Mason, June 16, 1913, Mason Papers.

90. Wheeling *Daily News*, June 19-21, 1913, and Wheeling *Intelligencer*, June 20-22, 1913. A copy of the "West Virginia Jubilee Song" may be found in Miscellaneous Collections, A&M 596, WVU.

91. Pepper, *Davis*, 204-209; S. Myers, *Myers' History of West Virginia*, 2:344.

Essay on Sources

The following essay is a selective one, emphasizing essential primary and secondary sources and books and articles that were useful in interpreting these sources. For standard reference works and such obvious sources as legislative journals and session laws, the reader is referred to the notes in the text.

Bibliographies. The West Virginia University Library has provided four invaluable bibliographical aids: Charles Shetler, *Guide to the Study of West Virginia History* (Morgantown, 1960); ———, *Guide to Manuscripts and Archives in the West Virginia Collection* (Morgantown, 1959); F. Gerald Ham, *Guide to Manuscripts and Archives in the West Virginia Collection, Number II*, 1958-1962 (Morgantown, 1965); and James W. Hess, *Guide to Manuscripts and Archives in the West Virginia Collection* (Morgantown, 1974).

Manuscripts. As the footnotes reveal, my greatest debt is to the archivists, past and present, of the West Virginia Collection, West Virginia University Library, Morgantown, who have gathered what must be one of the finest collections for post-Civil War state history in the country. The largest and most useful of the collections here was the Henry G. Davis Papers. Davis's letter books and those of C. M. Hendley and the West Virginia Central & Pittsburg Railroad offer a nearly complete view of his political and business activities over a fifty-year period. Incoming correspondence is filed under a variety of headings; chronological series of boxes labeled "Political," "Personal and Political," "Railroad," "Coal," and "Miscellaneous," all yielded political and business information. The Johnson N. Camden Papers form an equally voluminous and useful collection. My examination of the Camden Papers was greatly facilitated by the use of Professor Festus P. Summers's notes, made available to me through the courtesy of Dr. Glenn Massey and the late Professor Summers. By comparison to these two collections, the Stephen B. Elkins Papers are thin and fragmented, but this appears to be due to Elkins's peripatetic career and unsystematic record keeping rather than to any attempt to cull the papers. The most valuable items here concern Republican national politics during the 1880s and West Virginia politics, 1898-1910. Because White was at the center of Republican activities in West Virginia after 1889, the A. B. White Papers are an essential supplement to the Elkins Papers, especially as they contain the only large stock of letters from Nathan B. Scott and William M. O. Dawson. White's letter books and scrapbooks are a rich source for the period of his governorship (1901-1905), particularly for the tax reform controversy, 1903-1905. Also valuable for the formative years of the Elkins regime, and for earlier and later information about the "old-line" Republicans, were the John W. Mason Papers. The A. B. Fleming Papers yielded information about legislatures and lobbyists and constitute the key source of material on opposition to the tax reform movement. The Alston G. Dayton Papers are another such source, and are informative on earlier Republican politics as well. The William E. Glasscock and John J. Cornwell Papers are the major sources of information about Republican and Democratic politics, respectively, during the years after 1905.

The foregoing eight large (or, in the case of the Elkins Papers, small but rich) collections provide the foundation upon which my analysis of West Virginia politics in the transitional and industrial eras is based. Of importance for the preindustrial period are the papers of Gideon Camden, Jonathan M. Bennett, and David Goff, all of which reveal the links between antebellum and post-Civil War politics. The John J. Davis Papers form an important source on the Unionist opposition to statehood and contain fragmentary but useful information on the viewpoints of Democratic "bitter enders" and Agrarians during later periods. The typescript copies of Samuel Woods letters found in the Charles H. Ambler Papers offer indispensable insights into the constitutional convention of 1872. The Waitman T. Willey Papers and W. H. H. Flick Papers (Duke University Library, microfilm copy, WVU) are valuable on Republican viewpoints and activities during the two decades after 1865. The papers of Frank Hereford (private possession, microfilm copy, WVU) were disappointing on state politics during the period under study, as were those of Charles James Faulkner, Sr., and Nathan Goff, Jr., but each collection yielded individual items that made examination worthwhile. The diaries of William L. Wilson (Boston Public Library) and Henri Jean Mugler (private possession), both examined on microfilm at WVU, offer valuable records of politics during the transitional period from the standpoints, respectively, of a Democratic activist and a Republican onlooker.

For the later period covered here, the Charles W. Osenton Papers (Landsdowne Family Papers, University of Kentucky Library, microfilm copy, WVU) offer information on Democratic politics, 1898-1911. Two Republican legislators, Francis Marion Reynolds and L. J. Forman, left large collections of papers that illustrate the dilemmas of Progressives who rallied to the Elkins organization's reform platform. The papers of Harvey W. Harmer, another G.O.P. legislator whose career extended from 1903 to the 1940s, are valuable chiefly for Progressive party politics in 1914. The William M. O. Dawson Papers comprise a single box of miscellaneous materials collected by Don M. Blagg, plus Blagg's unfinished ms. biography of Dawson, and is more valuable for the gubernatorial contest of 1908 than for information about Dawson's governorship. The Granville Davisson Hall Papers, however, contain a valuable sheaf of letters by and about Dawson during his gubernatorial years. The papers of Henry D. Hatfield, Walter S. Hallanan, and Ira W. Robinson chiefly relate to later periods, but each contains items of interest deriving from or bearing upon the years before 1913. The John T. McGraw Papers, however, contain little that cannot be found in the Davis, Camden, or Cornwell collections or in William P. Turner's biographical study mentioned below.

The Library of Congress houses three series of presidential papers that were examined on microfilm copies in the libraries of Yale and the University of Notre Dame. Of the three, the Benjamin Harrison Papers proved by far the most useful. The Grover Cleveland Papers and the William McKinley Papers contain little of value for West Virginia politics. Also at the Library of Congress are the Garrett Family Papers, containing a few items on Davis's early political and business relations with the B&O Railroad, and the letters of Phil Waters in the Booker T. Washington Papers, which offer a rare insight into the thinking of black Republicans in West Virginia. The Richard Olney Papers and the Theodore Roosevelt Papers yielded information on Elkins's activities as chairman of the Senate Interstate Commerce Committee. More valuable in this respect were the Records of the Interstate Commerce Commission, housed in the National Archives in Washington and Springfield, Virginia, which provide insights into the politics of railroad consolidation and regulation in both state and national settings. The map collection of the National Archives and the Archive of Folk Song at the Library of Congress yielded a few items that supplemented more conventional sources, although the Library's collection of labor and protest songs relating to Appalachia is richer for eastern Kentucky than for West Virginia and derives chiefly from the period after 1930.

The papers of Ulrich B. Phillips in the Yale University Library contain many items of interest bearing on economic, social, and political life in antebellum transmontane Virginia and the upper South generally and also some early letters of the West Virginia historian, Charles H. Ambler. Also at Yale are the John W. Davis Papers, which contain a few letters of interest on West Virginia politics of this period. Three letters from Elkins to New York financiers in the Frank A. Vanderlip Papers, Columbia University Library, conveniently summarize twentieth century Davis-Elkins railroad and banking activities. A later series of letters from John J. Cornwell can also be found in the Vanderlip Papers. The

Thomas B. Catron Papers in the University of New Mexico Library, Albuquerque, contain a few items of value on Elkins's western activities and associates.

Another unpublished source of value is the typescript of testimony in *Alexander Shaw v. Henry G. Davis et al.*, 78 Md. 308 (1893), a bound volume in the West Virginia University Library, which offers a thorough airing of the quarrel between the B&O and West Virginia Central.

Newspapers and Trade Periodicals. Two essential newspaper sources are the Wheeling *Register* and Wheeling *Intelligencer*, the leading (and for many years, the only) daily newspapers in West Virginia. Despite its conservative editorship, the *Register*, as the semi-official Democratic party journal, avoided committing itself on intra-party issues and rivalries until they had been resolved, and used its exchange column as a means of giving all combatants an airing. The *Intelligencer* was narrower in its points of view, and, on the whole, more partisan than its rival. The Morgantown *Post* led the agitation against the Republican organization in 1899-1900. Later under different ownership it became a strenuous advocate of railroad regulation and tax reform, while the Fairmont *Times* spoke for conservative Democrats and anti-taxers. The Charleston *Labor Argus* was an independent journal oriented to the American Federation of Labor from its founding in 1905 until 1910. Then it became an organ of the Socialist party and remained such until its suppression by Governor Hatfield in 1913. Thanks to its location at the fount of patronage and an important rail center for travelers between northern and southern West Virginia, the Washington *Post* was well informed on state politics, especially for developments in 1891-1892 and 1903-1905 that West Virginia newspapers intentionally or unavoidably misrepresented. The Baltimore *Sun* also gave some attention to West Virginia politics. Specific issues of the Romney *Hampshire Review*, Charleston *State, State-Tribune*, and *Gazette*, Fairmont *Index* and *Free Press*, Wheeling *Daily News*, New York *Times, Tribune*, and *Herald*, Chicago *Tribune*, San Francisco *Chronicle*, and Washington *Star* were also consulted. My examination of other West Virginia and metropolitan newspapers was aided substantially by the clippings files or scrapbooks found in the Elkins, Mason, White, and Glasscock collections at WVU.

The Coal Trade, the yearbook of the *Coal Trade Journal* (New York, 1869-1937), offers a convenient summary of yearly coal production and price data, as well as market surveys and some political comment. It was, however, oriented toward the highly centralized and railroad-dominated anthracite industry rather than to bituminous producers. The *Engineering and Mining Journal* (New York, 1866-   ), represents more consistently a mining, as opposed to railroad, point of view,

particularly with regard to railroad consolidation after 1899. *Coal &
Coke* (Baltimore, 1894-1911) more frequently spoke for smaller producers than did the other two. *Poor's Manual of the Railroads of the
United States* (New York, 1868-1924) provides a variety of data on
railroad development in general and on the growth and ownership of
individual companies. Its railroad maps are indispensable to those who
wish to visualize the battlefield of railroad conflict.

Printed Documents and Contemporary Accounts. Edgar B. Sims,
compiler, *Sims' Index to Land Grants in West Virginia* (Charleston,
W.Va., 1952) is an indispensable reference work on antebellum land
speculation. Virgil A. Lewis, *How West Virginia Was Made: Proceedings
of the First Convention of Northwestern Virginia at Wheeling, May 13,
14, and 15, 1861, and the Journal of the Second Convention . . .*
(Charleston, W.Va., 1909), and Charles H. Ambler, Francis H. Ambler,
Francis H. Atwood and William B. Mathews, eds., *Debates and Proceedings of the First Constitutional Convention of West Virginia*
(1861-1863) (Huntington, W.Va., 1939) are key sources for the statehood period. West Virginia Tax Commission, *Preliminary Report and
Second Report, State Development* (both Wheeling, W.Va., 1884) spell
out a heretical interpretation of the development faith. Important for
the politics of 1894 is U.S. Congress, House, Committee on Ways and
Means, *Tariff Hearings before the Committee on Ways and Means, First
Session, Fifty-Third Congress* (Washington, 1894). A unique source on
railroad consolidation is U.S. Congress, Senate, Committee on Interstate Commerce, *Railroad Consolidation in the Eastern Region, Part I:
Before 1920* (Senate Report 1182, 76:3 [Washington, 1940]). Through
lavish use of the subpoena power, the authors have assembled and
reprinted documents, otherwise inaccessible to researchers, from the
files of such corporations as the Pennsylvania and New York Central
railroads, United States Steel Corporation, and Drexel, Morgan and
Company. West Virginia Commission on Taxation and Municipal Charters, *Preliminary and Final Report* (n.p. [Charleston, W.Va.], 1902),
doubles as a reference work and a primary source. West Virginia Legislature, House, *Report of the Committee appointed under resolution . . . on February 24, 1905* (Charleston, W.Va., 1907), a copy of
which may be found in the New York Public Library, offers a look at
the seamier side of West Virginia politics. Elizabeth Cometti and Festus
P. Summers, eds., *The Thirty-Fifth State, A Documentary History of
West Virginia* (Parsons, W.Va., 1966) contains a useful selection of
documents, better for the antebellum and statehood periods than for
the industrial era.

J. H. Diss Debar, *The West Virginia Handbook and Immigrant's
Guide* (Parkersburg, W.Va., 1870), is a pioneer expression of the development faith. In George W. Atkinson and Alvaro F. Gibbens, *Promi-*

nent Men of West Virginia (Wheeling, W.Va., 1890), one of the state's leading politicians reiterates the articles of the faith while providing an important reference aid, an achievement that Atkinson repeated in his *Bench and Bar of West Virginia* (Charleston, W.Va., 1919). William A. MacCorkle, *Recollections of Fifty Years of West Virginia* (New York, 1928), is a political memoir as candid and entertaining as any historian could hope for. Fred Mooney, *Struggle in the Coal Fields, The Autobiography of Fred Mooney,* edited and with an introduction by J. William Hess (Morgantown, W.Va., 1967), offers a valuable first-hand account of the "mine wars" in a careful scholarly setting.

Books and Articles. Charles M. Pepper, *The Life and Times of Henry Gassaway Davis* (New York, 1920), and Oscar D. Lambert, *Stephen Benton Elkins, American Foursquare* (Pittsburgh, 1955), are both commemorative volumes authorized by the subjects' families. Pepper omits a great deal of interest in Davis's career, but the value of the book is enhanced by many quotations from the now-missing Davis journal. Numerous errors and an inchoate literary style limit the value of Lambert's book for any purpose. Festus P. Summers, *Johnson Newlon Camden, A Study in Individualism* (New York, 1937), is a compendium of information about business and Democratic politics in West Virginia, presented in a highly readable style. The same author's *William L. Wilson and Tariff Reform* (New Brunswick, N.J., 1953) deals more with national than state politics, and is indispensable for the tariff struggle of 1894. Harvey M. Rice, *The Life of Jonathan MacCally Bennett, A Study of the Virginias in Transition* (Chapel Hill, 1943), is a scholarly account of Bennett's political life but focuses weakly on economic and social factors. G. Wayne Smith, *Nathan Goff, Jr., A Biography* (Charleston, W.Va., 1959), is an official treatment that maintains good standards of scholarship. Charles H. Ambler, *Francis H. Pierpont, Union War Governor of Virginia and Father of West Virginia* (Chapel Hill, 1937), illustrates the anomalous position of the statemakers in late nineteenth century politics. John R. Lambert, *Arthur Pue Gorman* (Baton Rouge, 1953), exploits the limited materials available to present a highly favorable but not uncritical view of the Maryland leader. The same may be said of David Saville Muzzey, *James G. Blaine, A Political Idol of Other Days* (New York, 1934). Harry J. Sievers, *Benjamin Harrison, Hoosier Statesman, From the Civil War to the White House, 1865-1888* (New York, 1959), suffers from the blandness of the subject's personality, but offers a detailed scholarly account of presidential politics in 1888. Allan Nevins, *Grover Cleveland, A Study in Courage* (New York, 1932), Theodore Clarke Smith, *The Life and Letters of James Abram Garfield* (2 vols., New Haven, 1925), Joseph Frazier Wall, *Henry Watterson, Reconstructed Rebel* (New York, 1956), and Mark D. Hirsch, *William*

C. Whitney, *Modern Warwick* (New York, 1948), were all, like Elkins, useful at odd times.

Secondary sources for the statehood period are given in Chapter 1, note 1. Otis K. Rice, "Seventeen Years of West Virginia History," *West Virginia History* 17:1 (October 1956), 90-96, is a review that illustrates the extent to which statehood and sectional politics prevail as topics of interest in West Virginia historiography. But hopefully Rice has blazed one path of departure in his *The Allegheny Frontier, West Virginia Beginnings, 1730-1830* (Lexington, Ky., 1970). There is no comparable work for the post-Statehood era. Two general works by Charles H. Ambler, however, *West Virginia, The Mountain State* (New York, 1940), a college textbook, and *A History of Education in West Virginia from Early Colonial Times to 1949* (Huntington, W.Va., 1951), are unique in their skeptical attitude toward the development faith and the value of the industrialists' political leadership, but this theme is a muted one in all of Ambler's work. I have also consulted the 1933 edition of the first-named book, which contains some comments omitted from the later edition, and the revision completed by Festus P. Summers in 1959, which updates Ambler's account of the twentieth century. Robert F. Maddox, "Four Eminent Historians," *West Virginia History* 27:4 (July 1966), 296-308, discusses Ambler's career in conjunction with those of his West Virginia University colleagues, James Morton Callahan and Oliver Perry Chitwood, and of his protege and successor, Festus P. Summers. Callahan's *Semi-Centennial History of West Virginia* (Morgantown, W.Va., 1913) and his *History of West Virginia Old and New* (3 vols., Chicago, 1923) are useful for reference, particularly for the essays by contemporary figures in the former work and the biographical volumes of the latter, but neither meets the standards achieved by Callahan's scholarly work in American diplomatic history.

Richard Orr Curry, *A House Divided: Statehood Politics and the Copperhead Movement in West Virginia* (Pittsburgh, 1964), provides an illuminating background to the period of Reconstruction in West Virginia, as do the essays collected by Curry in *Radicalism, Racism, and Party Realignment, The Border States during Reconstruction* (Baltimore, 1969). James Henry Jacobs, "The West Virginia Gubernatorial Election Contest, 1888-1890," *West Virginia History*, 7 (April, July 1946), 159-220, 263-311, is a careful examination of an important incident in state history. Rosemary Stevenson Turney, "The Encouragement of Immigration in West Virginia, 1863-1871," *ibid.*, 12 (October 1950), 45-59, deals with an important theme. Kyle McCormick, "The National Guard of West Virginia during the Strike Period of 1912-1913," *ibid.*, 22 (October 1960), 34-35, offers reliable information on a controversial subject. Carolyn Kerr, "A Political Biography of Henry D. Hatfield," *ibid.*, 28 (October 1966, January 1967), 35-63,

137-170, and Lucy Lee Fisher, "John J. Cornwell, Governor of West Virginia, 1917-1921," *ibid.*, 24 (April, July 1963), 258-289, 307-389, are uncritical but useful summaries of some later political developments, as is Elizabeth J. Goodall, "The Charleston Industrial Area: Development, 1797-1937," *ibid.*, 30 (October 1968), 358-397, in the economic sphere. Phil Conley, *History of the West Virginia Coal Industry* (Charleston, W.Va., 1960), is a modern expression of the development faith that is of little value as social or economic history. Quite the opposite is Eugene D. Thoenen's thorough and scholarly *History of the Oil and Gas Industry in West Virginia* (Charleston, W.Va., 1964). Conley, however, provided a useful reference work in his *The West Virginia Encyclopedia* (Charleston, W.Va., 1929).

Two older and popular treatments of the Gilded Age, Harry Thurston Peck, *Twenty Years of the Republic, 1885-1905* (New York, edn., 1917), and Matthew Josephson, *The Politicos, 1865-1896* (New York, 1938), have been displaced by recent scholarship in H. Wayne Morgan, *From Hayes to McKinley, National Party Politics, 1877-1896* (Syracuse, 1969) and John A. Garraty, *The New Commonwealth, 1877-1890* (New York, 1968). Contrasting viewpoints on the Progressive Era are provided by George E. Mowry, *The Era of Theodore Roosevelt, 1900-1912* (New York, 1958) and Gabriel Kolko, *The Triumph of Conservatism, A Reinterpretation of American History 1900-1916* (Glencoe, Ill., 1963). Samuel P. Hays, *The Response to Industrialism, 1885-1914* (Chicago, 1957), William Appleman Williams, *The Contours of American History* (Chicago, 1966), and Robert H. Wiebe, *The Search for Order 1877-1920* (New York, 1968), range imaginatively and provocatively over wider time periods. Two books that bear indirectly but suggestively upon the subject of the present study are C. Vann Woodward, *Origins of the New South, 1877-1913*, (vol. 9 of *A History of the South* [Baton Rouge, 1951]), and Harry M. Caudill, *Night Comes to the Cumberlands, The Biography of a Depressed Area* (Boston, 1963).

Howard Roberts Lamar, *The Far Southwest, 1846-1912, A Territorial History* (New Haven, 1966), sheds as much light as is likely to be shed on Elkins's early activities and associates. Robert W. Larson, *New Mexico's Quest for Statehood, 1846-1912* (Albuquerque, N.M., 1968), and Jim Berry Pearson, *The Maxwell Land Grant* (Norman, Okla., 1961), are also helpful in this respect. Charles C. Tansill, *The Foreign Policy of Thomas F. Bayard, 1885-1897* (New York, 1940), and Ernest Greuening, *The State of Alaska* (New York, 1954), provide keys to the seal fisheries episode. Two old and partisan accounts remain the standard guides through the tariff maze: F. W. Taussig, *The Tariff History of the United States* (New York, edn., 1914), and Edward Stanwood, *American Tariff Controversies in the Nineteenth Century* (Boston, 1903). Arnold M. Paul, *Conservative Crisis and the Rule of Law: Atti-*

tudes of Bar and Bench, 1887-1895 (Ithaca, N.Y., 1960), and David J. Rothman, *Politics and Power, The United States Senate, 1869-1901* (Cambridge, 1966), show how the formidable concentrations of conservative power existing at the turn of the century gradually evolved at the expense of older legal and legislative ideas and institutions. But John M. Blum, "Theodore Roosevelt and the Legislative Process: Tariff Revision and Railroad Regulation, 1904-1906," in Elting E. Morison and Others, *The Letters of Theodore Roosevelt* (8 vols., Cambridge, 1951), 4: 1333-1342, argues that the system could work against the conservatives with determined presidential leadership. The importance of moving beyond traditional approaches to political analysis is stressed in William N. Chambers and Walter Dean Buraham, eds., *The American Party Systems, Stages of Political Development* (New York, 1967), Samuel P. Hays, "New Possibilities for American Political History: The Social Analysis of Political Life," in S. M. Lipset and Richard Hofstadter (eds.), *Sociology and History: Methods* (New York, 1968), 181-227, and Richard J. Jensen, "American Election Campaigns: A Theoretical and Historical Typology," unpublished paper delivered to the Midwest Political Science Conference, May 1968.

Joseph T. Lambie, *From Mine to Market: A History of Coal Transportation on the Norfolk & Western Railway* (New York, 1954), is a model of scholarly transportation history. The best official railroad history is George H. Burgess and Miles C. Kennedy, *Centennial History of the Pennsylvania Railroad Company, 1846-1946* (Philadelphia, 1949); others are Edward Hungerford, *The Story of the Baltimore & Ohio Railroad, 1827-1927* (2 vols., New York, 1928), and Harold A. Williams, *The Western Maryland Railway Story, A Chronicle of the First Century, 1851-1952* (Baltimore, 1952). Warren C. Scoville, *Revolution in Glassmaking Entrepreneurship and Technological Change in the American Industry, 1880-1920* (Cambridge, Mass., 1948) is a useful example of scholarly business history, as is Ralph W. and Muriel E. Hidy, *History of the Standard Oil Company (New Jersey); I: Pioneering in Big Business, 1882-1911* (New York, 1955). Earl Chapin May, *From Principio to Wheeling, A Saga in Iron and Steel* (New York, 1945), and William Haynes, *Chemical Pioneers, The Founders of the American Chemical Industry* (2 vols., New York, 1939), are undocumented but generally reliable accounts. Alfred D. Chandler, Jr., "The Beginnings of 'Big Business' in American Industry," *Business History Review* 33 (Spring 1959), 1-31, and Allen D. Pred, *The Spatial Dynamics of U.S. Urban-Industrial Growth: Interpretative and Theoretical Essays* (Cambridge, Mass., 1966), provide important reformulations of conventional analytical frameworks in their respective fields.

The controversy between progressive and revisionist historians over the character and contributions of nineteenth century business leaders is reviewed from different points of view by Edward C. Kirkland, "The Robber Barons Revisited," *American Historical Review*, 66 (October 1960), 68-73, and William Miller, "The Realm of Wealth," in John Higham, ed., *The Reconstruction of American History* (London, 1962), 137-156. Both agree that Charles and Mary Beard, *The Rise of American Civilization* (New York, 1927), and Matthew Josephson, *The Robber Barons, The Great American Capitalists, 1861-1901* (New York, 1934), are starting points for the discussion from the progressive point of view. David Graham Phillips, *The Treason of the Senate*, George E. Mowry and Judson A. Grenier, eds. (Chicago, 1954), takes a muckraking view of Davis and Elkins. Arthur H. Cole, *Business Enterprise in Its Social Setting* (Cambridge, 1959), Thomas C. Cochran, *Railroad Leaders, 1845-1890, The Business Mind in Action* (Cambridge, 1953), and Edward C. Kirkland, *Dream and Thought in the Business Community, 1860-1900* (Ithaca, N.Y., 1956), attempt to understand the social and psychological pressures under which contemporary entrepreneurs worked. Two studies of the impact of big business on national policy decisions that uphold the progressive tradition are Gabriel Kolko, *Railroads and Regulation, 1877-1916* (Princeton, 1965), and James Weinstein, *The Corporate Ideal in the Liberal State, 1900-1918* (Boston, 1968). Robert H. Wiebe elaborates the revisionist viewpoint in *Businessmen and Reform, A Study of the Progressive Movement* (Cambridge, Mass., 1962).

Unpublished dissertations and theses: William Patrick Turner, Jr., "From Bourbon to Liberal, The Life and Times of John T. McGraw, 1856-1920" (Ph.D. dissertation, West Virginia University, 1960), is useful, but Elmer Guy Hendershot, "Tax Reforms in West Virginia during the Administration of Governor Albert Blakeslee White, 1901-1905" (M.A. thesis, West Virginia University, 1949), fails to exploit more than a fraction of the sources available.

Index

Absentee ownership, 184, 186
Adams, John Quincy, 36, 63
Africa, 140, 174
African Village Company, 208
Agrarians: opposition to Camden, 8, 41-44 *passim;* geographic basis of appeal, 8-9, 11; racial views of leaders, 9; position vis-a-vis other Democratic factions, 14; role in 1894 campaign, 61; and silver issue, 69; weakness after 1896, 77, 107; their pressure on corporations differs from labor unions', 198-99; mentioned, 120, 124, 134. *See also* Democratic party, factionalism
Alabama, 37, 227
Alaska, 16, 80, 208. *See also* Seal Islands
Alderson, John D., 63, 211, 270 n. 171
Aldrich, Nelson, 36
Alsace-Lorraine, 170
Ambler, Charles Henry: on political corruption, 16, 129; on West Virginia's conservatism, 248-49; on West Virginia's lack of pride, 254
American Can Corporation, 153
American Coal Trade Committee, 21
American Flint Glass Workers Union, 153-54

American Iron & Steel Association, 32
American Revolution, 255
American Sugar Refining Company, 22
Anti-organization Republicans: avoid directly challenging Elkins, 82, 103; character and leadership in 1900 campaign, 96-103 *passim. See also* Elkins organization, Republican party
Anti-pass legislation, 134-35
Anti-Saloon League, 239
Anti-tax movement, 224-28 *passim. See also* Tax reform movement
Appalachia, 1, 2, 254
Appalachian coalfields, 188
Appalachian highlands, 1, 193
Arthur, Chester A., 31, 36
Ashby bill. *See* Mine safety legislation
Asia, 174
Atkinson, Edward, 58
Atkinson, George W.: background, 11, 12, 48; Republican party credentials, 48, 101, 102; urges support of Blaine, 1892, 51; relations with Elkins and his organization, 52, 53, 84, 144; and governorship, 53, 79; aspirations for judgeship, 80, 93; senatorial aspirations, 83-85;

and 1899 senatorial contest, 91-93; and 1900 campaign, 95, 104; labor record, 98-99, 201-3, 217; and patronage, 134, 144; appointed U.S. attorney, judge, 145; on economic development, 170; and state fiscal crisis, 206-7; and 1901 legislature, 209, 214, 217; supports tax reform, 224; mentioned, 86
"Augusta County," 117

Baker, Lewis: relations with Davis, 33, 126; becomes editor of Charleston *Gazette*, 86; mentioned, 41, 59
Baldwin-Felts Detective Agency, 251
Baltimore, Maryland: mentioned, 15, 20, 24, 25, 51, 57, 72, 75, 86, 127, 130, 134, 136, 139, 149, 155, 157, 187, 226, 255, 277 n. 132
Baltimore & Ohio Railroad: relations with West Virginia Central, 23-24; business dealings with Camden, 24-25, 172; Davis serves as lobbyist, 78; supports Elkins organization, 100; relations with Standard Oil Company, 151; role in railroad consolidation, 155-56, 159-60; wins lower taxes, 204-5; lobbies in 1901 legislature, 212; mentioned, 9, 32, 33, 42, 48, 64, 69, 70, 115, 134, 137, 139, 180, 205, 245
Baltimore United Oil Company, 151
Baran, Paul, 186
Barbour County, 113, 242
Barbour *Democrat*, 90

Barnum, William H., 39
Barton, Isaac V.: record as labor commissioner, 99, 201-3; mentioned, 132
Bayard, Thomas F.: presidential candidacy, 1884, 38-39; mentioned, 32, 35, 76
Bayard, West Virginia, 169
Beech Creek coalfield, 19
Belmont, Mrs. August, 35
Benedum, Michael L., 187
Bennett, E. A., 300 n. 144
Bennett, Lewis, 127
Benwood, West Virginia, 60, 178
Bergoo, West Virginia, 169
Bering Sea controversy, 29
Berkeley County, 113, 114, 141
Berkeley Springs, West Virginia, 183
Berkshire, Ralph T., 81
Beverly, West Virginia, 117
Bittner, Van A., 193
Bituminous coal. *See* Coal industry
Blaine, James G.: and New Mexico statehood bill, 28; personal and political relations with Elkins, 29-32, 51-52; presidential candidacy, 1887, 32; urges Elkins to vote in West Virginia, 268 n. 127; mentioned, 33, 34, 45, 140
Blaine, West Virginia, 169
Bland-Allison Act, 75
Blizzard, Reese: career as retainer and politician, 137-38; and 1902 coal strike, 147; role in tax reform controversy, 222, 225, 306 n. 111; and legislature of 1905, 231; and controversy over fee-splitting, 235, 286 n. 84; backs Scherr for governor, 237; loses federal job, 239; mentioned, 241

Bluefield, West Virginia, 169, 177
Board of Control, 234-35
Board of Public Works, 204-5, 225, 236
Bolshevist Revolution, 193
Boone County, 115
Boston, Massachusetts, 20, 58
Boston & Maine Railroad, 20
Bowers, George M., 50, 79-80, 81
Braxton County, 113
Bretz, C. L., 63, 108
Bribery, 245
Brooke County, 113
Bryan, William Jennings: nominated for presidency, 1896, 71-72; campaigns in West Virginia, 76; renominated, 1900, 106-7; mentioned, 68, 72, 74, 77, 109, 124, 127, 161
Buckhannon, West Virginia, 168
Buffalo, New York, 208
Burke, E. A., 39
Burlington Railroad, 100
Butler, Benjamin F., 39
Buxton, Harry A., 108

Cabell County, 113, 114
Cabin Creek District, 123-24, 251-52
Caldwell, Charles T., 231, 235
Calhoun County, 113
California, 16
Camden, Johnson N.: relations with John D. Rockefeller and Standard Oil, 3, 8, 150-51, 152; early political activities, 4, 5, 6-7, 8; relations with Davis and Elkins, 5, 13, 22, 24-25, 34, 66, 87; alliance with Kanawha Ring, 11; not a good public speaker, 13; and federal patronage, 13, 35, 130; senatorial contests, 15,

41-44 *passim*, 55-56, 60, 61, 62; business enterprises and relationships, 24-25, 137, 155; and campaign expenditures, 64-65, 120, 126, 128-29; comments on 1894 campaign, 65-66, 68; role in 1896 campaign, 68, 71-72, 77; comment on 1898 campaign, 88; comment on 1900 election, 109; backs conservative Democrats, 106, 139, 146, 202; political pressure on employees, 120; use of railroad passes, 135; unostentatious living habits, 149; disregards anti-trust laws, 156; and Virginia Debt controversy, 161, 293 n. 43; economic aspects of political career, 161, 162, 163, 170-71; praised for helping poor, 165; tries to develop resorts, 183; as philanthropist, 187; influence on legislation, taxes, 196, 198, 204, 211, 304 n. 73; and tax reform movement, 226, 227-28; retirement, death, 229; mentioned, 29, 32, 38, 59, 100, 134, 140, 142, 164, 168, 186, 189, 253, 276 n. 106, 297 n. 118
Camden, Johnson N., Jr., 297 n. 118
Camden Consolidated Oil Company, 150
Camden-on-Gauley, West Virginia, 169
Campaign expenditures: industrialists control and use of, 13-14, 125, 126, 127, 129; in 1892 campaign, 53-54; in 1898, 87; distribution patterns, 102, 141; in 1900, 105,

106; how money was used, 127-28; in 1904, 228
Cannelton, West Virginia, 124
Caperton, Allen T., 8
"Caperton lands," 6, 25
Carbon, West Virginia, 169
"Car branding" bill, 212, 217
Carlisle, John G., 57
Carnegie, Andrew: Davis and Elkins solicit funds from, 58; role in railroad war, 157; mentioned, 30, 150, 187
Carter Oil Company, 156
Cassatt, Alexander J.: and railroad consolidation, 154-60 *passim;* mentioned, 30
Catron, Thomas B., 27, 241
Census Bureau, 178
Central Glass Company, 153, 289 n. 17
Chaffee, Jerome B., 27
Charleston, West Virginia: growth as government center, 10; voting behavior, 11, 122, 123, 124, 193; quarrel over post office, 96, 97, 98; economic ambitions, 130; mentioned, 12, 41, 67, 73, 79, 83, 86, 91-96 *passim,* 102, 106, 133, 137, 139-42 *passim,* 145, 146, 187, 199, 211, 215, 216, 220, 232, 235, 239, 244, 247, 250, 255, 256
Charleston Gang. *See* Kanawha Ring
Charleston *Gazette,* 69, 85-86, 183
Charleston *Mail-Tribune,* 83, 133
Charles Town, West Virginia, 133
Chemical industry, 173-74, 188
Chesapeake & Ohio Canal, 130
Chesapeake & Ohio Coal Agency, 148, 155

Chesapeake & Ohio Railroad: completed in 1876, 10; political activities of, 63, 64, 71, 100, 107, 212; role in railroad consolidation, 155-56, 160; control of coal shipments along route, 155, 159-60, 200; gets plant site sought by West Virginia Central, 180; mentioned, 19, 134, 137, 138, 167, 169
Chesapeake Bay, 23
Chicago, Illinois, 39, 169 n. 208
Chicago World's Fair, 197
Chilton, Joseph: and senatorial contest, 1893, 56, 61; and senatorial contest, 1899, 91-92; mentioned, 107
Chilton, William E.: as Democratic party official, 13, 72, 73; and silver issue, 70-71; reaction to Davis, 1896, 77; and 1898 campaign, 85; and 1899 senatorial contest, 91; on fees accepted while secretary of state, 206; Davis recalls loan from, 229; and senatorial contest, 1911, 244-45; mentioned, 68, 183
Chilton, MacCorkle & Chilton, 9
Cincinnati, Ohio, 56
Civil disorders, 1894, 60
Civil service, 131
Clark, E. W., and Company, 152
Clarksburg, West Virginia, 25, 100, 108, 180, 189
Clay County: voting behavior, 1876-1900, 115, 122; in campaign of 1910, 242-43
Clay, Henry, 36, 63
Clayton, William C., 136
Clearfield coalfield, 19, 160, 261 n. 12
Cleveland, Frances Folsom, 35
Cleveland, Grover: and tariff is-

330

sue, 26, 45, 46, 266 n. 73; and patronage, 34; visit to Deer Park, 34; presidential candidacy, 1884, 38-39; mentioned, 13, 22, 23, 33, 48, 57, 58, 69, 70, 76, 79

Cleveland Administration, 29, 130

Cleveland, Ohio, 15, 149, 150, 151, 152, 155, 161, 186

Coal, anthracite, 21, 37

Coal, Canadian, 20, 21, 37

Coal & Coke Railroad, 158-59, 169

Coalburg, West Virginia, 124

Coal industry: impact in West Virginia, 17, 175, 176, 187-92 *passim;* competition in, 19-20, 159-60; regional character of markets and production, 19-20, 188, 189, 261 n. 12; output and prices, 20, 25, 156, 188; role in 1894 campaign, 64; concentration of offices at 1 Broadway, 148; and consolidation movement, 154-57 *passim,* 159-60, 189; "captive mines," 188; environmental impact, 189-90. *See also* labor, strikes, tariff

Coalton, West Virginia, 169

Coal towns, 181-82, 190-91

Coketon, West Virginia, 169

Confederates, 4

Colcord, E. C., 222

Colcord resolution. *See* Tax reform

Colombia, 80

Colonial economy, 174-75, 186

Colorado, 27-28

Committee of Four. *See* Tax reform

Committee of One Hundred, 210

Community of Interest: as part of consolidation movement, 154-55, 156; railroad war with Wabash system, 157-58; benefits from coal "rationalization," 159-60; uses coal car distribution against rivals, 189; mentioned, 209

Company stores, 87, 190

Connecticut, 39, 170

Conservation, 183-84

Consolidation Coal Company: relations with B&O, 24; New York office, 148; merger with Fairmont Coal, 155; becomes Rockefeller property, 158; mentioned, 20, 250. *See also* Fairmont Coal Company

Consolidation movement, 150-60 *passim,* 186, 189. *See also* specific industries and localities

Constitution of 1872, 7-8

Constitutional amendments, 216

Constitutional convention: in 1872, 7-8; discussed but not called in 1901, 210, 216

Converse, George L., 39

Copperheads, 4

Cornwell, John J.: and Democratic leadership, 146; in legislature of 1901, 211, 215; first gubernatorial nomination, defeat, 228; as *comprador,* 245-46; relations with Rockefeller interests, 312 n. 50

Corporation license taxes, 213, 215, 216, 217

Corporations: legislative pressure against, 198; paid lower taxes in counties they dominated, 205; increased taxation of, 208-9; resistance to tax reform, 22, 224; well-treated in West Virginia, 249-50

333

honeymoon there in 1886, 35; conference between Davis, Elkins, and Harrison, 1887, 45; mentioned, 44, 46, 49, 51, 52, 149, 296 n. 106

Delaware, 19, 170, 178, 208

Democratic National Convention, 13, 38, 39, 40, 56

Democratic party: factionalism, 4, 6-14 *passim,* 55, 73, 226-27; and tariff issue, 17, 39-40; Davis's subversion of noted, 64-65; campaign strategy, 1892, 54-55; platform in 1896, 68; and silver issue, 69; and 1896 campaign, 76; resurgence in 1898, 87-88; conservatives revive in West Virginia, 106-7; organization after 1896, 146; and race issue, 227, 229; defeat in 1904, 228-29; regains control of legislature in 1910, 243-44; mentioned, 134

Democratic State Convention, 10

Denmark, 170

Denver, Colorado, 150

Detroit, Michigan, 255

Dillon, Charles W., 233-34, 236, 253

Doddridge County, 95, 113

Dominion Coal Company, 22

Donahue, Patrick J., 182, 190

E. W. Clark & Company, 152

Eastern Panhandle, 114, 141, 146, 157

Economic depression of 1894, 59-60, 110

Economic development: benefits industrialists politically, 57; character of increases importance of patronage, 130-31; colonial character of, 150;

West Virginia attitudes toward, 166-73 *passim;* slow start in 1870s, 167-68; sector theory of, 172, 173, 174; effect of tariff policies on, 173-74, 192; as justification for statehood, 179; role of regional specialization, 185; tax reform held a threat to, 223

Education, 198

Edwards, William Seymour, 82-83, 95, 100, 247

Election campaigns: general character in West Virginia, 110-25 *passim;* 1870, 6; 1878 to 1886, 10; 1884, 30, 33, 141; 1886, 41, 46; 1888, 46-47, 49-50; 1892, 53-55; 143; 1894, 15, 59-66, 68; 1896, 76-77; 1898, 83-84, 86-88, 89; 1900, 109; 1904, 126-27, 141, 226-29; 1906, 235; 1908, 127; 1910, 239-43; 1912, 247-48, 252-54; 1918, 246

Elk Garden coalfield, 19-20

Elkins, Davis: biographical, 3-4; senatorial contest, 1913, 134-35, 246; warns father against Glasscock, 240-41; appointed U.S. senator, 242; opposition to progressives, 247; mentioned, 191

Elkins, Hallie Davis: marriage, honeymoon, 5-6, 263 n. 42; distress at uncle's congressional nomination, 108; social ambitions, 149; entertains legislators, 215; mentioned, 160

Elkins, Stephen B.: biographical, 3; and Henry G. Davis, 3, 5-6, 17, 28-29, 73-74, 86, 87, 226-27; move from New Mexico to West Virginia, 4, 6, 15;

334

marriage, honeymoon, 5-6, 263 n. 42; and West Virginia Republican party, 15, 51-54 *passim*, 94-95, 105-6, 235-38 *passim;* and tariff controversy, 19-20, 21, 22, 59; business dealings with Camden, 24-25; New Mexico phase of career, 26-28, 29, 30, 31, 78; military record, 27, 101; senatorial ambitions and contests, 27-28, 31, 46, 55, 66-67, 92, 93, 94, 215, 234; career in national politics, 28, 29, 30, 31, 33, 50-51; and James G. Blaine, 29-32 *passim*, 51-52; economic aspects of political career, 29, 160-64 *passim*, 293 n. 44, 311 n. 26; character of political leadership, 30, 78, 79, 82, 142, 276 n. 106; problem of his residence, 31, 32, 47, 268 n. 127; and 1888 campaign, 45, 46, 47, 49-50; campaign contributions, 53, 84, 126, 129; and labor issues, 60, 147, 164, 191, 202-3; and 1894 campaign, 63-66 *passim*, 68; and patronage, 80-83 *passim*, 130, 133, 140, 215; and Albert B. White, 104-6, 222, 230; and Randolph County seat controversy, 117; on Charles D. Elliott, 129; office at 1 Broadway, 148; social ambitions, 149; and consolidation movement, 156-60 *passim;* tries to develop resorts, 183; as philanthropist, 187; as legislator and lobbyist, 196, 200, 211, 215-17 *passim*, 231-32, 240, 241, 292 n. 40, 294 n. 58; and tax reform, 216, 219-20, 223-27

passim; relations with William E. Glasscock, 238-41 *passim;* final illness and death, 241-42; and Henry D. Hatfield, 253; position on Spanish-American War, 276 n. 111; mentioned, 14, 42, 58, 71, 74, 96, 100, 102, 105, 107, 125, 132, 133, 136, 137, 138, 146, 165, 169, 173, 244

Elkins, West Virginia: founding, 48; becomes Randolph County seat, 117; attempts to develop as a resort, 296 n. 106; profits in sale of lots, 299 n. 139; mentioned, 51, 68, 73, 74, 86, 149, 169, 187, 191, 305 n. 92

Elkins organization: completes modernization of West Virginia politics, 12, 140-41; formation of, 80-82; acquires Charleston *Mail-Tribune*, 83; relations with Atkinson, 84; opposition to, 98-103 *passim*, 104, 105, 106; and patronage, 143-44, 217; and progressive movement, 195, 219, 233-38 *passim*, 247-48; and state fiscal crisis, 203; and tax reform movement, 225-26, 229-30; gubernatorial contest of 1908, 236, 237, 238; disintegration, 248; need for representatives from southern West Virginia, 253

Elliott, Charles D.: and 1900 campaign, 98, 106; colleagues mistrust, 129; as retainer and lobbyist, 138, 139, 211, 213-14; Scott finances newspaper for, 142; appointed U.S. marshal, 145; role in tax reform controversy, 222-23,

229-30, 231, 306 n. 111; and 1908 gubernatorial contest, 237; and 1910 campaign, 239, 243; loses federal job, 239; and Progressive party, 247-48; works as agent for school book company, 304 n. 76

Elliott, Mortimer F., 148-49, 289 n. 2

"Elliott letter," 231

Employment, 181

Energy consumption, 180

Engineering and Mining Journal, 189

Erie Railroad, 19, 169 n

Eskdale, West Virginia, 181

Eureka Pipeline Company, 156

Europe, 74

Factionalism: basis in Democratic party, 11-12, 14-15; development in Republican party, 94-103 *passim*

Fair, James H., 152

Fairmont, West Virginia, 85, 100, 117, 129, 140, 179, 242

Fairmont Coal Company: origin, 139; New York office, 148; expansion, merger, 155; and Monongah mine disaster, 190, 191, 192; lobbying activities, 196, 220-21; mentioned, 3, 138, 189, 205, 219, 232, 250, 286 n. 84, 297 n. 118. *See also* Consolidation Coal Company

Fairmont coalfield: impact of tariff reform on, 22; strikes, 60, 147; use of campaign funds in, 128; mentioned, 98, 117, 120, 138, 147, 251

Fairmont *Index*, 142

Faulkner, Charles James, Sr., 8

Faulkner, Charles James, Jr., 44, 55, 56, 71

Fayette County, 60, 94, 96, 106, 115, 118, 128, 182, 278 n. 162, 279 n. 172

Fee-splitting investigation, 231, 235, 308 n. 141

Fee system, 207, 216

Fillmore, Millard, 36

First National Bank of New York, 161

Fish hatcheries, 80

Flagler, Henry M., 148, 149, 163

Flat Top coalfield, 119, 169

Fleming, Aretus Brooks: biographical, 3; and 1896 campaign, 68, 71-72, 77; and 1898 campaign, 87; campaign expenditures, 126-27; as Standard Oil retainer, 138-39, 149, 212; and 1902 coal strike, 147; attitude toward anti-trust laws, 156; on water pollution, 183; on Monongah mine disaster, 192; vetoes school levy increase, 198; opposes labor legislation, 200-201; and tax reform controversy, 220, 224-25, 226, 228-29, 228-32 *passim;* becomes leading Democrat after 1904, 229; praises West Virginia's treatment of corporations, 249-50; mentioned, 109, 134, 146, 234, 250

Flint, Michigan, 187

Florida, 148, 149

Flour industry, 176-77

Flournoy, Samuel L., 86

Floyd, John B., 82-83

Flynn, James W., 136

Forest industries, 175-76

Forman, Lewis J., 223, 234, 236

France, 184

Freer, Romeo H.: gubernatorial candidacy, 95-96; connection with G.A.R., 101; supported by black Republicans, 102; personal history leads to withdrawal from race, 104-5; opposes tax reform, 224; and 1908 gubernatorial contest, 237; mentioned, 99
Freight rates, 20, 23, 156
Frick, Henry Clay, 157
Fuchs, Victor R., 178
Fusionists, 122-24

Gaines, Joseph, 83, 95-96
Garden, Anthony D., 62, 271 n. 8
Garfield, James A., 30, 31
Garrett, John W., 23-24, 32
Garrett, Robert, 24
Gilmer County, 113
Glasscock, William E.: relations with Elkins, 140, 238-41 passim, 310 n. 26; appointed collector of internal revenue, 145; nomination for governor, 237-38; supports severance taxes, 238; gubernatorial administration, 238, 239, 240; relations with Scott, 240; appoints Davis Elkins senator, 242; works to contain 1910 quarrels, 243; and campaign of 1912, 247; orders troops to coalfields, 251-52; follows operators' wishes on mine inspector, 251; and senatorial contest, 1910, 310 n. 24; mentioned, 182, 253, 255, 312 n. 43
Glass industry, 153-54, 175, 177, 179-80
Goff, Charles, 51, 52
Goff, Nathan, Jr.: background, rivalry with Elkins, 48; and

election of 1888, 49-50; accepts judicial appointment, 51; turns down cabinet post, 79; Elkins organization fears senatorial ambitions, 84-85; role in 1899 senatorial contest, 92-93; business interests, 100; and patronage, 134; and 1902 coal strike, 147; elected senator, 1913, 246; snubbed by semi-centennial celebration, 256; mentioned, 66, 80, 89, 101, 254
Gompers, Samuel, 99
Gorman, Arthur: role in tariff controversy, 22, 39, 59; Davis aids in 1895 campaign, 68; mentioned, 32, 33, 35, 36, 38, 64, 70, 76, 130, 136
Gorman, Peter, 293 n. 46
Gormania, West Virginia, 169
Gould, George J., 156, 157, 158
Grafton, West Virginia, 52, 96, 100, 110
Grand Army of the Republic, 101
Grand Trunk Railway, 169 n
Grant, Edward M., 98, 100
Grant, Ulysses S., 33, 56
Grant County: voting behavior, 95, 114, 115, 273 n. 48, 278 n. 162; mentioned, 90, 234
Great Britain, 29, 174
Great Kanawha River. See Kanawha River
Greeley, Horace, 13, 36
Greenback party, 11, 122-24 passim, 134, 218
Greenbrier County, 112
Greenbrier Valley, 25, 137, 169, 253

H. G. Davis & Brother, 18, 20, 136
Hagans, John M., 81, 131

West Virginia, 1, 4, 12-13, 15-16, 107, 109, 147; resistance to among Democrats, 4, 6-7, 12, 13-14; personal and political relations among themselves, 5-6, 78, 164, 276 n. 106; prefer sectional to economic issues, 8; influence with press, 13, 142; and political realignments of 1890s, 110, 125; political influence on employees, 119-22; campaign expenditures, 125-29, 141; investments in supporters' enterprises, 140; social and business stature in nation, 149-50; motives for involvement in politics, 161-62; economic leadership increases political strength, 165, 166; interest in legislation, 197, 211-13; oppose constitutional convention, 210. *See also* Johnson N. Camden, Henry G. Davis, Stephen B. Elkins, Nathan B. Scott

Inflationists, 75. *See also* Silver issue

Ingalls, Melvin E., 63, 71, 106-7

Interstate Commerce Act of 1887, 134

Interstate Commerce Commission, 35, 160, 163, 222

Iron and steel industry, 152-53, 175, 177

Italian Embassy, 250

Jackson, Andrew, 36, 63

Jackson, John Jay: as federal district judge, 93; anti-labor views, 99; resigns as federal judge, 144; and 1902 coal strike, 147; gets free coal from Camden, 286 n. 70; mentioned, 138

Jackson, Malcolm, 213, 214, 215, 304 n. 73

Jackson, Thomas J. ("Stonewall"), 255

Jackson County, 113

Japan, 174, 184, 186

Jefferson, Thomas, 36, 63

Jefferson County, 115, 116, 118

Johnson, Okey, 43

Jones, Benjamin F., 30, 32

Judgeships, 134, 144, 145

Junior, West Virginia, 169

Kanawha & Michigan Railroad, 168-69

Kanawha Coal Exchange, 199

Kanawha coalfield, 22, 60, 155, 168

Kanawha coal operators, 270 n. 171

Kanawha County: government, 83, 207; and 1900 campaign, 99, 106; voting behavior, 115, 122-24, 278 n. 126; legislative ticket includes labor representatives, 201; and 1910 campaign, 242; mentioned, 94, 182, 200, 218, 228, 251

Kanawha Ring: membership and methods, 9-10, 130; geographic basis of appeal, 10-11, 12; and other Democratic leaders, factions, 10-11, 13, 14, 72-73, 106-7, 146, 229; role in 1894 campaign, 60-63 *passim;* and silver issue, 69, 70, 71; and campaign of 1898, 86; demands Negro disfranchisement, 127; and campaign expenditures, 1904, 141; wins local elections, 1904, 228; and senatorial contest, 1911, 244-45; men-

tioned, 34, 71, 83, 91, 118, 139, 183, 253
Kanawha River, 9, 25, 169, 183
Kanawha Valley: center of opposition to Elkins, 94-95, 106; progressivism strong in, 97; third party strength in, 122-24; chemical industry, 174; mentioned, 93, 102, 138, 179, 199, 251
Keller, Benjamin F., 144-45, 147
Kenna, John E.: leader of Kanawha Ring, 9; and federal patronage, 34; reelection to the Senate, 1889, 50; death, 56; appropriation for statue of, 197; mentioned, 14, 46, 118, 132
Kenna & Watts, 9
Kentucky, 87, 119, 168, 177, 188, 189, 190
Kerens, Richard C.: buys into Davis-Elkins firms, 24; connection with Star Route scandal, 28; solicits campaign funds for Elkins, 100; on pressures of consolidation, 156; seeks favors from Elkins, 163; on company towns, 191
Kerens, West Virginia, 169
Keyser, West Virginia, 76
Kingwood, West Virginia, 105, 149
Knight, Edward W., 137, 138

Labor: Republican attitudes toward, 98-99; spokesmen oppose transfer of troops, 164; early legislation benefiting, 198-99; leaders try to influence elections, 201-2
Labor commissioner, 198
Labor legislation: meets increasing resistance, 199-203 *passim;* agenda for 1901, 203; in

legislature of 1901, 213, 214, 215, 217, 218; legislators deceive spokesmen, 250
Labor relations, 250, 251, 252
Lackawanna Railroad, 155
Laing, John R., 251
Land, 7-8, 10, 26, 27, 28
Landstreet, Fairfax S.: role in 1894 campaign, 63; political activities, 135; and labor relations, 191; as lobbyist, 212, 213; assumes Davis will protect corporations, 220; opposes tax reform, 226; and 1904 campaign, 228; later business career, 297 n. 118; mentioned, 108
Latin America, 174
Laughlin, George A., 209-10, 212, 214, 217
Leadsville, West Virginia, 48. *See also* Elkins, West Virginia
Legislature: use of caucus to expedite bills, 143; lack of accomplishment, 1889-1899, 196; session of 1864, 166; session of 1866, 5; session of 1879, 172; session of 1883, 198; session of 1887, 41-44 *passim*, 81-82, 198; session of 1889, 53; special session of 1890, 196; session of 1893, 197-98; session of 1895, 67, 200; session of 1897, 196; session of 1899, 89-90, 93-94, 201; session of 1901, 144, 197, 203, 211-18 *passim*, 218-19, 305 n. 93; session of 1903, 222-23; session of 1905, 230, 231, 232; session of 1907, 234; session of 1909, 234, 239; session of 1911, 243-44; session of 1913, 254; session of 1915, 254

340

Lehigh Valley Railroad, 155
Lewis, John L., 193
Lewisburg, West Virginia, 220
Lewis County, 113
Libbey, Edward D., 154
Libbey-Owens-Ford, 154
License taxes, 213, 215, 216, 217, 221-22
"Lieutenants," 147
Lincoln, Abraham, 93
Lincoln Club, 95
Lincoln County, 115
Loans, 125-26
Lobbyists: Davis works as, 134; corporations deploy routinely after 1890, 196; numbers and pressure increase, 200-201; in legislature of 1901, 211-18 *passim;* reported change in style, 214; lead resistance to tax reform, 220-24 *passim;* in legislature of 1905, 231-32; mentioned, 92
Lodge, Henry Cabot, 146
Lodge Election Bill, 54, 70
Logan, John A., 30
Logan County, 115, 117
Loree, Leonard F., 155
Los Angeles, California, 163
Louisiana, 38, 39
Louisville, Kentucky, 252
Lucas, Daniel B.: biographical, 9; and senatorial contest of 1887, 43-44; supports tariff reform, 44; supports free silver, 69, 71; abandons gubernatorial campaign, 107; and labor legislation, 198-99; mentioned, 137
Ludwig II of Bavaria, 184
Lumber producers, 64

MacCausland, John, 224
MacCorkle, William A.: on economic opportunities in

Charleston, 10; campaigns on race issue, 54; uses troops in 1894 strike, 60; urges Democratic unity, 69; and 1899 senatorial contest, 91; and 1892 campaign, 118, 119; on patronage pressure, 131; changes state nickname, 170; on water pollution, 183; opposes increases in mine inspectors, 196, 201; administration lowers railroad taxes, 204-5; mentioned, 52, 255
McDermott, Joseph H., 234, 242
McDonald, Joseph E., 32
McDowell County: voting behavior, 115, 118; use of campaign funds in, 128; property valuations decline, 205; mentioned, 155, 189, 252
McGraw, John T.: aids Elkins, 1895, 66; and silver issue, 69, 70, 71; feud with Kanawha Ring, 72-73; relations with Davis, 72-73, 77, 85-86, 89, 91-92, 229; and 1898 congressional campaign, 86, 88, 90; backs conservative Democrats, 106-7; relationship of business to political career, 137; leadership among Democratic professionals, 146; mentioned, 34, 62, 108, 139
McKell, Thomas G.: opposition to Scott, 93; and 1900 campaign, 95-96; and labor relations, 99, 279 n. 172; as absentee coal operator, 102; mentioned, 100
McKinley, William: campaigns in West Virginia, 54; offers Goff cabinet post, 79; relations with Elkins, 79; promises Atkinson Judgeship, 93; men-

341

tioned, 72, 82, 109, 120, 144, 215
McKinney, Owen S., 139-40, 142, 146
McKinney, William T., 102
McPherson, James A., 39
Madison, James, 36, 63
Maine Central Railroad, 21
Mann, Isaac T., 137, 246, 253
Mann-Elkins Act, 241
Manning, Daniel, 69-70
Mannington, West Virginia, 242
Mannington oilfield, 100, 117, 152
Manufacturing industries, 175-76, 178
Marion County: voting behavior, 113, 116-17, 120-21; property valuations decline in, 205; campaign of 1910, 242; mentioned, 117, 139
Marlins Bottom, 118
Marlinton, 118
Marshall, John, 138
Marshall County, 113
Martinsburg, West Virginia, 177
Maryland, 5, 19, 20, 39, 51, 64, 68, 76, 85, 87, 126, 178, 180, 188
Mason, James Murray, Jr., 184, 300 n. 144
Mason, James Murray, III, 185
Mason, John W.: and 1894 campaign, 65; relations with Elkins, 50, 82, 132-33, 144; Republican party credentials, 81, 101; and labor relations, 98; and 1900 campaign, 95; business interests, 100; involvement in Virginia debt, 293 n. 44; mentioned, 52, 105
Mason County, 94, 113, 242-43, 278 n. 162
Massachusetts, 39, 170, 221

Maxwell Land Grant & Railroad Company, 28
Mayer, Charles L., 64
Mercer County, 115, 118, 155, 242
Mexico, 16
Miami, Florida, 163
Migration, 111
Miller, William H. H., 50
Mills, Darius Ogden, 29
Mine guards, 182, 251
Mine inspectors, 196, 200-201, 251
Mineral County: and election recounts, 1898, 89, 90; voting behavior, 113, 114, 119, 273 n. 48; mentioned, 86, 87, 101, 136
Miners, 99. See also Strikes, United Mine Workers of America
Mines, Federal Bureau of, 251
Mine safety legislation, 198-99, 212, 214
Mine wars, 185, 251-52, 256
Mingo County, 115, 117
Minnesota, 86, 177
Moffett, James A., 186, 295 n. 86
Monetary issues, 198
Monongah, West Virginia: voting behavior, 120-21; as company town, 190-91; mine explosion, 1907, 191-92, 250-51; mentioned, 25
Monongahela River, 158
Monongahela Valley, 65, 94, 114, 139, 145
Monongalia County: Court House ring, 98; voting behavior, 112-13; and 1910 campaign, 242; and 1912 campaign, 247, 278 n. 162; Elkins's interest in local offi-

342

cials, 311 n. 26; mentioned,
117
Monroe, James, 36, 63
Monroe County, 113
Monroe Doctrine, 88
Montana, West Virginia, 120-21
Montez, Lola, 184
Morgan, J. Pierpont, 150, 155,
157-58
Morgan, John Tyler, 37, 227
Morgan County, 114-15
Morgantown, West Virginia: and
1900 campaign, 95-96, 98;
punitive legislation aimed at,
217; mentioned, 100, 125,
140, 149, 234, 241
Morgantown & Kingwood Rail-
road, 158-59
Morgantown *Post*, 93, 99, 104,
170
Morrill, Justin, 36
Morrison, William R., 39-40
Morton, J. Sterling, 39
Mott, Charles S., 187
Moundsville, West Virginia, 96,
99, 102
Mountainous terrain, 3, 11-12,
180-81
Mugler, Henri Jean, 110

Napoleon III, 184
National Civic Federation, 164,
221
National Civil Service Reform
League, 145
National Democratic Party
("Goldbugs"), 71-72, 76
National Guard, 239, 255
National Lead Company, 152
Natural gas, 175-76
Natural resources, 249-50
Naugatuck Valley Railroad, 21
Neal, George I., 146
Negro disfranchisement, 127,
237, 247

Negroes: Republican leaders unhappy with Elkins, 102-3; impact on voting patterns, 111,
116-19 *passim*
New England, 16, 19, 20, 155,
173
New Haven & Northampton
Railroad, 21
New Haven Railroad, 20
New Jersey, 19, 39, 170, 179,
208
New Mexico: Elkins's career
there, 26, 27, 28, 78; mentioned, 30, 46, 160, 163
New River Coal Company, 155
New River coalfield, 19, 60,
155, 168
Newspapers, 12
New York (state), 38
New York, New York: as headquarters for West Virginia
firms, 149-50; as Standard Oil
refining center, 151; mentioned, 15, 19, 20, 23, 29,
30, 57, 58, 72, 139, 147,
152, 159, 174, 186, 212,
245, 252, 261 n. 12, 277 n.
132
New York Central Railroad,
154-55, 159, 169
Nicholas County, 113
Norfolk & Western Railroad:
supports Elkins organization,
100; acquires Pocahontas
Coal Company, 155; role in
railroad consolidation, 155,
159-60; economic impact in
West Virginia, 168-69; mentioned, 19, 117, 137, 189,
205, 252
North American Commercial
Company, 29
Northcott, Elliott, 140, 145,
223, 235-36

Northern Panhandle: impact of consolidation movement in, 152, 153, 154; mentioned, 111, 157, 175, 178

Oak View Conference, 45
Ober, Gustavus, 75
O'Brien, ——, 86
Odd, West Virginia, 169
Oglebay, Earl W., 187, 297 n. 18
Ohio: glass industry, 153-54; imports West Virginia natural gas, 175; mentioned, 22, 39, 54, 102, 111, 166, 170, 177, 178, 188, 189, 244
Ohio County: voting behavior, 113, 114; labor representatives in legislature, 201-2; property tax valuations, 206; officials' fees, 207; mentioned, 70, 105
Ohio River, 9, 114, 115, 177-78
Ohio River Railroad, 25, 151-52
Ohio Valley, 54, 61, 94, 151
Ohio Valley Trades & Labor Assembly, 199, 201, 202, 203, 210
Ohley, William A.: as Democratic state chairman, 85, 146; and 1899 senatorial contest, 91-92; as retainer and lobbyist, 139, 201, 211; injured in train wreck, 271 n. 8; and anti-tax conference, 306 n. 111
"Old-line Republicans," 100-101, 125, 145, 237, 242
Olney, Richard, 62
Ontario, Canada, 22
Owens, Michael J., 153-54, 180
Owens-Illinois Corporation, 154

Paint Creek, 148, 169, 182, 251-52
Panamanian Revolution, 80

Pan American Exposition, 206, 214, 217
Parker, Alton B., 146
Parkersburg, West Virginia: Camden's economic role in, 151, 172; mentioned, 61, 73, 129, 140, 149, 170, 186, 231, 247, 295 n. 86
Parkersburg News, 142, 223
Parkersburg State Journal, 81, 142
Patronage: importance in West Virginia, 12, 129-34 passim, 249; during Cleveland Administration, 13, 34, 56; Elkins's use of, 46, 50-51, 79-80, 80-83 passim, 143-44; role in 1900 campaign, 96, 98; enhances industrialists' power, 129-37 passim; and Republican leadership, 145, 209
Paul, James W., 201, 251
Payne, C. H., 97, 102, 105
Payne, Oliver H., 152
Pendleton, George H., 32
Pendleton County, 113, 207
Pennsylvania: mentioned, 19, 20, 21, 22, 25, 54, 111, 166, 170, 175, 177, 178, 188, 189, 221
Pennsylvania Railroad: relations with West Virginia Central, 23-24; and consolidation movement, 154-60 passim; mentioned, 137, 169 n, 292 n. 39
Peonage cases, 250
Petroleum industry, 117, 152, 175
Phelps, William W., 30
Philadelphia, Pennsylvania, 20, 88, 119, 128, 149, 152, 154, 174, 249
Philanthropy, 186-87

Randolph County: and 1898 election results, 90; voting behavior, 113, 273 n. 48; county seat war, 117; property valuations, 205; mentioned, 48, 74, 88, 180

Reading Railroad, 155

Redeemers: defined, 7; attitudes and basis of support, 7-8; position vis-a-vis other factions, 11, 14; economic attitudes, 184-85; mentioned, 127, 253. *See also* Democratic party, Factionalism

Regulars, 13-14, 49, 61. *See also* Democratic party, Factionalism

Republican National Committee, 29

Republican National Convention, 30, 51-52

Republican party: factions and divisions, 4, 78, 94-103 *passim*, 218, 225, 233, 235-38 *passim*; support of Davis in 1877, 7; strength and weakness in various regions, 11, 13; Elkins's leadership of, 17-18, 52-53, 143; and tariff issue, 18-19; strength in West Virginia, 32, 46; potential West Virginia leaders, 48-49; and campaign of 1892, 54; and campaign of 1894, 65-66; victory in 1896, 76; impact of black voters, 111, 116-19 *passim*; identification with "progress," 115; leaders monopolize patronage, 145; new leadership after Elkins's death, 246, 252, 253, 254; legislators show greater unity in 1901, 305 n. 93

Republican state conventions, 52-53, 106

Resort industry, 183

"Retainers": principal ones listed, 137-38; distinguished from "lieutenants," 147; arrogance in 1901 legislature, 219; and tax reform movement, 224, 306 n. 111

Reynolds, Francis M., 101-2, 223

Reynoldsville coalfield, 19

Rhode Island, 170

Richmond, Virginia, 256

Richwood, West Virginia, 169

"Ripper legislation," 142-44, 217

Ritchie County, 95, 113, 278 n. 162

Roane County, 115

Roanoke, Virginia, 251

Robinson, Ira E., 223, 287 n. 88

Robinson, John A., 71

Rockefeller, John D.: and Camden, 3; wants to phase out West Virginia refining, 150-51; mentioned, 8, 150, 187

Rockefeller interests: employ Fleming as retainer, 139; New York headquarters, 148; acquire Western Maryland Railway, Consolidation Coal, 158; warned of tax commission report, 220; relations with Cornwell, 312 n. 50; mentioned, 245

Rogers, Henry H.: supports Elkins organization, 99; New York office, 148; and Virginian Railroad, 156; mentioned, 151, 168

Roosevelt, Theodore: and 1912 presidential campaign, 247-48; mentioned, 80, 131, 143, 144, 146, 183, 228, 235, 286 n. 84

Roosevelt Administration, 235
Rucker, Edgar P.: background, 83; as Norfolk & Western retainer, 137; and tax reform movement, 224, 306 n. 111; death opens way for Hatfield, 252-53; mentioned, 144, 216
Rush, Harry Welles, 129
Russia, 184

St. Clair, J. W., 138
St. Louis, Missouri, 24, 163
San Francisco, California, 152, 157
Santa Fe Ring, 26, 78
Scherr, Arnold C., 237-38, 239, 241
Scott, Nathan Bay: biographical, 3; relations with Elkins, 52, 80; campaign contributions, 53-54, 84, 102, 126, 128-29; legislative record, 1887, 81; becomes federal official, 82; and senatorial contests, 83-85, 89-94, 239-41, 246; describes election as cake walk, 88; wants to publicize Freer's problems, 104; advises White on strategy, 105; comments on Charles Elliott, 128; dislike of civil service, 131; acquires newspaper, 142; explains Republican organization, 143; wants tighter control over patronage, 144; business career, 150, 153, 154, 290 n. 17; on loyalty to Republican party, 162; economic motives in political career, 163, 211, 212, 213; as philanthropist, 187; approves White's biennial message, 230; acts as Republican peacemaker, 238; relations with Glasscock, 240; and

campaign of 1912, 247; motivation for political career, 293 n. 52; mentioned, 15, 82, 95, 96, 100, 136, 145, 214, 231, 232. *See also* Industrialists
Scott, William L., 22
"Scrip," 198-99
Seaboard Steam Coal Association, 21
Seal Islands (Pribilof Islands, Alaska), 29, 51
Seaman Committee, 308 n. 141. *See also* Fee-splitting investigation
Semi-centennial celebration, 2, 255-56
Senate, U.S., 164-65
Senate Committee on Interstate Commerce, 100
Senatorial contests: 1871, 7; 1875, 6, 8; 1877, 7, 127; 1881, 6; 1883, 7; 1887, 7, 15, 41-44, 81, 171; 1893, 55-56; 1895, 66-67; 1899, 89-94 *passim;* 1911, 244-45; 1913, 135, 253; 1918, 191
Severance taxes: proposed by 1903 tax commission, 212, 221-22; defeated again, 230, 232, 233; proposed for natural gas only, 238, 239, 240; significance of defeat, 249; mentioned, 230
Sewall, Arthur, 74
Shaw, Alexander, 24, 262 n. 22
Sheridan, John, 70, 71, 136
Sherman, John, 32, 36
Showalter, Emmett M.: colleagues' mistrust of, 129; as retainer and lobbyist, 138, 139, 211, 217; appointed U.S. marshal, 145; opposition to tax reform, 220, 222
Sillman, Peter, 140

Silver issue, 68-72 *passim*, 75, 88
Sistersville oilfield, 100, 115, 152
Socialist party, 124, 193-94, 254
Solvay Collieries Company, 182
Sommerville, James B., 137, 196
South Branch Valley, 114
Southern Historical Society, 58
South Penn Oil Company, 99-100, 156, 205, 219
Sprigg, Joseph, 136
Stalnaker, Randolph: as retainer and lobbyist, 137, 196, 212, 219; opposition to tax reform, 221, 222, 306 n. 111; mentioned, 140, 241
Standard Oil Company: and Camden, 3; and B&O Railroad, 24-25, 151; expansion in West Virginia, 99-100; retains Fleming as representative, 139; New York headquarters, 148; phases out West Virginia refining, 150-51; interest in legislation, 212; mentioned, 8, 22, 29, 35, 138, 172, 186, 219, 230, 231, 234, 295 n. 86
Star Route scandal, 28, 31
State government: financial crisis, 1900-1901, 203-4, 234; expansion of public services, 203-4
Statemakers: economic expectations, 2; driven from power, 1870, 6; laid foundations of modern politics in West Virginia, 12; they and heirs lose out to Elkins, 15; original Elkins men identified with, 81; mentioned, 101
State tax commissioner, 221
Statuary Hall, 197
Steck, Harry, 201
Stevenson, William E., 81

Strauss, Isidor, 58, 62
Strikes: coal miners, 25, 60, 147, 250, 251, 252; pottery workers, 59; railroad workers, 60; iron and steel workers, 60; Flint Glass Workers, 153
Strother, David Hunter, 130
Sturgiss, George C.: Elkins secures appointment for, 50; and senatorial contest of 1895, 66-67; identified with Elkins, statemakers, 81; and 1900 campaign, 95, 98; business interests, 100, 140; forced to resign as university regent, 217; supports tax reform, 224; elected to Congress, 235; and gubernatorial contest of 1908, 236; works against Scott, 239; on campaign of 1910, 243; mentioned, 82, 101
Summers County, 113
Supreme Court of Appeals, 43, 199
Sutherland, Howard, 101, 136
Swisher, Charles W.: business relations with Elkins, 140; implicated in Elliott letter, 231; conservative record as legislator, 234, 236; as gubernatorial candidate, 236, 237, 238, 253
"Switzerland of America," 166, 183-84
Syracuse, New York, 182

Taft, William Howard, 239, 247
Tariff: on bituminous coal, 7, 16, 18-19, 22, 36, 37, 56-57, 59; Morrill Tariff (1863), 18; debate of 1872, 18; of 1875, 18; Mongrel Tariff (1883), 36-37, 38, 173; Morrison bill (1884), 37, 40; Wilson bill

217, 304 n. 90; mentioned, 48, 57, 131, 132, 133
Wetzel County, 113, 205, 242
Wheeling, West Virginia: impact of depression, 59-60; and glass industry, 153-54; impact of consolidation movement on, 152, 153, 154, 186; accounts for much of West Virginia's industry, 178; Socialist gains in, 193; progressive reform movement in, 209-10; semi-centennial celebration, 255-56; mentioned, 3, 5, 9, 12, 14, 25, 33, 41, 48, 54, 61, 62, 70, 71, 110, 127, 142, 145, 151, 152, 182, 187, 199, 214, 215, 216, 217, 220, 252
Wheeling Board of Trade, 209-10
Wheeling Boom Convention (1888), 47, 172
Wheeling electric bill, 210
Wheeling *Intelligencer:* Elkins buys into ownership, 47; becomes independent of Elkins, 80; on corporation taxes, 208-9; and campaign of 1912, 247; mentioned, 51, 52, 60, 66, 142
Wheeling & Lake Erie Railroad, 157
Wheeling *Register:* and silver issue, 69; and 1896 campaign, 74; comments on Republican factionalism, 100; on economic development, 168; on labor legislation, 200; mentioned, 142, 211, 214
Wheeling Steel Corporation, 153, 186
Wheelwright, Jere H., 297 n. 118
Whigs, 4
White, Albert B.: relations with

Elkins, 50, 81, 140, 203; heads Republican delegation, 1896, 79; role in 1899 senatorial contest, 89; gubernatorial candidacy and campaign, 94, 104-6; promises friendship to B&O, 100; appoints new boards and officials, 144; urged to block reform legislation, 212; conservative economic views in inaugural, 219; appoints tax commission, 220; and tax reform controversy, 222-26, 229-30; calls special legislative session, 225; and fee-splitting investigation, 235, 286 n. 84; declines to run for governor, 1908, 236; becomes state tax commissioner, 236; and Progressive party, 247-48; mentioned, 73, 82, 83, 96, 101, 144, 146, 252
White, Theodore H., 130
White Sulphur Springs, West Virginia, 183
Whitmer, R. F., 88, 108
Whitney, William C., 23, 69
Whyte, William Pinckney, 136
Willey, Waitman T., 81
Williams, Luther Judson, 220
Wilmington, Delaware, 174, 185
Wilson, E. Willis: Agrarian spokesman, 9; elected governor in 1884, 9; and senatorial contests, 41, 42, 43, 44, 61, 62, 63; vetoes railroad bills, 44; and silver issue, 69, 71; introduced pioneer labor legislation, 198; beneficiary of fee system, 207; mentioned, 14, 137
Wilson, William G., 211
Wilson, William Lyne: character

and background, 14, 57-58;
relations with Davis, 14,
40-41, 56-60 *passim;* renomination to Congress, 1884, 40;
tariff debates with Goff, 49;
and 1894 campaign, 62-66;
economic troubles solved by
patronage, 131; mentioned,
68, 70, 74, 76, 82, 88, 110,
192
Wilson, Woodrow, 247
Winding Gulf coalfield, 148, 169
Windom, William, 32, 35, 50
Windom, West Virginia, 169

Wirt County, 113
Wisconsin, 34
Wisconsin, University of, 186
Wood County, 113, 114
World War I, 1, 188
World War II, 2
Wyoming County, 111, 115

Yakatog Gold Mining Company,
208
Yale University, 138, 149
YMCA, 187
Youngstown, Ohio, 181